The

GOD
I LOVE

Books by Joni Eareckson Tada

All God's Children: Ministry with Disabled Persons (with Gene Newman)
Barrier-Free Friendships: Bridging the Distance between You and Friends with Disabilities (with Steve Jensen)
Diamonds in the Dust: 366 Sparkling Devotions
Heaven: Your Real Home
Heaven: Devotional Edition
Joni
The Life and Death Dilemma: Suicide, Euthanasia, Suffering, Mercy
More Precious Than Silver: 366 Daily Devotional Readings
A Step Further (with Steven Estes)
When God Weeps: Why Our Sufferings Matter to the Almighty (with Steven Estes)

The GOD I LOVE

JONI EARECKSON TADA

A LIFETIME OF WALKING WITH JESUS

ZONDERVAN™

GRAND RAPIDS, MICHIGAN 49530 USA

ZONDERVAN™

The God I Love
Copyright © 2003 by Joni Eareckson Tada

This title is also available as a Zondervan ebook product.
Visit www.zondervan.com/ebooks for more information.

This title is also available as a Zondervan audio product.
Visit www.zondervan.com/audiopages for more information.

Requests for information should be addressed to:

Zondervan, *Grand Rapids, Michigan 49530*

Library of Congress Cataloging-in-Publication Data

Tada, Joni Eareckson.
    The God I love : a lifetime of walking with Jesus / Joni Eareckson Tada.— 1st ed.
       p. cm.
    Includes bibliographical references.
    ISBN 0-310-24008-5
    1. Tada, Joni Eareckson.   2. Christian biography — United States.
  I. Title.
    BR1725.T2A3 2003
    277.3'0825' 092—dc21

                                   2003008391

This edition printed on acid-free paper.

Published in association with the literary agency of Wolgemuth & Associates, Inc.

Interior design by Susan Ambs

Printed in the United States of America

---

03 04 05 06 07 08 09 /❖ DC/ 10 9 8 7 6 5 4 3 2

CONTENTS

The
GOD
I LOVE

For Tyler Eareckson Kinnamon,
my fourth cousin with whom I share a birthday . . .

And to Ken Tyler, Cody, and Jesse,
my great-nephews with whom I share Ocean City memories . . .

The Eareckson line may be ended,
but the adventure goes on.
Keep the story alive, boys!

The GOD I LOVE

 Part One

My son, preserve sound judgment and discernment, do not let them out of your sight; they will be life for you, an ornament to grace your neck. Then you will go on your way in safety, and your foot will not stumble; when you lie down, you will not be afraid; when you lie down, your sleep will be sweet.

Proverbs 3:21–24

I dug my toes into the sand of the Delaware beach, hugged my knees, and drew as close to the campfire as I could. The flames warmed our faces while behind us the night air chilled our backs. Huddled with my sisters and cousin, I smelled the burning logs and breathed in the fire's heat. We all sat in awe of my father. He stood across the campfire from us, a figure a-swirl in rising heat and smoke, his face underlit by flame as if he were a prophet on Mount Sinai. We clutched each other as he wove his story. And we didn't dare look over our shoulders toward the ocean, lest we catch sight of—

"The Flying Dutchman!"

My father's eyes widened as he fixed his gaze on us. "Just a few hundred yards across the water, he was, standing on the bow of his ship. He was so close I could see the glow of his pipe!"

The campfire crackled and popped, a burst of sparks twirling upward in the smoke. Another wave crashed on the sand, *shissh-SHING*, spilling its white foam over the ridge of the beach. Each wave edged closer to our campfire than the last one. Now I couldn't help myself. I peered over my shoulder, wondering if the Flying Dutchman's phantom schooner was out there, somewhere on the dark ocean.

"All the mates on board our ship had nearly given up," my father intoned. "Our vessel had been caught for five days in the Sargasso Sea. The thick seaweed had entwined our rudder and held us fast in its deadly grip. The water supply was gone, and our tongues were cracked and swollen. We knew our hope was spent when—"

"You saw the Dutchman," my sister whispered.

"Oh-*hoh*! you're a sharp lassie," Daddy commended.

We knew the legend by heart. It started on a wind-whipped, stormy night in the 1600s, when a Dutch sea captain steered his ship into the jaws of a gale at the Cape of Good Hope. The mounting waves hammered the vessel's sides, and the ship began to sink. As raging waters flooded the deck, the captain raised his fist and railed, "I *will* round this cape, even if I have to keep sailing until doomsday!"

As the legend goes, he did. And anyone who had the misfortune of sighting the old Flying Dutchman would surely die a terrible death. To this day, if you see the dark clouds of a gathering squall looming on the horizon, beware. You may spy the old Dutch sea captain smoking his pipe, and if you do, you too may seal your fate.

"But if you saw the Flying Dutchman when you were caught in the Sargasso Sea," one of us asked, "why didn't you die?"

We knew the answer. But we had to hear it again.

"Your daddy isn't afraid of any old curse," our father declared. "Why, I looked over the bow of our ship, and I spotted a great devil-fish. That gave me an idea."

I didn't know what a devil-fish was. But as Daddy spread his hands wide and flapped his arms, I knew it was something really big and powerful, like a giant manta ray. "I called for a harpoon," he gestured, "and waited for that devil-fish to float by. Slowly, I took aim—and I hurled the spear into his back!"

I grimaced.

"The great fish strained against the rope, but I held tight, calling for my shipmates. 'I say, *you*, Angus Budreau, and *you*, Georgy Banks! Tie the end to the capstan!' They moved quickly while the fish pulled harder. 'Up with the foresail and mainsail and the mizzen! Set the jib and the flying jib!' I yelled.

"Slowly, our ship began to creak and groan. She was inching forward, pulled by the two-ton fish, straining and flapping his wing-fins with all his might. I could feel the weeds snapping beneath our hull—"

Our own muscles tightened at the mighty fish's effort—

"—and suddenly, we broke free. The sails began to flutter and fill with air. Finally, a gust caught the mainsail. The crew let out a cheer. Our ship was freed from the grip of the Sargasso Sea! As that tired old devil-fish sank into the murky depths, having spent his strength, we waved our sailor's caps farewell. And once again, we hit the high seas."

I felt sad that the devil-fish had to die. But I was glad my father had lived to tell the story. So was Mom—I could tell by the way she looked at him. I always searched her face after Daddy ended a story, to see whether the tale was true. She never gave anything away, though. She just stood up to throw another log on the fire. If one of us asked, "Mommy, is that true? Did that really happen?" she gave a sly grin. Maybe she didn't believe Daddy's stories as much as we did. But to her credit, she didn't let on. She always left us thinking there may be some truth to his tales, with her faithful answer: "Good story, Cap'n John!"

A burst of sparks exploded from the fire, and a gust scattered them in the night.

"There's his pipe!" someone cried. "I see the sparks!"

"No you don't."

"Yes I do!"

"Don't."

"Do!"

It went back and forth that way, *don't-do, don't-do*, until Mother stopped the motor, shushing, "Quiet, you girls."

"So, what happened to the Flying Dutchman?"

My father stood silent for a long moment. All was quiet except for the pounding of waves. Smoke and flames danced in the wind, causing shadows to flicker in all directions. Daddy slowly ventured a few steps toward the blackness that was the ocean, the stars, and the night. I grew nervous as he moved away from the well-lit safety of our campfire. He stopped, placed his hands on his hips, and peered into the distance as if searching for someone.

"I escaped the Dutchman," he said softly. "Not many do, but I was one of the blessed ones." My three sisters and our cousin, little Eddie, leaned forward to search the darkness too.

"Don't look too hard for that old seaman," Daddy warned, "for you may not be as fortunate as I was." His voice took on an ominous tone: "You may one day hear, 'Heh-heh-heh!'" With that, he turned around swiftly, rubbing his hands and snickering in sinister glee.

We squealed and grabbed onto one another, kicking sand to keep the ghost at bay. But the tale-teller was finished now. He gave a swooping bow, and we applauded generously.

"Please, *please* tell another one!" we chanted.

No, enough was enough. My father was always one to leave us hanging for more. I was glad for that. It made whatever else we did next sweeter. Like singing. When the stories ended, it was usually time for songs. Campfire songs, Girl Scout songs, hiking, sailing, or cowboy songs.

My mother and father crisscrossed more logs on the fire, creating an inferno, and we kids backed away our blankets. We had all spent the day digging for clams on the other side of the barrier island. The shallow, clear water of the Indian River inlet there concealed hundreds of fat clams just inches below the sand. The day's labor had been successful, and now our white-canvas Keds were lined up by the fire to dry out. My father's best friend—Uncle Eddie to us—ambled over and plopped a couple of ice buckets next to his son, little Eddie, "our cousin." They were filled with clams.

We each reached in and took one. Squinting our eyes against the heat of the campfire, we carefully placed the clams on the end of a log near enough to the flames to steam them. Soon the clams were bubbling around the edges. One by one, they popped open. Using our thumb and forefinger, we gingerly picked up a hot, half-opened shell, *ouch!*-ing and blowing on them until they cooled. We could hardly wait to get the clams, wet and salty, hot and chewy, into our mouths.

Daddy tilted his sailor's cap and began dancing a silly jig. He launched into a song written for him by an old sweetheart from his merchant marine days, in the early 1900s. It was a song to eat clams by.

> *I would not marry an oyster man, I'll tell you the reason why:*
> *His boots are always muddy, his shoes are never dry.*
> *A sailor boy, a sailor boy, a sailor boy 'twill be.*
> *Whenever I get married, a sailor's bride I'll be!*

Reaching farther down into the ice, past the clams piled on top, we pulled out fresh oysters. Our Uncle George, Daddy's brother, was in charge of knifing them open. This was one of those artful

Maryland skills we hoped we too would one day excel in. It requires piercing the shell, heart, and muscle in a way that keeps the oyster plump and intact.

Uncle George passed out the opened oysters to us, and I held mine up, comparing its size to my sisters'. To hold in your hand the biggest and juiciest was a triumph in the art of gross. Balancing mine just so, I flattened my bottom lip, pressed the edge of the shell to it, tilted the oyster slightly, and slurped. I had seen some people swallow an oyster whole, but I preferred Daddy's way: chewing it. It tasted better that way, releasing a musty, salty flavor. The ritual never seemed odd when I was a child, but years later I would understand what people meant by the phrase "acquired taste."

Sea songs eventually gave way to cowboy songs, and then, when Daddy was sure we'd squeezed all the play we could from the evening, we sang hymns. Suddenly, the scene around the campfire was transformed from one of clam-slurping, sand-kicking, and tall-tale camaraderie into a sanctuary under the stars. The glowing sparks that rose now didn't come from a seaman's pipe, and the Atlantic Ocean no longer held fearful secrets of Davy Jones's Locker. Even the hissing foam of the retreating waves sounded soothing. Never was there a sweeter satisfaction than to lie back on a blanket, my hands under my head, and gaze at the starry dome above while singing a hymn.

I forgot all about tall tales as my father, full of warmth and tenderness, led us.

> *On a hill far away stood an old rugged cross,*
> *The emblem of suff'ring and shame;*
> *And I love that old cross where the dearest and best*
> *For a world of lost sinners was slain.*

We all joined in on the chorus. I loved adding harmony, fitting my notes under my parents' melody. We swelled the first part, like the flowing of the tide, and then sang gently on the last part, like the tide as it ebbed.

> *So I'll cherish the old rugged cross,*
> *Till my trophies at last I lay down;*

I will cling to the old rugged cross,
And exchange it some day for a crown.

As the rest of the family went on to the second verse, I stopped singing. I was listening to a larger song, one that came from the star-splattered heavens. With my knees bent heavenward, the fronts of my legs caught the heat and light of the campfire. A deep, cool shadow was cast over the rest of me as I lay listening to the universe drift by. Tiny clusters of stars and great constellations speckled the night, while the surf pounded away. The Atlantic Ocean was yet another universe of mysterious currents, touching the toes of Ireland and England, places too far away for me to believe they were real. And here we were, huddled around our small fire, a tiny ember on a beach stretching north and south for miles, with nary another camp in sight. We were a single point of light among thousands that night on the eastern seaboard, a coast on one of many continents, all on a planet dwarfed by galaxies spinning above.

I had never felt so small. Yet so safe.

Safe, secure, and significant. I couldn't imagine a kid anywhere else on the planet that night, much less among the sand dunes of the Delaware coast, who felt as safe as I. Part of that feeling was the stories. Most of it, the hymns. When someone started up, "I come to the garden alone, while the dew is still on the roses," I felt as though God himself were among us, illuminated by the fire and breathing a sigh with each wave.

My earliest recollections of being stirred by the Spirit happened through hymns. Soft, sweet, old hymns—the kind my Aunt Kitty liked to sing when she and Uncle George visited us on Friday nights, to go over the books from Daddy's business. Or the kind we sang at our little church in Catonsville. The sort of hymns we sang in the truck as we came over the Chesapeake Bay Bridge to the eastern shore, down Highway 1 through Queen Anne's County, over the bridge to the barrier island and our camping site. The same hymns whose words I knew by heart yet could not explain.

I know whom I have believ-ed and am persuaded
That he is able to keep that which I've committed
Unto him against that day.

I treasured this family hymn, but as for its meaning, I was clueless. It didn't bother me that I couldn't grasp it. Five-year-olds are able to tuck words into cubbyholes in their hearts, like secret notes stored for a rainy day. All that mattered to me now was that these hymns bound me to the melody of my parents and sisters. The songs had something to do with God, my father, my family, and a small seed of faith safely stored in a heart-closet.

"Come on, everybody!" Daddy clapped his hands and roused us from our blankets. "Up on your feet and try this one."

Climb, climb up sunshine mountain, heavenly breezes blow

We climbed the air and waved our hands hula-style—

Climb, climb up sunshine mountain, faces all aglow

—made flower-faces with a smile—

Turn, turn from sin and sadness, look up to the sky

—we frowned on the word *sin* and lifted our faces on the word *sky*—

Climb, climb up sunshine mountain, you and I.

—we pointed to someone else's heart, then to our own.

A hymn or Sunday school song that included hand motions demanded to be performed with no less confidence than a secret clubhouse handshake. Anyone who missed making like a flower, or looking sad when singing *sin*, was demoted to the last rung of the clubhouse ladder and thereby eyed carefully on the next motion-song. One had to keep up.

The hours around the campfire passed too quickly. Mother hadn't piled any driftwood onto the glowing coals for a while, and now the embers merely breathed small ghosts. We closed out the campfire with my father's favorite hymn. It was a hymn of the sea:

Brightly beams our Father's mercy
From his lighthouse evermore;
But to us he gives the keeping
Of the lights along the shore.
Dark the night of sin has settled,
Loud the angry billows roar;

Eager eyes are watching, longing
For the lights along the shore.
Trim your feeble lamp, my brother!
Some poor seaman, tempest tossed—
Trying now to make the harbor,
In the darkness may be lost.
Let the lower lights be burning,
Send a beam across the waves!
Some poor fainting struggling seaman,
You may rescue, you may save.

When the ocean mist began to overtake our campfire, we gathered our blankets and trekked back over the dunes to our tents. A flashlight led the way to the top of the barrier dune, between the beach and the smaller sand mounds where our tents nestled. The youngest Eareckson, I trudged behind my father, dragging my blanket.

As we crested the top of the mountainous barrier dune, we paused. To the south I could spot the Fenwick Island lighthouse. To the north, the glow of the town of Rehoboth Beach, miles up the coast. We were high up enough to see the starlight shimmering on Indian River Bay, several hundred yards to the west. The peak of sand we stood on was the only defense between the dark, dangerous ocean and our home continent. I reached for my father's hand.

"Daddy, what does it mean, 'Let the lower lights be burning'?"

My father looked out over the bay. He lifted a hand and pointed straight ahead, into the night. "See those?" he said.

I looked into the dark. A red light on the bay blinked on, then off. A green channel marker did the same.

"Those are the lower lights," he said.

That fact alone amazed me. I was always amazed when some mysterious word or line in a hymn found its counterpart in my world. Seeing a cross on a hill far away. Or coming into a garden alone, where the dew was still on the roses. The first time I ever won a trophy in a Brownies contest, I clutched it tightly and happily, "'til my trophies at last I lay down" on my dresser that night. I was amazed to think heaven might have a judge with trophies to hand out. And here, amazingly, were actual lower lights.

"Lower lights mark where the water is deep enough for a boat to sail safely," Daddy explained. "If those lights go out, sailors won't be able to tell where the sandbar is. Ships have wrecked on many shores for want of channel markers."

"So, why are they called 'lower lights' in the song?"

"God is the lighthouse, and we are his lower lights. We point the way, we show where it's safe to go," he explained. "That's what you do."

"I do?"

He held my hand, and together we slid down the side of the dune.

"Yes, you do," he said. He pronounced it as a fact about me, a fact I knew I was too young to absorb. "It's like what you've learned from the Lord," he said, shifting to a more serious tone, "'Let your light so shine before men.'"

I didn't know much stuff from the Bible. But the way my father said the words made them sound like something King James said, if not the Lord. Or like something Daddy would make up. Whichever, my father expected me to let my light so shine before men. I didn't quite understand what my light was or how I should shine it before men. But that was okay. I could never quite keep straight when things were from the Bible or from my father. This was probably because of the impressive way he shifted his tone of voice, as though he were speaking *ex cathedra*, like a real prophet with a message from heaven. Or it might have been the way he pronounced *Lord* with an Irish brogue. He never did that with any other important word beginning with *L*—only with *Lord*, as if he were Spencer Tracy playing the Irish priest in *Boys Town*. I figured the accent came from my Scots-Irish grandmother, Anna Verona Cacy, whom I never knew. Like Daddy, she was the source of many adventure stories. My father and grandmother had a corner on the *Laard*.

My dad, born John King Eareckson in 1900, should have been born a cabin boy on a clipper ship. He might as well have been. One of his earliest jobs was serving as errand boy for a crew of carpenters and shipbuilders who worked at the Baltimore dry docks, repairing wooden clipper ships. Those men's names were Angus Budreau and Georgy Banks—yes, the same guys who showed up in Daddy's stories—as well as Joe Dowsit and Pete DeVeau, sailing with him out of the Sargasso Sea or prospecting gold in Wind River Canyon. They could handle an adz with the best, and they were rowdy ruffians who drank heartily and cursed loudly. Yet when they tried to entice my father to drink, he refused, as he often told us proudly. He chose instead to go for ice cream made on Pratt Street, near the harbor. Naturally, they dubbed him Ice Cream Johnny. I was convinced my father had made up the rhyme, "I scream, you scream, we all scream for ice cream." I found out otherwise only later, when the Good Humor man told me so.

When Johnny Eareckson became old enough to harness horses, he was up before dawn, hitching the family wagon and making deliveries for his father's coal company. He never completed his schooling, for reasons of which I'm not sure. By the age of nineteen, though, he had started his own flooring company, hurrying to and from jobs on his bicycle. He had to scramble to keep up with his three more-learned brothers: Uncle George, an accountant, Uncle Vince, an architect, and Uncle Milt, a preacher.

John usually came home late to the family's small, brick row house with marble front steps on Stricker Street. He was exhausted every day from heavy labor—a kind of labor different from what his brothers did at their desk, drawing board, or pulpit. There was hardly a night when, creaking open the back door, Johnny didn't encounter his mother, Anna Verona, sitting in the kitchen by the coal stove, an afghan on her lap and a Bible in her hands. She was reading and praying for her boys. Especially for Johnny, the son who didn't fit the mold of his brothers, the one whose heart was a bit more tender and tumultuous, full of passion and adventure. How Anna Eareckson loved her Johnny, she said with an Irish lilt.

And he loved her.

"I'll never forget," he said, shaking his head, "I'd come home from wrestling at the YMCA, my brothers from school and work downtown, and Mother would say to us, 'We need coal for the stove tonight. Vince, it's your turn.' My brothers and I would be clowning around by the sink, snapping towels at each other, and Vince would say that it was George's turn. 'Not mine, it's Milton's,' and Milt would point at me, and I would push Vince and . . . before you knew it, there we'd see Mother, smudged with black dust, trudging up the cellar steps in her long skirts, carrying a heavy bucket of coal in her frail hands. It about busted my heart open."

My father's mother died young. She worked herself into an early grave. It was something Daddy never seemed able to forgive himself for, as if a family of four strapping, healthy boys could have—*should* have—somehow eased their mother's labor. It explained why, whenever my father spoke her maiden name, *Anna Verona Cacy*, he did so with such fondness of heart and with that Irish lilt. It also told me why he loved to sing "Let the Lower Lights Be Burning," one of my grandmother's favorite hymns.

> *Let the lower lights be burning,*
> *Send a beam across the waves!*
> *Some poor fainting, struggling seaman*
> *You may rescue, you may save.*

When Daddy and I got back to camp, we plopped our things down by the picnic table. Uncle George was closing up the Coleman stove. He had fried his prized soft-shell crabs for dinner that evening. Nearby, aglow with the light from the hissing propane lantern, my mother and a few aunts were putting things away in the coolers. Taking the lantern in hand, Mommy led my sisters and me to the little pup-tent beyond our camp, which served as our makeshift latrine. From there, she lit the way back to our huge army tent and through the wooden screen door. We slid off our sandy shorts and donned sweatshirts over our damp underwear. That's what I liked about camping at the beach—we could sleep in something fun beside pajamas.

Brushing the sand off our feet, we ducked under the mosquito netting and climbed into our cots. My cot was in the corner, and I loved it when the weather was pleasant enough to keep the tent's sides rolled up. That way, I could hear the adults whispering and the hissing of the lantern. As a night breeze flapped the netting, I would nestle into my pillow, clutch my stuffed rabbit, and fight off sleep as long as I could. I wanted to savor the taste of salt air, the aroma of coffee being prepared for tomorrow's breakfast, the hushed conversation of my mother, father, and relatives, and the cotton down of my warm sleeping bag. I knew no mosquito buzzing overhead could invade. Under the protective netting, I was safe. As safe as under the covers in my own bedroom, gazing at my favorite bedside plaque, the one of the little girl in her boat.

> *Dear God, my little boat and I*
> *are on your open sea.*
> *Please guide us safely through the waves*
> *my little boat and me.*

I wondered what adventures tomorrow would bring. I hoped I would be wakened by the smell of sizzling bacon. Maybe Daddy would make his poached eggs—an egg fried in a hot skillet, a cup full of water splashed in at the last minute, a lid to cover, and salt and pepper to season. I hoped Uncle George had put the ice from Lewis Dairy into the big milk jug, so the water would taste icy-cold from the dipper. I wondered if my cousin Little Eddie and my sister Kathy and I would discover any horseshoe crabs or conch shells in the tide pools. Or if we would play horse, galloping up and down the sand hills that stretched for miles on either side of our tent. I hoped the day would be bright and hot, so that when I lay on the sand with my cheek against my forearm, I would smell the sweet Coppertone.

I hoped we would make castles in the sand with Aunt Lee and Uncle Eddie, dig after burrowing sand crabs, watch the waves erase our footprints, shower when the sun went down, and slather Noxzema on our sun-pinkened skin. In the evening, after crab cakes, we'd help Mom wash the pots and pans in the ocean. Then we would drive to Rehoboth Beach, to walk the boardwalk and have ice cream or hot french fries with vinegar. Most of all, I hoped we would enjoy another fire on the beach. And another story from Daddy. Or Uncle George singing "Ramona," while holding up his cigar and leading us all like an impresario.

Whatever I hoped, I would not be disappointed. The flapping of the mosquito netting hypnotized us into sleep. "Goodnight, girls," I heard Daddy whisper. Or maybe—*I hoped*—it was God.

I don't know if they make many fathers like the one who raised me. No, I don't think so. How many daddies saw the Wright Brothers plane fly over Baltimore, or one of the first Model-T Fords chug down Howard Street? How many dads weave their children into a whole world of adventure, through the tales they spin by heart? My father traded with Indians in British Columbia and fought bears near the Yukon border—yes, I'm sure he did fight that bear with his hands, and that it wasn't just a story. Really. But even if the one about the bear didn't happen, I knew my father's tender heart and fine character and love for the Laard were real.

The next evening, just as I'd hoped, we returned to camp from Rehoboth Beach early enough for a fire. Soon the driftwood that my sisters, Linda, Jay, Kathy, and I had collected during the day was roaring, and the stars were sprinkled above us from one horizon to the other, like vast powdered sugar. The curling of the waves glowed phosphorescent from the red tide, and my Uncle Eddie had just finished singing "You Are My Sunshine."

"Do your poem, Daddy," I chimed, "the one about the bar." Ever the literalist, I had only recently discovered that this, my father's classic recitation, wasn't about a saloon.

Daddy stuck his hands in the pockets of his baggy pants and stared at the fire. Then he began his litany, which was more Eareckson than Tennyson. The poem came from somewhere deep down in my father's breast. As he spoke its haunting lines, I wanted badly for someone to please reach up and hold onto him, lest he turn toward the waves and cross the bar without me.

> Sunset and evening star,
>   And one clear call for me,
> And may there be no moaning of the bar,
>   When I put out to sea.
>   But such a tide as moving seems asleep,
>   Too full for sound and foam,
> When that which drew from out the boundless deep
>   Turns again home.
>   Twilight and evening bell,
>   And after that the dark!
> And may there be no sadness of farewell,
>   When I embark;

For tho' from out our bourne of time and place
The flood may bear me far,
I hope to see my Pilot face to face
When I have crossed the bar.

No one ever broke the silence that followed one of my father's poems. We simply kept listening while the lines settled in, the way you'd listen to a retreating sheet of surf before the next heavy wave crashed down. I didn't understand the poem, except for the part about seeing the Pilot—I surmised that was God. But my heart nearly twisted in half to think that my father loved a poem about dying.

I remember reaching for Kathy's hand. I knew she would understand my fear. We shared a bed together back home. Often, after Daddy finished telling a bedtime story, and we heard him walk down the stairs, we lay in the dark listening to our breathing. I reached for her hand once then and murmured, "What if something awful happens?"—I wanted to add "to Daddy" but couldn't choke out the words.

"I know what you mean," my sister whispered back. "I know what you mean about Dad." She held my hand then, and she held it now too, in the dancing shadows formed by the fire.

Daddy closed the poem with the same beautiful hymn we'd sung the night before. My sisters and I crescendoed on the line,

Some poor fainting, struggling seaman,
You may rescue, you may save.

Once again, all felt safe.

Surely my father rescued poor, fainting, struggling seamen. If not on the Sargasso Sea, then for certain during his merchant marine days. Yet never did I dream then that, in the not-too-distant future, I would be the poor, struggling, fainting one, going down for the third time, drowning in waves of grief higher than any surf. More terrifying than any Dutchman's curse.

And even Daddy wouldn't be able to help.

CHAPTER TWO

Listen, my sons, to a father's instruction; pay attention and gain understanding.

Proverbs 4:1

Memory means everything to me. I was the kind of kid who could look at an African violet on a window sill and later retrace in my mind the blue-green of the stamen, the fuzzy leaves, and the soft purple flowers, when others might forget there was even a window sill.

My memory became all-important to me in 1967. That was the year I was paralyzed in a diving accident.

I remained in the hospital for nearly two years. Most of that time I spent on a Stryker frame, lying face-up staring at ceiling tiles or being flipped face-down to stare at floor tiles. With a body that could basically no longer move or feel, I pulled up from my memory bank every jaunt to the beach, every horseback ride, every tennis game, every song, *everything*, and turned it over like a diamond, savoring its color and light. If I couldn't use my hands anymore, I would bear down hard to recall what it felt like to hold a bottle of Coke and feel the ice-cold droplets run down the glass and over my fingers. If I could never walk, I would revive every sensation of bending, stretching, stooping, running, or wiggling my toes.

Memories were all I had back then. They became as reassuring to me as gazing up from our beach campfire to check how far a constellation had drifted. Or snuggling under the covers back home in bed and gazing up at the stars my father had painted on my bedroom ceiling.

Back in 1955, I think I was the only kid in my neighborhood— maybe in our whole town—who went to sleep each night under the stars, even if they were only painted. Daddy seemed to understand that children love sleeping under a night sky, and so, since we couldn't always be at camp, he brought camp to us. And since Daddy was a housing contractor, he built our rambling, rustic stone-and-timber, lodge-like house where all the nooks, crannies, arches and banisters, gables and dormer windows—all hand-crafted in warm oak and Douglas fir—and all the massive stone chimneys, crowned by elk and moose horns, just waited for children to appear. Living there was like living at camp. It was fun.

From any room you could hear, "Ready or not, here I come!" because ours was the perfect house for hide-and-seek. Terror and joy seized our hearts as our feet frantically raced to find the ideal hiding spot. You could choose the second-story balcony. Or dive behind the big wooden chest in the nook at the top of the back stairs. Or hide behind the large drop-leaf table in the dining room. Or wrap yourself in Mother's raccoon coat in her closet, if you could stand the smell of mothballs. I didn't worry that my heavy breathing or stifled giggles would give me away; our large home embraced us and played along with our every game.

Other rooms joined in. The living room with its tiger rug in the corner, bear rug in the middle, and elk antlers on either end, could be on one day, a jungle; on another, the Northwest Territories. "Daddy bagged those when he was trading with Indians in the Yukon," I said of the antlers. I had no idea what the Yukon was, but it sounded far and distant, wild and exotic, a place where my father could really find elk that big. Linda even got in on the game, insisting the gigantic logs supporting the ceiling "really came from Captain Hook's ship. Really."

For years our living room played along, keeping our childhood secrets safe. I always assumed our house was typical, until I went to other kids' houses to play. I discovered homes with white carpet, low ceilings, "do not touch" silver services on buffet tables, and porcelain Marie Antoinette figurines atop fireplace mantles. Even the couches were covered in clear, stiff plastic. Those houses had sheer curtains, see-through china cabinets, and absolutely nowhere to hide. It was then I realized something that would stick with me for years to come. The Earecksons were different. And maybe a little odd.

It was a fact I pondered under my bedroom-ceiling stars. Actually, it wasn't my bedroom, it was Kathy's. She was slightly older than I was, and she had the room first. That meant she had dibs on the best dresser drawers, the larger side of the closet, and the best side of the bed—next to the door. Usually before lights out, Kathy would kneel on the bed, draw an imaginary line down the middle, and say, "See this?" From the headboard to the baseboard, her finger traced the demilitarized zone between us. "This is *my* side of the bed, and you better not cross this line."

I was five years old at the time, and the last of four girls. I was afraid to cross her, or her line.

Rooming with my sister was not that bad, although I was constantly reminded to close the bathroom door after a shower so the moisture wouldn't warp her dresser. She had neatly taped cotton balls on all four dresser corners to protect the wood from me and my toys. I couldn't understand why she prized that dresser so—it wasn't as if she was about to get married at the age of nine. No matter. It felt good to lie in bed next to someone, feel her warmth under the covers, listen to our parents' hushed conversation downstairs, and through the glow of the hall light, gaze at angels on our bedroom wall.

Yes, angels. Three of them. A brunette, a blonde, and a redhead.

Our bedroom was a little like an attic dormer, and Daddy had painted the angels on the slanted wall to our left. *There's no one like my dad,* I prided myself in him. *He can sing, tell stories, and paint angels!* Not only that, on the entire wall behind our headboard Daddy had oil-painted Jack climbing a beanstalk, an old woman living in a shoe, rock-a-bye baby in a tree top, the Pied Piper with children in tow, a cow jumping over a moon, and finally, Humpty Dumpty sitting on top of the door jamb. In the middle of this menagerie, he hung a simple painting he rendered of a dog and a boy kneeling by his bed in prayer.

Sometimes I twisted around on my elbows and peered up at the nursery-rhyme and fairy-tale characters or the dog-and-boy painting. But mainly, it was the angels that captured my attention.

The three angels nearly filled the slanted wall-ceiling, all singing with sheet music, their mouths open like big O's, and their feet firmly planted in the clouds. The first angel looked like my oldest sister, Linda. That made me chuckle. Linda was anything but an angel. Almost ten years older than I, she was into James Dean, slicking back her hair with Vaseline, rolling up her jeans and rolling down her socks, scuffing her new saddle shoes, and wearing oversized cotton shirts with the collar turned up. At school, it was too-tight sweaters with straight skirts. Elvis was king and Pat Boone was a nerd—milk and white bucks were not her style. Not that Linda walked on the wild side; she just played the part. Once, when I had to sleep in the room she and Jay Kay shared, she turned out the lights, climbed into bed next to me, and, after a few minutes of silence in the dark, turned and whispered in my ear, "Would you like to see the werewolf that lives in my closet?"

It was from Linda I learned the spirit song for Milford Mill High School:

> *I go to Milford Mill, so pity me*
> *There are no boys in the vicinity*
> *And at nine o'clock they bolt the doors*
> *I don't know why the heck I ever went there for*
> *And then it's on the bus and homeward bound*
> *I'd like to burn that durn school to the ground*
> *I'd like to smoke, drink, cuss, neck,*
> *Be a wreck, what the heck*
> *I go to Milford Senior High.*

That year, my parents placed her in an all girls' school.

The angel in the middle had blue eyes and a thick tousle of blonde curls. I guessed that was Jay Kay, except for the fact my sister had brown eyes. Jay was my favorite angel. She was a few years younger than Linda and tamer. She liked Elvis, but less for "Jail House Rock" than for "Oh, Let Me Be Your Teddy Bear." Jay looked just like Betty, the fair-haired girl with the ponytail in all the *Archie* comics. She didn't treat me like a tagalong. She liked me. "Jonathan Grundy," she affectionately called me. When Jay played "Sentimental Journey" on our upright piano, I tried to mimic her. When she sewed skirts, I gave it a try. When she artfully messed with her hair, I twisted mine up. I couldn't understand why Bob Barker didn't want Jay as Miss Maryland every September when the Miss America Pageant came on.

It was never clear who the red-headed angel was. Kathy and I hadn't yet been born when Daddy painted them, so maybe he filled the space with Linda's next-door neighbor friend, Audrey Espey, who had auburn hair. That bothered me. I studied the mural to try to figure out a way my father could paint me in it. There I'd be, the hazel-eyed towhead angel, with pigtails that stuck out like the ears of a Yorkshire terrier. I was Rocket J. Squirrel's niece.

Then again, maybe Kathy should be painted next, not me. Kath-Kath, as I called her, deserved it. She was, well, different. Chubbier, with a generous splattering of freckles and a silly grin, she was often the brunt of much teasing by Linda and sometimes Jay: "Fatty, fatty, boomba-latty," they chided. Sometimes at night, lying next to me, I heard Kathy crying.

It was not easy being the youngest. I wasn't teased the way Kathy was, but I was the end of the line. I didn't have first dibs on the T-bone from Daddy's plate at dinner. It was hand-me-down jeans, dresses, and underwear, used bikes, scuffed skates, and musty sleeping bags. The real insult was when I was dumped at Grandmom's house on Saturday mornings, after which Daddy and my sisters drove away to the horse stables.

"You can't go horseback riding with us. You're a twerp. You'll slow everybody down," Linda said.

As if that weren't bad enough, I faced the boredom of watching Mom clean my grandmother's house all day. And so, as Daddy's truck pulled away, I wrestled against my mother's grip, wailing and kicking the curb with my cowboy boots. "Enough of this!" Mother demanded. Since she was the chief disciplinarian of the family and could swat a behind pretty hard, I'd clam up.

Underneath, however, my fierce competitive spirit festered. Anger too. I was not about to be left in the dust. Or told I was too little to ride a bike. Or that I could not go horseback riding until next year. I would insist my sisters respect my "Seat saved!" when I got up for a snack during *The Red Skelton Show*. I scrambled not only to keep up but to excel. I would learn how to play the piano better than Jay, learn the words to more Elvis songs than Linda, cross Kathy's stupid line in bed if I wanted, handle a tennis racket as well as Mother, and—*and what about my father?*

The thought of outdoing Daddy was unthinkable. Yet, as I lay in bed pondering the angels, I wondered if I could paint. Perhaps as well as Daddy. *I felt guilty*. But I couldn't deny it. As I examined the painted angels, it occurred to me their hands looked funny. *Hmmm, he didn't get the hands right . . . I bet I could do better.*

Life was a competitive race to keep up with older, more athletic sisters and a father and mother with their own swimming, diving, wrestling, and tennis medals. There was no time to gripe over the fact that God had assigned me the lowest rung of the Eareckson ladder. No chance for whining or hanging onto anyone's coattails. It was keep up with the rest or get left behind.

For all the competitiveness, there was still room—lots of room —for gratitude. I'm not sure how my parents cultivated a spirit of gratitude in us, but it was commonplace for us to express appreciation for everything from food to Friday night roller-skating at Vernon's Roller Rink. "Daddy, *thank* you," or "Boy, Mom, this tastes great!" Maybe showing appreciation came from seeing the way Daddy always said, "Mommy, you're something else!" I remember noticing during dinner at a friend's house how no one said anything as bowls of food were placed on the table. I felt badly for the mother. Around our table, gratitude was ingrained early on when, with a nod from Mother, our father would lead us, saying:

> *Come Lord Jesus, be our guest*
> *let this food to us be blest.*
> *Make me kind and make me good,*
> *help me to love Thee as I should.*
> *Amen.*

If I knew safety on the beach at Delaware, it was peace I knew at home. Yes, there was the occasional slammed door and "You took the blouse out of my cupboard! Gimme it back!" and "You said *what* to my boyfriend?" There were nights when I crossed Kathy's line, kicked her in bed, she pinched back, and I screamed bloody murder, to which our mother threatened from the bottom of the stairs, "I better not hear another peep from you girls, or I'm coming up there!"

Still our home reflected peace. The kind of peace I sensed when lying in bed and listening to the night breeze rustle through the tall oak trees outside the open window. Or the way the wind would tinkle the glass chimes at the back door. Or how, when the breeze subsided, I could hear the crickets call. Or the peace that would wash over me just knowing the angels on the wall were watching. Most of all, that my parents were downstairs, talking in friendly, low tones, eating ice cream and watching *Mitch Miller* and his men sing on TV. It was pure peace. It all made me believe the Lord Jesus really *had* come and been our guest.

On special nights after dinner, Daddy pulled out his paints. He kept his large wooden paint box underneath his desk, a box I was forbidden to touch, let alone open. My heart raced and I squirmed while holding onto the end of his desk. "Oh boy, we're going to *paint!*"

"No," my father would remind me, "*I'm* going to paint."

Painting was my father's sole hobby. I kept my distance but watched closely. Setting his tubes of color in a row to the left—he was left-handed—he poured turpentine and linseed oil in little metal cups, wiped the edges with his rag, and placed the cloth out of the way. The aroma of paint filled the room.

Daddy took each of his brushes and began gently bending the stiff bristles, eyeing me the whole time. "Want to open that tube of blue for me?"

I eagerly twisted off the little cap on the wrinkled tube and handed it back to him, at which point he squeezed a generous glob of shiny, dark blue color on the palette. Then red, yellow, and a big glob of zinc white. The colors had fascinating names like cobalt blue, burnt umber, crimson red, and Payne's gray, and they sat on the palette like wet jewels. Daddy then propped a large piece of white Masonite against the bookshelf that backed his desk. He adjusted his desk lamp, picked up a large wide carpenter's pencil, and began sketching.

"What are you drawing?"

"You'll see."

I leaned on my elbows and observed how he lightly touched his canvas here and there, making broad, big lines. I spied a *National Geographic* magazine to his right, opened to a photograph of an Indian on a horse. I figured that's what he was drawing, but the marks he made on the canvas didn't resemble a horse at all.

Remembering the funny hands on the angel painting in my room, I felt I must remind him of this.

"That doesn't look like a horse."

"I know. But it will." He worked on in silence.

"When will it look like a horse?"

"When I finish the composition."

"What's a compo-o-o?"

"Composition. It's what is underneath the painting," he said, looking at me over his glasses.

Whatever that compo-zit-thing was, I still wasn't sure why Daddy didn't just start painting or, at least drawing, the horse. The stuff underneath the painting couldn't be *that* important. After many long pauses, erasures, and corrections, he put down the pencil and leaned back to look at his work. It was an interesting but obscure combination of squares and circles, none of which resembled a horse or an Indian.

"See what I've done?" my dad asked as he adjusted the lamp. Parents are funny. They know you don't know the answer to the question asked, but they ask it anyway.

I leaned over. "Hmmmm." I was embarrassed for him.

"That's my composition."

Now I was really disappointed. He had worked all this time to produce *that?*

"Joni, the composition is the most important part of a painting. If I don't get it right here," he said, pointing to his canvas with the pencil, "then I won't get this right," he patted the *National Geographic.*

I looked at the array of squares, lines, and circles. "But nobody will see this stuff," I said.

"That's why it's so important. A composition is like the bones underneath your skin. Like the foundation of this house. My horse and Indian won't look right unless I make a balanced arrangement of these squares and circles." He paused a long moment, and then added, "It's like having the Lord in your heart. Nobody can see him inside you," he said, pointing to my chest, "but he makes everything right on the outside."

The Lord in my heart. Now there was a statement that raised weird questions. Like, how does he get in there? I kept imagining a tiny Jesus figure living inside my heart, making everything go smoothly on the inside, like a little traffic cop. There were many times I wasn't so sure he was in there, but Daddy seemed to think so. I think he believed if we sang the following hymn often enough, the lesson would rub off on us.

> *Since Jesus came into my heart,*
> *Since Jesus came into my heart,*
> *Floods of joy o'er my soul*
> *Like the sea billows roll,*
> *Since Jesus came into my heart.*

I felt floods of joy fill my soul when we held out that last note, where the sea billows rolled. But then, an hour later, when I found myself playing with matches or coloring in the little white tiles on the bathroom floor or sneaking change off Daddy's dresser, I knew in my heart of hearts that Jesus wasn't there. Or if he was there, I'd thrown a wet blanket on him. I wondered if there was really a balanced arrangement of spiritual squares and circles inside of me.

Daddy went back to his squares and circles while I sat on the floor and pulled out my Roy Rogers coloring book. I flipped to my finished crayoned pages of Trigger. "Look, Daddy." He would smile and suggest I do another one.

Mother especially prized a crumpled church bulletin I had once scribbled on. We were visiting a church, the sermon was boring, and I was given the bulletin and a pen to keep me quiet. I was intrigued by the photograph of the church building on the front—it had many gables, a steeple and belfry, a side building, steep steps at the front, and bushes all around. While the speaker droned, I sat slumped, swinging my feet and studying the photo. After staring for a while, I got an idea. I took the pen and drew a little devil on the sidewalk getting ready to swing his pitchfork through the stained glass window. In the belfry I drew an angel aiming his machine gun at him. Other devils cropped up behind the bushes only to find bigger, stronger angels with pistols and swords, poised, ready to chop them down. One angel I drew was sliding down the steep slope of the roof in order to ambush a devil doing graffiti on the church's welcome sign.

While Daddy kept painting, I colored. They say the mark of artistic talent in a child is when he or she grabs any old color and begins smearing it willy-nilly all over the page, that real talent can be spotted when a youngster is brave enough to color outside the lines as would a budding Picasso or Andy Warhol. I disagree. And I would have disagreed as a kid had someone told me that. To me, the prescribed lines in the coloring book were—lo and behold—composition. Somebody who knew better than me had put those lines there, and I instinctively obeyed them, reserving my bravery for the coat of the horse where I'd shade tan into soft brown into dark brown, so as to contour the neck muscles or accent the legs. The face of Roy Rogers required at least four tones of pink and peach. Bullet, the German Shepherd, had to have gray, brown, and black.

Finally I finished another Trigger drawing—this one also had in it Buttermilk, Dale Evans's horse. I stood up and showed it to my father.

"He-e-ey, this is good." He was impressed.

Nothing catapulted me into art more vigorously than his approval. A few words, a glance, a smile, or a nod of the head can strike a match to a child's creative spirit, and I wonder if fathers understand this power of casting a vision. It's like surf-fishing at the ocean, where you lean back and cast a long line, throwing it out there for all you're worth. You're bound to get a bite. My father cast far, knowing full well I was bound to get hooked on art.

"Come over here," Daddy said. I stood up, and he hiked me up on his knee and swung me around. There I sat, front and center, at eye level with his canvas. He reached for a brush and wrapped my short fingers around it, just so, as though he were a tennis coach instructing the proper grasp on a racket. He then covered my right hand with his left. Together we jabbed the brush into the blue paint, smeared it on the palette, added a tad of yellow, and mixed well. There before my astonished eyes, we produced green. A much smoother, truer green than using crayons.

"Hold on," he said, proceeding to lift my hand with the paint-laden brush to the canvas. I was mesmerized as together we swept and swirled our way into the forest behind the squares and circles.

We moved quickly, adding a bit of tan here and a touch of blue there. I tried to second-guess his strokes, but whenever I started to wield strength, I heard, "Relax a bit." I tried to go limp in his grasp, but we were moving too fast. None of it made sense to me, but the euphoria of creating something big and beautiful with my father kept me breathless. I could hardly wait to see what we were doing.

The time went by too quickly, and I was disappointed when Daddy released our grip from the brush. Placing it down, he asked, gesturing toward the picture, "You did pretty good, don't you think?"

To my amazement, I saw the shape of an Indian on a horse, appearing out of a forest and hills. Just like in *National Geographic*. It was stunning. "But I didn't do that," I corrected him.

"Yes, you did."

There went Daddy again, giving me credit for things I knew I didn't and couldn't do. Things I knew I wasn't, like a lower light showing lost people the way or having a heart in which Jesus lived or being an artist who could create masterpieces worth framing. Then again, as I reflected on how much at home I felt in front of the canvas, perhaps my father wasn't far off. Maybe my Triggers and Buttermilks could turn into magnificent steeds on which Indians with bows and arrows would sit, hands to their brows, shielding their eyes from the western sun, scouting the wide horizons. Perhaps compo-whatever was something I did possess. In my life and on a canvas.

"Boy, did you luck out," Kathy whispered that night in bed.

In the dark, I smiled a Cheshire cat grin. Our father wasn't the sort who naturally hugged his little girls, reaching down to pick them up and give them a squeeze or a kiss on the cheek. In fact, I hardly remember him ever hugging me—maybe people weren't brought up to do that in his day. But to sit like a princess on the knee of the king of our most magnificent home, to be invited to join him in his private hobby, to touch his untouchable paints, and to create with him a scene worthy of the real Trigger, well . . .

The angels must have been smiling on me that night. And they were. Blonde- brown- and red-haired ones.

CHAPTER THREE

*Do you give the horse his strength or clothe his neck with a flowing mane?
Do you make him leap like a locust, striking terror with his proud
snorting? He paws fiercely, rejoicing in his strength, and charges into the
fray. He laughs at fear, afraid of nothing; he does not shy away from the
sword. . . . In frenzied excitement he eats up the ground; he cannot stand
still when the trumpet sounds.*

Job 39:19–24

I heard about broken necks from the horse's mouth.

Black Beauty's, to be exact. He was a horse, and horses by
nature are honest, forthright, and without guile. Why wouldn't
he tell me the truth about both happy and sad things in life?

I knew this about horses from *The Black Stallion, The Black
Stallion's Sulky Colt, Son of the Black Stallion,* and *The Black Stallion's
Revenge.* You might think horse sense wouldn't address things like
a broken neck, but Black Beauty mentioned it in the book he wrote.
I was sure he penned his autobiography, and not Anna Sewell. To
me, horses were not only able to love and feel deeply, they could
communicate. And no one communicated better than Black Beauty.

I was introduced to him one night when a baby-sitter tucked my
sister Kathy and me into bed. As we nestled under the blanket, the
sitter opened Black Beauty's book and, by the glow of the bedside
lamp, began to read. The murmur of her voice was mesmerizing,
but I struggled to stay awake, especially since she paused often to let
us look at the sketches on the pages. There were drawings of Black
Beauty when he was a colt with his mom and playing with other
colts and fillies in their pasture.

I was startled by one particular drawing of a hunt scene. I will
never forget the words of Black Beauty on the opposite page.

Before I was two years old a circumstance happened which
I have never forgotten. It was early in the spring; there had
been a little frost in the night, and a light mist still hung over
the woods and meadows. I and the other colts were feeding at

the lower part of the field when we heard, quite in the distance, what sounded like the cry of dogs. The oldest of the colts raised his head, pricked his ears, and said, "There are the hounds!" and immediately cantered off, followed by the rest of us to the upper part of the field, where we could look over the hedge and see several fields beyond. My mother and an old riding horse of our master's were also standing near, and seemed to know all about it. . . .

"Now we shall see the hare," said my mother; and just then a hare wild with fright rushed by and made for the woods. On came the dogs; they burst over the bank, leaped the stream, and came dashing across the field followed by the huntsmen. Six or eight men leaped their horses clean over, close upon the dogs. The hare tried to get through the fence; it was too thick, and she turned sharp round to make for the road, but it was too late; the dogs were upon her with their wild cries; we heard one shriek, and that was the end of her. One of the huntsmen rode up and whipped off the dogs, who would soon have torn her to pieces. He held her up by the leg torn and bleeding, and all the gentlemen seemed well pleased.

As for me, I was so astonished that I did not at first see what was going on by the brook; but when I did look there was a sad sight; two fine horses were down, one was struggling in the stream, and the other was groaning on the grass. One of the riders was getting out of the water covered with mud, the other lay quite still.

"His neck is broke," said my mother.

"And serve him right, too," said one of the colts.

I thought the same, but my mother did not join with us. . . .

Many of the riders had gone to the young man; but my master, who had been watching what was going on, was the first to raise him. His head fell back and his arms hung down, and every one looked very serious. There was no noise now; even the dogs were quiet, and seemed to know that something was wrong. They carried him to our master's house. I heard afterward that it was young George Gordon, the squire's only son, a fine, tall young man, and the pride of his family.

There was now riding off in all directions to the doctor's, to the farrier's, and no doubt to Squire Gordon's, to let him know about his son. When Mr. Bond, the farrier, came to look at the black horse that lay groaning on the grass, he felt him all over, and shook his head; one of his legs was broken. Then someone ran to our master's house and came back with a gun; presently there was a loud bang and a dreadful shriek, and then all was still; the black horse moved no more. . . .

Not many days after we heard the church-bell tolling for a long time, and looking over the gate we saw a long, strange black coach that was covered with black cloth and was drawn by black horses; after that came another and another and another, and all were black, while the bell kept tolling, tolling. They were carrying young Gordon to the churchyard to bury him. He would never ride again. What they did with Rob Roy I never knew; but 'twas all for one little hare.

It was not the best story to read at bedtime.

Over the following weeks, I took the book off the shelf several times and turned to the hunt scene. The picture showed a man sprawled on the ground by a stream, his head turned at an awkward angle. I couldn't help being strangely pulled to the sketch, and I kept rehearsing the words, "His head hung back and his arms hung down . . . they carried young Gordon to the churchyard to bury him. He would never ride again."

My head agreed with the colt: "Serves him right!" But my heart wrenched for the man with the broken neck. He was young, fine, and tall, and the pride of his family. I felt so sorry for him and his daddy.

I was also terrified. I was five years old, and I rode horses too. Big horses.

Back in the fall of 1954, I had finally been released from Grandmom's house and allowed to go to the stables with my father and sisters. I broke in riding behind the roll of Daddy's saddle as together we perched atop his sixteen-hand-high palomino, Cherokee. My father would swing me up behind him and say, "Hold on tight to my belt, Joni." He then tapped Cherokee with his heels, and off we'd go, galloping alongside Linda on her horse, Bobcat,

Jay on Monica, and Kathy on Cactus. The dust billowed behind us as we tore up the trail. "Hold on!" Daddy's voice carried on the wind.

I clasped the leather of my father's belt in a sweaty death grip. Cherokee's back was broad and, bouncing this way and that, I could barely squeeze my thighs around his barrel. But I was staying up with the family—I was hanging in there. The grooms at Wakefield Farm where we boarded our horses got a kick out of helping my family saddle up every weekend. No one rode with more speed and courage than we girls, they bragged.

But now it was the summer of 1955. This year would be different. My father thought it was time I had my own horse. Not a pony—ponies couldn't keep up with Cherokee and the others. So, with my mother's blessing—Mom enjoyed sitting down by the chestnut tree near the pasture fence rather than ride—I was handed the reins to Thunder.

Thunder was the family's hand-me-down. My older sisters had learned the basics on her, and now it was my turn to ride the docile old Appaloosa mare with the short, ratty mane and tail. Never did God create a kinder, gentler horse than Thunder. She seemed to understand that the flyweight sitting atop her could barely hold on to the saddle horn. For all my bravado, I could barely manage two reins and a horn. And Thunder was huge. She wasn't a merry-go-round horse at Gwynn Oak Amusement Park. And she wasn't one of the little ponies you could ride for ten cents at the far end of the park. Being on her certainly wasn't the privileged seat I had come to enjoy behind my father and his saddle. Now I was out there all alone on a very large horse, even if she was old and docile.

There were plenty of wide open pastures in which to run—I mean *really* run. Wakefield was a sprawling farm that not only boarded horses like ours but raised Maryland thoroughbreds for hunting and jumping. Every time we entered Wakefield's gates, I pictured Black Beauty grazing in the fields. A large white barn stood at the end of the drive with the clubhouse and white-pillared mansion on the left. A glorious chestnut tree shaded the paddock area, and huge weeping willows draped over the creek where mares and foals gathered. White fences separated the many pastures that bordered the woods of Leakin Park. It was hard to believe such a stately manor was only five miles up the road from our home on Poplar Drive.

The first day I rode Thunder by myself was a family milestone. Daddy plopped a child-sized saddle on her back, and as he tightened the girth, Thunder shook her head. I saw that it was impossible for me to reach the stirrups, even if I used the mounting steps by the paddock. So my father grabbed me by the waist and heaved me up onto the saddle. I shook the reins and flailed my little legs to get the old mare to go. When she ambled over toward the watering trough, I turned and gave my dad and mom a big grin.

From that day on, I couldn't wait for Saturday mornings. Kathy and I would leap out of bed before the rest and pull on our cowboy boots over our pajama bottoms. We retrieved the fresh bottles of milk from the backdoor step, slurped off the cream, poured ourselves Cheerios, and—anxiously waiting for the rest of the family to get up—sat cross-legged in front of the small, black-and-white TV in Daddy's den. First, we watched *My Friend Flicka* followed by *Fury.* Then there was *Hopalong Cassidy* in his broad-brimmed black hat with silver conches, and *The Roy Rogers Show* with Roy on Trigger and Dale Evans on Buttermilk, wishing my sister and me "Happy Trails."

But my love affair with Saturday morning horse programs found its most thrilling consummation in *The Lone Ranger.* Nothing got my heart pumping faster than when the masked man galloped Silver to the top of a hill and reined him around to face me, as I sat wide-eyed at the bottom of the trail. He yelled, "Hi-ho, Silver!" and his beautiful white stallion with flowing mane reared, nostrils flaring, head tossing, and magnificently pawed the air. I wondered if I could get Thunder to do that.

After we stacked our bowls in the kitchen sink, we rushed upstairs, pulled on our jeans, and loaded our cap pistols for a gunfight in the backyard. Nothing sounded neater than the bang of a successfully smashed gunpowder-circle, followed by that wonderful acrid smoke. Finally, when the rest of the family was ready, we crammed into my father's old green truck, a Dodge cab with a covered, open-sided flatbed Daddy had hand-welded. The vehicle was as odd as us Earecksons. Years later I would catch my breath the first time I saw the opening scene of *The Beverly Hillbillies*. "That's our truck!"

It was a short drive to Wakefield, and as soon as we parked, my sisters and I raced to the barn to see our horses. The stable hands had left them in the pasture most of the week, but on Saturday mornings our horses were in their stalls and ready for saddling.

There was a method to this Saturday-morning madness of Daddy's. I'd heard rumors that sometime in the future we would be heading to Two-Bars Seven Ranch in Tie Siding, Wyoming, to see Uncle Ted. He was another one of Daddy's friends, but I was too little to remember him. All I knew was he owned a seven-thousand-acre ranch and—could it be? Were we really going to mount up on horses and help Uncle Ted herd his cattle? I imagined us yippee-ty-yi-yo-ing all the way to the stockyards. Now all our Saturday morning horseback rides through the fields of Wakefield and the trails of Leakin Park had a purpose: we had to become expert horsewomen.

Horseback riding was second nature to me. Something magical happens between a horse and a little girl when tender young hands bend the will of a massive and superior animal. To be on top of something so mountainous and muscular, living and breathing, with fine intelligence and a sensitive spirit, and then to have him arch his neck so he can nuzzle yours—that is sublime. To a five-year-old, it's the closest thing to walking on air. Whether it's the awesome awareness of your supreme authority over and complete responsibility for this pleasant beast beneath you, or the primal wonder of watching grace and courage in motion, a small girl can't help but swoon for a beautiful horse. Nothing matches the euphoric feeling of destiny and grandeur when a horse's mane flows in rhythm with a girl's, as the two, perfectly melded, consume the ground beneath them. Boys may be enthralled by trucks, with all their impersonal, mechanical moving parts, but only horses can seduce little girls.

And I was captured. It was another one of those celestial things. Being on a horse was like lying on my back on Rehoboth Beach, gazing at the stars and sensing the entire universe could fit into my small soul. In God's order of creation, a horse slid under the wire in a close second behind the universe. I could look into the animal's eye—a pastime that fascinated me—and see light and life. Where did that come from? Who made that?

A horse couldn't whisper secrets in your ear, but he still somehow had personality. Cherokee was the John Wayne amongst the others in the pasture. Monica was as buxom and sassy as Aunt Jemima on the syrup bottles. Bobcat was a gangster, and Cactus, with his crazy, sticking-out mane, was as corny as Alfalfa on *Spanky and Our Gang.* How could something that wasn't human be so . . . *human?*

Best of all, I was able to "hear" the messages horses seemed to communicate. It was like listening to the night sky at Rehoboth. Did other kids hear—no, *feel*—this language too? I felt as though something bigger was behind horses and stars, some universal principle forever seeking local expression through things, forever sharing the same message that seemed to touch me so deeply. Maybe it was God talking. And anything so closely connected to God had to be safe.

I got my proof of this pudding one Saturday morning as I trotted Thunder across the pasture to Wakefield's show ring. The day was breezy, sunny, and bright, and I was confident in my balance on top of Thunder. Maybe too confident. A gopher or something frightened her, and she darted sideways. Suddenly, I lost my stirrups, and without a good grip on the horn, I began sliding down the side of the saddle. Thankfully, I was still clutching the reins. That broke my fall, allowing me to gently slip and then plummet the remaining short distance to the ground.

Still gripping the reins tightly, I was wrenching Thunder's head down and sideways, so that she slobbered on my hair. When I realized my predicament, my tears quickly turned to heaving sobs.

Thunder shook free of my grip, perked her ears toward the barn, and whinnied loudly. While the reins dangled from her, she circled me a time or two, then planted both front legs firmly on either side of my body. I could look straight up into her chest and underbelly. She whinnied again.

Within minutes, Daddy came running across the field to discover me in the high grass under Thunder's belly. Nervous and out of breath, he pushed the horse back. "Good girl," he said—I wasn't sure if he meant me or the horse, but either was fine. Even though I was unharmed, it felt good to have my father's arms around me.

"Are you okay?" he asked, feeling my arms and legs. I rubbed my eyes and nodded.

"The good Laard was sure watching out for you," he whispered anxiously.

"So was Thunder," I sniffed.

Daddy understood what I meant and reached to stroke the bridge of the old mare's nose. For a moment, a brute beast had become enlightened, as sure as any angelic emissary from God. From that day on our family spoke often and with great fondness of the horse who called for help, who planted herself firmly over me like a mother hen covering a chick. The fact I could have seriously injured myself never made it into the story. I quickly learned why.

"Joni, you must get back up in the saddle."

I stood next to my father, finger in mouth, holding his hand. I stared up at the empty saddle. Thunder stamped her hoof and swished her tail at a fly. She swung her head around, cocked her ears toward several horses in the next pasture, and neighed so loudly her whole body shook. Her chivalry had disappeared. She was back to being an ordinary horse.

"Daddy, no-o-o, please no," I cried.

"Look at me," he said in all seriousness. "You must get back up on this horse, or you will be afraid for the rest of your life."

I knew I didn't have to get back up on that horse to prove I'd never be fearful. But I understood the point Daddy was driving home. It was an issue of pride and propriety. And of being an Eareckson. Earecksons were to get up, brush themselves off, and try again.

My stomach was in knots. My body stiffened as my father lifted me on top of Thunder. He handed me the reins and stepped back. Our eyes met. The thought that flashed in my mind was furtive but clear: *Daddies shouldn't make their kids do these kinds of things. Especially on big horses.*

But I knew my father was not like other daddies. It never crossed my mind to protest my father's wisdom. If he insisted I should get back up on Thunder, it must be okay. It must be safe.

"Well?" he said.

Sulking, I flapped Thunder's reins, and she began a lazy walk toward the barn. Daddy kept pace beside us, his hand resting on Thunder's hind quarter. With each clop of her hoof, the fear drained from my body. It was replaced by embarrassment. How could I have balked at the idea of getting back up on a horse? I was *Daddy's* daughter.

It was less of a test of my horsemanship and more of an initiation into Eareckson-hood. By the time we arrived at the barn, I was older. I had found my courage and conquered something big: fear. Obeying my father had resulted in a strange sensation of destiny and freedom: Destiny in the sense that I was stepping into the person my father wanted me to be. Freedom in the sense that I never felt more like Joni.

I had met my father's expectations. I had not disappointed him.

At least in this sense. In other ways, I was always a little concerned that I had disappointed Daddy, at least a little. My father was an alternate on the 1932 Olympic wrestling team, a national AAU champion, a coach and captain in the Boys' Brigade. And he longed to have a male heir.

After my three older sisters were born, Mom and Dad resolved to try for a boy, to give it a final shot. Whoever came out—and of whichever sex, boy or girl—would be named "Johnny," after my father. On October 15, 1949, they held their breath in the delivery room as my mother bore down hard one last time. I slipped out and—oh!...

They would have to spell it "Joni."

My wrestler "uncles" and Daddy's contractor buddies razzed my father mercilessly, taking potshots at his manhood. It made me furious. Had they forgotten that Daddy was once on the Olympic team? I kicked Uncle Eddie in the shin with my cowboy boot for the way he kept teasing Daddy about us four girls.

I was determined to make my father proud. I tirelessly corrected people whenever they called me "Joanie" rather than "Johnny." And I decided I would be as good a rider, as good as any boy. I would learn how to tighten my saddle girth, sling manure, lift hay bales, and spur a horse as well as my sisters. I would pretend-wrestle, hike, swim against the high waves at Rehoboth Beach, build campfires, sling an ax, do whatever it took to keep up.

And I did. My rank, as we rode single file on the trail, was always immediately behind Daddy on Cherokee.

Summer vanished into fall, but the cool weather didn't keep us off the bridle paths. Every trail on which Daddy led us became a lesson. This was an elm tree and that was a tulip poplar. Maple leaves were shaped like this, oak leaves like that. If the moss was on this side of a tree, north must be that way. That call sounded like a mockingbird and over there, a bobwhite. This creek flows into the Patapsco River, which flows into the Chesapeake Bay, which flows to the ocean, which covers most of the earth.

Lessons on horseback were also gleaned at night. Many a late evening we would fill our thermoses, drive out to Wakefield, stuff everything into saddle bags, and start out across the fields on horseback under a full moon. The pastures of the elegant old farm were an Ansel Adams photograph, muted in mist and tinted in soft silver and steel gray, with the branches of Mother's chestnut tree spreading like metallic lace against a black sky. We passed under its moon shadow and looked up to admire the twigs wearing stars like diamonds. Crickets chirped and frogs called from down by the creek. The weeping willows were sleeping giants, the stream an iridescent ribbon of pale moonlight. Fireflies floated by us in the pasture as we entered the woods; they glittered mysteriously from behind the trees, as if beckoning us to come deeper into the forest. Owls hooted and night birds echoed through the black stillness of Leakin Park.

"Are you girls set?" my father's silhouette asked quietly. Once we'd nodded, Daddy urged Cherokee into a lope down a familiar dirt road through one of the fields. It took my breath away to canter through the night, watching the shadow of a horse and girl sailing alongside. That dark figure keeping pace seemed like a mythical centaur, half horse and half human, and wholly magical. To run through the fields on the wings of a steed was blind trust—trust in the horse, in Daddy, and in this beautiful moonlit night. A fairy-tale book could not hold more enchantment.

Even when winter came, my father's spirit of adventure kept us saddled up. One snowy night, my parents lined us up at the back door and began dressing us in our coats and scarves.

"Daddy, why are we going to Wakefield *now?*" my sister Jay asked. "There's no full moon. It's not time to go riding."

"You'll see," my father said, a gleam in his eye.

Our truck rumbled through the quiet streets of town toward the stables. The windshield wipers slapped away wet snow, and the engine whined as our tires slid. It was almost Christmas, and the houses in our neighborhood were covered in blankets of white, with sparkling colored lights lining the eaves, windows, and doors.

Within an hour, we were back on those same streets—not in the old truck, but on horseback. With thermoses full of hot chocolate in our saddle bags, we guided our horses up Poplar Drive and down Birch, stopping under every lamppost to sing Christmas carols. It felt strange and surreal to sit on top of my horse and look down on the same sidewalks where I rode my bike in summer. And it was wonderfully strange to wave to our neighbors as they opened their doors to chime along on "Silent Night."

I didn't know what transcendence was, but if asked I probably would have pointed to my father and attributed the warmth and wonder in my heart to him. Yet now, sitting on my horse and watching the snow swirl under the street lamp, I felt as though the Christmas hymn we were singing was turning a key to one of my heart closets: "Silent night, holy night, all is calm, all is bright . . ."

When we began the trek back to Wakefield, sitting on my hot water bottle, I pondered the words we sang, as I so often did with hymns: "'round yon virgin, mother and child" was, to me, a plump, young girl from Virginia next to a mother and child. I didn't understand much more than that, but I knew it was a pleasant, warm scene focusing on baby Jesus. Looking up, I wasn't sure where Jesus and God were sleeping in heavenly peace, but I was certain they were up there together somewhere. And oh, the stars! Surely God made those constellations. No matter what season it was or whether I was at the beach or on horseback, I felt drawn to the sky, a universe so massive that Orion was now over there to the south, rather than there, the north. With snow softly falling and the warm lights of Wakefield in sight, I realized this was no fairy tale from a book. This was far more real.

As winter melted into spring that year—my first year of school, Brownies, and many other things—we continued our Saturday horseback riding rituals. Now, there are certain spring mornings when one knows he or she has passed a personal milestone. Maybe no one around takes much notice, and those who do might soon forget, but when such a thing occurs to you, you know you've experienced a true life-change. It's as though a wrench has loosened a bolt on something inside you. This happened to me on the morning Thunder was sick.

Sensing my horsemanship had improved, my father placed me on Monica, Jay's horse. I can't remember who Jay was riding that morning; all I know is, the family cantered a good distance ahead of me, across a flat stretch of Leakin Park. Suddenly, Monica began prancing. I tugged on her reins with all my strength, but she was far more willful than Thunder. Setting her strength squarely against mine, Monica lunged ahead, fretful to catch up with the others. I was breathless with fear. Jay's horse didn't know me—or if she did, she knew I was a lot weaker than my older sister. As my heart raced, I saw Daddy slow down ahead and turn my way.

Monica was now out of control, galloping and straining to eat up the dirt beneath her. I couldn't do anything but release the reins and hold onto the horn in desperation. Feeling her freedom, the horse ducked her head between her front legs and began to buck. Everything turned into slow motion: the horizon going askew, my hands leaving the horn, my body floating through the air, seeing the ground rise toward me, and—bang!—hitting my head.

Everything went black, with stars swirling all about. Then a dull, thudding pain filled my head. Dirt and grass pressed against my cheek, and as I tried to move a wave of nausea overwhelmed me. In the curious acoustics, I heard Monica cantering away while the hooves of another horse—my father's—galloped up. I lay motionless, wondering what happened.

Daddy raced over to me, regret and panic in his breath. "Oh, no, please, what have I done?" he half-cried, cradling me.

My head was spinning, and I couldn't bring myself to talk or even cry. But even so, I didn't want my father feeling too sorry for me. I struggled in his arms to get up on my feet. Daddy brushed my hair back—looking for blood, bumps, anything—but miraculously, I hadn't been seriously harmed. For several long minutes, we stood there until my wobbliness disappeared. Finally, I managed a few shaky steps.

"Why, *why* did I put you on that horse?!" my father berated himself.

I stopped for a moment and held onto my father's hands. Things stopped spinning, and our breathing calmed down. Daddy held my face in his hands to examine my eyes, saying half to himself, "I need to get you back to the barn."

I slowly walked toward Cherokee, who was still standing at the place where his reins were dropped. I turned and weakly asked, "Let me ride behind you, Daddy."

My father pushed his hat back, puzzled. "You want to *ride?* Don't you want to walk? Or let me carry you piggyback to the barn?"

A warm breeze lifted his hat, the same breeze tossing my hair. Father and his youngest stood a foot apart, facing one another, both knowing they were laying a landmark. I appreciated his concern, but my mind was made up. I repeated, "I can ride behind you on Cherokee."

The decision wasn't meant to evoke pride from him. It was just . . . *my* decision. He deferred and proceeded to mount Cherokee, gathering the reins and then leaning down to help me up. "Here, take my hand," he said tenderly, as though I were wearing a purple heart. I grabbed hold and, with a tug, Daddy hoisted me up behind his saddle.

We plodded back to the barn, my father trying his best to turn the tragedy into a triumph for me, patting my leg and saying, "That's my girl." I was quiet mostly. The invisible wrench inside had loosened something in me, and it ratcheted me up a notch. If growing up means becoming slightly more autonomous than when you pulled on your cowboy boots that morning, that's what I experienced. And with such self-governance comes a feeling of immunity from danger.

But not for Thunder. Later that year, she had to be put down. Someone came with a gun, and there followed a loud bang and a dreadful shriek. Then all was still; the horse moved no more.

As for me, I was no son of Squire Gordon. No church bells tolled for me, no one was burying me, and I was still young and fine and able to ride perhaps even Black Beauty. Broken necks, I decided, happened only to others.

CHAPTER FOUR

Your eyes will see the king in his beauty and view a land that stretches afar.

Isaiah 33:17

I n 1957 space was the final frontier. Sputnik proved that. The whole country seemed on edge about the little chrome ball with its funny antennae, spinning around earth on the threshold of space. Newspaper photos made Sputnik look the size of a basketball. Pretty harmless, I thought. But as everybody told me, the Russians could now spy on us. It was the talk of third grade at Woodlawn Elementary School: *The Communists will know where to drop their bombs.*

"And if ever there's an invasion, they'll come for our guns too," my father observed, flipping the page of his newspaper.

Would people in gray uniforms really bust down our doors looking for guns? I wondered. I glanced at Daddy's antique squirrel rifle above the dining-room entryway. I thought about my own Daisy air rifle. Would the Communists also come for my Roy Rogers holster set, with the spring-action trigger and caps?

I must have lived that year in denial. Even as every student at Woodlawn Elementary hit the floor, hiding under a desk when the firehouse siren went off for an air-raid drill, it still seemed surreal to me. Why did the Russians hate us? They couldn't possibly be afraid of our country—we were too nice.

I'd heard that some people beyond Woodlawn were building bomb shelters, but I couldn't believe that Nikita Khrushchev would aim his missiles at us.

"You don't think so?" Linda challenged me. Indignant, she pulled out a map from the bookshelves above Daddy's desk. "Look, here's Woodlawn," she said, pointing to a tiny speck west of Baltimore. "And here's Washington, D.C.," she added ominously, sliding her finger a fraction of an inch south and west. "Boy, are you dumb."

As close as we lived to our nation's capital—ground zero for nuclear-crazed Communists—it simply didn't sink in with me. I felt immune to any danger. If my tumbles from tall, galloping horses were no threat, how could something as distant in my mind as an atom bomb be? If there was a bomb shelter of any kind for me, it was an enormous, invisible shield of innocence, protecting Wakefield Farm, Gwynn Oak Amusement Park, Leakin Park, Woodlawn Pond with its swans, and our cozy wooded neighborhood.

So as my parents followed Sputnik on *Walter Cronkite and the Evening News*, Kathy and I set up our plastic-cowboy-and-Indian fort in the basement and happily blasted each other with cap guns, screaming, groaning, feigning wounds, collapsing dead on the hardwood floor. Ours was a benign war. And the make-believe battles somehow reinforced our immunity against intercontinental ballistic missiles and nuclear warheads.

Maybe while we slept, Sputnik beep-beeped overhead, keeping an eye on us, but even as the Russian satellite charted new frontiers, so did my father.

"Pack up, everybody, we're heading out West!"

"Where?" My sisters and I gathered in varying stages of wonder.

"The Two-Bars Seven Ranch."

"Really? Where is it?"

"Virginia Dale, Colorado—"

"Wow," we gasped in unison.

"—*and* Tie Siding, Wyoming."

"A ranch covering two states?" We were incredulous.

The idea of a cattle ranch spreading over 7,000 acres was as unfathomable to me as the Communists' bombs: *Naaah, how could it be?* Jay tried explaining it to me, saying it was like a zillion Leakin Parks. But her words were wasted. All I cared about was the chance to bring all my equestrian know-how to bear on a new, true Western horse.

A few days later, we lugged our sleeping bags and duffels to the driveway, and stuffed ourselves into every corner of Mother's big white Buick. Three sisters would sit in the backseat, with one in the front between Mom and Dad, rotating seats with every stop along the way.

As the smallest, I never got a window seat in the back. It was always the middle for me.

"You're the only one who can fit there, what with this big humpy thing," Jay ruled, pointing to the hill on the floor that covered the drive shaft.

It was so unfair. I was already short. How could I see any scenery if I sat in the middle?

Suddenly, a plan came to me. I turned around and knelt, facing the rear of the car. With the huge back window all to myself, I realized this wasn't too bad. I could watch the world go by, even if it was backward. I could also crawl up on the back ledge and lie down against the window. It would be private there, and my purple rabbit with the plastic smiley face and I would have a great view.

My father had us all bow our heads before he started the engine. "Dear Lord," he intoned, "guide our journey, and go before us."

Yep—that was my God and my daddy. Always going before us, leading everybody on an adventure of up and down, sideways, through the creek and spur, on up the other ridge.

We started out cruising along old Route 40, heading west toward the Appalachian Mountains. *Mountains!* The very idea thrilled me. I wondered if I would experience the same blissful feelings standing on top of a mountain as I did gazing out onto the expanse of the endless sea, the way I did at Rehoboth.

I didn't have long to wait. As the Piedmont Plateau began to rise and the Blue Ridge came in view just beyond Frederick, Maryland, we spotted one sign after the next: Scenic Point—Two Miles Ahead. I don't think our family ever passed one up. At least not while my father was driving. We'd barrel along until someone would see one of the familiar brown-and-white signs, and suddenly our journey took a new twist. *Intrigue and enchantment were up ahead*, I thought, pressing my purple rabbit against the window, putting my face next to his, and asking softly, "What's over the hill? What will it be like?"

We piled out of the car at every scenic point on the old Pennsylvania Turnpike, with virtually every stop a vast painting of green valleys and patchwork-quilt fields. My folks, doubly joyful at seeing it all through our eyes, constantly beckoned, "Girls, look at this!" and we gladly complied. We ate bologna sandwiches on the car hood and breathed in the scent of pine and the thin, cool air. We handled rocks whose names I could never remember, tried to scale cliffs that loomed large and foreboding. I breathed in every scene and experience, wondering all the while, *How can the Rockies and Two-Bars Seven Ranch match the grandeur of the Appalachians?*

When our Buick finally descended into the Ohio River Valley, I couldn't understand why we had to leave these gentle mountains. Why not do a U-turn, go back, pitch a tent, sit around a campfire, and do what we always did? Sing and tell stories. *Uncle Ted's ranch can't be any neater than the Appalachians.*

How could I know I was far too easily pleased?

Over the next few days, our gallant old Buick sailed past sweeping fields of wheat and acres of corn. We waved at everyone we passed, from engineers on trains to farmers riding their tractors alongside miles of white fences and Burma Shave signs. We clattered across wooden bridges and hooted at barefoot boys in overalls as they waded in streams; they seemed to appear straight out of *Tom Sawyer* and *Little House on the Prairie*. My third-grade teacher was right: there really was a Mississippi River—and banjos and paddleboats. And there really were upside-down horizons, with dark gray skies and bright golden fields.

Those endless green meadows eventually spilled us out onto the dry prairie. Every so often we pulled off the old highway and stopped for Cokes in little towns where brick-faced buildings lined quiet main streets. Pushing farther west, we turned off the highway and onto a gravel road leading to Dodge City, Kansas. My sisters and I scanned the range for outlaws, singing all the songs from *Rawhide, Sugarfoot, Gunsmoke, The Rifleman,* and my favorite, *Death Valley Days.* I kept expecting our Buick to pass the Twenty-Mule Team Wagon from the Borax commercial. In the end, Dodge City was, well, Bat Masterson and Wyatt Earp country, so we sang their songs too.

Dodge was the small, dusty Western town I hoped it would be, just like in the TV shows, except the road down the middle was paved. As the wind kicked up dust from Front Street and I heard some window sashes flapping, I suddenly wished I'd brought my Daisy air rifle. Kathy and I could make up a great gunfight here.

But the historic town before us was adventure enough. We poked our heads in the Long Branch Saloon and hiked up to Boot Hill. We explored around a few tombstones, and I couldn't resist ducking behind one, aiming my finger at Kathy, and letting go one big "Ka-pow." She ka-powed back a few times, then finally, we descended on the general store—a big, touristy place with real Indian headdresses hanging from the beams and an immense buffalo head on the wall. We were allowed to fill up on licorice sticks, jawbreakers, and post-cards, while my father bought a set of long steer horns and roped them to the grill of the car. When we finally pulled out of Dodge City, we stuck our finger pistols out the back window, ka-pow-powing at invisible posses who chased us out of town.

The rolling vista of golden wheat we passed crept no farther than western Kansas, drying up into cattle country and sagebrush as we crossed the state line into Colorado. Now we were *really* on the frontier. I propped my rabbit up on the edge of the front seat so he could see.

Is this still America? I heard him ask. I leaned my chin next to his.

Sitting in the middle was okay after all, I decided. My view of what lay ahead was clear and uncluttered.

As the miles rolled by, turning the high, hot sun into late afternoon, a strange, purple-jagged line appeared above the landscape far ahead.

"There they are," Daddy beamed.

We all craned to see.

"The front range of the Rockies," he told us, "the purple mountains' majesty."

As the peaks slowly began to rise, still many miles in the distance, our father stretched his arms against the wheel and leaned back. Then, with his hair wildly blowing from the open window, he belted out another hymn:

> *O beautiful for spacious skies*
> *for amber waves of grain—*

We rolled down the windows and joined him at the top of our lungs:

> *For purple mountain majesties*
> *above the fruited plain.*
> *America, America, God shed his grace on thee.*
> *And crown thy good with brotherhood,*
> *from sea to shining sea.*

After a while, we came upon a high ridge, and Daddy slowed to pull the car onto the gravel. We all got out to stretch and to admire the town of Colorado Springs below. It was tucked at the base of a massive and imperious wall of peaks, which rested like silent, wise giants dusted in snow. The air was cool and the landscape was heavy with silence, except for the whining of truck wheels farther down the highway. I had a hard time remembering the Appalachians.

"See that big one in the middle?" my father said, pointing to the highest point. "That's Pikes Peak. And you know what happened to me on *that* mountain, don't you?"

This was no tale like the Flying Dutchman. We had heard Daddy recount the details of this story many times, and we never doubted it was true.

It was 1933, and my father had invited a group of his YMCA wrestling buddies, along with some other young people from the Sunday school he supervised, to climb Pikes Peak. They all crowded into his old green truck and headed west. Days later, when they reached the base of the mountain, they rose up early in the morning, pulled on their gear, and began the hike up the front ridge.

By late morning, the sky had become overcast, winds began to bluster, and a few in the group turned to go back. Daddy continued on with his wrestling friends. Soon a light rain began to spit, and his buddies stopped to consider the danger of going on. When the rain didn't lighten up, they decided to call it quits.

Knowing he was only a short distance from his goal, my father yelled to them above the wind, "I'm going to try for the top."

"Don't do it. You're crazy," they called back.

"I'll be okay. You fellows get started down, and I'll catch up with you."

My father plowed on. Yet as he hiked higher, the rain turned to snow. He tightened the collar of his plaid wool jacket against the thick flurries and pressed on. He felt certain that any minute he would reach the mound of stones crowning the top of Pikes Peak.

When the terrain began to flatten slightly, he figured he had arrived. But he couldn't find the mound anywhere in the swirling snow. The icy wind was howling now. He kept looking but found nothing like stones; everything around him was pure white. Finally, he decided to head back.

As he turned around, he looked down for his footprints, to follow them back down the mountain. But they were gone. They had disappeared behind him, under a blanket of snow piling higher by the second. As he looked up, he realized he was in the midst of a blinding blizzard. He had lost the trail.

All my father could see in front of him was gray and white. His chest tightened as he sensed that the gray was growing darker. *The day is escaping*, he realized. *Nighttime is coming.*

"I must keep walking, I must keep walking," he murmured over and over, hoping his feet would feel a path. But soon darkness fell, and his tired muscles ached. Tiny icicles formed on his brows and lashes. He wanted desperately to sit down in the snow to rest for a moment or just lean against a rock, anything. But he knew that would be suicide. *I must keep walking ... keep walking ...*

He walked all through the night. When the darkness began to turn into grayish white, he knew dawn had come. He squinted and saw a couple of small pine trees in the distance. *I must be at a lower elevation*, he reasoned. When he came to within a few feet of the trees, the snow underneath him collapsed. Tumbling and turning, he somersaulted down what had to be a cliff, thudding to a halt against a huge tree trunk. Those small pines had been the tops of trees, sticking out of a snow bank!

For three days, my father floundered his way through the whipping wind, stumbling, dropping to his knees in the snow, straining to get back up, and all the while whisper-singing, "Some poor fainting, struggling seaman, you may rescue, you may save." He never stopped singing until finally he stumbled upon railroad tracks. He followed them all the way to a miner's cabin in Cripple Creek, a little gold-rush town on the back side of Pikes Peak. When the miner heard thumping on his door, he opened it against a blast of wind and saw a near-frozen man standing in the snow. "What in the—! ... Get in here quick!" he exclaimed.

That night, Daddy sat down for the first time in forty-eight hours.

The miner offered him a plate of beans and whisky, but when he held up the bottle, Daddy clutched the blanket around him tighter and asked in a weak, gravelly voice, "Do you have anything besides liquor?"

The miner looked at him as if he were crazy.

"That was the first time, *and the last*, I ever drank a cup of coffee!" Daddy laughed, resting on the hood of our Buick. We let the story settle, and Mother said what she always did at this point: "This isn't one of Daddy's tales. Remember seeing the newspaper clippings?"

We all were familiar with the headline banner on the front page of the *Evening Sun*: "Baltimore Athlete Found on Peak!" Because John King Eareckson was the city's favorite son in the '32 Olympics, the mountain-climbing incident had been the main story in '33. Now that same mountain—a real one, huge and foreboding, having nearly claimed our father's life—stood before us. I held my rabbit up for a long, serious look, turning him slowly from the south end of the wall of peaks, all the way to the north where they disappeared.

Everybody had stopped talking, and no cars were coming either way on the road. A spacious silence settled over us as we stood in awe. Soon it begged to be filled, so Daddy began to softly sing. We joined in on harmony.

> *Rock of Ages, cleft for me,*
> *Let me hide myself in Thee;*
> *Let the water and the blood,*
> *From Thy wounded side which flowed,*
> *Be of sin the double cure,*
> *Save from wrath and make me pure.*

We drove on in silence, remarking on how Pikes Peak kept changing the closer we got to it. Once we arrived at the foot of the mountain, we discovered that a winding dirt road had recently been cut to the top. Our big V8 Buick was able to chug all the way up.

When we got out, the thin air was freezing. We quickly dug inside the trunk for sweaters. Once everyone was wrapped and warm, Kathy and I ran toward the edge and stopped in awe. We were stunned by the expansive view; it felt like we could see forever. We were higher than we'd ever been, and as we turned to look at each other we trembled with wonder.

The sky was bright and blue, and as I shielded my eyes, I saw the tops of clouds below us. To the south was the Sawtooth Range in northern New Mexico, and to the north, Denver. As I pulled in more oxygen, I realized it wasn't only the thin air that made me breathless. *This is no Pennsylvania scenic point*, I sighed.

"Here they are," Daddy announced behind us.

Kathy and I wandered over and saw our father standing by the mound of stones he had missed so many years ago. A few feet away was the actual trail he had hiked.

We went into a small shop, but I kept going back outside, trying to gather into memory as much of the awe-inspiring view as I could. I had the strangest sensation I had been here before; it was like leaning on my elbows in bed and staring at the puffy clouds Daddy painted on the wall behind the angels. *Was this heaven? Or at least its vestibule?*

Descending Pikes Peak, we turned north toward our final destination: Virginia Dale and Two-Bars Seven Ranch. Daddy kept an eye on the rearview mirror, watching his mountain diminish until it was almost out of sight. "I never dreamed I'd see that peak again," he murmured.

My own dreams came true on that journey. We finally pulled up to the ranch house, and as my parents unloaded, my sisters raced to the corral to see the horses. I stayed behind when I heard Uncle Ted call to us from inside the house. He let the screen door slam behind him as he strode up to give Daddy a slap on the back and Mom a hug. I couldn't take my eyes off his cowboy hat. It was nothing like my red felt Dale Evans version with the white chin strap. His was big, worn, dusty, and *real.*

That week, I rode a steed as grand as Thunder and watched Uncle Ted rope calves. I handled branding irons and learned to square dance. Finally, we saddled up and spurred out on a three-day trek to the Frontier Days Rodeo in Cheyenne, Wyoming. With the Rockies to our left and the rolling plains to our right, we traveled north, pitching our tents next to the chuck wagon after every sunset. We watched Mom help the cook make Dutch-oven biscuits. (Rarely did we see her on a horse the whole trip; she was much more at home with a skillet than on a saddle.) Every morning we drank from gurgling brooks and tried to catch prairie dogs.

When we arrived at the rodeo, I was presented with a Frontiersman certificate. As it turned out, I was the youngest rider ever to log the hundred-mile trip there on horseback. My parents rewarded me with a pair of red hand-tooled cowboy boots from Laramie, and I strode out onto the town's boardwalk, thumbs in jean pockets and the brim of my cowboy hat cocked low. *This*, I thought, *was the real final frontier, and I've reached it.*

On the ride back to Two-Bars Seven Ranch, our pace was slower and more reflective. At times, I discovered a beauty so big it was frightening. One night, sitting by the twilight campfire, I looked over my shoulder only to be startled by giant layers of dark, brooding mountains. They were almost . . . *beckoning* me. Like the sirens in the Greek myths, something mysterious out there was whispering to me, urging me to leave the familiarity of the fire and walk off into a world that was sublime, enchanting, and maybe even dangerous. The sensation was hypnotic, not unlike being at Rehoboth and watching Daddy venture a few steps into the night, away from the campfire, all the while feeling my heart pound, so fearful he might disappear, yet desiring to follow him.

I knew I fit in that alluring landscape. It was as though I was born to be in this environment, or somewhere very much like it. A place of majesty and splendor, glorious and grand, holy and awe-inspiring. Several years later, I would feel the same way, standing with my mother on the edge of the Grand Canyon—an impossible expanse, a yawning chasm so monstrously deep and wide, so full of ancient color and timeless mystery, so silent and frightening, I held tightly onto the guardrail for fear that if I let go, I'd fly away or be swallowed up. *The Rockies can't match this*, I thought then. I was discovering that souls can be too easily satisfied, that there is always a higher and more glorious plane.

When it was time to go home, Uncle Ted stood by the corral with his rope on his hip, smiled, and waved good-bye. As we began the long drive eastward, watching the mountains disappear behind us, I was slightly troubled. My feelings of euphoria seemed to dissipate with every mile.

Several days, hundreds of miles, and dozens of landscapes later, we reached western Maryland, pulling into a gas station by the

Cumberland Gap. We weren't far from home, and it felt good to take a break. Since this would be the last time we would see real scenery, I took my purple rabbit off the ledge of the backseat to walk him around and show him the river and steep hills.

"Now I realize this isn't like the Rockies," I whispered in his ear, "but you have to remember these sights so we can tell the others back home." I was thinking of Kathy's stuffed animals. Or maybe I just wanted to hold onto something that had *been there* with me, something that had experienced the same enchantment I had and could somehow remind me of it.

As I meandered back to the car, I encountered Linda leaning on the trunk, drinking a bottle of pop. "Are you still talking to that idiotic rabbit?" she said. She took another swig, wiped her mouth, then set her bottle down. "Here, let me have that thing."

Before I knew it, Linda grabbed the stuffed animal out of my hand. Then she drew back her arm and smashed her fist into his plastic face.

Horrified, I stood speechless. As I watched pieces of plastic fall to the ground and saw the huge cracks in my rabbit's smile and eyes, I lost it. I rushed at my sister with both fists, pounding and swinging at any part of her body I could reach. I cursed and kicked as hot tears spilled down my cheeks. Linda was sixteen, and she could easily hold me at a distance. "Hee hee," she kept laughing.

"Daddy, Mommy!" our sisters screamed. "Linda and Joni are fighting!"

My father and mother came running. "Cut it out, you two!" Daddy yelled, but I kept trying to kick Linda.

"I said cut it out!" Daddy insisted, this time louder in his gruff, wrestling voice. He reached down and pulled me away by my beaded Indian belt.

I heaved great sobs as I tried to tell him what Linda had done to my rabbit. He picked up the tired, old stuffed animal and ran his hand over its damaged face. My parents made Linda sit in the backseat and told her she was not to make a sound until we were home. I was made to sit in the front in between my parents. I cradled my damaged rabbit and sniffed back tears all the way to Baltimore. Embittered, I heard Linda muffle a giggle in the back, as if things were normal. *Somebody should smash her face in*, I told myself.

I now had a dilemma—one much bigger than a fight with my sister. It was clear I couldn't hold onto the awesome beauty I saw on top of Pikes Peak or around the campfire by the brook or at the ranch with the horses. And I couldn't clutch the beautiful feelings I had experienced in all those places. The largeness in my soul had been deflated. And instead, anger and cursing were now close to the surface. (Thankfully, my parents hadn't heard me say "damn," and, mercifully, Linda hadn't tattled.)

Stewing in the front seat as we drove east on Route 40, I felt the sun set behind me. I was back to being me. *A twerp, a dummy*, I fumed, slumping and kicking my feet under the dashboard. It was the first time I realized I didn't like who I was.

Like Sputnik, I had left the final frontier and fallen to earth.

When we got home that night, my father helped me place my purple rabbit in a little bed that Aunt Lee made—a cigar box painted black, with clothespins for bedposts. The rabbit was way too big for it, and his arms and legs flopped over the sides. But still, the little bed was a good place for me to doctor him until he got better. I set him on the floor of my closet, and he stayed there for a long time, so I could check on him as a nurse would.

I prayed for him, but he never got better. That bothered me. Sometimes prayer seemed to work and sometimes it didn't. My father had said it was prayer that kept him going on the top of Pikes Peak. And of course he made sure we said our "Now I lay me down to sleep" every night before bed. Still, I wasn't sure how prayer operated and what the real requirements were.

Pray as I did, my rabbit never improved. Maybe I needed to pray like my classmate Kathy Carski. The Carskis' house was up the hill beyond our wooded neighborhood, where a newer development had been built. I often played at her place and was fascinated with one or two small crucifixes I saw on the walls. The Carskis were Catholics, and they faithfully attended church (Kathy called it Mass) every Sunday.

Kathy was a frail girl with fair skin and jet black hair, a full mouth and large brown eyes. She was also a ballerina, or, as she corrected me, a toe dancer. She didn't use ballet slippers; she had graduated to toe shoes. The Carskis' home was orderly, one of those with Marie

Antoinette figurines on the white fireplace mantel, and, with only two children, it was a very quiet home. We would play with her dolls, leaf through her Nancy Drew books, and she would let me try on her old ballet slippers. She was so ... *feminine*.

Kathy Carski didn't talk much about prayer, but I knew she understood it. Once, when I went with Kathy and her parents to her church, I observed them genuflect. They knelt on kneelers and fingered rosaries. I didn't much like the statues or the fancy gilded altar or the priest with his robes, but I was drawn to the formal way Kathy and her parents stooped and bowed and prayed. They were connecting with God, and I imagined he looked favorably on their religious sincerity.

Not long after my visit to their Catholic church, I became inspired. I dragged the little metal vanity stool from the bathroom and situated it next to my bed. My sister Kathy watched.

"What are you doing?" she asked, her tone implying that she should call the shots about furniture placement in our room.

"You'll see." I turned the stool this way and that, next to my bed. When it was just so, I placed on it a lace doily from downstairs and a small framed picture of Jesus with happy children. I finished it all off with a little candle in a crystal holder.

"What is that?"

"An altar," I said casually.

"You're going to get in trouble."

I ignored her warning and stepped back to admire my arrangement.

"Bedtime!" we heard Mother call from the bottom of the stairs. Daddy would soon be coming up to tell us a bedtime story, so Kathy and I finished putting on our pajamas and brushed our teeth. When we heard Daddy's footsteps on the stairs, we hopped into bed. He came in and reached for the large red book of fairy tales on the bureau and walked over to my side of the room.

He stopped. "What is this?"

I was proud to show Daddy my prayer altar. I leaped off the bed and knelt in front of the vanity stool. I was just starting to light the candle when he interrupted. "What are you doing?"

"I'm getting ready to pray, Daddy. This is an altar."

"Don't do that. Put it away," he instructed.

I gave him a funny look, sensing something was not quite right. When I didn't move right away, he put down the red book and grabbed the framed picture, candlestick, and lace doily, tucking it all under his arm. "Put the stool back."

"But it's for praying."

"Told you," Kathy sing-songed.

I stood there, bewildered. My father didn't wait for me to lift the stool. He picked it up and put it back in the bathroom.

"But, Daddy, Kathy Carski has—"

"I don't care what Kathy Carski and her family do. This is not what you do, what we do. You don't pray this way."

I could tell I had done something wrong, and I flushed hot with embarrassment. I climbed back into bed, red-cheeked and my eyes wet. It dawned on me this was more than a prayer-altar thing. This was a _Catholic_ thing. It was unfair. Kathy Carski was my best friend. I was mad at Daddy, yet I also felt sick that I had disappointed him. And I hated that my sister Kathy was right.

There was no bedtime story that night. Before my father turned out the lights, however, he paused. "Joni, I know you meant well, but God is bigger than ... than _that_," he said, gesturing to where the little prayer altar had been. "Much bigger."

I was confused.

I stayed on my side of the bed that night, thinking hard. I thought about Kathy Carski and her ballet slippers and tutus and the crosses in her house. About her single bedroom and the fact that she had no older, bossy sisters. I thought about her peaceful, orderly house, and our loud, rambunctious one. And about my sad little rabbit on the floor in the dark closet. I thought about my room, the angels, and the little silhouetted girl on the plaque on the closet door. I couldn't help but grope in the dark for the familiar, so I prayed with the silhouette:

> _Dear God, my little boat and I_
> _are on your open sea._
> _Please guide us safely through the waves_
> _my little boat and me._

My last thoughts that night were of our recent trip to the frontier, to all those glorious places that beckoned me, to vistas where my soul felt larger. It was then that I rested in my father's words: "God is bigger . . . much bigger."

CHAPTER FIVE

Even a child is known by his actions, by whether his conduct is pure and right.

Proverbs 20:11

Y ou're coming with me right now. This instant!"
The words strike fear in your heart, especially when pronounced crisply and with resolve and with a hand squeezing your wrist so tightly it turns your fingers purple. When it happens, you'd better not drag your feet. Yet to save face in front of your friends or sisters, there must be an obligatory—

"But Mom!"

If you utter such brazen words, you only run the risk of her grip tightening and tugging on you so sharply you'd swear your shoulder's being ripped out of joint. But it's worth it. Nothing hurts more than the humiliation of being scolded in front of your friends. And especially your sisters.

I had failed to get a ride home with Linda, as I was supposed to, so now my mad-as-a-hornet mother had driven to Wakefield Farm to find me. My afternoon piano recital had already started in the auditorium of Woodlawn Elementary. The other girls and boys were all sitting prim and proper on the front row, dressed in flouncy frocks with patent leather shoes or stiff shirts with little bow ties. I should have been among them. Instead, I had let the morning slip by, staying way too long at Wakefield for their annual Horse Pageant. It was a kind of costume parade on horseback, in which one could win a nifty trophy dressed as the Headless Horseman or Paul Revere or, as in my case, Davy Crockett.

I was simply having too much fun riding my horse in my coonskin cap, fringed leather jacket, and cowboy boots, and brandishing my Daisy air rifle. Daddy had even tied a squirrel skin to my belt, and skillets and pots to my saddle. The thought of having to go home from the pageant early and miss all this fun, then take a shower and put on a dress to rush to a piano recital—it all seemed like a drag. And so, when the sisterly suggestion came, "It's time to go home," I had turned a deaf ear and ridden off to the hamburger stand. Maybe the recital would go away.

Not that I didn't enjoy piano. I loved it. But my affection for it had been born out of boredom on those Saturdays when I had to go to my grandmother's house with Mom, and I had to do something to occupy myself while she dusted, polished, and scrubbed floors. My grandmother, firmly German and rigid in her Lutheran rules, was as stiff as her home, a tall, narrow dwelling with heavy brocade curtains and inflexible furniture. Nothing about Grandmom or her house was soft, except for the lush grape arbor that graced the side of the house. While my mother mixed Spic & Span, I either went outside to squash bees with my boots as they buzzed around the fallen grapes or I fooled around with the old box-upright player piano in the parlor.

I wasn't allowed to touch much at Grandmom's, but she didn't mind my being around the player piano. It was an ancient thing, left over from the thirties when relatives would lift their steins and make it play Strauss waltzes. Next to the piano was a cardboard box of spindles that held rolls of thick, waxy paper, perforated with zillions of little holes. I would sit on the piano bench, slide open the doors of the center compartment, and snap the roll inside like toilet paper, then hook its little ring to a clasp on the bottom roll. Under the piano, instead of pedals, there were two pumping platforms. I could barely reach them, but once I got a good rhythm going, the rolls began moving and air began to wheeze and suck at the paper. Suddenly, the black-and-white keys began to dance, and the happy, cascading tune of "Yosemite Falls" filled the parlor. To pick up the pace of the song, I grasped the two ends of the bench with all my might, to get a good angle on the pumping. It was exhausting, but I was delighted to give Mother music to clean by.

At home, we had a similar-looking piano in the basement—not a player type but one just as boxy and ancient. Jay took lessons on it, and I often mimicked her on the keys. She taught me the bottom part to "Chopsticks."

One day, I began to experiment with a couple of tunes. I heard my mother pause at the top of the basement steps.

"Joni, are you playing what I think you are?"

"Yep!" I knew she recognized "Yosemite Falls."

The next week, Mother marched me up the long, concrete walk to a three-story French Provincial apartment building on the edge of Woodlawn. It was where Miss Merson, Jay's piano teacher, lived. As we entered the foyer, everything echoed with elegance and culture. A winding staircase took us up past a hanging chandelier to the third floor, and Mother knocked on Miss Merson's impressive door.

When the door opened, before us stood a slightly built, aged woman in a long black skirt, with a gypsy scarf knotted around her gray hair-bun. With her pointed nose, long chin, and longer fingers, she looked a little like the Wicked Witch of the West. But that's where the similarity ended. I loved Miss Merson.

"You must be Joni," she said in a deep, rich voice, like Talullah Bankhead. As she escorted us in, I inhaled the scent of cinnamon and lemon oil. She and Mom started small-talking, and I glanced around at the oriental carpets, chintz sofa, and floor-to-ceiling windows, with their sheer curtains billowing in the breeze. In the corner was her upright piano.

"Come over here," she instructed sweetly, patting the piano bench. "Place your thumb here," she said, pointing to what she described as middle C. "Now try to stretch an octave. That's eight keys."

This was a test I was not about to fail. I might pull a ligament, but I would widen my thumb and pinky and very well make that octave. When I pressed the two keys, proving I was old enough to begin lessons, Miss Merson smiled with satisfaction and announced, "We shall begin next week."

And so, every Monday after school I carried my books—including the beginner's little red piano book—and walked up the street, past Balhouf's Bakery and the Equitable Trust Bank, to the tree-shaded concrete path that led to piano lessons. Something about Miss Merson reminded me of that strange enchantment I felt out West, when I had been enraptured by the distant, dark, brooding mountains. Being around her gave me the same sublime fascination. She was so . . . arty. And unusual.

I never encountered Miss Merson away from the piano, but if we had ever bumped into each other at the soda fountain at Woodlawn

Drug Store, I would have frozen. She didn't come from Woodlawn. She came from another world. A world of European class, of tall windows where the sun poured in like buttercream, where there was always a gentle finger under my elbow to remind me to gracefully arch my wrists, always a gold star for doing well, always demure applause, and always a chocolate with a cup of tea, if I wanted it, at the lesson's end. Even "Are You Sleeping, Brother John?" sounded tasteful and exquisite at Miss Merson's.

Practicing at home was a pleasure, but I also quickly learned to "play by ear." It was less work and a lot more fun. I would hit the bass-note rhythm of "You Give Me Fever" and pretend I was Peggy Lee, squirming on the bench and pouting my way through the melody, singing as stupidly and sexily as I could. Other times, I sang Doris Day songs with charm and innocence. And sometimes, I just pressed the third pedal—the one that made everything echo—and slowly struck all the keys, making for the biggest, richest, and most complex chord I could invent. I held it, so large and sweet, until the sound disappeared. It made my eyes fill.

My love of piano pleased my mother to no end. She longed for her daughters to be refined and skilled in more social graces than simply holding a knife and fork properly or answering the phone correctly. She was getting tired of her girls always horsing around and bragging about slinging manure, weary of having to shake sawdust out of our clothes and emptying horseshoe nails from our pockets. I don't recall my parents ever arguing, but at times they had to knock heads over the way we were being raised. I sensed it whenever Mother loaded us in the car and carted us off to tennis or badminton lessons at Mount Washington Country Club.

Mom was especially delighted when I came home from Kathy Carski's one day and asked if I could take ballet lessons. That's all it took. From then on, every Thursday I hopped the streetcar by Woodlawn Pond and clickety-clacked up to Gywnn Oak Junction at the edge of the city line. Miss Betty Lou's Dance Studio was on the second floor of a storefront building there, just down the street from the Ambassador Theater. Though the music we danced to was produced on an out-of-tune piano played by a portly man who always chewed on a cigar, to me it was graceful and refined.

At first, wearing a ballet outfit felt odd. A little dorky, even embarrassing. But soon I got comfortable in my pink tights, slippers, and black leotard. I stretched my neck and arms, wanting desperately to look demure and feminine in the mirror as I slowly did first, second, and third positions (fifth was my favorite) in the long line of little girls, all of us looking like princesses. A few months later, when I performed onstage at the Lyric Theatre—I was an apple in Miss Betty Lou's dance recital—twirling across the floor, a red blur in a long line of other apples, nobody was happier than my mother sitting in the tenth row. Afterward, my parents came backstage—a world not unlike a Degas painting—to congratulate me. They gamely made their way through gaggles of giggling girls, stage props, and the theater crew to find their apple— or, during other years, their flower or their bird—to give me a hug and a "You were great!" Daddy made that backstage visit only once. After the ruckus that year of the apple, he waited in the lobby.

No wonder my father preferred us to be horseback riding. Piano was okay to him, but I think he considered the world of ballet to be totally off the map, with its gaunt women, effeminate men, and French-sounding eccentricities, such as pirouettes and pliés. Besides, any discipline that encouraged a kid to stay transfixed on his or her image in a mirror for two hours had to be suspect. Playing tennis at Mount Washington wasn't much better. The country-club world, with its highbrow socialites, was not to his liking.

If there were ever an honest-to-goodness tug-of-war between my parents for the manner in which we were to be raised, my father won by the mid-fifties. That's when he purchased an old, run-down farm twenty-five miles west of Woodlawn. It was seven hundred acres, way out in the country, adjoining Patapsco State Park, and a perfect place to keep our horses. No longer would we have to board them at Wakefield Farm. In an agreement with the YMCA, my father also decided to turn the farm into a working YMCA camp. With the help of a family friend who would live on part of it, we would raise horses, hay, corn, and cattle.

Daddy christened the farm the Circle X Ranch. It was nothing like Wakefield, with its Kentucky bluegrass and white fences. Instead, it was a rootin'-tootin' cowboy camp, complete with a weekend rodeo. From then on, we would spend our weekends on the farm.

Never were there sweeter summers for me than those in the fifties. We packed our suitcases and settled in for the season up at the Circle X, diving right into country life. While Daddy and his crew fixed up the barn and the old farmhouse, my sisters and I explored. The house was surrounded by mounds of honeysuckle and a sloping hill that led down to a stone spring house where we could keep watermelons cool. The old barn had bales of hay we could build forts with and a tack room where we could shine our saddles. At the far end of the field, near the edge of the woods, Kathy and I could hammer and nail together a tree house. Or we could wander down the old, narrow dirt road, bordered by sweet blackberry bushes and leading to secret streams and waterfalls and mysterious little dales and meadows. The old road eventually ended at the Patapsco River, where we could catch fat fish using handmade poles and worms on safety-pin hooks. We would be our own Huckleberry Finns.

There was also the old, dirt River Road, which took you to Sykesville, where you could get a great ten-cent ice cream cone from the drugstore. Or, if you took it in the opposite direction, you'd end up at Marriottsville General Store, where you could share a Coke with your horse—you just tipped your horse's head up, stuck the bottle in the corner of her jaw, and let her slurp down and slobber all that sugar water. By 1959, I had graduated to a sharp-looking brown mare named Tumbleweed, and she and I quickly learned which trail led to the Coca-Colas for her and the best ice cream for me.

I learned the art of relaxation on that horse.

If heaven at all reflects earth's memories, I hope once again to lie back on my mare's haunches as she ambles up River Road, home to the farm. Her head will be low, her gait easy, the reins drooped, and I will lick my ice cream and watch the branches of the trees go by above me, the sun sparkling and playing hide-and-seek behind green summer leaves.

If heaven replays our memories, I hope to climb into Daddy's old truck and squeeze between him at the wheel and his door, while my three sisters fill out the front seat to his right. We will sing all the way from Woodlawn to Sykesville, harmonizing on—

Tell me the stories of Jesus I love to hear;
things I would ask Him to tell me if He were here:
Scenes by the wayside, tales of the sea,
stories of Jesus, tell them to me.

And as the truck pulls off of Route 32, and we turn onto River Road, Daddy will stop so we can run to the back and hop up on the tailgate. There we will jiggle and bounce over the dips and ruts, all the way to the farm, laughing and holding onto the roof-rings for dear life.

If heaven has clubhouses, I hope to recreate with Kathy the one we made on the second floor of the corn shed. She was vice president, a neighbor friend was president, and I was secretary of the Horse and Dog Club, or the HD Club, as we called it. We held our hands over our hearts and dedicated ourselves to the advancement of dogs and horses.

We even held our own horse show. We gathered old horseshoes and painted them gold for our first-place trophies, and we made signs, nailing them up and down Route 32 and in Sykesville. We really didn't think many people would show up, but on the morning of the show, trucks and horse-trailers came rumbling up River Road from everywhere. Glossy quarter-horses and sassy thoroughbreds exited from their upscale trailers, and riders saddled up their steeds with shiny leather tack. Kathy and I looked at one another and gulped. The horse show gamely went on, but Daddy had some explaining to do with several serious contenders, who were irate over their trophies, sticky with gold paint.

If heaven puts on dramas, I hope to do an encore of *Oklahoma!* with Kathy, just as we performed for some of the YMCA kids and folks on the farm. We will find the old flatbed truck, throw the tattered quilt over a clothesline for a curtain, and strut out onstage, singing with all the gusto of Gordon McRae, "Oh, What a Beautiful Morning." We will play the old LP on the record player behind the curtain, make up the lines as we go, square dance, doe-si-doe, and at the end, lead everybody in singing, "O-k-l-a-h-o-m-a, Oklaho . . . MAH!" We will bow and eat up every ounce of applause we can siphon from our farm audience who, sitting in beach chairs and sipping lemonades, will beg for more. And we will do it for them, if they toss in another twenty-five cents.

Putting on musicals was one thing, but the year 1957 also found Kathy and me playing more serious games. I was nine years old when the cowboy-and-Indian fun with my sister graduated to a new level.

"Here," she said, handing me a bottle of gentian violet. "You can use this to paint Tumbleweed like an Indian horse."

"Why would I want to do that?"

"Because we're going to do what we've always done—play cowboys and Indians. But this time," she said coyly, "on our horses."

I was intrigued. I painted a violet-colored circle around Tumbleweed's eye and dabbed a fake brand on her hind quarters, the way I saw Indians do it in the movie *Broken Arrow*. I threw a little blanket over her back and hopped up on her with no saddle. We followed Kathy to the far field where the wild bucking horses for the rodeo were pastured. It was a real herd, with even a stallion. Just enough to play the game.

"Okay, I'm the sheriff and you're the Indian," Kathy called from her horse, her air rifle in hand. "You're going to try to steal this herd and rustle them to Mexico."

"Where's Mexico?" I yelled back.

"Across the stream, beanhead!"

"Oh, why didn't you say so, *bigger beanhead?*"

As I looked at the horses, who gazed lazily back at us, a thought crossed my mind: *I wonder what Mom would think of this.* But she was over at Grandmom's, helping out; she only came up to the farm occasionally, when the YMCA put on a special event, or sometimes for the rodeo. It made her too nervous to watch Kathy and me trick-riding and barrel-racing on our horses. Mostly, she stayed around Woodlawn and probably prayed.

"Are you ready?" Kathy called. "Come and get the herd!"

I dug my heels into Tumbleweed and cantered into the heavy woods lining the pasture. Like a good TV Indian, I sneaked through the trees, looking for the best position from which to ambush the herd. My plan was to burst out of the woods whoop-whooping like a savage, making the wild horses stampede toward the stream and into Mexico before Kathy knew what hit her.

After several minutes in hiding, I kicked my mare out of the woods, yelling and galloping and brandishing my air rifle like chief Crazy Horse. Suddenly, the stallion and his mares stopped munching and jerked their heads up. I popped off a shot, and the horses began scattering down the hill, terrified, in the direction I was hoping they'd go. Tumbleweed cantered hard behind the herd, and I glanced over my shoulder to see where Kathy was.

Pow! I heard her air rifle explode to my left. The she-varmint was hiding in a large, scrubby tree and had bushwhacked me. Caught up in the moment, I threw my hands up in the air—I'd been "shot," after all—released the reins, and flung myself off while in full gallop. I hit the ground with a thud and exhaled a dying gasp.

Kathy's eyes widened. She galloped her horse up next to me and asked anxiously, "Are—are you okay?"

I was slightly stunned by the fall, but I got up in one piece and began brushing myself off.

"You crazy beanhead," she said. "Why'd you go and do a fool thing like that?"

"I don't—I'm not sure why," I said, feeling a little dizzy. "I guess I really got into the game."

"Yes, and I can't believe you did that," Kathy scolded. "I just can't believe you let go of the reins!"

I was touched by my sister's concern. But when I thanked her, all she said was, "Thank me? Yeah, you can thank me after I find your stupid horse, who's a mile away by now, with that stallion. Thanks for nothing!" She turned in a huff and spurred her horse to go find mine, mixed up somewhere in the herd.

The next spring, Tumbleweed gave birth to a foal.

Wasn't life supposed to be like this? An adventure, a game, an odd mix of what's real and make believe?

That's what I thought until one late winter, when it snowed for days and the wind piled huge drifts across the dirt road leading to Sykesville. We were snowed in. At first, it seemed like one more of Daddy's wonderful adventures, something he and God had planned, something worthy of a chapter in *Little House on the Prairie*. The first night of our captivity, Kathy and I bundled up and ventured outside the old farmhouse to marvel at the cool, pale moon and how it turned the snow-covered pasture into a field of sparkling silver.

The next day, however, the wind was still piling the drifts higher. My father gathered together the rodeo cowboys, who were staying in trailers through the winter. He was concerned for the cattle. High snow banks had bent the barbed-wire fence in some places, and cows had gotten out. We had to find them to bring them back to safety, food, and water. Every man—and kid—was needed on his horse for the search.

I saddled up Tumbleweed, feeling tremendously important that I, a nine-year-old, could be called on for real ranch duty. This wasn't one of Kathy's games. Our cows were in trouble. The snow fell softly as we fanned out in different directions; I was ordered to stay with one of the cowboys, a nice man on a good horse who could rope very well.

The herd had scattered onto distant parts of the farm and the state park. Several hours passed as we regularly called to each other across the woods, slowly closing in on the hapless cows. The afternoon was getting on, the snow was picking up, and the temperature was dropping. As the cowboy and I rode up from the Patapsco River, looking right and left for strays, we heard a plaintive bawling from behind a snow-covered shrub.

A red-and-white heifer was on her side, her belly swollen with her unborn calf due in a month or so. In the heavy snow and freezing wind, she must have fallen down and gone into labor. We urged our horses closer, and I made out a tiny pair of cloven hooves protruding from under her tail. Blood spurted and stained the snow. The cow tried to lift her head. She dropped it back and cried again.

My throat tightened as the cowboy jumped off his horse and gave me his reins to hold.

"Please, do something," I pleaded hoarsely, the stinging wind biting into my cheeks.

He pushed on the cow's side, urging her to stand up, but she was too weak. After several tries, he moved to her backside, grabbed the unborn calf's legs, and pulled with all his might. It wouldn't budge.

"It's a breech," he said. Breathing hard, he rested back on his knees and wiped his brow with his glove.

It was beginning to get dark and the snow wasn't letting up. I was paralyzed by every emotion an animal-lover like me could feel: pity, horror, helplessness. It hurt to look into the cow's doleful eyes. "Isn't there *anything* you can do? Should I get Daddy?"

The cowboy ignored me. Instead, in one last-ditch effort, he untied the rope off his saddle and looped the noose around the little calf's feet. He swung himself up on his horse and proceeded to slowly rein him back, stretching the rope until it was taut. The cow began to bellow in great puffs of frosty air, but still she could not expel her calf.

"Do you have to?" I called above the wind. Tumbleweed shook her head and stamped her hoof to go home.

The cowboy backed his horse a bit more until the whole cow began to slide in the snow. Still, the calf could not be dislodged. Shaking his head, the cowboy nudged his horse forward to relax the rope.

The cow stopped bawling. She now lay completely still. The cowboy told me he was sorry but that there was nothing more we could do. As he gathered in his rope, I took a last look at the cow on her side. Then we urged our horses toward home.

We were the last to arrive back at the barn. I didn't, I couldn't, say much to the others. We had left hurting animals—a mother and a baby—back in the darkness, in snow so heavy they surely had to die. It was that simple. And I felt simply numb. Numb from cold and from horror.

Even as we warmed up inside, I felt like someone had taken a hammer and had chiseled away at something important in me—at my sense of wonder, perhaps. My carefree abandonment on the farm was replaced that day by a dull ache of reality. I couldn't shake the image of the mother cow in pain, a helpless animal who hoped that we—humans, wise and good—would rescue her and her baby.

I realized that as I'd stood watching, shocked and breathless, I learned that every living creature has its terrifying side, and every soft moment a razor edge. It was the beginning of a terrible understanding: that every lighthearted day does its best to stave off the darkness and that life is difficult and dangerous. In such moments, everything can seem so disconnected from God—or maybe it's that God seems disconnected from it. Life gets back to normal, as it did after that snowstorm passed—but a tiny corner of my soul had seen too much, and a part of my heart had hardened.

Maybe this was why, deep down, I preferred the safety of our home on Poplar Drive. It was home as home should be. On many Sunday nights, after we drove back to Woodlawn from the Circle X Ranch, I would unpack my suitcase in relief. I kicked off dirty boots, pulled off filthy jeans, and showered away barn dust, to sleep clean and secure under the gaze of angels. On Monday morning, I would be back at school with Kathy Carski and my regular friends, purchasing U.S. Savings Stamps, conducting a science experiment, visiting the library, and waiting for the 3:30 bell to head to Miss Merson's. As I walked up the path for my lessons, I saw her curtains billow from the third-floor window and heard Chopin wafting in the air. My eyes became wet every time, just as they did when I held down a big chord until the sound disappeared.

This was why, on the day of the horse pageant, my "But Mom!" was no real protest. It was why I endured the sharp tug on my shoulder and my fingers turning purple. Way down deep, I *knew* where I belonged.

And moments later, I was sitting in the front row of the auditorium at Woodlawn Elementary, next to fifteen other girls and boys, waiting my turn at the piano recital.

The auditorium was abuzz with parents and relatives, filled with the fragrance of ladies' perfume, whispering with the rustling sounds of little girls' crisp dresses. Although I was late, I was able to slip in behind Alan Silverstein, who had just finished playing. I peered over my shoulder. My mother sat a couple of rows away, watching my every move. As Alan returned to his seat, Miss Merson gave me a nod, and I proceeded up the side steps to the stage. I felt the scrutiny of everyone's eyes as I walked across the wood floor to where the piano waited at center stage.

I sat down, pulled up the bench, lifted my wrists, and began to play "Swaying Daffodils," an artful, lovely piece, delicate and sweet. When the last note disappeared, I inhaled deeply, relieved to have made it all the way through with no mistakes. I stood and curtsied to everyone's applause. When I walked across the stage to the side steps, however, I could tell everyone's eyes were still riveted on me.

It must have been my cowboy boots clopping on the hardwood floor, if not my coonskin cap and fringed-leather jacket.

CHAPTER SIX

Surely you desire truth in the inner parts.

Psalm 51:6

I
n the end, horses won out over piano, painting, and ballet. The arts provided me with platforms to express my wonder at life. But the horse *was* the wonder. I did things in toe-shoes, on a canvas, with the keys of a piano—but the horse did things to me. Besides, it had a soul. Or so it seemed, to a ten-year-old.

All animals had souls, as far as I was concerned. Which is why, to this day, I get a sick feeling when I think of the time I kicked—and kicked again—a puppy who stole my candy bar. I'm sure a psychologist could link my angry outburst to some familial aberration that might excuse my behavior, but I wouldn't buy it. And I wouldn't have bought it then. When I gathered the whimpering puppy in my arms to beg forgiveness—the fright in its eyes broke my heart—I was torn apart with guilt. I knew I was the stronger one, the smarter one, yet I had used my size and strength to terrorize. The punishment I dished out to this creature did not fit the crime.

Apart from that incident, and one or two flailings on Thunder's hindquarters with my crop, I felt that most animals—especially horses—were my soul mates. And I tried my best to tell them so.

I think of Christmas week in 1959, when the clouds were low and gray and hung as far as I could see. As the snow fell in light, dry flakes, a gray-white haze made the barn and spring house almost disappear. I was leaning on my elbow looking out the window, while my mom and sisters busied themselves in the kitchen, cooking and setting the table. An aunt and uncle were visiting, along with a neighbor and a few friends. The house was busy with a pleasant bustling about, and crackling Christmas carols drifted from the kitchen radio into the living room, where I sat on the window seat staring at the out of doors. I was just a kid, so I had no particular responsibilities for the preparations.

Sometime during the late afternoon, when the clouds were billowing like goose down, I pulled on my jacket and boots, stuffed a few carrots in my pockets, and slipped outside. My cheeks stung from the cold as I hiked through the drifts to the stable. I felt sorry for the horses in the barn. Our farmhouse was warm and light; their barn was dark and cold. All of us were talking about Christmas gifts—and I didn't want the animals to be left out.

I kicked a small mound of snow away from the barn door, dragged it open, and stepped into the long, dirt aisle lined with stalls on either side. Everything was quiet and still. I breathed in the aroma of leather, sweet feed, and hay, and the cozy odors of dry manure and horses' coats. I blinked—the light in the barn was the same muted-rose color as one of my favorite crayons. I took a few steps, and several of the horses whinnied softly as they heard me begin to unlock the feed bin. I knew that someone had already fed them that morning. But I wanted to give each horse an extra handful of oats, as well as a carrot. I wasn't needed back at the farmhouse, but I was needed here.

I opened Tumbleweed's stall and smoothed her mane and bangs. She was the demure one, the polite, feminine mare who would never dare be caught hogging her way to the trough, pushing others aside, the way Monica did. For being so good and kind, I gave her an extra carrot and thanked her for all the rides, pressed my nose against her muzzle, and wished her, "Merry Christmas."

Next, I visited Baby Huey, Monica's full-grown colt, in his stall. Baby Huey was huge, as big as his mother, and so was named after the large baby duck in the comic books. I gave him his carrot and stroked his forehead. He didn't know it, but I had helped to geld him. I wasn't quite sure even then what it meant, but when Dr. Loper, our veterinarian, needed help, he spotted me sitting on my haunches at a distance, watching as I always did.

"Want to hand me a few of these instruments?" he asked, peering over his glasses. He was the typical vet—intelligent looking, sporting a plaid vest, pocket watch and chain, and having just enough "farm" in him to soften his medical side.

I was stunned by the request. I looked over my shoulder to make sure he really meant me, and then happily got up to go help.

"Here, hold these snippers . . . careful, only hold the handle," he instructed in a businesslike tone.

I couldn't believe it—Dr. Loper actually needed my assistance, as if I were a nurse in an operating room. I opened my palms to make a flat little table for his snippers; I didn't want to touch the ends for fear of spreading germs. I scooted closer to Baby Huey, who had been tranquilized and was lying on his side. Hunching slightly, I saw Dr. Loper's hands flatten the colt's groin area—a soft, gray place with no hair that looked very tender. Taking his scalpel, Dr. Loper gently made two slices into the flesh. Blood began trickling, and I held my breath.

"Snippers, please," he said quietly. I offered him the instrument on my hand-table.

As he dug around up inside the two incisions, I tried hard to remember that this was all for Baby Huey's good. Finally, the doctor found what he was looking for—two small, yellow, egg-like organs. He pulled on them slightly until they were extended outside the colt's groin, and then—*snip! snip!*—the "eggs" dropped into Dr. Loper's hands.

"Want to take these?"

For fifteen minutes I had been the epitome of professionalism. I was as composed as the last time I'd helped Dr. Loper, when he allowed me to slice a boil on one of the horses' withers. I didn't lose my poise even when the smelly, mustard-colored puss spurted all over my jeans. But this was different. I didn't offer Dr. Loper my hand-table. Instead, I pushed the surgical tarp closer to him with my foot.

"I'm glad you don't remember that, Huey," I whispered now, and he nodded, crunching his carrots.

I went from stall to stall, making certain I spent an equal amount of time with each horse, telling them my favorite stories about their antics, and whispering any messages I thought my sisters might want them to hear. Cherokee had recently been shod, and I commiserated with him about the farrier cutting too close to the frog of his hoof. "I hope you didn't feel the nails going in," I said, kissing that soft, raspy place on a horse's nose right above the lip.

The wind howled and shook the barn door, pushing a blast of icy air down the aisle. I snuggled against Cherokee's warm, long winter coat, clasping my arms around his neck. Then the wind subsided and the stable fell quiet again. I listened to the hush, as though it had a voice. For a long time, I listened and remained still. Something about the peace and silence warmed me through and through—as warmly as if I were sitting by the fire back at the farmhouse. Maybe it was because I was alone. Maybe it was that I took time to think while watching the horses crunch their gifts.

But I think it was because I was, well . . . in a barn. I knew enough of the Christmas story—what Mary and Joseph and the Baby Jesus went through—to understand that being in a stable on a cold evening, surrounded by animals, was somehow . . . right. It was also fitting that I thank God for the peace and quiet. I may have only been ten years old, but I knew my rough-and-tumble tomboy life had in it too little quiet. And maybe not enough peace.

Ginger, the brown mutt-mother of the puppy I had kicked, came ambling up the aisle, her tongue hanging and her breath frosty. I squatted and ran my hands over her head, flattening her ears just as she liked. I couldn't remember what happened to her puppy, and I wished he were around so I could somehow make it up to him. Suddenly, my mood shifted—I realized I'd never have the chance to show the puppy I wasn't the person he thought I was. I wasn't mean.

I looked around the stable. All my thoughtfulness toward the horses couldn't whitewash the fact that I was the object of my own lesson: *I* was the living creature that had its terrifying side, and even this moment of soft beauty had a razor edge.

When the cold finally crept into my bones, I bid the animals good-bye, closed the barn door, and turned to trudge back up to the house. The wind caressed the snow-laden pine trees, blowing a swirl of white off their tops. Almost all color had vanished from the winter landscape. I was walking through a darkening world of grays, blacks, and heavy blues, all except for the two squares of golden, happy light from the farmhouse windows.

Night had fallen, and I hurried toward the chatter and noise of the farmhouse.

CHAPTER SEVEN

Blessed is the man who does not walk in the counsel of the wicked or stand in the way of sinners or sit in the seat of mockers. But his delight is in the law of the LORD, and on his law he meditates day and night. He is like a tree planted by streams of water, which yields its fruit in season and whose leaf does not wither. Whatever he does prospers. Not so the wicked! They are like chaff that the wind blows away. Therefore the wicked will not stand in the judgment, nor sinners in the assembly of the righteous. For the LORD watches over the way of the righteous, but the way of the wicked will perish

Psalm 1:1–6

God was only a little bigger than my father. The Lord may have filled the universe, but my dad filled mine. Whereas God kept the planets orbiting, my father was the center of our orbit. And whatever he commanded us was spoken not so much with words but through the sheer force of his own good character.

In the spring of 1961, it was God's responsibility to show young President Kennedy how to run a country, to keep the Russians on their side of the earth, to bring Adolf Eichmann to trial, to keep the Bomb from falling on Woodlawn Elementary, and *The Creature from the Black Lagoon* in his swamp and out of our neighborhood. Everything else was Daddy's responsibility.

Actually, there *was* something else that was God's responsibility. That was the fifty-yard dash—the one I was going to run at Play Day, a track-and-field competition between Woodlawn, Catonsville, and Pikesville Elementary Schools. Every year, I couldn't wait for this tri-school competition. Running came naturally to me, and during our foot races at recess I left most other girls my age in the dust. Now, at Play Day, all my eleven-year-old physical prowess would be on display.

I realized there was nothing my father could do to engineer a victory for me in the race—but God could. God was a little bigger and able to shift fate. He could make me a winner.

I knew I had to help, though. God was, well, the kind who liked a little cooperation. So, while other girls jumped rope or the guys played Greek Dodge, I spent all my recess time running the perimeter of the playground. I didn't run the ordinary way—I galloped like a horse. I figured it had to make me go faster. That's the way horses did it, and if it worked for horses, it must work for people.

"Hey, Horse-Face," Rocky Krien would call from the dodge ball court, "we're puttin' our money on *you*."

I hated being called Horse-Face. But I didn't hate it enough to stop running to the beat of *The William Tell Overture* in my head.

After school, I clutched my Roy Rogers book-bag tightly in one hand, slapped my thigh with the other, and—glancing around to make sure nobody heard me—I cried a "Hi-ho, Silver, away," galloping all the way home from our school: down Main Street, past Woodlawn Pond, down the two blocks along Gwynns Falls Creek, then up to the top of Poplar Drive, to my house. Under normal circumstances, I would have meandered my way home, maybe stopping at the pond to feed the swans with leftover lunch crumbs or taking the back way to our house up through the woods. Not this week, though. I was in training.

The fifty-yard dash for Play Day was all-consuming. After dinner, I practiced racing around the property line of our home—starting at the back door, jumping our flagstone entrance like a stream in a steeplechase, powering up our front bank, gliding down the back steps, cantering up the side driveway, swooshing past the play log cabin in the backyard, striding over the bank behind the garage. Finally, with knees weak and lungs bursting, I gathered my strength to vault the picket fence, then slapped my side and galloped the last few yards to the back door. Half horse and half human, I pranced and tossed my head to the cheers and applause of the admiring throngs.

Having someone to race against made it more interesting, especially if it was someone you knew you could beat. Sometimes I was able to talk Joe, the little kid next door, into running with me. I knew if I could win the 2321 Poplar Drive Steeplechase, I was a shoo-in for the fifty-yard dash.

I hoped—no, I was sure—God was observing it all. I felt I had to check in on him, though, to make certain he was clued in to the victory I needed. Occasionally, when I had a few minutes to kill after school before piano or ballet, I checked in with him at St. Luke's Methodist Church. It was directly across the street from school, and I knew it was a place where I could find God. Anyone was sure to have an audience with him in the beautiful, white-clapboard church with double doors and a steeple with a bell. Our town had only two churches—St. Luke's and a Catholic one, and there was a synagogue a mile or two up Windsor Mill Road. With so few houses of worship in Woodlawn, the doors to all of them were always open.

The front flagstone steps of St. Luke's were set just off the sidewalk, with a neatly trimmed lawn and bushes on either side. I walked up the steps and turned the knob of the heavy door. Even though our family didn't attend St. Luke's, it didn't feel like I was trespassing; after all, this was where I attended Girl Scout meetings and had come for kindergarten. Now, as I slipped in, I clicked the doors behind me and reverently approached the altar. I guessed that was the name for the high white table with the gleaming gold cross. When I reached a pew, I genuflected and made the sign of the cross, although I wasn't exactly sure how to move my hand. I just knew it was the sort of thing Kathy Carski did at her Catholic church.

Dealing with God was a little like approaching a larger-than-life parent. You weren't always conscious of his presence, but there was always the thought he was somewhere around, keeping an eye on you. And because he was watching, you were mindful that he—not always, but more times than not—was probably standing in front of a large blackboard, poised with a piece of chalk, ready to tabulate your good and bad behavior.

It was not a particularly pleasant image, but in my mind there wasn't much of an alternative. To not believe God was up there was, well, impossible. For one thing, there were the Ten Commandments posted at the front of our classroom, right underneath the American flag. No day at Woodlawn Elementary—at least back in the fifties and early sixties—dared start without a series of rituals: a U.S. Saving Stamps pitch to keep our country strong; the Pledge of Allegiance, to assure liberty and justice for all; the collection of lunch money (thirty-five cents for grilled cheese sandwich, tomato soup, carton of milk, and a Nutty Buddy); all capped off by a daily reading from the Bible.

Each day a different kid was selected to come up front, pick up the big, black King James Bible off Mrs. Hunt's desk, and choose a portion to read aloud. For the up-front, leader types, it was a chance to show off, reading a passage with "withersoever" or "vouchsafe" in it. Others not so gifted spread the word that, "If you want to get it over with fast, pick Psalm 117. You can speed through it in a single breath." So, most kids, trying their best to look cool and casual, as though handling a Bible were something they did all the time, flattened their faces against the page and read,

> *O praise the Lord, all ye nations:*
>   *Praise him, all ye people.*
> *For his merciful kindness is great toward us:*
>   *and the truth of the Lord endureth for ever.*
> *Praise ye the Lord.*

The Jewish kids in our class were the ones who most often picked the Ten Commandments. Kids like Arvin Solomon and Alan Silverstein. I couldn't put my finger on why, but they stood a bit straighter than the rest of us, as if reciting Scripture in front of people wasn't new to them. I'm sure it wasn't. Maybe the Commandments and the Psalms were familiar territory to Alan and his friends because of Bar Mitzvah or Passover. Or perhaps their pride in saying "Thou Shalt Not Kill" had something to do with the awful things we'd learned in class about what the Nazis did to the Jews in Europe.

I didn't know much about the Nazis and Jews, except that the war in Europe had been an historic bad-guys-versus-God-guys matter. It never came up much at the dinner table when the meat and potatoes were being passed around. My mother was German, and although the Allies may have had good reasons—even great ones—for plummeting Deutschland, Mother hated the bad press aimed at her parents' homeland.

"Those Nazis weren't true Germans," she'd mutter.

Her father, Maxmillan Landwehr, had immigrated from Hamburg, and her mother had been brought to America in the nineteenth century as one of many German orphans. As a young girl,

Grandmother was made to work in the fish market down on Broadway near Baltimore's harbor. It was there she caught the eye of Max, and shortly thereafter they were married. Pop, as my mother called him, loved Strauss waltzes, hard work, and strong lager. During the Great War, when hate began to fester against Germans down by the Baltimore docks, Max Landwehr began to drink harder. Then he left. He just up and disappeared, leaving his family of six to fend on their own. To help make ends meet, my mother began selling flowers on the street corner when she was still a little girl.

"But, Mom," I once asked as I helped her twist-tie flowers in bunches by the corner of Loudon Park Cemetery, "why are you still selling flowers? We're not poor." I was very young at the time, but I knew it was a stupid question. My mother and her sisters had always sold flowers on that street corner, probably since they'd been my age. It was just something the Landwehr girls did. Ever since their father had left.

My mother said Maxmillan had been driven from his job by taunting and rock throwing. She never talked much about him or Germany, Jewish people, or the war. She never talked much about the Ten Commandments either.

My Jewish friends had something I knew I lacked. When Arvin Solomon wore his *kippah* to class on a high holy day, I noticed that no one teased him or any of the other Jewish kids. In the aftermath of so many horrors during World War II—gruesome things they showed on *MovieTone News* in the theaters—most of us understood that our Jewish classmates had endured something sobering. In fact, we understood it more than most adults gave us credit for. When Adolf Eichmann was captured the year before, in the Spring of 1960, every kid in the cafeteria lunch line let out a cheer. It was as if the devil himself had been apprehended, and the Lord Jehovah Almighty had personally crushed the serpent's head with his foot. Jewish kids, however, had a special corner on the deeper meaning of that announcement. I envied that a little.

Wanting to be equally as religious, I waited with great anticipation to be called on to take the Bible from Mrs. Hunt's desk, stand erect, and read with great importance a *long* psalm. I figured God couldn't help but chalk one up in my celestial column as I stood under the American flag and boomed out Psalm 1. It had great words like "whatsoever he doeth shall prosper" and "the ungodly are not so, but are like the chaff which the wind driveth away." It was the sort of psalm that underscored how God favored the good guys. And I wanted very badly to be good.

Yet the words from the Bible prodded and pricked. They touched something deep inside me, like the churning inside I felt whenever Alan Silverstein read, "Thou shalt have no other gods before me!" Words like those hit my heart heavily. I didn't think my prized collection of plastic horses or my crush on Michael Coleman constituted idol worship, but my conscience knew a warning when it heard one. I may have been clueless as to what my conscience was or the role it played, but I knew that, like God, it existed. It was just ... there. And I knew I couldn't ignore it, just as I knew it was impossible *not* to believe God was there.

Yes, God was *there*. The fact was inescapable. I constantly had the impression that God was always saying something, not with audible words, but inaudible. It was as if he spoke on a different wavelength, like an ultra-high frequency. This was especially true on a breathtaking night when Casseopia crested the moon like a diamond tiara. It was as sure as the constellations, as certain as the Big Dipper pointing to Polaris, as predictable as Orion in summer: a Designer had to be up there, choreographing the dance of stars and suns. I even heard words for it once, when some kid in class read from Psalm 19 (KJV):

> *The heavens declare the glory of God;*
> *and the firmament sheweth his handiwork.*
> *Day unto day uttereth speech,*
> *and night unto night sheweth knowledge.*
> *There is no speech nor language,*
> *where their voice is not heard.*

Something, Someone was definitely on display in the earth and the heavens. That impression was confirmed on a class trip to the old Maryland Academy of Sciences, where we looked at their model of the solar system.

"Here are Mercury, Venus, Earth, and Mars," the curator noted, gesturing with his pointer at the glassed-in, wooden model of small planets spinning.

"Where is Jupiter?"

"Over there. By the wall."

"And Saturn?"

"Keeping scale, it would be over there in the next block," he pointed out the window.

"Wo-o-ow," we all breathed.

The curator then geared up for his *pièce de résistance*, announcing, "And, keeping in mind the scale, children, Pluto, the outer planet, would be located beyond Ohio."

It was too much to take in. I was hands-down, slam-dunk hooked on the heavens. And earth too. All of it whispered about God. Just the way the harvest moon, every year on time, crested the eastern horizon at the same minute the sun sank in the west. Or how a breeze left a silvery trace through the undersides of the leaves. Or the strange light and life in a horse's eye. A heart can't help but recognize a message that keeps insisting, "I am here . . . you are not alone . . . the world is even bigger than what you see." It was the same "beckoning" I sensed in Colorado. Maybe even the strange enchantment I felt with those wonderful big chords on the piano.

Yet it was about more than experiences. God seemed to be whispering from behind them all. You heard the whisper when you turned over a horseshoe crab in a tide pool on Rehoboth Beach and marveled at the intricate design of shell and membranes, joints and tiny claws wriggling and thrashing. Realizing this creature had been swept on shore from the deep, and there you were, the only person on earth to have ever revealed its underbelly to the light of day— it felt almost like an act of creation. I found it in my delight in sneaking a can of condensed milk to feed hungry barn cats at the Circle X Ranch and feeling pleasure in their grateful meows. Knowing I could give enjoyment to an animal made my heart feel divine. I remember my mother handing me a leaf of fresh kale by the sink. "Look at these beautiful colors," she exclaimed. That leaf should have been framed and mounted at the Baltimore Museum of Art. I turned it over and over in my hands, admiring the delicate purple veins webbing through shades of green to blue, purple to rose. It must have been designed by Someone.

All of this—every psalm and commandment, every balancing act with the constellations, all of Arvin Solomon's religiosity—now hung precariously and profoundly on the scales for me. God was in the dock as I sat in that moment in St. Luke's United Methodist Church.

Because now it didn't involve science, Nazis or Jews, astronomy, or the world of art. It involved the fifty-yard dash.

I did my best to rest against the stiff pew, trying to think pure and upright thoughts so God would hear me. I decided to sing something worshipful to set the mood, so I began reverently:

> *Praise God from whom all blessings flow,*
> *Praise him all creatures here below;*
> *Praise him above, ye heavenly hosts;*
> *Praise Father, Son, and Holy Ghost.*

I held out nice and long the "A-a-a-men," knowing God must have been pleased with my pretty good pitch. Once the echo had disappeared, I prayed, "Oh God, I know I don't often talk to you, you know, all proper and everything. And it's not often I come to you asking for stuff, but—"

It's not often you come, period, my conscience suddenly spoke up.

"—God, I need your help, please, to win the fifty-yard dash at Play Day next week."

Joni, my conscience interrupted again, *talking to God is no different than talking to Aunt Kitty. You shouldn't ask for stuff right off the bat.*

"You are powerful and great."

That's better.

"I guess you've seen me practicing running every day. You can probably tell I'm trying very hard. And, God, it's not that I expect you to come through for me or anything—"

Then why are you here, stupid?

"Well, to be honest . . . I just wanted to ask if you would be so kind as to help me win. I promise I'll tell everybody you had a part in it, and I'll speak up for you, really. I promise you'll get all the credit."

I put my hand on my chest in a cross-my-heart-and-hope-to-die gesture.

"I promise you, you'll really be proud of me if—if you'll only make it so I'll win. Amen."

I started to get up, then remembered something they always said in church after they prayed.

"I mean, 'in Jesus' name, Amen.'"

Well, you did the best you could. You should be proud of yourself.

I picked up my book bag and left the church satisfied I had that base covered. And on the way home, I did my usual horse-gallop.

The pressure was on—on me and God. Everybody at Woodlawn Elementary knew I was the fastest student in sixth grade, boy or girl. Kids were already tallying which boys and girls would win their events to ensure a first-place trophy for our school. They didn't bother to deliberate over me. I was a sure thing.

On the final week leading up to Friday's Play Day, I visited St. Luke's one more time to pray. Then, on Friday morning, I borrowed Kathy Carski's St. Christopher medal and clasped it around my neck. By the time I climbed on the bus to head for Catonsville Elementary, where the games would be held, I felt sufficiently religious. I had performed every spiritual requirement known to a ten-year-old, short of paying indulgences. The scales of justice were sufficiently weighted in my favor, but I dared not say it aloud, either to myself or to God. I had simply stacked my training, and all my visits to the church, on one side of the scale. And I trusted that God, always fair and impartial, would lift his blindfold, take a peek at my hard work, and be happy to tilt fate my way. God could always be trusted to help those who help themselves.

When we arrived at Catonsville, kids were pouring out of buses, cheering and yelling as they brandished banners and bundles. The day was hot. I looked around, amazed at the number of kids and teachers. Soon the track-and-field events started, and I waited for what seemed to be hours before my number and name were called. Finally, when I heard the summons, I walked over to the starting area.

I could feel the heat rising from the track. I glanced to my right and left and smiled at the other sixth-grade racers. I didn't know any of them. Tall, long-legged girls ambled up to the starting line, exuding confidence. More than one or two of them were black girls from Catonsville, the school bordering the Baltimore city line. They were wearing shiny running shorts and important-looking shoes.

The track supervisor called us to the line. I squeezed my medal and breathed a quick prayer, "God, this is it."

"On your mark—"

I glanced to my right and noticed one of the Catonsville girls in a Wilma Rudolph stance: legs bent, back arched, shoulders perfectly balanced over fingers edging the starting line. Her muscles were stretched and spring-loaded for action. She was completely focused on the red tape stretched across the track fifty yards away.

"Get set—"

I sort of crouched and hunched my shoulders.

"—Go!"

I have run many races in my life, some literal and many figurative, yet of all those races, I still can feel the sting of defeat in my chest and the taste of embarrassment in my mouth from this one. Huffing halfway down the track—not near the finish, but halfway—I strained with all my might just to stave off the dumpy kid from Pikesville and the skinny beanpole girl with baggy shorts.

Our school came in third. I didn't say much during the bus ride back.

"Too bad, Horse-Face," Rocky jeered. He tossed a wad of paper at the back of my head.

I may have hated that name before, but now it brought hot tears and burning resentment. A few kids proudly showed off their medals, but all I could feel was the notion that everyone's eyes were boring through the back of my head. Most kids on that bus were probably thinking about weekend stuff by the time we pulled into our school's parking lot. Not me. I knew exactly what I wanted to do the minute I got off the bus.

I waited around until most of my friends had left with their parents. Then, as the last car left the lot, I stuffed my hands in the pockets of my shorts and kicked a stone all the way over to the school crossing. I stood on the edge of the curb for a moment, staring at the white clapboard church across the street.

Something was different. Monumentally different. Oh, the town looked the same. On one side of the church was Monaghan's Bar and its tree-shaded parking lot, and on the other were the storefronts of Balhof's Bakery, the hardware store, the barber's shop, and the Equitable Trust Bank. Main Street was still lined with trees, and I still felt the happy security of being part of a rural village that knew you and your family as well as it knew the Balhofs and their famous sugar-twist buns. But something bigger than all these things was different now. Something about the church had changed. I had thought its Occupant could be trusted, but now I wasn't sure.

There was no school crossing-guard that late in the afternoon, and so I looked both ways before stepping off the curb and walking across the street to the steps of St. Luke's. This time, as I entered the doors, I didn't go up to the front. I didn't genuflect or cross myself either. I just sat in a back pew for a long time, until the burning in my cheeks cooled.

The last rays of the day washed through the stained-glass windows, catching little bits of dust floating in the air. The place was quiet, the kind of quiet that makes you want to think. A dog barked outside, and I heard people talking in the church basement. The voices reminded me that I used to know this church well, that I had gone to kindergarten downstairs. It was where I'd met Kathy Carski, Rocky Krien, and Michael Coleman. We had played Marines in that room, stacking up big wooden blocks like a gunner's turret to keep the Koreans at bay. Rocky made a great General Eisenhower although he always had his wars mixed up.

The thought of Rocky brought me back to why I'd come here. I hated that he called me Horse-Face. I hated that my galloping-like-a-horse had achieved me nothing—absolutely nothing, except for feeling foolish. Most of all, I hated that I had let down my classmates. I was no longer "the best." I was sure Daddy would have expected me to win. How would I face him when I got home? I was afraid he'd be disappointed in his pal.

Yet what hurt most was, quite simply, my humiliating and resounding defeat. It made me very disappointed in God.

The God who resided in this church was supposed to be the same God I knew down on the beaches of Delaware and along the bridle paths near the Patapsco River. The God I was familiar with was the one I Christmas-caroled about on horseback, the one I sang about in church hymns. He was the one who smoothed the tops of the clouds below Pikes Peak. He was wild and free, and he spoke through the eyes of horses and danced among the fireflies and echoed along with mockingbirds in the woods. He was the God who invited gulls to play on his wind and painted glorious sunsets over the Chesapeake Bay, who delighted to observe from heaven his children playing in his tide pools and catching his sand crabs. The God I knew delighted in entertaining me with his awesome creation and was perfectly agreeable. Surely he had to notice my hard work. Surely he realized how much this race had meant to me. My request was so small, not very demanding. Why couldn't he have lifted his little finger to push me across that finish line ahead of the others?

I looked up at the wooden rafters. I noticed a couple of cobwebs and a strange thought flitted through my mind: *I wonder when was the last time someone dusted up there.* That the house of God could gather dust seemed ironic. I wanted to say something to wound or hurt him, but I couldn't. I couldn't bring myself to spite him, so I figured the best tactic was to sulk silently. So I waited for a few minutes, and then I got up to leave. I decided the white clapboard church had tamed God too much.

It was getting late, and I worried that Mom might be ringing the dinner bell soon. I ran home, leaving the church behind. As well as something of my childhood.

The
GOD
I LOVE

Part Two

You will hear of wars and rumors of wars, but see to it that you are not alarmed. Such things must happen, but the end is still to come.

Matthew 24:6

On October 22, 1962, President Kennedy filled the screen of our television set and declared, "We have no wish to war with the Soviet Union, for we are a peaceful people who desire to live in peace with all other peoples.... The cost of freedom is always high, but Americans have always paid it. And one path we will never choose, and that is the path of surrender, or submission."

I was just another thirteen-year-old, sitting on the floor, hugging my knees and huddling with my family around the tube. NBC had switched from a commercial to a special report from President Kennedy, announcing the discovery of Soviet missile sites in Cuba. The president made it clear that any missile attack from Cuba would trigger an all-out attack from us on the Soviet Union.

How could an eighth-grader like me grasp the terrifying possibility that nuclear war was imminent? In the Atlantic, Soviet ships—presumably carrying more missiles—were steaming toward Cuba, while the U.S. Navy was mounting a blockade. In Florida, nearly 200,000 soldiers were being concentrated in the largest invasion force ever assembled in the United States.

My world could be snuffed out in a nanosecond. In a mere twelve minutes, a nuclear bomb could drop on our country. Yet it was hard for that terrible fact to sink in after President Kennedy went off the air, and we were reminded that "You'll wonder where the yellow went, when you brush your teeth with Pepsodent."

Everything was changing. Everything was in upheaval. People all over the country were praying about the standoff between the United States and Russia. Churches were having midweek services. Even the bells down at St. Luke's rang at odd times, signaling a prayer meeting. Could God really sway a bunch of atheists on the other side of the earth?

It was like a gigantic chess game. I had learned chess during a class train trip to New York City and was impressed at the older kids who were able to think three moves ahead. I felt that's what the Soviets were doing, sitting across from us Americans and always thinking three moves ahead. Could truth and right really checkmate them? Was God listening to people's prayers? Could he stop the inevitable?

Sometimes I dared think the more obvious question: what if *God* were the one playing chess, and we, along with the Soviets, were his pawns?

I got the impression from my parents that thirteen-year-olds weren't supposed to concern themselves over Cold War tensions or the Berlin Wall. Once Daddy and Mother were away from the Walter Cronkite report and the radio, they tried to diminish the crisis. Yet I had no doubt that the Soviet-American-Cuban chess game was what caused so much edginess and nervous joking in the hallways of Woodlawn Junior High. Then again, my friends in homeroom didn't seem bothered much about the possibility of nuclear war. They seemed more worried about learning "The Loco-Motion" or the "Monster Mash" in time for the sock-hop than about any Cuban missile crisis.

Had my peers forgotten the days of doing duck-and-cover back in elementary school? Had they forgotten the fear of hearing the Woodlawn Fire Department's siren go off, signaling everyone to stop what they were doing, dive under their desks, and clasp their hands over their heads? "You can't believe the Russians are really going to drop a bomb," a boy had once chided, as we came out from under our desks and brushed off our knees. Maybe it was just that horrible siren. It sounded like the European sirens, the real ones you heard on the MovieTone news reports in the theater. And Woodlawn Elementary was only a block from the fire department, making the siren's wail vibrate through every bone. The terror was real.

But that was elementary school. This was junior high. And now we had an entirely new crisis, with real missiles just ninety miles away in Cuba, missiles aimed straight at us. I didn't know what to think or whom to believe. Did someone really have a finger poised over a red missile-launch button? Were we going to have to cancel the sock-hop on Friday night? Was all this a political ploy or something just to fill the space between commercials?

God seemed to be the only one who knew anything. Well, God and Mr. Lee.

Mr. Lee was our eighth-grade CORE teacher, a three-period class that grouped English and social studies together. Current events were Mr. Lee's thing, and he made quite a point of President Kennedy's speech. He would come to class every morning with the latest headlines in hand, drilling us about Castro and Batista, the CIA and the Bay of Pigs. I leaned on my elbow, riveted on every word and enraptured with every detail. I could quickly grasp dates and figures, and I shot my hand up fast to be first with the correct answers. I wasn't moved so much by current events as I was, in the midst of all the missile madness, by my huge crush on Mr. Lee. He was the reason I made the honor roll both semesters in eighth grade.

My straight A's certainly didn't come because I ogled Mr. Lee from the third row. But my scholastic success *was* one-sided, motivated solely by a passion to please my teacher. I was discovering at thirteen that nothing rouses the soul quite like love. Doesn't matter if it's puppy love or the real thing—the point is, it's potent. Nothing shoves you into high gear quicker, stretches your attention span longer, or makes you hit the alarm button faster in the morning than love.

My mother and father were impressed that I would zoom up the stairs immediately after dinner so I could hit the books. "My, what a change! That teacher of yours—you say his name is Mr. Lee?— must be quite interesting," they observed with amazement. I would grab the banister in mid-flight, pause on one foot, smile, and say demurely, "Yes, he is," then bound up to my bedroom to study.

My bedroom was another thing that had changed. I no longer shared a room with Kathy. Linda, who shared the bedroom at the far end of the house with Jay, had gotten married soon after high school. She and her husband now lived at the Circle X Ranch. And that meant that half of a nice, big bed opened up in her old room.

A big closet too. And a beautiful balcony so close to the front yard's oak trees that you could almost reach out and touch a branch. You could sit on the balcony on any night, listen to the crickets, count the fireflies, hear the rustling of leaves inches away, and strum your guitar to your heart's content. You could also spot any cars coming up Poplar Drive—a feature that would be useful later in high school, when I began dating.

When Jay asked if I wanted to leave Kathy's room and come share hers, I jumped at the chance. Who wouldn't want that big, wonderful bedroom? Besides, how could I refuse the sister who let me shift gears in her Buick Skylark from the passenger seat? The one who played the piano with me? Who called me "Jonathan Grundy"? This was my big chance to strengthen the ties that bound me to Jay, my "new" big sister.

The change happened one afternoon when Kathy saw me hauling hangers of clothes over to Jay's room. "What are you doing?" she asked.

"I'm moving out," I said matter-of-factly.

Kathy grew quiet. "Why?" she finally asked.

I didn't stop to think about the ties that had bound me to her for so many years. The many happy cowboy gunfights we enjoyed around the Ping-Pong table in the basement. The Saturday mornings we skimmed the cream off the milk bottles, scarfed down Cheerios, and watched horse programs on TV. Or the Saturday afternoons we tied our horses to a tree on the bank, rolled up our jeans, and waded into the Patapsco River to catch crayfish. I didn't think about the meetings of the HD Club up in the corn shed, when we wrote fan letters to the stars of *Wagon Train*. I didn't pause to consider—or to say thank you for—those lonely nights when Kathy held my hand under the covers. Or the times we raced steeplechase on foot, jumping every stone wall and running up and down every terrace around our home. Or dragging the many big pieces of driftwood back to our tents for the campfires at Rehoboth Beach. Or especially clinging together the times when we were left out because Jay and Linda thought we were too little. I didn't think about any of this.

With a pile of clothes in my arms, I answered Kathy's "Why?" with a standard shrug of the shoulder and, "Cuz." Then I turned and left her with Jack and the Beanstalk, the Pied Piper, and the angels on the slanted wall. I was Jay's roommate now.

Jay's room—I should say, my new room—was fit for a thirteen-year-old. The bedroom was far away from Mom and Dad's and Kathy's, and it had its own private staircase, with a door with a lock and key. The room was sunny and airy, full of windows, and the walls were papered with big roses, not dorky, fairy-tale stuff. Its outer door opened onto the covered balcony, which ran along the room's length. So whichever window you opened, you could lean out and look eye-to-eye with a squirrel or reach farther and almost touch a bird's nest.

I had my own desk, with a place for books and a new slanted wall on which to tack pennants from Poly or Mount St. Joe's, the two arch-rival schools from downtown. I could leave the bathroom door open and let the steam out without worrying about warping anyone's furniture. I could tack up my certificates from the Honor Society, and listen to Peter, Paul, and Mary to my heart's content. I loved my room. It was easy to study there in the afternoon and easy to dream at night.

Sometimes my studies and dreams overlapped. When Mr. Lee taught a course on American poetry, we all were assigned to pick a poem by Edgar Allen Poe, memorize it, and be prepared to recite it by heart in front of the class. Several classmates and I had chosen "The Raven." Come Monday morning, I observed the way most of the kids walked stiffly up to the front, stood awkwardly behind the lectern, and stumbled through their poems. I eyed Mr. Lee in the back with his grade book. *I need to do better than this*, I thought, knowing my turn was tomorrow.

I had an idea. That night, I dug around in my mother's closets and located a couple of yards of black fabric. I scrounged for an old drippy candle and a holder. I stuffed the fabric and the candle in a duffel bag and then got ready for bed, rehearsing "The Raven" line after line until I had it right.

The next day, the second group of students waited their turn to be called. By the third or fourth kid's recitation, everyone was getting bored. Near the end, Mr. Lee called my name, and I went to the coat closet to retrieve my duffel. Then, silently, I made my way along the side of the classroom and began closing the blinds. Finally, I placed the candle carefully on the lectern, lit it, and turned off the classroom lights.

A couple of boys whistled and gave a smattering of applause. They knew something fun was up.

Next, I draped the black cloth over my head and clutched it under my chin.

"Hey, it's the midnight hag!" Arvin Solomon jeered.

I put my face as near to the candle as I could, knowing its glow would cast macabre shadows under my eyes, nose, and mouth.

"It's a witch!"

I smiled in agreement. That brought more applause. Mr. Lee adjusted his glasses and leaned forward with his grade book in hand.

I mustered all the Scarlett O'Hara, hand-over-forehead theatrics I knew and proceeded to pour all the drama I could into my reading:

> *Once upon a midnight dreary, while I pondered, weak and weary,*
> *Over many a quaint and curious volume of forgotten lore,*
> *While I nodded, nearly napping, suddenly there came a tapping—*

At that point, I rapped on the lectern, cupped my ear as if to urge, "Hark!" and continued:

> *As of someone gently rapping, rapping at my chamber door.*
> *"'Tis some visitor," I muttered, "tapping at my chamber door;*
> *Only this, and nothing more."*

On the fifth line, I realized I was doing a pretty good Vincent Price. I hunched over the lectern and cruised through the rest of the verses, crescendoing on the last one, trading in my Vincent for Boris Karloff:

> *And the raven, never flitting, still is sitting, still is sitting*
> *On the pallid bust of Pallas just above my chamber door;*
> *And his eyes have all the seeming of a demon's that is dreaming;*
> *And the lamplight o'er him streaming throws the shadow on the*
> *floor;*
> *And my soul from out that shadow that lies floating on the floor*
> *Shall be lifted—nevermore!*

Arvin Solomon leaped to his feet in applause. My friends called, "Bravo! Encore!" like Marcello Mastroianni, and I twirled my black cape and threw it to my fans in the classroom. Then I blew out the candle, à la Lauren Bacall in *Key Largo*.

I got an A++.

Mr. Lee insisted I repeat my poem for the rest of the junior-high English teachers the next day. Afterward, when one of them suggested I have a part in the school's upcoming rendition of *Macbeth*, I was thrilled. My bubble popped, however, when I was given my "big part": I was to play one of the three witches in the opening act. Even so, no one ever recited, "Double, double, toil and trouble; / Fire burn, and cauldron bubble" with more pathos.

On every front, life seemed great. Whether I was playing the piano in band, painting posters for art class, spiking volleyballs in gym, or raking in credits with after-school activities, I appeared to be handling life's changes and challenges pretty well. I waved hi to friends in the hallways, and I had people to sit with in the cafeteria. I did my homework, took on extra assignments, and was well-liked by my teachers.

So why did junior high leave me feeling so empty?

Good grades and mediocre popularity weren't cutting it. Class plays and talent shows, band practice and choir rehearsals weren't either. Instead, sour, rancorous emotions constantly competed for my peace of mind, and sullen feelings had me bursting into tears for no reason at all. Sometimes I'd be huddled with girlfriends, hanging outside of homeroom before the morning bell, when suddenly I thought, *Where's the center of this? Is the real center happening somewhere else? Is it down the hallway in front of someone else's homeroom? I know it's not. The center isn't there. And it sure isn't here.*

I tried pushing the thoughts out of my head, so I could listen to a girlfriend's chatter about which Beach Boy song would hit number one that week. But her eyes kept darting up and down the hallway, as if she were watching for someone more interesting to come along. *Why does this feel so hollow? Why am I standing here talking about which disc jockey I like better on WCAO? Why do I sound so ... empty?*

Down deep, I knew the stakes in life were getting higher. It felt the same way as when the Cuban missile crisis ended: Khrushchev had offered to remove the missiles in return for an American pledge not to invade Cuba ... but that only meant the Cold War had warmed from 85° below zero to 75° below. A breathless world was breathing again, but its blood pressure was still high. Things had changed in the waters off Cuba, but the world still was not safe. Life still felt tenuous. The chess moves were happening too fast, and there was no way a kid in junior high could keep up.

Not even my feelings for Mr. Lee could quiet my inner restlessness after the bus dropped me off at home. Why did I sit on my bedroom balcony at night, mournfully strumming "Michael, Row Your Boat Ashore" and singing as if my heart would break? Why did I feel that Arvin Solomon had it more together? That Kathy Carski was light years ahead of me in social graces and the pursuit of real meaning in life?

Proof of that happened the year before in 1961. Mrs. Carski had taken us shopping at the new Mondawmin Mall, so we could buy angel blouses. It was the blouse every girl was wearing, with frilly sleeves and an empire waistline that made you look pregnant. Kathy and I found our sizes and went into a dressing room, where we proceeded to get undressed. With my blouse halfway off, I turned to tell Kathy something but froze in mid-sentence. Kathy was wearing a bra.

I hadn't expected my friend to be wearing a bra. I didn't know what to do but was already committed to a course of action. So I continued to get undressed, revealing my undershirt.

Kathy saw me in the full-length mirror. "Oh, Joni, you really need a bra," she said in a slightly superior tone.

"Uh—well, I left mine home," I lied.

"Really? What size do you wear?"

I had no idea what bra size I was. "I can't remember," I lied again.

"Well, you know that without your bra, you should probably get a bigger blouse size."

Right there—that was it, that comment. It was why I was convinced Kathy Carski was years ahead in grasping the meaning of life. She spoke with such authority, not only about her own blouses and her body, but about mine. She exuded confidence. She groomed her nails, and she knew that one day she wanted to teach piano, if not ballet. When we had been in sixth grade, it was Kathy Carski, not me, who went to the special personal-hygiene session where they showed *The Film*.

My parents had thought I was too young to see *The Film*. Besides, they didn't believe it was the school's responsibility to educate adolescents on personal hygiene. That stuff was reserved for family discussion. The only problem was, at home we never got around to officially talking about birds and bees and bras. My parents probably figured sex education would filter down to me from my older sisters, like Maxwell House coffee. Maybe they thought I knew enough from watching horses and dogs on the farm. Whatever the reason for their discomfort, they hadn't signed my permission slip for *The Film*. So, while Kathy Carski and the other girls in my class pursued new levels of maturity and life-meaning in the film room, learning about menstruation and boys' bodies—while they found *the center*—I sat with two or three other girls in our classroom, reading *Smokey the Cowhorse*.

For a tomboy like me, missing out on that experience set me on an inevitable collision course with junior-high hormones. I was about to get a crash course with life changes. Suddenly, I didn't know what to do with towhead blonde hair that now had turned mousy. Or pigtails that now looked little girlish, freckles that were giving way to pimples, and a mouth full of teeth that now required a full set of braces. I didn't feel comfortable in my old, black Jack Purcell tennis shoes anymore, and I certainly wasn't comfortable with plucking my eyebrows. Some of the old dresses I was still wearing—the one-piece jumpers with buttons up the back—were getting awfully tight around my chest. And I couldn't, for the life of me, get those little garter hooks to secure my nylons. Should I shave my legs like everyone else? My underarms? Use deodorant? I couldn't keep up with my body's changes.

And it wasn't only about hormones. It was life in general. Everything I'd come to treasure was rapidly changing—the weekend rodeos, sharing Cokes with my horse ("Eew, did you really do that?" a friend would say), planning dramas with the HD Club, everything. Remarks from old classmates in elementary school didn't help: "Remember the time Eareckson brought that big old, ugly bear rug in for 'Show 'n' Tell'?" and "Yeah, and that scrawny pine tree she brought in for the Christmas play?" That last comment really hurt. I remembered the tree: I was only in fourth grade at the time, but I saddled up my horse on a winter's day, rode out to a small pine grove on the border of our farm, and chopped it down myself with a hand ax. I tied my lariat around its base and dragged it all the way back to the farmhouse.

Those days had changed forever. One moment I would long for the old days when my sister Kathy and I nailed little blocks of wood together as boats, set them to sail on the creek, then ran along the bank, watching them dip and swirl in the current, waiting to see how far they'd go before hitting a rock and sinking. But the next minute, I found myself resenting those very days, for the way they beguiled me into believing life could really be that simple. Building and sailing wood-block boats seemed passé. At least to girls who wore bras.

Little wonder I felt I didn't fit in junior high. While I desperately kept up pretenses—volunteering for a solo in choir or continuing to impress Mr. Lee with my grasp of the Limited Test Ban Treaty—in my heart I retreated to the balcony of my bedroom. Joan Baez and Mary Travers became my heroines, and I strummed and sang every plaintive song on their albums, finding words for my woes.

Hang down your head, Tom Dooley, because the fruit of your poor lemon is impossible to eat, and besides, where *have* all the flowers gone? If only I had a hammer, and if only life would quit changing. If only life weren't so impersonal and mechanistic, if only algebra wasn't so hard, if only my girlfriend would quit looking up and down the hallway for a better friend. If only Mr. Lee wasn't married, and I didn't feel so hollow and empty, and God was—well, more like he used to be.

In English class, I learned "These are the times that try men's souls" and wrote it on the front of my three-ring binder. I hated junior high. If I wasn't retreating to the balcony with my sketch pad, I found solace at my piano. I had long graduated from the old upright down in the basement and now proudly played a black baby grand my parents had purchased from Carski Piano Company. I could hardly believe this glorious instrument was mine, resting as it did in the corner of our living room, on top of the Bengal tiger rug. When I struck its keys, the sound filled the spacious room and echoed off the vaulted ceiling.

On weekend evenings in late spring or early fall, I opened the tall windows in the living room, letting the breeze waft in on one side and carry the piano's melody out the other. As I sat and played, I remembered every artful admonition from Miss Merson. I found myself bending and yielding to the keys and chords, gracefully crescendoing and retarding with every note in every measure. Music provided the atmosphere that, for a little while, at least, allowed me to rise free of things around me. Just as with my guitar on the balcony, I *fit* at the piano.

Whenever I played, I hoped deep down that my father, working hard in his den office, could hear me. *Oh, Daddy, are you listening? Would you please leave your work at your desk, and come help me find the center? Come listen to me play my piano?*

With his office just across the hallway, I know he could hear me. And, joy of joys, occasionally he would leave his desk, or one of his paintings, and walk to the living-room door. As he leaned against the door frame, watching me play, I felt his eyes on my back. And I felt his smile. After a while, he would step down into the living room and take a seat in the comfortable chair next to the piano. I would glance and see him resting his head back with his eyes closed. He'd heard the strains of one of my homemade arrangements, beckoning and inviting him to listen—and he had thought my playing was worthy of interrupting his work or hobby. Often he asked, "Mind if I join you?" in a respectful tone.

Daddy had always been attentive to his girls, but now that we were growing older, I'm not sure he knew what to do with us. We weren't quite his "pals" anymore, as he liked to call us. We no longer helped him mix cement at the farm, and we'd stopped nibbling food off his plate. Jay, Kathy, and I had put away our Daisy air rifles. Our Roy Rogers cap guns too. We had graduated from riding Western-style, like cowboys, to riding English.

I'm sure my father hoped we still wanted to hear a bedtime story. That we wanted to catch frogs down by the spring house. Yet maybe he didn't know what to hope. My father had to be facing the same thing I was beginning to face: that we couldn't remain little girls forever.

I wanted ever so badly to help him ease through the transition. The transition of our growing up. If I couldn't deal with my own changes, maybe I could at least help him.

So I did what I knew best. I played my piano. Here, nothing had changed. I fit at the keys. And Daddy fit there, listening. At the piano I had certitude—as much as Kathy Carski, maybe more. And I found no greater pleasure, whether in class or on the volleyball court, than when I was able to perform a private recital for my father. Maybe I wasn't his pal, but I was still the young girl he loved. He proved that by entering into my domain, my music.

Those moments were timeless. When they happened, the upheaval of junior-high change receded, and peace flowed in. There was no cold war raging inside my heart, no terrible game of chess with an enemy out to capture my king. Maybe here, playing Aaron Copeland or Chopin—here in this beautiful, old living room, filled with so many memories, my father at my side, he still the king and I the princess— maybe I would find the real center.

CHAPTER NINE

In his heart a man plans his course, but the Lord determines his steps.

Proverbs 16:9

How would I ever learn to be a lady if I couldn't give up my boots? My rough-out, suede-bottom cowboy boots, with the hand-stitched, tan leather tops, that went so well with my Levis?

I had worn those boots for ages. But, to quote Bob Dylan, the times they were a-changing. Not only were my dress and jean sizes growing, I also jumped from a 6M to 8M in boots overnight. If I was going to change along with my body and start wearing a bra, maybe I'd better change my Tony Lamas too.

I did the ladylike thing: I left cowboy boots behind and purchased a shiny pair of black, stove-top English riding boots. Then I scrounged more for the rest: a pair of jodhpurs, a starched high-collared shirt, a tweed riding jacket, a black-velvet skull cap, and a crop. Standing in front of the mirror in my full riding regalia, my hair pulled back in a bun and cap in hand, I looked like a painting from the nineteenth century. I looked almost . . . beautiful.

Daddy thought I looked pretty special too. Enough so that he bartered a used English saddle off of a friend, repaired some of its leather fixings, and presented the saddle to me in the fall of 1962. I immediately saddled up Tumbleweed—the horse I had always ridden Western-style—and began testing her over a few low fences in the show ring.

"She looks pretty good jumping over those rails," Daddy called from the gate where he stood leaning. "She has good form, an easy gait. Nice manner. Keeps her head down."

"Yeah, she's a natural," I called back.

"You are too!"

After several fences, I reined her over to where my father stood. Letting the reins relax, I patted Tumbleweed's lathered neck. "I don't think we should raise the fences on her," I observed. "She's only a little over fourteen hands high. I think a three-and-a-half-foot fence is her limit."

Daddy didn't answer, but I could see an idea beginning to mull in his head. A few days later, he drove me to the Maryland Livestock Auction Yards. A nearby thoroughbred farm was having a liquidation auction, and Daddy thought we might pick up a good horse for a fair price.

Before the auction began, we walked the dirt aisles behind the arena to look over the choice of horses. The air was full of hay dust. Men barked orders from across the barn. The horses, frightened by all the strange and loud surroundings, kept whinnying in distress. We saw plenty of classy thoroughbreds, but they were way beyond my price range. Others, thin and tired, peered at us from behind their stall doors, looking homeless and hopeless. I couldn't bear it. A few had scars on their shoulders, reminding me of Black Beauty and Ginger. I realized these were the horses—aisles and aisles of them—that were probably marked for dog meat.

Late in the morning, after the best geldings and mares had been paraded by, the hands escorted into the ring a tall, gangly thoroughbred. He was chestnut-colored, with a white blaze running down the front of his large head. Nothing about him was attractive, and my heart wrenched when I heard the starting bid: it was low, and that meant the glue-guys and dog-meat people had a good shot at him.

Then the ring-groom began to lunge the horse, warming him up to go over a fence. That's when I sat up. The horse began to prance. His ears perked up. He seemed eager to show off his stuff. The groom angled him toward the fence in the middle of the arena, gave a click, and the long-legged animal sailed over it easily.

"That was four feet," I said to Daddy, amazed.

"That horse could easily do four-foot-six."

During a break, we had a chance to look over the big chestnut gelding. We ran our hands down his legs and examined his hooves and teeth. He was generally sound. And so, tabulating my baby-sitting earnings and what I had in my bank account, Daddy and I decided on our bid. We would offer that amount and no higher.

As it turned out, I didn't have to worry. Hardly anyone else wanted the ugly, large-headed horse.

I named him Saint Augustine, after a little book I kept on my shelf called *Confessions of St. Augustine*. It was like a lot of little books I'd been collecting lately. I'd read some of them because I'd seen older, Beatnik-looking fans of Peter, Paul, and Mary reading them. I had accumulated an eclectic array: *Catcher in the Rye* and *Franny and Zooey* by J. D. Salinger, *Siddhartha* by Hesse, *The Western Book of the Dead*, and this one by Augustine, an early church father.

"I christen you Saint Augustine," I said to my new horse, patting his head. I soon tired of speaking about him in four syllables, however, so I shortened it to two. He became Augie.

Augie and I began making the rounds on the horse-show circuit, and soon we were known among our competitors—people who rode sassy-looking thoroughbreds and sat on nicer, newer saddles. Augie's and my best class for competition was "Modified Olympics," in which we would tackle a complex maze of fences, odd-shaped obstacles, triple-bar spreads, and no jump under four feet high. It was a rigorous and dangerous competition.

First, we enter the paddock. Augie prances. Gate opens, and horse explodes into show ring. I muscle the reins and head toward the first fence. Hooves pound dirt . . . snorting, breathing . . . I clasp his mane, whip his shoulder, and—*Uff!*—up and over the fence we fly. Come down hard with a grunt. Gather reins. Eyes alert, ears up . . . angle horse to next fence and take deep breath.

"I can't look! I won't look!" my mother would cry, covering her eyes. She often volunteered to man the hamburger booth during those horse shows, but she always took a break when she heard the loudspeaker announce that "Miss Joni Eareckson on her horse, Saint Augustine" was now entering the arena. Mom insisted, "You're going to break your neck one of these days!"

Eventually, I put Tumbleweed out to pasture, and spent more time riding Augie along the trails of the Patapsco. One of the trails took me up past the Cauthorne estate, on the other side of the river. Mr. Cauthorne was the epitome of a gentleman-farmer; I often saw him standing on the white-columned porch of his mansion, with his favorite foxhound by his side. Whenever I trotted Augie up

Gorsuch Switch Road—mostly a wide, rutted, dirt path—Mr. Cauthorne waved if he was standing on the lawn or walking down by the barn.

One day, after seeing Augie and me sail over one of the fences bordering his farm, he called me over. "Joni, how would you like to go with me on our next fox hunt?"

"Me? You want ... *me* to ride with *you* on the heels of the hounds?"

Early on Thanksgiving Day, after I had wrapped Augie's shins and braided his mane, my dad helped me trailer Augie to the Howard County Hunt Club. We parked our van, and I unloaded my horse, giving him a palm full of oats for being good. Within minutes, I had the girth on my saddle tightened, and I mounted Augie, gathering the reins in my hands.

I looked around for Mr. Cauthorne, and spotted him by the red barn. He was sitting atop Pepper Pot, his well-seasoned thoroughbred. Mr. Cauthorne had on his red coat and black cap and was talking to several other huntsmen on their horses. Anxious hounds circled Pepper's legs. The dogs barked, the horses whinnied, and matrons from the hunt club greeted everyone with cups of hot cider.

The morning air was damp with the sweet freshness of new-mown hay. Or maybe it was leather polish. Or just the horses. Everything smelled wonderful.

Someone tested a bugle, and the dogs became more restless. Just then, Mr. Cauthorne called me over to his circle of riders. When I trotted up, he tipped his hat and made introductions. "Miss Eareckson, I would like you to meet Mr. Carroll of Doughoregan Manor," he would say, and the huntsmen would answer, "It is my pleasure to meet you, young lady," or, "The pleasure is mine, Miss Eareckson," raising themselves slightly in their saddles and tipping their hats.

Finally, the master of the hounds sounded his horn. Our horses' hooves clattered on the cobblestone, and when we hit soft dirt, riders and mounts broke into a thudding canter.

I reined in line behind Mr. Cauthorne, observing how he deferred to the hunt master. We crossed a stream and trotted onto the first field, where I spurred Augie into a slow gallop. I can still feel my hands holding the reins, knees squeezing the saddle. I can hear hooves tearing up thick clods, the blast of the hunt horn, the creaking of leather, dogs baying, and horses heaving and breathing. I can smell the November air, sharp, dank, and earthy, the sweetness of shaven cornfields, and the pungent odor of dead leaves, mud, and sweat. I can sense the lightness in my stomach as we'd gallop toward a stone wall, the suspension of gravity as my horse and I would fly over it, I would catch my breath, and we'd head for the next fence. Flinging his mane, tossing his head, snorting, and chomping his bit between every jump—my happy Augie was right at home.

We never caught that fox. After we cleaned down our horses, Mr. Cauthorne took me to the Howard County Clubhouse for tea. When we entered the ambling old farmhouse, I was taken aback, for it had the same elegance as Miss Merson's apartment. A string quartet was playing, and there were holly and ivy, candles and linen. Butlers ladled punch from silver bowls and placed trays of meats, cheeses, and breads on the tables. Everywhere I turned, people talked gaily about the day's ride.

I looked down at my boots, still muddy and scuffed, and at my jodhpurs caked with horsehair and sweat. I caught myself in a mirror and busily tried to fix my hair, now falling slightly askew from the bun. I was struck by my image—a smudge of dirt on my cheek, but a cup of punch in hand—and I decided, *I look like a lady. I am in this place of candle and crystal and manure and mud and—look at me!—I can ride a horse and still be a lady.*

That night, when I joined my family back in Woodlawn for Thanksgiving dinner, I jabbered like a magpie around our holiday table. "And Augie and I didn't skirt any fences—pass the potatoes, please," and, "I got a chance to meet the owner of the hunt club, and—who's got the cranberries?—and everybody said my horse was so cool, and ... and ..."

After dinner, my father led our Thanksgiving tradition with each of us around the table sharing something we were thankful for that year. Linda and her husband were expecting again. Jay had met a neat guy from Denison University during spring break in Fort Lauderdale. Kathy was thankful that she and her horse, Reds, were once again Maryland State Barrel Racing Champions that year.

I was so excited, I could hardly wait for my sisters to finish. All day I had been living in a Currier and Ives print, surrounded by romance and nostalgia. Junior-high-school blues were history. No longer did I feel conflicted. That day I had been graced with a brilliant vision and was now able to see forever into my future. All was perfect. Absolutely perfect. I knew what I would say when Kathy finished talking.

"Your turn, Joni," someone finally said.

"I'm thankful I have my life planned. I'm going to get good grades in high school, apply to a veterinary college, marry the man in the Marlboro cigarette commercial, live on his ranch in Wyoming, breed and raise horses, and qualify for the equestrian team and go to the Olympics."

It sounded like the center to me.

CHAPTER TEN

So justice is far from us, and righteousness does not reach us. We look for light, but all is darkness; for brightness, but we walk in deep shadows.

Isaiah 59:9

There wasn't a man in Maryland who could build a stone wall like my father. Dad was able to combine his building skills with his artistic talent to design walls that resembled something out of a Robert Frost poem. Weathered sentries, they were, all gray and old, balanced and sturdy. When my father would build a wall, he wouldn't rush. He'd take his time. He and Mr. Tom would unload a big pile of uneven boulders and rounded stones, and then sort through them, putting aside the ones for the wall.

I watched them from a distance. Dad would pick up a rock, brush off the dirt, turn it over in his hands, and line it up, this way and that, placing it just right in the row. Mr. Tom would come behind Dad with the cement and trowel.

"Here you go, Mr. John," he would say, pouring the cement into the cracks between the rocks.

"That's it, Tom."

"More cement?"

"Mm."

They worked like a well-oiled machine, each one fitting into the other's pace. Slowly and meticulously they'd lay the wall. First they built one along the side of the barn, and a second by the spring house. Another bordered the patio in front of our farmhouse.

Yes, in the summer of 1963, walls were being built. My father was lining the farmhouse driveway with one. And Mr. Tom, ever by his side, was helping him. Now that my father was getting older—he had turned sixty-three with the year—he needed someone to work beside him: an extra pair of hands to reach for things and an extra pair of legs to compensate for his arthritic knees. Tom Chappel was that man. A slight-built black man with a quiet, gentle demeanor,

Mr. Tom loved my father and enjoyed shouldering extra weight for Daddy. All of us in the family appreciated Mr. Tom. That's what we called him; "Mr. Chappel" was too formal for so congenial a family laborer, but plain "Tom" was too disrespectful. So it was "Mr. Tom."

He and Dad would begin the day's labor early in the morning and hardly took a break under the hot sun as they sweated and strained to position the heavy rocks. By noon, my father would strip off his T-shirt, but Mr. Tom usually kept his shirt on, as well as the tidy brown tam on his head. Jay would make lemonade and fetch lunch, but mostly, Dad and Mr. Tom looked out for themselves. Mr. Tom seemed devoted to my father. He was ever in agreement with my dad's views on everything from politics to the pay scale.

Sometimes I would ride home from the farm with Dad and Mr. Tom. We took the roundabout way to Woodlawn, passing through Gwynn Oak Junction, so we could drop off Mr. Tom at his house— a place my father owned—on Plateau Avenue.

Occasionally, we also drove by another house on the same street. It was a pleasant, red-brick-and-white-clapboard home where Miss Thelma, a distant aunt on the Eareckson side, lived. She was an elderly woman, short, plump, with gray hair, thin spectacles, and a gratifying smile. Miss Thelma lived alone, and Dad often stopped by to see if she needed anything or if there were any repairs to be done.

I liked Miss Thelma, but I felt sorry for her. She had no husband and therefore no children. Yet she was so nice. I couldn't understand why she'd never caught a man's eye. I was just grateful that Daddy and the rest of us enjoyed an abiding friendship with her. And now that Jay and Kathy had their drivers' licenses, they often ran errands for Miss Thelma or helped her clean house.

Although Mr. Tom and Miss Thelma only lived a few houses away from each other, their worlds never touched. And neither could possibly know how their lives would touch mine.

In 1963, God was beginning to take the stage in America, front and center. His name was bantered and brandished, spotlighted and highlighted in every Beatnik song, poem, and political speech of that day. Writers questioned him, musicians doubted him, and Joni Mitchell, one of my favorite singers of the sixties, even wondered how we might get ourselves back to his Garden. God was sermonized by some and eulogized by others who claimed he was dead.

But nobody played the prophet quite like Martin Luther King Jr. as he stood on the steps of the Lincoln Memorial that hot August afternoon before scores of thousands, and proclaimed:

> I have a dream that my four little children will one day live in a nation where they will not be judged by the color of their skin but the content of their character. . . . I have a dream that one day every valley shall be exalted, every hill and mountain shall be made low, the rough places will be made plain, and the crooked places will be made straight, and the glory of the Lord shall be revealed, and all flesh shall see it together.

It seemed God was taking sides. And he appeared to be on the side of Martin Luther King Jr. and not George W. Wallace. Federal troops had just forced Governor Wallace to honor a court order desegregating the University of Alabama, and President Kennedy went on television, asking, "Are we to say to the world—and much more importantly, to each other—that this is the land of the free, except for the Negroes?"

I thought of Mr. Tom and the walls my father was building.

I wanted to be on God's side. So I became one of a mass of young people who searched, as one poet put it, for God and truth and right. Some of my passion was fostered by class discussions on segregation. We were assigned to read a book called *Black Like Me* by John Howard Griffin, the true story of a white man who colored his skin black and journeyed south to experience firsthand the stigma of segregation. The hate and horror this man faced left a deep impression on me. My search for truth and right began heating up.

I memorized the protest songs of Peter, Paul, and Mary, as well as Joan Baez. I paid attention as the pastor of the little United Methodist Church we attended up by the farm pounded his pulpit about racism and social inequalities. I hung on every word of Mr. Lee as he urged us to examine the issues that were ripping society apart. We discussed injustices in the classroom and brought to light things that needed changing. "Let justice roll down like the mighty waters!" went the Bible verse, quoted from pulpits and coffeehouse stages alike. Yes, God was in.

And if I was going to be on God's side, I had to get better connected with him. I asked my sister, "Jay, could you drive me to Bishop Cummins church this Sunday?"

"Why? What's wrong with our Methodist church?"

Nothing was wrong with the Methodist church. It's just that Bishop Cummins Reformed Episcopal seemed to be the right place to find spiritual roots, especially if you were an Eareckson. Daddy's brother, Uncle Milton, had served as pastor there for years, and many of our relatives, near and distant, filled the pews. I couldn't help feeling comfortable and at home there. The front pages of so many prayer books had inscriptions such as "In memory of Ruth Eareckson" or "In honor of Vincent Eareckson Jr."

All of which raised a good question: "Why didn't we attend Uncle Milton's church on Sundays?" I wondered the question aloud to my Dad one day.

"We're up at the farm on weekends," he answered pleasantly.

I wasn't entirely satisfied with his answer. "But it's neat being with everybody, the cousins and all."

"It's too far to drive," he countered. His tone shifted slightly, and I realized I was not to pursue the matter further. That was okay; I decided it *was* probably a long drive in from the farm on Sundays, so I let it rest.

That is, until the following Sunday, when I once again encountered my cousins. I put my head together with a couple of other soon-to-be fourteen-year-olds and tried to trace our family tree. Vince, Nicki, and Lois were my cousins, although I was more the age of their children, Roger, Vicky, Paul, and the others. Vince Jr. married Elva, and they had Vince III, or Trippy, who was Jay's age ... and so on. It was complicated.

I wondered where Miss Thelma Eareckson fit in. Kathy seemed to know her best, so one Saturday afternoon I went with her to take Miss Thelma shopping. I decided I would ask my aunt where she fit on the family tree. But once we'd unloaded all the packages on Miss Thelma's kitchen table and left, I realized I'd forgotten to ask her.

On the way home, I asked Kathy, "Is Miss Thelma an aunt-once-removed or a great aunt or what?"

"You mean you don't know?" Kathy asked, a little surprised.

"No. Who is she?"

My sister gave me a look that said, "I don't know if I should tell you." Then dropped the bomb: "She's Daddy's first wife."

I felt my mouth drop open.

"Daddy was married to Miss Thelma a long, long time ago."

"You mean he's been—" I gulped, "—he's been divorced?"

"It's not like you think," Kathy stiffened, rising to Dad's defense.

This was a seriously bad conversation. It dawned on me we were using words about my father that at any other time would have meant a mouth-washing with soap. *Divorce? Daddy was married before?* Impossible. People were only supposed to get married once. Besides, if they divorced, they were supposed to hate each other. But we loved Miss Thelma. All of us, including Mother, had nothing but respect and affection for her. And there was another matter altogether: Mother. What about her?

"You can ask Daddy about it, you know," Kathy said.

That was unthinkable. No way, no how could I ever broach this subject with my father, even if it were true.

But I could with my mother.

I had a decision to make before I approached her. First, I could forget the whole thing and shelve Kathy's bombshell as stupid sister talk. I would never raise the subject and play dumb as if I'd never heard anything. On the other hand, if I broached it with my Mom—bringing it into the open, out of the closet, and into fresh air—things would never be the same. Never.

I decided it was too important to play ignorant. I waited for a moment to catch my mother at the kitchen sink, while she was at work. I took a deep breath and let the cat out of the bag: "Mom, is it true, is Miss Thelma really Daddy's first wife?"

My mother stopped wiping dishes. "Yes," she replied. "Yes, Miss Thelma was married to your daddy."

I watched my mother say the words, but they didn't seem to fit. They didn't go with her. It was as if she'd said, "We've been lying to you: white is really black, and black is white."

"How did it happen?"

My mother took me back to the years just before 1920 and recounted the story as she had learned it. My father was the strapping, happy Captain John in Company C of the Boy's Brigade at Bishop

Cummins Church. Everyone loved "Cap'n John." Quick with a smile and Christian encouragement, he was everybody's favorite at church. Eventually, he was named Sunday school superintendent, and he worked well with his brothers, Milton, the pastor, and Vince, the vestryman. Anna Verona couldn't have been more proud of her sons.

By the time the early twenties rolled around, couples were pairing off at Bishop Cummins and wedding bells soon followed. Everyone, it seemed, was getting married except for two people: my father and Thelma who, although sweet and soft-spoken, was also a leader in the church. During Sunday socials and picnics, they were often paired together—after all, Cap'n John and Thelma were the only two remaining single young adults. But back then, a man didn't sit with a young woman at a church social unless he had serious intentions. People began to push them together a bit harder. Expectations rose. And pressure mounted. With Thelma's stern mother giving Daddy the eye, and everyone elbowing him and jibing, "When are you two going to tie the knot, John?" he finally did what he thought was the chivalrous thing. He married Miss Thelma.

"But did you ever *love* her?" I would ask him years later.

He would reply, "Love? We were such good friends that we felt, well . . . love would come later on."

It never quite did. Miss Thelma realized this. They tried to start a family, thinking that children in the house would bond them together, but they were unable. Nothing seemed to be helping. Especially Miss Thelma's demanding mother. And so they quietly agreed to an amicable divorce.

"I was just a youngster in the Girl's Legion," my mother added. "I didn't know all the details myself, being fourteen years younger than your father. Of course, many years later, after I'd grown up and got to know your daddy, well—we were married in 1940. I guess there were a few people at Bishop Cummins who didn't like the fact that your father remarried. There was a lot of gossip and . . . I never felt—" Mom's voice got softer, "—accepted."

This explained everything about Bishop Cummins. About why we weren't members there, and why we went to the little church near the farm.

My father had remained committed to providing for Thelma, which included the red-brick-and-white-clapboard home up at Gwynn Oak Junction. He had promised to meet all her financial needs. And he did that and more. Years later, we girls became Miss Thelma's helpers, offering on our own to help with housekeeping and errands. We became, like Mom and Dad were, her friends.

None of this softened the blow, though. I was ashamed there were skeletons in the Eareckson closet, and I wrestled with conflicting emotions. I was resentful at the truth, yet bewildered over the secret. I felt sorry for Miss Thelma one minute and sad for Daddy the next. I anguished over the word *divorce* and how it stained the family name. Then I thought, *But we wouldn't even have a family—my sisters and I never would have been born—had Daddy stayed married to Miss Thelma. God had to know that!*

Most of all, I was disheartened that my father—my strong, able adventurer, the one who called me his pal, whom I had placed on a pedestal all my fourteen years—had toppled. He'd fallen from grace. Why hadn't he told us? Why did he lead us to believe our family was special, different, even perfect?

An odd thing occurs when you unveil someone else's sin, especially when you're a self-righteous teenager on God's side. You take fiendish glee in pointing out everyone else's wrongs. After all, God is the God of truth and right, and by gum, we have to drive home his point to the one who has broken the rules. Pick up that stone. Aim it and throw hard.

Stones. Yes, that's it. Daddy and his walls. Daddy using Mr. Tom to build those walls. Could Daddy be hiding something else? I calculated how and when I might approach him. I decided it should be on some afternoon after we dropped off Mr. Tom on Plateau Avenue. As we passed Miss Thelma's house, driving along in silence, I aimed and threw: "Daddy, how much do you pay Mr. Tom?"

"How much do I *pay* him?"

I was clearly raising a subject I knew little about and was none of my business. But I pressed him further: "Mr. Tom does so much, and he works so hard alongside you—"

Daddy interrupted me: "Tom receives a fair salary for his work."

"Minimum wage? That's fair?" I pounced on my prey. "Daddy you know you've got him working hard, from early morning to late in the day. I think the Lord would want you to be more generous with Mr. Tom."

My father didn't answer. We drove the rest of the way home without speaking. Somehow, I felt my stone had hit its mark. Especially since I'd weighted my words with God's name.

I went to my room that night thinking I was Mr. Tom's great white hope. I had vindicated him from oppression and injustice and had fought for rights he was perhaps too meek to claim. As I sat on my bed, proud to be on the side of God and truth, I rehearsed the conversation a couple of times. Finally, I slapped my knees and stood up to get ready for bed. But as I brushed my teeth and put on pajamas, I kept wondering, _So why do I feel so rotten? I'm right and Daddy's wrong. So . . . why don't I feel good about it?_

I opened the window, then climbed into bed. I punched my pillow a few times and lay back to listen to the wind in the trees, the tinkle of the glass chimes at the back door, and the songs of summertime crickets. It reminded me of nights when I was a child, nights that were so enchanting I'd force myself to stay awake just to listen to the soft sounds in the dark. The sound of the radiator thumping and the floorboards creaking. Or the gentle, peaceful voices of my mother and father drifting up the stairs. Of Daddy calling softly from the bottom of the steps, "Goodnight, Joni."

I turned over in bed and sobbed into my pillow.

"You beanhead," Kathy chided the next day. We were riding our horses along the Patapsco River, she in the lead and me behind. "You said _what_ to Daddy?"

"I told him he ought to be paying Mr. Tom more."

"Why would you say that?" she said in disbelief.

"Because. It's right."

"You don't know nothing," she muttered.

"Whaddya mean?" I dug my heels into Tumbleweed to get alongside my sister.

Kathy twisted around in her saddle to look me in the eye. "Joni, do you have any idea of the arrangement Daddy has with Mr. Tom on his house?"

I shook my head.

"It's not only a good arrangement, it's a very generous one. Daddy holds a no-interest mortgage, and Mr. Tom and his family will be able to easily own that house in a few years. And if Mr. Tom dies before the mortgage gets paid, his family will get the house free and clear."

"Really? Are you sure?"

"Yes, I'm sure," she said. As she turned to face the trail again, she added a final, "Beanhead."

It may have been one of the few times in the many years Kathy and I bickered that I truly felt like a beanhead. I was sick to my stomach. Sick that I had spoken rashly to my father and more sick that I had attacked him with no good cause. The very stone I'd cast had ricocheted back and struck me. And it crushed me like a boulder.

My face was hot now and my eyes burned. I whipped my horse around and spurred her toward home, full of resentment. I wanted to strike out and hurt someone, but there was nobody to take my anger out on. No one was responsible for this but me.

I wish I could explain what happened after the summer of 1963. All I know is, I got angrier. I was a stupid beanhead, a fact I could have let drive me to my knees. But my anger wouldn't allow it. Neither would my pride. So I did what so many teenagers of that day were doing: I rebelliously began building my own walls. Walls against my parents, my past, and my better judgment.

I knew a couple of girls, who knew some boys from Mount St. Joe, who knew where a fun party would be held that weekend. This meant telling my parents I was going to hang out with so-and-so down the street but not *really* telling them where I was going. It meant catching a ride on the corner in a friend's car. It meant walking into a party that was always in a low-lit basement in a friend-of-a-friend's house. It meant sauntering through the noisy, red-lit, smoke-filled room like I knew the ropes, moving to the music of the Rooftop Singers, who invited me to "Walk right in, sit right down, baby, let your hair hang down." I did just that.

There were actually only a handful of basement parties I snuck away to, but those were enough. I had never felt more alone, more alienated. All the time I sat on a couch with a boy's arm around me, all the time I draped myself over him while dancing, laughing at jokes I didn't get and people I didn't think were funny, I knew beyond a shadow of a doubt I was dying inside. I had pushed a self-destruct button, and I didn't know how to disengage. The Joni I'd been raised to be was suffocating and shriveling. I was dying from lack of air, of peace and safety, of joy and a sense of belonging. *Oh God, oh Daddy, please find me. Here I am, please find me.*

Sunday morning would arrive, and I would get ready for church—I had decided to keep attending Bishop Cummins. Thankfully, I hadn't regressed to the point of hating church, and most every Sunday I stood with the rest and prayed from *The Book of Common Prayer:*

> *Almighty God, Father of our Lord Jesus Christ,*
> *Maker of all things, Judge of all men;*
> *We acknowledge and bewail our manifold sins and wickedness,*
> *Which we, from time to time, most grievously have committed,*
> *By thought, word and, deed . . .*

My conscience was still able to whisper and convict me. But I knew that the more I chose those parties, the duller and more inaudible that God-whisper would become. Plus, the higher and thicker my walls would become. Down deep, I wanted my conscience to remain my friend, even though it had been like a thorn in my side the night before.

After church, I spent Sunday afternoons at the farm, saddling up and riding the trails along the state park with Kathy or Jay. We exchanged small talk as we rode along, mostly sharing memories of times when we were kids on the Circle X Ranch. But something wasn't quite the same. The sunlight still streamed through the leaves the same way, the creeks still gurgled, the squirrels played tag on the sides of trees, the hay smelled sweet, and the birds still called, echoing through the woods. . . . God's creation hadn't changed one bit. But I no longer felt at one with it all. I could see freshness and purity all around me yet felt anything but fresh and pure. I was stained, tainted, and oh, how desperately I wished I could get back to his Garden. *Please, can you find me? Will you rescue me?*

God must have heard me. He didn't part the heavens or reach down through the clouds to lift me above the walls I was building. But still he reached out.

"I'm going over to Miss Thelma's to help her move," Kathy said one day. "Wanna help?"

I found an excuse not to. But I was curious: "Where is she going?"

"To a retirement center."

"Why?" I asked. My concern was real now.

"Because she's old. She needs more help."

Looking back, I wish I would have joined Kathy that day. I wish I hadn't made excuses. Miss Thelma had ever been the gracious "aunt." Never once did she repeat the old gossip, and never once did she fail to defend Daddy's reputation. Walls were not to her liking. She loved God and, I believe, still loved my father as much as she loved all of us, his children.

Years later, when she passed away, I was surprised to learn my sisters and I had been included in her will. Miss Thelma didn't have relatives or many possessions. When we discovered she had remembered us in her estate, we were humbled and a little excited. It was the first time anybody had bequeathed us anything. I couldn't imagine what Miss Thelma had left me.

When Daddy returned home from settling her estate, he took me aside and said, "You do know how much Miss Thelma loved you—how you were her favorite, don't you?"

I nodded, a little embarrassed and red-faced. Daddy's face was a little red too. He was having a hard time finding words. Finally, he handed me a small box. When I opened it, I gasped. It was a beautiful, one-karat diamond ring in an antique-platinum setting.

"Oh, Daddy, this is beautiful. She wanted *me* to have this?"

He was quiet for a long moment. Then he answered, "She asked specifically for me to give this to you."

I turned it over in my hands to examine every facet.

"Here, let me show you something, though," he said. He took the ring and held it up to the light. "See that?" he pointed to one of the facets. I squinted until I saw, way down in the interior, a speck of black carbon. "It's got a flaw."

It didn't matter to me that there was a carbon speck. I'd never held in my hands such a big diamond. It was so big, in fact, that I never wore it. For years, I kept it tucked away, taking it out only once in a great while, so I could be surprised anew by its beauty. And by its fragment of black carbon.

Flaws or no flaws, I cherished it. It had been Miss Thelma's engagement ring.

CHAPTER ELEVEN

For he has rescued us from the dominion of darkness and brought us into the kingdom of the Son he loves, in whom we have redemption, the forgiveness of sins. He is the image of the invisible God, the firstborn over all creation. For by him all things were created: things in heaven and on earth, visible and invisible, whether thrones or powers or rulers or authorities; all things were created by him and for him. He is before all things, and in him all things hold together.

Colossians 1:13–17

If planets have feelings, what do they think when their sun's gravitational pull no longer holds them in orbit? Do they feel sad for their sun? What crosses their galactic brain when they find themselves drawn to some other supernova that has exploded onto the scene? Do planets have a say, or is it all a matter of centrifugal forces?

As I rested on my elbow in Mrs. Klingamon's tenth-grade science class, it seemed to me that planets couldn't care less. The universe was beginning to look awfully mechanistic, and all the king's horses and all the king's men couldn't put poor planets back in orbit again.

And for all his luminous personality, all his magnetic pull, my father was no longer able to hold me in his orbit. At least not in that fall of 1964.

I hadn't exactly been itching to spin off and away from Daddy. I was still charmed when he sat by my piano, and I felt honored when he saddled up and rode with my sisters and me. I was proud to show my friends around our house and pause by his trophy case in the den, pointing out his wrestling medals and diving trophies. At times, it felt a little odd to me; even in light of what I'd learned about my father's past, my respect for him had grown. He had become more human—more real.

So I wasn't dying to be released from Daddy's sphere of influence. But other universal forces had kicked in. Though some of these were packed with peer pressure, most were rather ordinary, like flipping a calendar to discover one day that suddenly you're a fourteen-year-old. In either case, these push-and-pull gravitational fields were taking me somewhere else. And besides, it was a new era: dreams and idealism had died hard alongside President Kennedy on that bloody day in Dallas, and now even the Beatles couldn't buy me love. I was on a teenage trajectory, having been separated from my booster Daddy-rocket. I was lost in space—not so much twirling off into nightmarish chaos, but just . . . drifting. I was a teenage planet whirling on my own axis, wondering what luminous star would dazzle me next. It certainly wasn't Mrs. Klingamon or her science class. Nothing she taught captivated my imagination—not even the time she breathed into a dead cow's lungs to illustrate the function of alveoli.

Ah, but history. Now *that* got my attention: the subject that asked where do we come from and where are we going? How does everything—us included—*fit?* History was packed with true stories of adventurers and conquerors, explorers and discoverers, all larger than life, their escapades documented in books with lots of pictures, graphs, and charts. Suddenly, I was off on a history orbit.

"Okay, everyone," Mrs. Krieble barked one day in world history class. We all sat down, startled; our teacher didn't normally raise her voice.

"I am dismayed at this class's performance on recent tests," Mrs. Krieble said, walking ominously from one side of the classroom to the other. "I want you all to pull out a plain piece of paper, a pencil, and get ready to take a pop quiz."

"Aw-w-w-w," we all groaned.

Mrs. Krieble marched briskly to the blackboard and raised the world map, revealing the quiz questions. She looked at her watch. "You have ten minutes to complete your answers. Begin!"

Everyone penciled feverishly. Yet just minutes after we started, Mrs. Krieble slammed shut the classroom door. Startled again, we looked up.

"That's it. I've had enough!" our teacher yelled, smacking her yardstick against her desk. "I am sick and tired of the cheating in this class. I will absolutely not tolerate this practice *anymore*—do you hear me?" She raised her voice: *"Anymore!"*

We looked around to find the culprit who cheated on the test.

"Eyes front!" Mrs. Krieble demanded. A couple of kids dropped their pencils. The teacher began slowly walking down each aisle, muttering threats. Someone began to cry.

Mrs. Krieble strode to the front and raised another map. Underneath this one, a pledge was written. It was made up of several demands, one of which was to turn in classmates if we suspected them of cheating. She told us to copy it down. Then: "I order each and every one of you to sign your name to this pledge."

This was weird. We were being forced to fink on each other.

A boy raised his hand. "Is this," he gulped, "is it *right?*"

Mrs. Krieble's eyes narrowed. "I define what's right in this classroom."

A few students crossed their arms, resistant. But the majority of the class picked up their pencils and proceeded nervously to sign their names to the pledge.

When we were finished, Mrs. Krieble erased the pledge from the blackboard. Then she quickly chalked down in large, fast letters: DEMAGOGUE.

Our teacher turned and smiled. "*This*, class, is today's lesson."

What in the world is going on? I sat stunned with everyone else.

Mrs. Krieble continued, "A demagogue is a leader who, through intimidation and fear, forces people to do as he says. Like—"

"Like *you*, Mrs. Hitler," a guy called out from the back. A sigh of relief swept the classroom.

"Yes, like him, and so many others," she said, rapidly writing the names of Mussolini, Stalin, and other frightening figures from World War II.

"Were you just scaring us? This wasn't a real quiz?"

Mrs. Krieble put down her chalk and said something I'll never forget. "Students, I want you to remember this: You will never truly know it here," she said, pointing to her head, "until you experience it"—she thumped her heart—"*here.*"

We now understood the meaning of demagogue.

My eyes widened. In one brief, visual moment, hearing just one short sentence, I felt the capacity of my soul actually stretch. It was as if someone had shown me how to really breathe. How to look for the real center.

Knowledge that only stays in my head—it's just a bunch of facts and figures. But if I can experience it—if my heart gets involved—then, wow, that's a whole different story.

I had always possessed a natural curiosity about life. Daddy had started that in me. But even as I memorized the constellations or differentiated kinds of leaves or devoured historical novels or grasped current events, I always sensed the presence of an underlying current. I knew there was a kind of knowledge that floated on the surface of science and history, astronomy and math, but I also knew there had to be a deeper, different knowledge. *What was underneath it all?* Why did my heart jump when Mrs. Krieble drove home her history lesson?

Her insight reinforced something crucial to me: knowledge was supposed to be personal. It had to connect to the heart. Suddenly, in an instant, the mechanistic and unrelated worlds of cow lungs and algebra formulas, constellations and Cuban missile crises gelled. All knowledge pointed to something deeper and higher, bigger and more beautiful than mere facts about life. It had something to do with the heart, with experience. It was not unlike Daddy's style of instruction. He helped me grasp things with my heart.

Yes, there was more out there. Like the beckoning of those darkpurple Colorado mountains. The *something* that was ever drawing and tugging at my heart.

Days later, I would feel my soul's capacity stretch even further.

"Hey, Jon, you wanna come with us to Club?" It was just the sort of thing you hoped a twelfth-grader would ask as you were taking off your hockey shoes after practice. I must have been doing pretty well, I figured, as center-forward on the junior-varsity hockey team to warrant this notice from Betsy, an upperclassman.

"Yeah," I responded with calculated casualness. "What's Club?"

I found out that Wednesday night. For the first time in years, I sat on the hardwood floor of the multipurpose room at St. Luke's United Methodist Church. I hadn't been inside the church since probably my elementary school days. Now I was packed like a sardine, shoulder to shoulder among scores of other teenagers, all singing, clapping, cat-calling, whistling, and urging friends on the edge of the crowd, "Come sit with us!" I was squeezed in between my hockey buddies at "Club," a Christian outreach to high school kids run by Young Life.

The next hour was packed with mixers, a game or two, and a wild array of upbeat songs about love and God. I recognized a few of Daddy's old hymns, except here my voice wasn't blending with my three sisters' but with a rousing, robust chorus of my peers. Then everyone quieted down as the Young Life speaker stepped forward, opened up his Bible, and launched into a short passage from somewhere in the New Testament. It wasn't King James, and he didn't have Daddy's Irish brogue when he said "Lord," but it was close enough. His simple opening of the Bible had struck a tuning fork in my heart. Something resonated inside me, and my face warmed. A universal force was kicking in.

That evening, I fairly ran home from St. Luke's Church. I couldn't wait to race up the backstairs to my bedroom, grab pen and paper, and pour out my thoughts to my Box. Other girls wrote in their diaries; I scribbled secrets on index cards and placed them in a cream-colored leather box next to ticket stubs, class notes, charms, and one-minute photo strips. I sat on the balcony and wrote:

> *Dear Box . . .*
>
> *I've always felt like I knew God, sort of, but tonight at Young Life was so neat. It was so cool to sit there with all kinds of kids, Catholics and Jews and people like me and just, well . . . it was so cool!! They talked about a weekend retreat at Natural Bridge, Virginia. I'm going to sign up!*

I wasn't content to loaf along in some outer orbit, like a Uranus or a Pluto. And I certainly wasn't about to get lost in an asteroid belt like so many small, spectator rocks. By the time I packed my Levis, sweaters, and softball glove, and climbed aboard the bus for Natural Bridge, Virginia, I was on a trajectory for the inner circle, where all the big planets were. Key kids like Betsy, the twelfth-grader who'd invited me to Club for the first time, and her friends. They had something I wanted.

The hills of Virginia were frigid in early fall, but my heart heated up just thinking of all the discoveries in store. The wooden floor at the conference center was just as hard as the one at St. Luke's, but this crowd was three times bigger. High schoolers from all over Baltimore County had come to the weekend retreat. And just like at St. Luke's, the speaker—this one's name was Carl—got up after the fun and games to give a message from the Bible. Only this time it was from the *Old* Testament.

"Did you know that God loves—I mean really loves—you?"

No surprise. The God I'd been hearing about for the last few weeks was not only cool but existed to make my life happy and more meaningful.

"Would you like to get to know him?"

I already know him, was my first thought, *from Daddy and Sunday school*. Yet this Carl guy up front—he doesn't look like a preacher or a relative. He looks "with it." So—

Yeah, I want to know more about God.

"Let's start at the Ten Commandments."

To me, it was an odd place to begin. But then, the Commandments *were* pretty basic.

"You've probably heard them since you were a child—"

My mind snapped a mental image of Alan Silverstein and Arvin Solomon.

"—well, God gave these commandments, and he did so not only as a guide, but as a standard. I guess you could say, a set of rules."

A good-natured groan rose from the floor.

"So-o-o," Carl continued, "as much as you hate rules, I have a challenge for you. I want each of you to measure your life up against each commandment, one-by-one, as I read through them. Got it? This is a little like *Truth or Consequences*. So, here goes—"

It was a contest. And I loved competing.

"Okay, try this one on for size from Exodus 20. 'You shall have no other gods before me. You shall not make for yourself an idol.... You shall not bow down to them or worship them.'"

This was a no-brainer. It obviously applied to people in India, with freaky gods on their mantels. I didn't worship Allah or Shiva or Buddha. Mine was the true God of the Old Testament and the New. The one big Judeo-Christian Prime Mover. And Jesus was his close relative. Nope. No idols here.

But Carl hadn't finished. "What do *you* worship?" he prodded. "What do you bow down to? Other kids' opinions? Affection and attention from that special guy or girl? What do you think about first thing when you wake up? In short, what takes up the bulk of your thought life?" He paused for a long moment. "Does God?"

This was getting serious.

"Let's try another one. 'You shall not misuse the name of the Lord your God, for the Lord will not hold anyone guiltless who misuses his name.'"

Inside I squirmed. I wondered if the God of the Ten Commandments would hold me guiltless for saying "Jeez" all the time. My Aunt Kitty once scolded me because she said it sounded too much like "Jesus." Surely God wouldn't be that picky. He wouldn't sweat the small stuff.

"'You shall not murder.' That means not hating anyone in your heart."

I thought of my oldest sister, Linda, and the fights I'd had with her and my other sisters. I thought of the times when my emotions seethed and raged. Times when I erupted like Mount Vesuvius.

"'You shall not steal.' Have you ever stolen attention from someone else when they deserved it? Taken credit for something you didn't do? Cheated on a test?"

A recent quiz in Mrs. Klingamon's biology class flashed by.

"How are we doing here, gang? Anybody got a perfect score yet? No? Well, let's go a little further." Carl continued reading, "'You shall not covet your neighbor's house ... your neighbor's wife, or his manservant or maidservant, his ox or donkey' or his GTO, his grade-point-average, his A in chemistry, her date for the junior prom, or her popularity."

The entire hall was dead quiet until Carl guffawed, "Uh, I made that last part up, guys. The stuff about the prom and the car."

A few kids laughed, breaking the tension.

Carl closed his Bible and looked at us straight on. "If you faltered on even one of these commandments, you've fallen short of the standard. You've missed the boat. Failed the test. You've not reached the high bar. It's called *sin*."

There it was—the "S" word. The word that nailed me when I was a five-year-old, squeezed between my parents in the front seat of the Buick, heading home from out west. The word that best described my stubbornness and peevish anger. The word that dug under my skin like a splinter when I fudged the truth to my parents. It was the same word that hung around my neck like a millstone when I went to those basement parties. I might be able to wrestle off guilt the next morning, but sin would be strangling me again a day later. *Sin.* I hated the word.

"God's holy and you're not," Carl pointed out. "You might not like it, you may think it's old-fashioned, but it's what describes us all. It's what describes you. We have all sinned and gone in the opposite direction from God. And if we're honest, not one of us really seeks him. No, not one."

That was it. Now I was really confused. All this time I would have sworn I *had* been seeking him. But now it was clear God wasn't going to let me get by with Ten Suggestions. He wanted all or nothing.

No longer did God appear very cool. He was more like the angry Wizard of Oz, sputtering out demands in plumes of smoke and fire. Mrs. Kriebel's chalked letters on the blackboard came to mind: DEMAGOGUE. It seemed unfair.

When the meeting ended, I pulled my sweatshirt around my shoulders and walked out into the cold autumn night. I wanted to be alone. As I meandered up a dirt path toward a hill, I was pricked by an odd fact: the more righteous God appeared, the more resentful I became. *Is this because of pride?* my conscience asked.

I found a large rock near a pine grove and sat down in a huff. My gaze turned upward, and I spotted Orion low on the southern horizon. A flood of memories washed over me—memories of when I felt much closer to the Maker of that constellation and so many others. Nights when we went beach camping or horseback riding at Wakefield Farms. *I'm comfortable with the God of the good old days*, I mused. *I can't reconcile that God with this one.*

Yet whether God existed wasn't the argument for me. Rather, it was in what form he existed—what shape, size, and character. If there was a one-and-only God, then he could be only one way, right? *Right*, I told myself. And since the God of the Bible was the only one I was clued into, I decided to be pointblank honest.

"If you're so great," I dared to say out loud, "then how can you give us a bunch of commandments you know full well we're unable to keep? Your laws are impossible. No human being can be perfect. You demand too much, God."

Not one minute after throwing my grievance out into the night—as soon as I paused to look at the stars and listen to the wind—a glimmer of faith flickered. And I knew—I just knew—this God was about to take on my challenge. I was convinced I was about to encounter him.

A holy God and a stiff-necked, stubborn people. How does it all fit together? I bore down on my brain as though I were in algebra class, trying desperately to solve a complex math problem. Suddenly, I sat up. It was as if a lightbulb had gone on overhead. It dawned on me. "That's why Jesus came," I whispered in amazement.

I wanted to make certain I had it right. I felt like I'd come to the end of a confusing linear equation, with only one or two constants and lots of variables. So I traced the steps out loud, counting on my fingers every single point.

"When you created us, we rebelled against your law. Got it. So you, a holy God, owe us rebels nothing. Check, got that.

"Yet, you are compassionate, and you didn't want to see us perish. So you became one of us. Except you didn't murder, lie, cheat, steal, or idolize anything. You kept the Ten Commandments, you hurdled the high bar, you lived the perfect life—"

I was running out of fingers, but it was stimulating to solve this one from the inside out.

"Jesus lived the perfect life, even though we weren't able. And—"

In one brief, visionary moment, I not only felt my soul's capacity stretch, I sensed something was filling it. For weeks, someone had been taking his hands, as it were, and widening my soul in order to create space for himself. My chest expanded, and I stepped forward onto a new level, speaking to this God as though he were a real person.

"—And this is why Jesus died on the cross. The wages of sin is death, and ... *somebody* righteous had to pay the penalty, so I might go to heaven and—"

I looked up into the stars. I could have sworn I saw the smile of God.

"—and it was *you*. It was you all along."

People say that word—*you*—all the time. A neighbor is a *you*, and a mother is a *you*. But I had never thought of God as an honest-to-goodness *you*. He had always been a benign force, a Prime Mover with the face of Grandfather Eareckson in that sepia, turn-of-the-century photo. But now God felt near and real, alive and vibrant, as if he were sitting next to me on the rock. God was a *person*.

The world was suddenly a lot less mechanistic and unconnected. There was a *person* holding it all together—a personal God, whispering through his creation and speaking through his Word. This was the meaning behind that beckoning I'd always sensed. No longer was my knowledge of him floating on the surface of life. I had discovered the underlying current, what was underneath. And what was underneath was a *who*.

All I could do was let the tears flow.

"Thank you, God. I'm so sorry, I'm so—"

I couldn't say any more. A movie reel ran before my eyes, images of me snapping at my mother, judging my dad, copying answers off a test paper, kicking that puppy, fighting with my sisters. Worst of all, I remembered the awful night I got up from a couch in a basement party, walked into the bathroom, saw my tired face in a mirror, and whimpered, *Who am I?*

I kept repeating, "Forgive me, please forgive me, please—" As I sensed the presence of this personal God beginning to fill that space in my soul, my tremors became chuckles. Then, muffled laughter, until I yelled, "Yahoo!" and threw my arms open wide.

The first word that came to my mind was *clean*. I felt clean and fresh. The pine trees and rocks seemed just as clean. The stars too. They looked like little pinpricks on a sprawling black dome, through which the pure, sweet light of heaven sparkled and streamed.

I ran back to my cabin, found Betsy, and told her what had happened, what I'd felt and heard. As I looked into her eyes, I sensed I knew her now in a different way. Not as a Woodlawn High senior or as a varsity hockey player but as . . . a family member. We shared something unearthly in common. We were like sisters. I wondered if she saw the same thing in my eyes.

"And Betsy, it's like I know God here"—I thumped my heart—"*here!*"

"It's not just a head thing, is it," Betsy smiled. "He's in your heart."

Suddenly, a childhood image of a tiny Jesus figurine flashed through my mind. A little cop directing traffic inside of me. But this was a whole different story. This was *real*.

That evening, I hugged my knees on the camp meeting floor and looked—really looked—all around me. Everything appeared different. The lights in the camp hall were brighter and warmer. The colors of my friends' clothes were more vivid, their smiles happier. Even the songs sounded different. Before, the hymns and gospel songs were fun to sing, but now, out of nowhere, I seemed to understand the words for the first time. I sang with heart and soul the verses to an old hymn my family knew. But this time it meant something *to me*:

> And can it be that I should gain
> An interest in the Savior's blood?
> Died He for me, who caused His pain?
> For me, who Him to death pursued?
> Amazing love! How can it be
> That Thou, my God, shouldst die for me?
> He left His Father's throne above,
> So free, so infinite His grace!
> Emptied Himself of all but love,
> And bled for Adam's helpless race!
> 'Tis mercy all, immense and free,
> For, O my God, it found out me.
> Long my imprisoned spirit lay
> Fast bound in sin and nature's night.
> Thine eye diffused a quick'ning ray:
> I woke—the dungeon flamed with light!
> My chains fell off, my heart was free,
> I rose, went forth, and followed Thee.

As everyone continued singing, I mulled over the stanzas. Twenty-four hours earlier, I would have sneered if someone had told me my spirit was imprisoned. Bound in sin? No way. But now, with Christ sitting on the throne of my heart, I knew beyond a shadow of a doubt

I had left behind nature's night. Chains had really fallen off. I thought about Mrs. Krieble's words, "You'll never truly know something until you experience it *here*," she said, thumping her heart. God had entered my heart, and I knew him—not just in my head; I experienced him in my heart. I had a new heart. I had hope.

I was a teenage planet now pulled by God's gravity, circling around him in a new orbit. Jesus was the luminous star that had me dazzled.

The maple-walled music room of Woodlawn Senior High School vibrated as the choir lustily and loudly—very loudly—belted out the refrain, "Glo———ri-a in excelsis Deo!"

It was just a few days before the school's Christmas concert, and there wasn't a kid in choir who didn't have his head back, singing his part at the top of his lungs. And no one more enjoyed singing this soul-stirring refrain than I did.

"Hold it, everybody."

Mr. Blackwell rapped his wooden baton on the piano top. "I said *hold it!*" he demanded.

Basses, altos, sopranos, and tenors trailed off, their various parts winding and heading off-pitch, finally crash-landing at a halt.

"Someone in the alto section. Second row. You, Eareckson!" He pointed his baton at me. "Miss Eareckson, you are not the primo-alto here. You are supposed to *support* the melody, my dear, not drown it out."

But I couldn't help it. I loved the song too much. This was the first Christmas I could honestly say I knew what it was all about. *Gloria in excelsis Deo. Glory to God in the highest, peace on earth and goodwill toward men.* Goodwill toward me. Plus, I was having way too much fun with all the runs in the first three measures. All those eighth notes, jammed together, begging to be sung like an opera star would in *La Bohème*.

"Hey, we'll take you in the tenor section," a boy said. "We need big girls with big voices."

There was a smattering of laughter, and somebody threw a wad of paper.

"Okay, enough!" Mr. Blackwell grabbed control before more paper started flying. He tapped the baton until everyone got quiet, raised his hands, nodded at the pianist, glared at me, and then with a 1–2–3–4 on the downbeat, our choir launched once again into *Angels We Have Heard on High.* This time I was careful to support my soprano friends, saving the mezzo-soprano Brunhilde-in-the-Viking-helmet act for some other time.

Snow fell softly outside the choir room window, covering our campus and its trees in white, and I could hardly see the athletic field through the flurries. The icy white landscape made me want to huddle next to my choir friends. I sang with a smile, standing in the alto section, halfway up the theater-like room, surrounded by sound, in the middle of the melody, lost in the harmony, and lifted by the happy-hearted unity a choir member feels in the midst of singing a great chorus with eighty others. I had a part to play, and it felt wonderful.

One of the first things I discovered as a Christian was that I *fit.* I knew who I was—or at least, who I was supposed to be—and the peace and well-being I felt couldn't help but overflow in my singing.

The Christmas of 1964 was much more to me than spiced cider and garlands on the banister, candles in the windows, or snow swirling around the street lamp on the corner. Christmas was Emmanuel, God with us. God with *me.* It was the first time I would personally ascribe to Christ all that the angels heralded in every carol.

I wasn't off on a trajectory, floating, lost in space, disconnected, or drifting.

I had found the center.

CHAPTER TWELVE

If some of the branches have been broken off, and you, though a wild olive shoot, have been grafted in among the others and now share in the nourishing sap from the olive root, do not boast over those branches. If you do, consider this: You do not support the root, but the root supports you.

Romans 11:17–18

High in the hills of western Maryland, near the border of Pennsylvania, lies the sleepy town of Hancock. It's apple country up there, where the Piedmont Plateau rises to meet the Appalachians. And it's the home of my Uncle Don and Aunt Emma. Uncle Don's little house nestles near the top of a ridge, from which a large orchard spreads below like a wide skirt.

It was late fall in 1965, and I had driven my parents to Hancock for the annual apple-picking party with Daddy's YMCA wrestling friends. I parked our car next to Uncle Eddie's on the edge of the orchard, number eight in a line of ten cars, their trunks all opened and boxes stacked around. Daddy was in his late sixties now and had to walk slowly with the aid of his Canadian crutches. Mom ambled beside him, between the rows of trees with a large basket, plucking ripe, red apples off the low branches. It was nippy in these foothills of the Appalachians, and I was glad I wore a heavy jacket.

I stuffed apples in my pockets and rubbed one on my sleeve before taking a hefty bite. It was just the way I liked apples—firm and crisp, snapping when I bit into it. I tossed it after a few bites and meandered at a slower pace, dropping behind my mother and father. I could see that the orchard was well tended to. The soil was tilled, the trunks of the trees were mulched, and the bark looked healthy.

On the far side of the orchard stood a grove of pine trees. In front of these pines, just inside the border of the orchard, sat a couple of dry, gray tree stumps. I noticed something close to the stumps, snapping in the breeze like a stiff flag. As I drew closer, I saw it was a sturdy little sapling growing out of one of the stumps. Uncle Don must have grafted it in the previous spring. The stump and sapling made an odd-looking couplet; under the brooding skies, the dead stump looked like a rock, while its little branchlet bobbed and bent in the wind, sprightly and green, full of life and energy.

I squatted and fingered the baby tree. As I ran my hand over the stump, I felt a bump where a crab-apple sucker shoot had been snipped off. Around the base, I saw other places where suckers had sprouted but were clipped back—a technique Uncle Don used to ensure a sapling's survival. Suddenly, a strong gust roared through the pine trees, ripping one or two tiny leaves off the sapling. Considering the elements and the suckers, I thought, Uncle Don had his work cut out for him.

I stood up, shoved my hands in my pockets, and stared at the happy sapling. It dared to think it would not only survive but might one day actually burst forth buds and blossoms, then bear fruit. It didn't know winter was coming.

I felt a kind of kinship with the young tree, as though I were really the vulnerable one under brooding November skies. My old life had been cut down and left for dead, and now I had a new life, fragile and fresh-faced and anxious to grow. I was the sapling itching to pop out peace and joy, kindness and love.

I no longer pursued the kind of peace that hippies were V-signing about the Vietnam war. Mine was peace of a different sort. And my love was of a different kind than Make-Love-Not-War. The peace and love I wanted in my life were the kind that pointed others to the God I had found. Peace that quelled a sisterly spat before it erupted. Love that reached out to Benjamin Wallace in the school hallway, when others razzed him because he had to take remedial reading. This was new and tender fruit, this peace and love. It was a bit timid and slightly unripened, but it was as real as the God who was producing it in my life.

Yet I was also the sapling fighting off sucker shoots. Suckers that kept trying to drain my spiritual energy and strangle my new life before I could yield lasting fruit. Watching the delicate little tree before me—so thin and green, and naive enough to think it could survive on the edge of the orchard, in the shadow of tall, grisly pines—I wondered if I could, or better yet would, be able to live up to all that I'd confessed.

God had his work cut out for him. That would be the story of my life for my remaining high school years.

In the flush of excitement on that magical night at Natural Bridge, Virginia, I had signed up and signed on, joined the army, put my hand to the plow, and poured new wine into new wineskins. In the euphoria that followed, I drew on a mysterious, divine, life-giving sap and experienced not only peace and love but a wide-open zest for living. I was proud to bring my Bible to school and place it on top of my books in homeroom.

No sooner did the first blossoms of real fruit appear, however, than the sucker shoots sprouted up.

That became evident as soon as I tried out for the swim team at Woodlawn Country Club. I loved rising early in the morning and driving past the village pond as the swans swam through the mist. Diving into the pool before practice, I delighted in the chance to burn my muscles with every lap, stretching, straining, slicing through the water. Swimming felt almost divine.

But when I hoisted myself out of the water and began horsing around with my teammates, another feeling struck me. I became acutely aware of everyone's bodies—much more so than ever before. Boys in their thin nylon Speedos stood hugging their chests, dripping and stomping their feet, trying to get warm in the frigid air. As water trickled over their muscles, their bodies looked handsome and chiseled, their legs long and lean, their suits too tight. Girls in almost-sheer tank suits stood in the cold air, hot and breathing heavily, steam rising from the flimsy nylon clinging to their breasts.

I wondered, *Are others looking at me this way?* Whether anyone did was beside the point. *I* was looking. More to the point, I was imagining and—*pop!*—a sucker shoot sprouted. I could have nipped it in the bud, but I didn't. I secretly let sensuality grow over the next year until lust entwined itself around my soul, drawing me into places like the backseat of a car, where it strangled my conscience and stole my purity.

Other sucker shoots sprouted during junior-varsity hockey. Our team was in the playoffs, and the bus ride to Parkville High, our opponents, was full of cheering, singing, and clapping. The afternoon was crisp and windy, perfect for field hockey. We were convinced of God's favor.

Just before the referee whistled to begin the game, Parkville's center-forward strutted up to the center line opposite me, looked me up and down, and muttered a snide remark under her breath. Not able to let it slide, I shot back something profane and stupid.

Immediately, another Parkville player shook her finger: "There, there, Miss Young Life. You Christians aren't supposed to say nasty things like that."

Her retort shamed me. But instead of bringing me to my senses, it made me madder. *These Parkville jerks take us for a bunch of religious wimps.* And for the remainder of the game, I played on the energy of anger. It didn't alter the score; we lost.

But something changed. The tender fruit of peace and contentment I had enjoyed went sour. And other sucker shoots of pride and anger took root.

I wasn't powerless to stop pride, lust, or anger. Sucker shoots of sin aren't indestructible, able to take over with a mind of their own. The fact was, I just didn't choose to reach for the clippers—I didn't muster the will to say no. And every time I allowed my passions to take control, my sapling-soul shriveled further.

I didn't know why I kept choosing my own way over God and his. I could point to the typical self-centered approach to life most teenagers have. But I knew better. I understood—I really did—what God had done for me and all he offered. I had tasted his joy and peace, I had experienced contentment and well-being. Yet I allowed it all to be choked by weeds and suckers, by passions and pride. In so doing, I denied God. And I denied the real Joni he wanted me to be.

Never was that more clear than in early 1967. The year before, I had purchased my sister Linda's old Sunbeam Alpine, a rusting but still-snazzy sports car, for $300. It was dented and had a nearly cracked engine block, but to me it was the hottest, most streamlined little car in the school parking lot. It was black, albeit faded and chipped, and had red-leather interior, not counting the duct tape hiding the cracks and splits. When I pulled up into the parking lot in the morning, I grabbed the space closest to the school entrance, where my friends hung out.

Then one day my mother insisted I pick up Little Eddie on the way to school. Little Eddie, my old playmate at Rehoboth Beach, when we went camping with Uncle Eddie and Aunt Lee.

"Aw, Mom! Do I have to?"

"Yes, you do."

"But—he's a sophomore, and I'm a senior!"

I didn't want to confess my real worry: that he was also a thin, loose-jointed nerd with thick glasses and a white plastic pocket-protector for his slide rule. Eddie was no longer the cute little boy we led through the dunes and built race cars in the sand with. He was now tall, gangly, and bore an uncanny resemblance to Jerry Lewis in *The Nutty Professor*. The thought of pulling into the school parking lot with Eddie in the car struck fear in my heart. Especially on days when he might wear his Boy Scout uniform.

I tried one last plea: "I'm too busy. I've got to be at school early for choir."

"How is it," my mother asked, "that you have time to zoom around with your friends, go to Young Life, play hockey, sing in the school choir, the church choir, take piano lessons, play your guitar, stay after school for art club, go to the library—and you can't squeeze in an extra five minutes to help your cousin?"

"He's not my cousin," I answered, as if that were the problem.

"You two grew up together. You *always* played with Eddie."

"I don't pla-a-ay with kids anymore, Mother."

The next morning I stormed out of the house, revved up the Sunbeam Alpine, and looked in the visor mirror to muss my hair. Today I would be taking a sophomore, a mere child, to school with me, and it required I put as many years and as much space between us as I possibly could. I must look like an adult. I reached into my handbag, pulled out my red Maybelline mascara box, licked the dry brush, and scrubbed it into the black clay. I touched my eyelashes, threw the box back in my bag, and slammed the gear stick into reverse.

Uncle Eddie and Aunt Lee lived only a few blocks up the street. When I arrived, Little Eddie wasn't waiting curbside, as I'd told him to. I laid on the horn and glanced impatiently at my watch. A minute later, he staggered out the front door under a load of books.

"Hi, Little Joni!"

Ugh. The *Little* irked me. It was okay when we were younger, to differentiate me from my dad, but I wasn't little anymore. Of course,

I didn't apply the same standard to Uncle Eddie's youngest son; to me, he would always be Little Eddie.

"Wow, nice car," he commented, running his hand over the leather seat.

Keep your hands to yourself, I silently scolded. *I don't want you touching the dash, the radio, visor, or the door handle.*

Little Eddie usually rode a bicycle everywhere. I imagined he would continue to ride it until he got his learner's permit. After that, his mode of transport probably would be his mother's boxy Ford Fairlane.

Eddie adjusted his glasses and folded his hands squarely on top of the books in his lap. The drive to the high school would be only a few minutes, but with every passing mile I squirmed, wondering how the scene would play out when I pulled into the parking lot with my weird cousin. Then I got an idea.

When we came to the border of the school property, I pulled over on the shoulder. We were still at least a block or two away from the red brick-buildings of Woodlawn High.

"What's wrong?" Eddie asked.

"Nothing. You're getting out here."

"But we're not at school yet."

"I don't care. This is your stop. It's as far as we go together."

I reached across Eddie to open his door, and our eyes met. I'll never forget the expression on his face. It wasn't so much bewilderment; he knew I thought he was a bookworm. And it wasn't shock—he obviously faced harassment from many upperclassmen. It was a look of disappointment.

Eddie and I had a long history together, and in many ways he knew me far better than half my friends at school did. He had looked up to me, at least until that point. I was the one he'd sat next to in my father's old green truck as we bumped along the dirt road bordering the Patapsco River, on our way to the farm to ride horses. We had walked home from elementary school together. We'd fed the swans at Woodlawn Pond in the summer and skated on it in the winter. He'd shown me his lizards. He'd played hide-and-seek with my sisters and me and traded his favorite comic books with me. And he knew Daddy's campfire stories backward and forward as well as I did.

We had tucked under our belts a million shared experiences over the years. And now—I was ashamed to be seen with him. All because of a few kids I shared milkshakes or class assignments with.

Eddie didn't say a word as he got out of the car. He just hiked his books under his arm and soundly shut the door. Our eyes met one more time. *I know what you're up to, Joni,* his eyes seemed to say. *While you're jerking me around, I want you to realize I know exactly what you're doing.*

I looked away. I shifted into gear and left him to walk the rest of the way with his load of books.

When I pulled into my parking space, I glanced in the rearview mirror to check my hair. Had I looked closer, I would have seen something else: another sucker shoot. This one, vanity.

Why, when I was given every chance, when I honestly knew better, did I keep choosing the darker path? Why could I not bring myself to nurture my sapling soul with good and godly things? With good thoughts and motives, habits and actions?

Apple trees had it a lot easier. They just yielded to the sun, rain, and the owner of the vineyard. Apple trees didn't resist the owner of the orchard whenever he came along to clip back sucker shoots. Trees didn't ignore the gardener. Young trees knew where they were planted; obedience was part of their nature. They were submissive saplings, and their obedience bore fruit.

Not me. I "grew apples" the wrong way around. I'd muster a little patience, fasten it to a big branch, dig a hole, and set the entire thing into the ground. There, I had it: fruit in my life. Or at least the appearance of it. Then it quickly rotted.

I kept going to Young Life, but afterward, when I talked to Betsy or my other Christian friends, I felt my peace was made out of plastic. The fruit in my life was fake. The joy was a veneer.

Watching Little Eddie in my rearview mirror now, I grieved that nothing about me seemed genuine. I was more miserable now than I ever was before that trip to Natural Bridge.

Sometime in early April 1967, on an unusually balmy spring evening, I walked out onto my bedroom balcony with my Box. Twilight touched the soft haze of green buds in the oak grove nearby, and I noticed how much closer the branches were since the days when I sat here strumming my guitar. I wished I could say I had grown as much. I sat down and wrote on the back of an index card:

Dear Box . . .

I am tired of saying I'm a Christian out of one side of my mouth and saying something else out of the other. I want to honor God with my life. And so God, I'm asking you to please, please do something in my life to turn it around, because I'm making a mess of it. If I'm going to call myself a Christian, I want to live like one!

I had to get connected back to God. I had to approach him as He-Who-Must-Be-Obeyed. Like the owner of the vineyard he was—and the owner of the tree, and the ground, and the roots, and the rain and sun, and even the clippers. I had to get back to drawing on his life-giving sap, so I could blossom and grow. Once and for all, I wanted to *be* the apple of his eye.

I didn't know how God would answer my prayer. But I knew he'd do something.

I certainly didn't dream that Uncle Don's orchard would hold the clue.

Springtime arrived, and we returned to the little mountain town of Hancock. This season, the broad skirt of apple trees spreading beneath the ridge provided a blanket of white. Row after row of trees was laden with fragrant, snowy apple blossoms.

There's nothing more magical than losing yourself within such a world of white, the spring breeze wafting a natural perfume and the sound of busy bees buzzing. Uncle Don's orchard was a Garden of Eden. And I was Eve in Levis and saddle shoes, walking in the cool shade of the fruit trees, at one with the blossoms and bees. I hadn't seen any big changes in my life, and I still didn't know how God would answer my prayer. Maybe the change would come with college in the fall—I had been accepted at Western Maryland College, not far from the farm. Or maybe it would happen during summer vacation, with the job I'd taken at Ocean City for the season.

Maybe something big would happen this Easter Sunday. I wanted so much to celebrate Easter the right way this year. As I ambled through the orchard, plucking small branches and tucking blossoms behind my ear, I thought about Christ and all that he had done for me. Here among the chattering of birds and the trees' perfume, it was hard to think that the God who created such beauty was the same man who once lay stone-cold dead, stiff with rigor mortis, on a slab in a tomb. Walking through this world of white blossoms—so fitting, it seemed, for Easter—I had a hard time picturing the fact of Easter: a gray corpse in the dark, suddenly stirring in his grave and rising to his feet. That the God of the universe chose to run a gauntlet on my behalf, ending in spikes driven through his heels and hands. It was so hard to imagine: God beaten almost beyond recognition by drunken soldiers? God shoved and kicked? More than that, the apple of God's eye turning brown with the rot of *my* sin, my pride, my lust? The whole idea humbled and sobered me.

God must have been smiling over me in the apple orchard. It held the secret to his death—and to the life I was still seeking.

Early spring is grafting time. Uncle Don would run his hand over the bark of an apple tree, find just the right place to peel it away, and make a slanting cut into the heart of the wood. He then took a small branch—sometimes one as small as a frail twig with a couple of buds—and made a long cut with a sharp knife. He pushed the graft down into the damp wood of the tree, centering it on the slit. Sometimes he hammered small nails to tighten the scion to the stock. Then he covered the union, to keep the graft cool and moist. Weeks later, new life emerged—blossoms to buds to fruit. Uncle Don said that a single tree can bear many different kinds of apples, but it never comes without a wounding in both the tree and the branch.

It was John Bunyan who wrote,

> Conversion is not the smooth, easy-going process some men seem to think.... It is wounding work, this breaking of the hearts, but without wounding there is no saving.... Where there is grafting there is a cutting, the graft must be let in with a wound; to stick it onto the outside or to tie it on with a string would be of no use. Heart must be set to heart and back to back, or there will be no sap from root to branch. And this, I say, must be done by a wound.

God was after my heart. He wanted more than my name in his book and my hand to his plow. He was after more than my signature on the dotted line of an eternal insurance policy. He longed for my heart. Heart and soul, bud and branch, blossom, sun, rain, and soil—everything.

I would have thought he had my heart, especially since I wrote my prayer in the Box earlier that season. But my prayers would be answered in due time; I soon would learn that God grafts those he loves.

And very soon, grafting would mean wounding. A terrible, horrible wounding.

CHAPTER THIRTEEN

All was well with me, but he shattered me; he seized me by the neck and crushed me. He has made me his target.

Job 16:12

I've always wondered why I broke my neck.

Not "why" in the theological sense of, "Why does God allow bad things to happen?" And not in the technical sense of, "Why couldn't I pull out of the pike dive fast enough?" Not even in the sense of fate, as in the times I've wheeled through a crowded mall, parting people like a fish swimming upstream, snapping mental photos of their faces, wondering as they pass, *Why not her?* or *Why not him?*

I mean in the sense of destiny.

As if . . . it was just bound to happen. Not because I was bad, although the discipline of the Lord is something to consider. And not because I dived recklessly, although my water safety instructor, who'd presented me with my Life Saver certificate just the week before, would disagree. It was just inevitable.

The first inkling should have been the ax I wielded at age five. Even now, whenever my family threads home movies onto the old 8mm projector and sits back on the couch, shoving down popcorn and elbowing one another, they jibe, "Here it comes, watch this, don't miss it, you won't believe it," as if no one's ever seen the stupid footage before. Suddenly, there we are, my father in his jeans, suspenders, and plaid shirt, looking like a lumberjack, and me in my fringed jacket and cowboy boots . . . holding the ax. I can barely lift it, it's so heavy. But I'm game, because Daddy is teaching me how to chop wood. No matter that the ax is taller than I am. And sharper than Daddy.

"Would you look at Little Joni? Isn't she cute with those silly pigtails!"

No one stops to think that my father, bless his heart, was silly for putting an ax in the hands of a five-year-old.

The very thought of it almost knocks the wind out of me. I keep wondering, "What if." At the time, however, cutting wood was one of those competitive activities I wanted desperately to prove myself in against my older sisters, the same way I tried to ride, run, and wrestle to keep up with them. And so, there we were, in jerky 8mm action, mugging for the camera, the two of us happily swinging away, chips of wood flying left and right.

There were other omens. I was determined, for instance, to ride a wild steer or bucking bronco at one of the rodeos held at the Circle X Ranch. On those lazy summer afternoons when we put on rodeos for the Y campers, long-legged cowboys saddled up their horses behind the stock pens, rosined their lariats, and creased their Stetsons. Some would sit on the corral fence, swigging Pabst Blue Ribbon and spitting tobacco, spinning yarns about the best saddle bronc or Brahma bull they ever rode, or wondering who they'd meet at the American Legion dance hall that weekend.

I sat on a post nearby, sketching them or maybe fingering my pigtail, hoping some of their bravado would rub off on me. Rodeo days were full of cutting and cattle roping, swirling dust, and the grunting of bucking horses, squealing and biting each other in the pen. There was the smell of manure and leather and the hillbilly sound of bluegrass music lilting over the arena's loudspeakers. I was only eight years old, but that didn't stop me from following the cowboys as they ambled toward the arena, gathering fistfuls of dirt and smearing them into my newly washed Levis so they'd look worn and faded. I thought I could ride as well as any of them.

Maybe it was inevitable that I swaggered up to Daddy before the rodeo one weekend and asked if I could ride the steers like my older sisters were doing. I realized it was dangerous. Wild and wiry steers with stubby horns would burst out of the chute, bucking and bawling, twisting and turning, doing their best to unseat one of the YMCA camp kids or sometimes one of my sisters. My siblings hadn't done badly. They had almost lasted the full eight seconds, which qualified one as having "ridden a steer."

"Daddy, I can ride, *please* let me ride!"

My father looked over the chute at the holding pens to see if there were any small calves that could be driven up. There were none. An older cowboy thought I was cute and assured my father that if he held onto the steer's tail, the animal couldn't buck as much. Daddy gave him a questioning look but eventually decided it was a safe plan.

A steer was driven into the chute, a cowboy lifted me up over the fence, and next thing I knew I was sitting astride a nervous animal. Suddenly, I sensed I'd gotten more than I bargained for.

"Hold on here," I was instructed, as another cowboy secured my hand under the bucking strap. "And hold tight!" he commanded, kneading my fingers into a tight fist around the rope. "Just lean back and your daddy will make sure the steer won't buck you off."

I nodded, a little jittery.

"Daddy," I called, "are you back there? Do you have his tail?"

"I got 'im," he called back.

The cowboy above me shouted, "Ready?"

I jerked my head up, the way I'd seen the Brahma bull riders do, and the door of the chute flew open.

All I remember is seeing the top of the steer's head fly upward as I felt my body catapult forward. My head exploded as it collided with his skull. I went limp and slid off the animal, dropping into the dirt, my face pushed into manure and dust. The steer had bolted out of the chute so suddenly that my father lost his grip on the tail.

I spent the rest of the afternoon on my bunk bed, with an ice pack on my head. But I still have in my Box a tattered piece of brown paper on which my father wrote:

June 15/58

Today Joni my little eight-year-old daughter rode a wild steer at the rodeo at Circle X Ranch. Although she was struck in the head by the steer's horns which made a terrible lump, she still made a wonderful ride. Her Daddy, John K. Eareckson.

Twice now I had suffered baseball-sized lumps on my forehead—one from that steer and one from my ride on Monica at Wakefield Farm. Knocking heads with horses and steers was just another confirmation that I had inherited not only my father's name but his daredevil DNA.

My mother also imparted to me her special style of adventuresome genes. She wasn't exactly a shrinking violet. Mother loved a good challenge, at least when she was young. This was the woman who refused to go by "Margaret Johanna," her christened name, but rather insisted on "Lindy," after her hero Charles Lindbergh. Why she chose not to look up to Eleanor Roosevelt or Madame Curie is a mystery to me. Yet that she chose a fellow who virtually invented the word "daredevil" is very much my mother.

It was Mother who, during a hiking trip out west in the thirties, accepted an invitation to climb into a cage-basket and be lowered over Mount Rushmore onto the rock-carved face of George Washington. A workman with his jackhammer had taken a liking to this spunky, athletic woman, and dared her to join him in carving away a little rock around Washington's nose. Lindy took him up on his challenge. Few would believe it happened without the yellowed photo we possessed of Lindy poised against the president's profile, rat-a-tat-tatting his nostril.

"I'd follow your father anywhere," my mother once told us while standing over our beach campfire, poking a stick into the wood. "Although there was one time we both nearly got ourselves killed."

"Are we going to tell them about the boat?" Daddy mock-whispered to Mom. The light of the campfire made their faces glow as though underlit by stage lights in a vaudeville theater.

"What about the boat?" Jay and Linda said.

"Yeah, tell us about the boat!"

"We want the boat! We want the boat story!"

"Well," my mother effused as she stepped onto center stage, "it was a large sailing ship anchored not far offshore in the Chesapeake Bay. And your father here"—Daddy took a sweeping bow with his sailor hat—"your father and some of the men from the Y were fancy-diving off the starboard side. They began daring one another to 'scrape the hull.'"

"What's that mean?"

Daddy explained that in olden days, when captains of sailing ships wanted to punish a crew member, they knotted his wrists to a ship's rope, threw him overboard, and dragged him down into the water and under the hull, pulling him up on the other side. Sometimes the crewman's body scraped against the barnacles, and he came up bleeding, sputtering, and gasping for breath.

"Some of them couldn't hold their breath long enough, and—" Daddy dropped to one knee and grabbed his throat, "—they drowned."

"And you made Mommy do that?" Kathy was wide-eyed.

"No, of course not," Daddy guffawed, standing up and brushing away sand.

"Your father waved from the water and challenged me to a dare," Mom went on. "He wanted me to dive in and follow him under the hull and up the other side. He called out, 'C'mon, Lindy, you can do it! When you're deep underneath and you reach the keel, just grab hold and push off of it with all your might.'

"I jumped in, ready to take your daddy up on his dare. Then, as I was treading water, I looked up at the sails flapping above me. The boat was massive, and I wondered how much more of it lay beneath the surface. Your father saw the hesitation in my eyes. 'You're not afraid, are you?' he said, and with that he did a flip-dive and was under.

"I was frightened to death," Mom said, "but not enough to keep me from huffing and puffing to grab a deep breath. I then dove for the keel."

"Did you make it?" I asked.

One of my sisters rolled her eyes.

Mom continued, "I kicked as hard as I could straight down, pushing water behind me, until it got darker and colder. I couldn't see your father at all. It was pitch black, and I groped in the darkness to find the hull, my hand touching slime and barnacles on the wood. Down, down I went, until my lungs started to burn and I was seized with fright.

"Finally, my fingers found the keel. By now my head was spinning, and I felt I would lose consciousness. But I mustered enough strength to swim under the hull, brace my feet against the keel, push off it, and swim toward the light above. I had to exhale long before I reached the top; bubbles were everywhere. Just when I thought I wouldn't make it, when I thought I was about to drown, I felt an arm pull me up. It was your father, smiling and looking so proud of me."

I tried to imagine the terror of being so far under, so much out of breath, with only blackness around me. I remember Kathy once holding me under the water when we were playing Marco Polo. It was horrible. The image now of my mother under water for so long was awful.

Mother shook her head at the story. Our beach campfire caught a fiery glint in her eyes, but I couldn't tell if it was a spark of passion or a flicker of fury. Perhaps both. I've often wondered if people who dare each other—who challenge themselves in risky, athletic contests—walk a thin line between romance and rage. Maybe they doubt themselves and half-hope that taking on a dare will prove they're anything but average. Now, watching the way the campfire cast towering shadows behind my parents, I was convinced they were giants. A god and goddess, larger than life, out to defy the mediocre and challenge the norm.

Hugging my knees around the campfire, I began to hope that I too might one day dive for the keel and come up the other side, brave and courageous.

I didn't need a boat to do that. I had a horse.

Augie and I had become seasoned professionals, he in English tack and I in riding boots and crop. One breezy, early-summer afternoon we had returned from loping along the bridle paths of the Patapsco River, where rows of trees on the banks swayed their skirts in the wind. The airy day had invigorated us both, and as I trotted Augie back to the barn I saw my sister Linda and her husband, Dick. I told them about a fallen tree blocking the bridle path and boasted about how Augie had easily flown over it.

"How high was the jump?" Dick asked.

"Oh, I don't know," I shrugged. "Maybe four feet."

"Bet he can't do four and a half."

I had always thought my brother-in-law was a jerk, and now he confirmed it. Dick had seen Augie jump in horse shows. And he was at the Howard County Fairgrounds earlier that year when Augie and I had won a blue ribbon.

"Of course he can do four and a half feet."

"Let's see you do it." A snake-like grin curled across his face.

Fifteen minutes later, we all were on the dirt flats behind Dick and Linda's house. Dick began to set up the single jump—two white standing supports, bridged with a single pole that could be adjusted higher or lower. I watched him. A gust kicked up the branches of the trees behind their house, rustling thousands of leaves in the wind. My big chestnut horse lifted his head, perked his ears toward the line of trees, and whinnied so loudly he shook beneath me.

Linda walked up to me and stroked Augie's forehead. "You don't have to do this, you know," she said quietly. I waved her off with, "No problem."

After Dick had set the bar at four and a half feet, I trotted Augie up to the fence. He flung his mane, arched his neck, and snorted, sniffing the rail and flicking his ears back and forth. He knew what I was about to ask of him, and I could sense his excitement.

I trotted Augie in a large circle, turned him squarely into the jump, and dug my heels into his ribs. Augie cantered confidently toward the fence as I gathered the reins, grabbed a fistful of mane, and leaned forward to match my rhythm with his. Up and over the fence he flew. I pulled him up at the end of the dirt flat and called back to Dick, "See?"

My brother-in-law didn't say anything. Then he called out, "So let's see him do five feet."

A five-foot jump was nothing to sneeze at. It was as high and as dangerous as the obstacles in national competitions or the Olympics. Augie tossed his head and chomped on his bit, stamping his foot. I couldn't tell if he wanted to jump more or if he was itching to go back to the barn. The breeze kicked up a dirt devil near the lone fence in the middle of the flat, obscuring it for a moment.

Dick called out again, "Well?"

I waved and told him to put it up a notch. I slowly trotted my horse back past the fence, eyeing its height and wondering if I should alter Augie's pace on the next try. I decided I'd give him a longer start. I stopped, turned, and smoothed his neck, whispering, "You can do it, boy. You can do it."

With that, I tapped Augie on the shoulder with my crop, and he lunged forward. The huge fence threatened ahead, and I crouched over Augie's neck, grasping his mane higher up to steady my balance. The mighty horse collected himself within a couple of feet of the fence, then lifted off the ground, sailing over the rail, just scraping it with his hind hoof. *Uff*—we landed safely. I breathed a sigh of relief.

Once again, Dick didn't say anything. This time he simply began to raise the pole to five and a half feet. He turned to me with his wry grin.

I should have stopped then. I should have waved him off and reined Augie toward the barn. Now my horse shook his head and strained against the reins, and this time I could tell he wanted to go home. He was tired from the trail ride and from this pointless exercise. Nevertheless, I urged him back toward the starting point.

What possessed me to take on my brother-in-law's dare, I can't say. All I know is, my heart was in my throat as I surveyed the towering obstacle. I thought Augie could do it, but it was a risk— a risk to both him and me. I remembered the tiny crack I'd discovered that morning on the top of his hoof. I thought of his fragile pasterns and hocks. I pictured what might happen if we crashed or if he stumbled and fell. In spite of my fears, I couldn't back down. I had to prove we could do it.

The late afternoon wind suddenly roared through the trees, blowing up more dust. I walked Augie several times in a wide circle, leaning down occasionally to rub his shoulder. Finally, I took a deep breath and headed him into the jump. I had no way of judging it accurately at this height; I could only hope our pace, timing, and distance to the fence were right. We got to within a couple of feet, and suddenly Augie veered, throwing me off balance and almost dislodging me from his back. He tossed his head. "Steady boy," I said.

"Aw, your horse is no big thing," Dick scoffed.

"Leave her alone," Linda said in defense.

"It's okay," I insisted, shooting a look at Dick I hoped would kill. "We just got a bad start."

I circled my tired horse again. Once again, we headed into the monstrous jump, and I wondered if we'd strike the rails and Augie might hurt his hoof. The wind and dust stung my eyes, and in the next instant I buried my face in his mane, clutched my horse's neck, and sensed his massive weight shift as his hooves pounded. I squinted my eyes as I felt him lift up, up, and over—with a grunt— a height of five and a half feet.

He came down hard on the other side, his knees nearly buckling. I slowly pulled him up at the far end of the dirt flat.

This time, I didn't look over my shoulder at my brother-in-law. I didn't want to see whether he was raising the fence to an unthinkable six feet, a height I had never—Augie had never—jumped. With my heart pounding and my horse breathing heavily, I walked back to the barn, leaving Dick in my dust.

The airy lightness of the day had dissipated now, and I felt no more brave or courageous than before. There had been nothing adventurous or soul-stirring about this dare. In fact, I felt a little used by my brother-in-law, as if I might be the brunt of one of his secret jokes. As I relaxed under Augie's slow clip-clop on the way to the barn, I realized my sister's husband couldn't have cared less about my safety or my horse's. I felt even more sick when I realized I'd given no thought to my safety or that of my horse. *I* was the one who was irresponsible. I had risked so much—me *and* my noble thoroughbred, with his great heart—on a dare that was as empty-headed and brainless as I felt.

But it *was* a dare. And I couldn't refuse a dare.

By the time I unsaddled Augie, the sun was sinking behind the hill in the hay pasture. I cooled him down with a vigorous brushing, then opened the gate to let him loose into the field, slapping his rump and shooing him off. He bolted and soon disappeared into the blackness at the bottom of the slope. The sound of his hooves faded, but his shrill neigh echoed as he searched for his horse friends.

I leaned on the fence and contemplated the "what ifs" in jumping a bar raised so high. I shuddered, thinking of *Black Beauty* and broken necks. Surely God wouldn't allow something like that to happen. Yet I wondered if he would allow danger to get within inches of me—so close I could feel its cold breath, so near that my skin prickled—yet not have it wound me.

Did God take risks with us? Not the crazy sort that would have us diving for the keel or hurdling a five-and-a-half-foot-fence—but a divine dare that really *is* noble and courageous. A risk where he really *does* look out for our safety yet at the same time propositions us with a hint of danger, as if to say, *I'm not satisfied with your mediocrity. I have something in mind for you that's above the norm. Can you follow me? You're not afraid, are you? C'mon, you can do it.*

I thought back to my prayer earlier in the year: "God, do something, *anything*, in my life to change me." I was convinced God was about to alter my life. I just didn't know what he would do or where, when, or how it would happen.

If my ears could have tuned in, I might have picked up the signal. I might have even heard God whispering, *"I have something in mind for you. Something above the norm. Can you trust me? Can you follow me?"* And if I had sensed the challenge, I believe—yes, I do believe—I would have taken the dare.

The weatherman promised that by mid-afternoon it would be sweltering.

I debated whether or not I should keep my tennis date. There were lots of options to choose from on that Saturday in July 1967. I could either meet my friend at the courts or get ready to go to my niece Kay's second birthday party at Jay's in-laws'. I'd already said no thanks to Kathy and her boyfriend, Butch, when they'd asked if I wanted to join them at the beach on Chesapeake Bay.

Whatever I planned to do, I had an hour or so to kill. So I decided to *Nice 'n' Easy* my hair—*Midnight Sun Blonde.*

An hour after coloring my hair and getting dressed, I was still waiting for a call from my tennis partner. When the phone failed to ring, I decided to go outside and do my nails. I was surprised to hear Kathy's Volkswagen beetle chug up the street. She and Butch were supposed to leave for the beach an hour before.

"Did you forget something?" I called.

"Yeah," Kathy answered as she got out of the car. "Money! Haven't you left for tennis yet?"

"I haven't heard yet, so . . ."

My sister paused for a moment. Then she asked, "Sure you don't wanna go with us?"

I scrunched my face. "I really should go to Kay's birthday party, if I do anything."

"Yeah."

While my sister went to get money, I mulled over the options again. I'd just washed and colored my hair, and I didn't want to get it wet . . . I hadn't yet purchased a present for the party . . . I could drive over to the tennis court to see what was going on . . . or I could head up to the farm and go for a ride . . . then again, wet hair can always dry again.

"Well?" Kathy said as she walked to the car.

"I'll go with you," I decided.

"You will? I mean, you *are?*" Kathy gave me a weird look. "You never go anywhere with me and Butch."

She was right. I didn't hang around with her and her boyfriend much. But I figured since I was heading off to college in the fall, I wouldn't have too many more times with my sister. So I ran back upstairs, slipped on my new Speedo from the Woodlawn swim team, and climbed into the backseat of the VW.

By the time we arrived at Maryland Beach, it was just as the weatherman had predicted—sweltering. While Butch headed to the Coke machine, Kathy and I left our things on beach towels and ran straight toward a giant water slide next to the cordoned-off swimming area. The water was cool and murky, but the bay beyond us was broad and blue, stretching for miles. I was glad I'd come.

"Hey, there's a sign on the ladder here," Kathy called from the foot of the slide. "'NO SLIDING. LOW TIDE.'"

My sister started back toward the beach. As I turned toward the big blue bay, I saw a raft anchored farther out. Some little kids were diving and jumping off of it. I decided to head there, and after swimming some thirty yards or so, I hoisted myself onto the raft. I slicked back my hair and stood with my arms wrapped around my chest.

"Look at me," a boy yelled at his buddy. "Betcha can't do this!" He cannon-balled into the water.

His friend called, "Watch me!" He did a belly flop.

"Oh yeah?" Another backed up to get a running start, then made a big jump.

"I dare ya!"

I enjoyed the boys' fun and games. When the raft was finally clear of their wild, scrawny bodies, I decided it was my turn. I aligned my toes on the edge and stared into the water. Waves slapped the side of the raft and sparkled like diamonds.

Yes, I was glad I'd come. To feel my body, to be blonde and tanned, fit and looking forward to college. *God is good*, I thought, summing it up. I smoothed my bathing suit, then stretched my arms above my head, arched my back, and jibed offhandedly to the boys, "Watch this," planning to show them a simple inward-pike dive.

And I dove for the keel.

The
GOD
I LOVE

Part Three

Be merciful to me, LORD, for I am faint; O LORD, heal me, for my bones are in agony. My soul is in anguish. How long, O LORD, how long?

Psalm 6:2–3

I thought it was my sister Kathy, but I wasn't sure. It was her voice, but not really. The image of the girl looking down at me was fuzzy around the edges, and her words sounded like a 33rpm record on slow speed.

I tried to move my head, but it was locked in position. When I strained harder, the sound of metal bolts creaked inside. I attempted to speak, but I couldn't form any words. All I heard around me was bleeping, machine-like sounds.

I inhaled deeply and recognized the smell of formaldehyde and alcohol.

"Ids a guud thin I cud she your bomb bare," the girl slurred again, her voice the sound of someone who's drunk.

I squinted, trying to communicate with my eyes. *What did you say?*

The girl's face came closer. "I said, it's a good thing I could see your blonde hair."

My hair. It became one of two miracles everyone whispered about those first few days at the University of Maryland Hospital. My shocking blonde hair had floated on the surface as I lay half submerged in the water. The other miracle was the blue crab that bit Kathy's toe just before she stepped out of the shallows and onto the beach. Any other time, Kathy would have bolted to escape what she was convinced were zillions of hungry crabs. But this time, she didn't race to the safety of her towel. Instead, she turned to warn her little sister. Her sister, whose bright-yellow hair, ebbing and flowing, told her something was wrong.

As those first few days in the intensive care unit blurred on, a few recollections came into frightening focus. I recalled diving and striking something hard, like a log. Immediately, I heard an electric buzz that I felt shooting through my body. I sensed that my arms and legs had suddenly curled up in a fetal position. They seemed locked. I tried to move but couldn't. As I lay face down in the water, small tidal currents lifted me and strange images from my childhood flashed through my mind: school friends, Miss Merson, horseback riding, Brownies. An eerie thought struck me: *Is this what it feels like to die?* Another swell lifted me. Then I heard my sister's voice in the curious underwater acoustics, and I realized my dreadful predicament. I was running out of breath.

Oh Kathy, please find me. Save me! my mind screamed.

"Joni, are you looking for shells?" I could hear splashing and Kathy's voice drawing nearer.

No! I'm caught down here. Grab me, I can't hold my breath any longer!

I started to see spots, sensing that everything was about to go dark. Just then, I felt Kathy's arms around my shoulders, lifting me. Even as she hoisted me, I felt I was falling. But just before fainting, my head broke the surface. Air! Beautiful, life-giving, salt-tinged, cool air. I choked in oxygen so quickly, I almost gagged.

"Oh, thank you, God—thank you!" I sputtered.

"Hey, are you okay?" Kathy asked.

My head flopped against her chest. I let out a groan, feeling dizzy and sick. As I blinked the water out of my eyes, things only got cloudier. I saw my arm slung over my sister's shoulder, yet I couldn't feel it. I could have sworn it was still tied to my chest. As I strained to look down, I realized with horror that my arm and hand were dangling motionlessly. I couldn't move them. I couldn't even turn my head.

"I can't move. Kathy, I can't move!"

Suddenly, Kathy realized this was deadly serious. She charged into high gear, screaming, "Butch!" She commandeered a rubber raft, and she and Butch placed me on it, dragging it to the beach and yelling for an ambulance.

In the next few minutes, I was being raced to the emergency room of University of Maryland Hospital in downtown Baltimore. All I remember there was a hard gurney, a dark hallway, a bright lamp, and a nurse approaching me with a pair of shears. After removing my high school ring, she stretched my Speedo shoulder strap and slipped the scissors under it.

"Hey, w-what are you doing? That's my new bathing suit. Don't cut it, it's brand new. I just got it—and it's my fav—"

"Sorry. Regulations." The heavy *ch-cluk, ch-cluk, ch-cluk* of the shears echoed off the walls. She pulled off the wet, ruined scraps of blue nylon and dropped them in a waste can. The suit didn't mean a thing to her. She pulled a thin sheet over my chest and left.

I sensed the sheet wasn't all the way up, and I was afraid my breast was exposed. Yet there was nothing I could do about it; I couldn't move. As male orderlies passed by, I shut my eyes in embarrassment.

Someone wiped my arm with a cotton ball and stuck in a needle. I felt nothing. The room began to spin, and I heard another *ch-cluk, ch-cluk*. In the corner of my eye, I saw chunks of blonde hair. Then I heard a high-pitched buzz near my head. It sounded like a drill— *Oh my God, it is a drill!* Someone held my head while a doctor began grinding into the side of my skull.

The room grew dark and the noise faded. It no longer mattered that I was lying naked on a gurney with a shaved head. The drill no longer seemed threatening, either. I drifted into a deep sleep.

"Joni, can't you hear me?" Kathy asked again. "It was your blonde hair. I never would have seen you if you hadn't colored your hair."

My head began to clear. The bleeping and huffing of the machines and the strange odors in the intensive care unit were working on me like smelling salts. I was coming out of the fog.

"What happened to me?" I asked.

Mom and Dad's faces appeared next to Kathy's.

"Joni, we're here. It's okay," my mother softly said. "It's been a day or two since your accident. The water where you took that dive was too shallow. They're saying you hurt your neck."

When I heard the word *neck*, I tried moving my head. I couldn't budge it an inch. Something like clamps were on either side, holding my head in place. I was forced to stay immobile.

I sensed I was lying in a very narrow, strange kind of bed. Later, I would be told it was a Stryker frame, a long flat canvas stretcher. Whenever I had to be flipped face down, they placed a similar long piece of canvas on top of me. Flipping me would help to prevent bedsores.

My parents' words flashed in my head: *They say you hurt your neck.*

My neck. *Is something wrong with my neck?* That could mean anything. It could mean I pinched a nerve or bruised some muscles or strained a tendon. Anything could be the problem. Surely I would get better.

"I'll get better, right?" I asked. I expected an automatic, "Sure thing." But everyone seemed distracted by something going on at the nurse's station.

The intensive care unit became my asylum for the next three months. And it was insane. The heavy drugs being pumped into my body fermented into nightmarish hallucinations. Every time the nurses flipped me over, face down, I shuddered. That's when I saw them: hairy, cloven hooves. Green, ugly hooves where nurses' feet should be. I shut my eyes against the warted feet, because I knew they were connected to demons hovering around my bed— monsters that gently lifted off the top canvas of the Stryker, then smoothed and straightened my sheets, occasionally patting my shoulder when they finished turning me. They couldn't trick me with their pretend kindness. Their cloven hooves gave them away.

"Get them away, Daddy," I pleaded.

"Get what away, honey?" he answered tenderly.

"Them," my eyes pointed to the other side of the bed frame, "*them!*" I couldn't believe he didn't see the hoary, frightening figures standing right next to him. I even heard the clacking of their hooves on the linoleum.

One night, after they flipped me face-up, I drummed up enough courage to ask a nurse as she tightened the last screw on the bed frame: "C-could you please look behind the curtain there? I know he's there." But when she lifted the curtain, the demon had disappeared. Later, after the lights were out, one of the demons sneaked back in and placed a large concrete block on my chest. I woke up, screaming, "Get it off! Please, get it *off.* I can't breathe!"

A nurse rushed over and looked at me oddly. She tried to console me, "Joni, it's only your hands on your chest. That's all, your hands were just crossed on top of your abdomen. You're okay. You're *okay.*"

I couldn't sleep that night. I was sure the nurses were in cahoots with the monsters.

Once in a while, the nightmares dissipated and I found myself clutching for some sense, any sense, of normalcy. In more lucid moments, I memorized the names and functions of the tubes and machines in my corner alcove. Maybe understanding them would strip them of their terror. When nurses drew my curtain in the alcove, away from most of the really sick people, I tried to pretend I was in my own little tent. Occasionally, on a balmy evening, they opened the window above my Stryker so I could hear the clip-clop, clip-clop of horses pulling vegetable carts on the street below.

My sister Jay brought a small radio for my little bed stand. Every time someone turned it on, the summertime hit was playing: "It was the third of June, another sleepy, dusty, delta day ... the day Billy Joe McAllister jumped off the Tallahatchie Bridge." I weakly half-sang my own version: "It was the end of July, another sleepy, dusty, summer day ... the day Little Joni jumped off the raft and into the Bay."

Every song had a morbid twist. Mother and Jay tried to cheer me up by keeping the conversation on things going on "outside." They told me how little Kay was handling the terrible twos or how changes were being made along Main Street in Woodlawn or how the elementary school had to give up its field to the new boulevard coming through. We talked about who was packing up to head off to which college and how Augie and Tumbleweed were doing.

"Well, not so good," Jay told me during one visit. "Tumbleweed took a fall and—" She hesitated, not sure if she should tell me. "—and she's—she's paralyzed."

"She's *what?*" I said, incredulous.

"The vet has had to catheterize her. Kind of like you. I'm sorry, Joni. They don't know if it's permanent or not."

This was completely bizarre. *My horse and me, both paralyzed?* My mind scrambled to click in, relate, identify. *Needing doctors. Sick. Down, unable to walk. Catheterized.* The parallel screeched to a halt with that final word: *permanent.*

My paralysis might be permanent. I rolled the idea around in my head. I repeated, *Paralysis permanent ... permanent paralysis ...* but the words were lifeless. Unequivocally flat, as if I were merely reading a dictionary. They possessed no threat, no looming prospect of evil. They simply bounced off my brain, traveling as far as the inner ear and then dying.

After those first three months, the hospital staff began putting up Halloween decorations. At any other time, I would have been fine with the clown-like face on the orange cardboard pumpkin. But now the jagged smile and empty black eyes seemed truly ominous. I asked Mom to have them take it down.

The get-well cards had dwindled, and the visitors had tapered off. My eighteenth birthday had come and gone. All my high school friends were either in college or holding down new jobs or getting married. It was too chilly now to have the window open, and I missed the summertime sounds of the vegetable hawkers on the street. I did find some cheer in the recent reports on Tumbleweed: the vet had her back on her feet and running. My cheer quickly fizzled, though. I hadn't been able to move an inch.

"I have good news for you, Joni," the doctor said one morning during his rounds. "We're going to perform a very critical surgery that will stabilize your neck. It means we'll be able to get you out of these tongs."

"*Really?*" I almost laughed—it was great news. The stabilizing tongs screwed into my skull all these weeks were finally coming out. This was improvement, progress. I was moving forward, getting better.

"We may even get you out of here and on the floor in a regular room," he added.

It was everything I'd hoped for. Immediately, my mom and dad infused new enthusiasm into our prayer chain, asking them—asking everybody—to remember my surgery in their prayers. I was convinced the operation would help me walk. The demons were gone now, and I kept thinking of Jesus' words in Luke 18:27: "What is impossible with men is possible with God."

Everything's possible with God ... everything's possible with God ... I murmured it over and over on the morning I was wheeled to surgery, like Dorothy in *The Wizard of Oz*, repeating, "There's no place like home ...," I just knew I would wake up walking or, at least, able to move my legs.

The surgery was a success. The doctor had scraped bone chips from my hip and pressed them like mortar in between the broken cervical vertebrae. The graft took very well, and the doctor also unscrewed the bolts in my head, liberating me from the tight grip of the tongs. When I was released from the intensive care unit, I was given a bed—a real bed—in a private room.

But the impossible hadn't happened. My fingers and feet were as limp and paralyzed as before. Nothing moved from my neck down.

Lying in the middle of my new room, I stared up at the high ceiling and listened to the quiet. Hospital workers padded softly and casually by the door and down the corridor. They were completely unaware that the new girl in the room they were passing was totally terrified. There were no beeping machines, only the sound of the radiator under the high window popping when the heat came on. And the windows were so high that the walls made every sound echo.

My friends wasted no time in covering every square foot with posters of Paul Newman from *Cool Hand Luke*, Steve McQueen on a motorcycle in *The Great Escape*, horses, and a couple of large cardboard Chiquita bananas, begged off a supermarket display.

"See that palm tree?" Jacque, my hockey-playing buddy, asked, patting a travel poster of the Caribbean. "That's where we're going when you get better. You just wait."

I was tired of waiting. I was tired of urinating through a tube and defecating in bed, smelling my matted hair and watching TV sideways. I was weary of *The Price Is Right* and soap operas, of eating lying down and being "up" for interns on their morning rounds. When visitors came, I desperately wanted to say yes, I was getting better, and yes, your visit was worth your while, and yes, your prayers were being answered. But I couldn't even assure them with a smile; my teeth had become blackened from the medication.

The clock ticked on. Shifts kept changing, as did the sheets. Nurses logged temperature, pulse, respiration, and how many cc's of urine had drained. The intercom endlessly paged doctors and announced visiting hours, the juice cart rattled down the hallway, and janitors mopped the linoleum. I counted the ceiling tiles over and over. I was weary of time dragging by; the snow piling on the window sill told me that another season was passing.

What's going on, God? Why aren't I getting better?

A creepy thought seeped into my consciousness: *Could this be . . . is it possible, God, that this*—I glanced at my bedside table and the four walls—*this is your way of answering the prayer I asked you?*

A large lump filled my throat. *The prayer about getting closer to you?*

My mind raced back to the blossoms in Uncle Don's apple orchard and to the balmy spring evening I sat on my balcony and wrote on the back of an index card: *Dear Box . . . I'm tired of saying I'm a Christian out of one side of my mouth, and saying something else out of the other . . . and so God, I'm asking you to please,* please *do something in my life to turn it around.*

I breathed slowly and deeply, to get rid of the tightness in my chest. Could it be that all the prayers offered in the visitors' lounge, all the praying of friends at church and across the country, counted for nothing? Could it be God wanted me in this situation? *Is this true?*

I pleaded to the ceiling as if it were heaven. I waited in silence, listening to the clock tick. The intercom paged a doctor.

The empty silence began to choke me. *God, you can't do this.* I squeezed my eyes to hold back tears. *I didn't mean something like* this *when I prayed.*

I began to cry. I hated it, because there was no one around to wipe my eyes or blow my nose. I let escape a long groan. *I can't even blow my own nose.*

It would be another couple of hours before my mother would arrive. *I must keep my mind occupied,* I told myself. *I must do something . . . think something.*

I looked around the boxy room. My eyes had already memorized every detail. Then I realized I'd never noticed how white everything was: the crown molding, the tiles and windows, even the walls underneath all the posters. Then there were the doctors in their white lab coats, the nurses in their white uniforms, hose, caps, and shoes. Even the air smelled *white,* antiseptic. Suddenly, everything seemed to morph into a huge sanitized laboratory. And there I was, lying naked under a thin white sheet, waiting, about to be experimented on.

I'm in the middle of a white, sterile box, I reasoned. *Stuck here by the force of gravity. Can't move or feel. Just breathing, eating, and defecating. That's it.*

I let the thought intrigue me. *Do people see themselves this way? As just existing? No*, I answered myself. *They don't know it, because they have too many things to distract them. They're busy doing stuff—holding down jobs, going to college, walking and running around.*

I stopped the experiment for a moment. And I pictured myself in the middle of this drama.

But me, aha. There's a guinea pig of a different color. Because I have nothing—I spit the words in a harsh whisper to the ceiling—"I have *nothing* to distract me. Did you hear that, God? *Nothing!*"

I was beginning to build up steam. Maybe I wasn't able to punch him in the nose, but I felt I could whip him with my words. I began to imagine myself in a science film, addressing a hidden camera in the ceiling: "I am a guinea pig, representing the entire human race. I am in this laboratory just . . . existing. All this is happening so that the question of existence might be tested on me.

"What is the meaning of life, *God?*" I hissed. "Do you bring people into this world just to breathe, eat, grow old, and die? Do you toss the dice and paralyze people along the way? Or throw in a little cancer? Or smash some brains in an accident? *Huh?*"

I spewed my next thought: "Why shouldn't I coerce one of my friends to bring me their father's razors or their mother's sleeping pills? Why not have the whole human race put a gun to its head, if we're here just to exist? Exist, is that it? Is that all?"

I said it again, louder, "Is that *all?*" my words echoed.

"Good morning," my mother's voice said cheerily. I looked up and saw her striding into the room. "What was that you said?" She put down her things.

"Nothing." I turned my head on the pillow.

"Would you like to read?" she asked, rummaging in her bag. "I brought a few books from your shelf. There's a couple of *Seventeen* magazines here, and *The Western Horsemen*. And let's see, *The Lord of the Rings* and something by Hermann Hesse—who's *he?*—and I found this thing by Viktor Frankl, and . . ."

Mother paused when she picked up a little black book she had often dusted. "I know you used to read this one. *Confessions*," she murmured, flipping a few pages.

The imaginary camera in the ceiling was still rolling. I really wanted to get back to my experiment, but I couldn't refuse my mother. She was always thinking of me. Always fighting the crosstown traffic to visit every day, always looking for a magazine, or bringing a sack of donuts or hanging my hockey stick on the wall—anything to brighten my spirits and make things more bearable. In fact, it twisted my heart to see her try so hard. I so wanted to ease her through this awful transition, just as I'd done with Daddy when I started to become a woman.

I turned off the camera. I chose a *Seventeen* magazine. Mother flipped open to the first article and took her place by my bedside. She held the page above my face. "Can you read it okay? Do you need it closer?"

"No, it's fine," I said and began reading the first paragraph. The hospital corridor was filled with the sounds of morning routines, but it was quiet here in my room, except for the breathing of my mother and me. After a page or two, she shifted her weight. A few pages later, she leaned on the guardrail with one hand and held up the magazine with the other. Then she went back to holding it with two hands. Although her tennis arms were strong, this had to be extremely fatiguing for her.

Suddenly, I wanted to cry again. I was glad the magazine hid my face from her. I was afraid if I looked into my mother's eyes, I would break apart. I kept thinking of all the times she'd dragged me to ballet or piano lessons or covered her eyes when I jumped Augie or the many summers she stoked our campfires on the beach and steamed clams on the logs, whispering softly, "Good night," as she tucked the mosquito netting around my cot. I kept thinking of our home in Woodlawn and the afternoons I bounded up the back steps, opened my bedroom door, and sniffed the fresh smell of clean sheets. How she rang the backdoor dinner bell, how she made our home such a wonderful place, how she prepared crab cakes, roast pork, and sauerkraut, all the hours she spent on her knees cleaning the tiger rug and waxing our hardwood floors. I may have been a headstrong, stubborn eighteen-year-old who hid things behind her mother's back, but I was human enough to recognize compassion and commitment when I saw it. And I couldn't miss it with her standing here now, holding a magazine for me.

The rims of my eyes welled, and the words on the page went blurry. I found myself back in my science film, scrambling to hold my emotions together. *There's got to be more to life than just being born, eating and sleeping, and dying. There must be more to it than mere existence.* My mother's simple gesture of helping me had to be part of the equation.

People like my mother made commitments and kept them. They made promises and honored them. People—like no other species on earth—could cry, reason, and love even the unlovely. They could forgive wrongs and inspire what's right. People were too significant just to *exist*. There had to be more. There had to be more for *me*.

Somehow, I sensed, my life was still significant.

As weeks dragged on, I dabbled in my science experiment every now and then. But each time, I was plunged from the whiteness of my surroundings into a blackness inside. I knew I was important and connected to other humans, yet I felt so isolated and alone. My neck was still broken, and my paralysis hadn't worn off, leaving me in a corpselike state. And I was in this gruesome predicament alone. No one, not even Daddy or Mother, could rescue me.

One night, I became convinced I was beyond rescuing. Once the room was dark and the corridor was quiet, I started jerking my head slowly, back and forth on my pillow. Without a neck collar, this was easy to do. I got into a rhythm. The jerking became a wrenching, an angry thrashing I hoped would break my neck at an even higher level. I stopped only when I realized it might not kill me but only make me more paralyzed.

My world got blacker and murkier. Sometimes, just before I fell asleep, I felt myself diving, down, down, until my lungs started to burn and I was seized with fright. *Oh no*, I panicked. *I can't see Daddy at all. Where's Mommy? Where's the hull? The keel? I'll never make it. I'm going to drown. When will I reach the keel?*

Then one night, in a fitful half-sleep, I thought I heard someone at my door. I turned my head and saw the silhouette of somebody crouching, casting a long shadow across the floor.

I blinked my eyes. The form drew closer, and my heart quickened a little. I knew visiting hours were over. No one was supposed to be here. "Who is it?" I demanded.

"Shh!" It was a woman about my age. As she reached my guardrail, I recognized Jacque, my high school friend.

"What are you doing here?" I warned. "If they catch you, they'll kick you out."

Jacque carefully placed her hands on the guardrail and quietly lowered it. She gingerly climbed into bed with me and stretched herself next to me on top of the sheet. Then she began cuddling her head on my pillow, as if she were snuggling with me at a pajama party.

We lay there for a long time, not speaking. I realized her presence had brought a touch of normalcy. When she finally spoke, she whispered that all this time she'd been hiding behind the couch in the visitors' lounge until the nurses went on break. I giggled at the thought.

"Shh-h-h," she giggled too, cupping both our mouths, trying to stifle any more chuckles.

In the darkness, I could make out Jacque's silhouette against the glow from the corridor. She moved her arm, reaching for something down by my side. It was my hand. I saw her raising my arm, her fingers intertwined in mine, clasping and holding our hands together in the air. For a long while, she held my arm aloft, our two arms forming an obelisk in the night. It looked like the silhouette of a monument or some kind of memorial. *A statement that I was significant.* I wasn't a corpse in a gruesome existence. I wasn't isolated and alone; I was connected to the human race. I was connected to a friend.

"Jacque," I said softly, "it's been so hard. So scary. I'm afraid."

This was the girl who, up until now, I had only shared milkshakes, gossip, hockey sticks, Young Life songs, and boyfriends with. But she instinctively knew how to provide comfort beyond the wisdom of her years. In the blackness, she began to sweetly sing:

> *Man of Sorrows! What a name*
> *For the Son of God who came;*
> *Ruined sinners to reclaim:*
> *Hallelujah! What a Savior!*

The old hymn possessed a strange power. It soothed and consoled me like a mother's lullaby.

We didn't talk much the rest of the night. We just lay together, listening to the steady rhythm of our breathing. *I fit,* I thought. I fit alongside my friend like a piece of a puzzle ... even though I couldn't feel.

For the very first time, it was okay. It was just . . . *okay*.

Once in a while, someone walked by the room, a moving shadow across the floor. For the first time in a long while, I didn't mind that time seemed to stand still. The night was tender, and I drifted off to sleep, feeling like I was at a girlfriend's house for a sleepover or maybe lying under the stars on the beach, with the *Flying Dutchman* and his curse far out at sea, listening to the steady rhythm of the surf wash away my fear.

CHAPTER FIFTEEN

Then Jesus said to him, "Get up! Pick up your mat and walk."

John 5:8

R ead it again. Just one more time."
Diana liked to read to me from the Bible. She was a good friend from high school, and she often asked, "Is there any special verse you want to hear?"

I always gave her the same answer, at which point she would sigh and flip to the now-familiar passage. It was a page I rehearsed over and over in my imagination. And so today, Diana stood by my bedside and began reading from the Gospel of John:

> Now there is in Jerusalem near the Sheep Gate a pool, which in Aramaic is called Bethesda and which is surrounded by five covered colonnades. Here a great number of disabled people used to lie—the blind, the lame, the paralyzed. One who was there had been an invalid for thirty-eight years. When Jesus saw him lying there and learned that he had been in this condition for a long time, he asked him, "Do you want to get well?" "Sir," the invalid replied, "I have no one to help me into the pool when the water is stirred. While I am trying to get in, someone else goes down ahead of me." Then Jesus said to him, "Get up! Pick up your mat and walk."

Diana closed the Bible and lowered her eyes. She didn't know what to say. Nobody ever knew what to say.

I was drawn to the passage like a magnet. Like my science experiment, it became a movie in my mind. When the day was dark and quiet, I imagined myself back in Judea two thousand years ago at the Pool of Bethesda, with its sun-baked pavement and colonnades. The day was hot and dry, the crowd at the pool restless and expectant. A donkey brayed. Dogs barked. Everywhere, people crowded up against one another, murmuring, shuffling, and straining to see if the angel had stirred the water yet.

I placed myself among the sick and paralyzed people, some of them slumped on the steps, others languishing by the colonnades. Then I was lying on a straw mat, a kind of stretcher, against a cool, shady wall. Someone was nice enough to cover me with a rough cloak, but others weren't as thoughtful—like the ones who stepped on my legs. Flies buzzed, the sun rose high and hot, and I hoped Jesus would come soon.

Finally, late in the afternoon, shouts rose from the crowd over by the colonnades. I looked up and saw the people parting for Jesus. He was stepping out of the shadows and into the warm sunlight by the pool. He stopped and turned, saying a few words to a small group by the pool that I couldn't hear, and then stooped to touch the eyes of a blind person. By the gasps I heard, I could tell the man had received his sight.

Suddenly, people began pushing and elbowing to get near Jesus. They knew this was the healer. They crawled on hands and knees, eyes pleading, arms reaching, begging for help. I wanted to crawl too, but I couldn't. Others were ahead of me, blocking my view. I had no one to drag me to Jesus.

Inside, I screamed at the top of my lungs, "Jesus, here I am. Don't forget me! I'm over here, Lord, over here!"

I waited for him to answer, to glance over his shoulder and see me. To say to the others, "Sorry, she's been praying and waiting a long time. I really must go and help her."

But the movie never ended that way. It always came off the reel and spliced into something else—a nurse coming to take my blood pressure or a visitor entering. And I fell back into the pool of disappointment again. Then I simply waited for another visitor, another time, to ask if I wanted to hear something from the Bible. And I would ask for the Gospel of John, load the reel, and play the scene one more time.

Oh, God, it seems like ages since I've been in this hospital, I worried. *Where are you? Why am I not getting better?*

There wasn't anything more the doctors at the University of Maryland Hospital could do. They decided to send me to Montebello Hospital, a state institution on the outskirts of town. "You'll improve there," they promised. "You'll see."

All I saw when I arrived at Montebello were a lot of people like me: quadriplegics, paraplegics, people whose limbs hung limp like mine. They languished in the lobby, playing cards, smoking, or staring at a TV. The place had a feel of permanence to it, as if everyone there expected to have a long stay.

I was placed in a ward with five other girls whose problems ranged from quadriplegia to multiple sclerosis. Thankfully, I was given a bed near the window. But life was slow and laborious, full of rules and regulations. My routine became the same old stuff: bed bath, cornmeal mush, pills, physical therapy in the morning and occupational therapy in the afternoon. Weeks passed, and the routine wore into a deep and inescapable rut.

At night, I played the Pool of Bethesda movie in my mind, always praying that my legs and arms would start moving. But I was always left disappointed that Jesus never pushed past the others to come my way. He never even seemed to be around as I lay awake while my roommates slept. He must have been walking down other corridors, visiting other wards, bending and stooping to touch the needs of other patients. _Are you there?_ I prayed to him, near tears. _Do you even care?_ The clock just kept ticking, and late-shift nurses padded quietly down the hallway.

Occupational therapy provided a small change of pace. The OT room was always abuzz with chatter and the clanging of weights, as therapists jabbered with their patients, cheering on stroke survivors, people with brain injuries, and others with spinal-cord injuries like mine. The room smelled of wool and paint, turpentine and dried reeds, and the radio was always tuned to WCAO. Jars of poster paint, brushes, and unfired clay pots and plates filled the shelves on one wall, and at the far end of the room, near the floor-to-ceiling mirror, were typewriters, easels, and tools for making potholders and baskets.

"Joni, can't you do better than this?" sighed Chris, my occupational therapist. She held up my most recent work of art. "I know that using your teeth to hold your pen isn't easy, but surely you can do better. Come on, you're an artist."

The page was completely covered in black ink. I had used up my entire hour of OT scrawling with my felt-tip pen, up and down, this way and that, until I'd nearly filled the tablet. The paper was ripped in places where I'd dug hard, and it smelled damp and toxic from all the ink it had absorbed.

I didn't answer Chris. I just leaned my head back and stretched. My neck muscles were sore from so many repetitive motions.

"I know you can paint more expressively than—" she reached for words to describe her mild irritation, "—than this abstract . . . *thing*."

I thought it was very expressive. It reflected an hour's worth of angry, crisscrossed black lines obliterating any vestige of white. And that expressed my state of mind perfectly. In fact, if you looked closely, the little scuffs revealed a pattern: chaos. When my reach with the pen zigzagged so far, I repeated the black patterns in other places, making scores of little chaotic mosaics across the paper.

It paralleled perfectly the black chaos in my life.

As well as the chaos beyond the walls of Montebello. Earlier that spring of 1968, the Viet Cong had launched the Tet offensive into South Vietnam, and Lyndon Johnson had committed more troops to the region. Every time the TV was on, I saw live pictures of young men my age running into a fray of bullets and bombs. It was crazy, but it was real. This was TV, but somehow it wasn't.

UCLA and UC-Berkeley erupted into hotbeds of political protest, and the musical *Hair* opened on Broadway. Then there was that bleak April day when a shot from a lone gunman killed Dr. Martin Luther King Jr. on the balcony of a Memphis motel. As the news reports flashed over the TV, I gasped, and in a flash recalled a report I'd written on civil rights in Mr. Lee's CORE class. I remembered the words of the "I've Got a Dream" speech. And I thought of old Mr. Tom and Daddy.

Where were the sweeter, safer days? Days when national crises remained on the pages of my tests and essays, when racism seemed to have a solution in legislation or Sunday sermons? The world— my world—was unraveling faster than a thread pulled from one of my sweaters. Army tanks were rumbling down the boulevards of Baltimore, and a curfew kept the streets deserted and window shades drawn. It also kept my family from driving across town to visit me as frequently.

I was frightened. The black aides shouted slogans in the halls of Montebello. Some walked into our ward, shaking their heads and warning no one in particular, "We shall overcome. We're gonna overcome, honey."

For days, the washcloth on my face was cool rather than hot. I was fed abruptly rather than carefully. At night, my pillows were tucked forcefully, not gently. Three of the girls in my ward were white and three were black. Never was I so aware of the color of my skin.

Gone was all innocence, all reason, all national hope. Plummeting and spiraling downward, the prevailing spirit was burn-the-flag and "Bye-bye Miss American Pie." It was break the cross, turn it upside down, and make a hippie symbol out of it. God seemed to be abandoning the music and the arts, the campuses, and the whole country.

Maybe America and I were too stubborn and rebellious. Maybe we'd gone too far in the backseat of a car, and now God had decided to pour his energies into other, more deserving people. Maybe he was looking for more compliant Americans, more obedient Christians, to focus on.

Was Montebello even on his radar screen? Or was he off somewhere listening to other people's prayers about cancer or divorce, drumming his fingers on a desk until they prayed hard enough? Maybe he was in the Middle East, cleaning up after the Yom Kippur War to keep the gears of prophecy turning.

Whatever God was doing, I would make certain he heard from me. I would get his attention with mental judo and throw back in his face some gift or grace, to add insult to injury. He'd given me the talent to draw, and I was going to use it, all right.

That's how it was in occupational therapy. I would aim my power chair for the tripod easel, strain my neck forward to reach for the black felt-tip pen in the holder, and attack the tablet. Scratch, scratch, scrawl, slip, scratch, back and forth, digging down into the pure, clean paper. *Jab to the left jaw, right hook, punch below the belt.* "*Take that and that!*" I fought as I drew.

Eventually, I spit out the pen. *I've had it. I hate painting with my mouth, I hate this wheelchair, this hospital, these people, this stupid routine and*—I stopped just short of saying it: *God.*

Instead, I devised other ways to strike out at him. No longer with hot, flailing words or jagged lines of black chaos, but with smooth digs, daggers, and darts, slicing to the point with cool precision. I began smoking, pulling deeply on a cigarette to fill my lungs and holding in the hot smoke as long as possible. Hey, my body was damaged goods anyway. Or I put up psychedelic posters in my corner of the ward. I snubbed the hymns of my childhood to wallow in *The White Album* by the Beatles or songs by Cream: *Ba-da-da-dah! Dah, dah, dah, da-dah, dah!* I learned the raw lyrics of Graham Nash and the Band, words that sank so deep into my muddled brain that I knew the words of "The Weight" backward and forward: "I pulled into Nazareth; was feeling 'bout half-past dead . . ." Yep, that was me—except I wasn't pulling into Nazareth, I was pulling out of it. Jesus had passed me by, and I was showing him how it felt. I would pass *him* by.

My anger fermented until one hot August evening in 1968. That was the night another gunman pulled a trigger, assassinating Senator Robert Kennedy. I blinked at the black-and-white TV images of him lying on a hotel-kitchen floor in a pool of blood. Like the scenes from Vietnam, it was strangely surreal. *Would you look at that,* I stared at the screen, *Robert Kennedy dying. They've killed him.* I wasn't sad. I wasn't even shocked.

I was numb.

As numb as when the doctors told me a few days later, "We're going to have to remove your fingernails." An infection under my nails had gotten worse, and, just like that, they had to come off. I was told how a surgeon would slice into the quick of each fingernail, grab it with pliers, and simply pull. It sounded like something the Viet Cong did to POWs, not to girls like me who carefully filed their nails before putting on a base coat, a filler, and the latest Revlon polish. Yet I was unfazed. I felt nothing. The doctors continued on their rounds. And I kept staring at the tube.

Reality was getting too hard to swallow. And when that happens, it's easier to let someone else do the living. I did that through the characters I watched on television. I disappeared into their lives, especially that of *The Prisoner,* the man in the sci-fi series who constantly hatched plots to escape an island where he was being held captive. Each Wednesday night I watched him begin a new and ingenious attempt at escape. But in every episode, a huge white ball—a kind of Big Brother—tracked the prisoner down and forced him back. The show even had a cruel twist: characters and circumstances always seemed to be on his side, working in his favor. But some overarching intelligence seemed to keep manipulating those characters; they ended up lying, becoming the prisoner's enemies.

Near the end of the season, there was one particular episode when I was sure the prisoner would finally escape from the island. There had been so many foiled attempts all along, I was certain he would make it this time. In the final scene, the prisoner cleverly thwarted his captors, climbed a fence, and dove into the sea. He had escaped, and was happy and breathless, still swimming hard a half mile out. Freedom was in sight, and the music began to crescendo. The prisoner smiled with every stroke, feeling relief.

Then, suddenly, the music went minor. Out of the water popped the dreaded white ball. The series ended. The prisoner would never, ever escape.

What? As the credits scrolled, I kept shaking my head no. It had ended on such a despairing note—and I was choking with hopelessness. "Did you see that?" I called to a roommate who was watching with me. "How could they do that?"

"Huh?" another roommate looked up from *The Enquirer*. By this time, commercials for soap detergent filled the screen. Soon my viewing roommate was glued to the next show, and the other was flipping through her magazine.

"Never mind," I muttered to myself. But I did mind. It was crazy, but I'd felt something. A television show had hit me harder than the thought of pliers pulling out my nails or the image of Robert Kennedy lying dead. *I* was the prisoner. *My* life was ending on the same despairing note.

Panic seized me. *Please, I can't live like a prisoner. I can't live this way.* Suddenly, the ward had the smell of death. So did the hospital. Things weren't living here—they were only biding time until they shriveled and died. Everything was decaying, but nobody realized it. They just turned the TV dial to *Laugh-In*. Sock it to *me*? I didn't get it. *I don't fit. I don't belong here.*

It was the same feeling I had in the science experiment—the one where I played the guinea pig, and all of life's big questions were being tested on me. *There's got to be more to life than just being born, eating and sleeping, and then dying. There must be more than mere existence. I have to have some significance.*

"God, you've got to be up there," I whispered hoarsely in the dark. "This crazy war. The commercials. Everybody getting killed. More commercials. And then my fingernails. Everything's so bizarre. I have no hope, no hope, no hope," I repeated rapid-fire.

I stared at the ceiling. "You *have* to be up there. Somebody *better* be up there." My whisper became a cry, desperate and urgent and insistent. "And you must—I know you must—*care.*"

I shot the prayer into the air like a basketball tossed at the hoop in the final seconds. I didn't know where it would land, but I knew where I was aiming.

Then something happened. Quietly and calmly, there in the shadows of the ward, I sensed an infinitesimally tiny ray of light penetrating my dark heart. Suddenly, I was transported back to that cool, autumn night in Virginia. The ray was just enough to illumine my thinking, just as it did then. And now, once again, my soul began to stretch its capacity ever so slightly, making room for faint and familiar faith.

Memories began to dawn—fuzzy memories of Young Life and Natural Bridge, the rock and the trees, the stars in all their freshness and purity. I squeezed my eyes shut, trying hard to remember the wood floor, the bright colors of everyone's clothes, the warm glow from the hanging lamps above. I remembered everything—especially saying, "I don't want to choose hell, Lord. I want to choose heaven."

I looked again at the ceiling. I murmured, "Well—I've had a taste of what hell is like."

The paramedics from Johns Hopkins University Hospital came to pick me up. They bundled blankets around, placed me on a stretcher, and loaded me into the ambulance for the short drive to downtown Baltimore. I was going to have my fingernails pulled out today.

A young, chunky, red-haired fellow with freckles sat in back with me, cracking gum. His blue shirt was open at the collar, and whenever we hit a bump, his large frame jiggled.

"You okay?" he asked loudly above the clattering of oxygen tanks.

"Yeah," I answered. I had a blasé feeling. I wondered if I would be this casual about losing my fingernails if I were still on my feet.

We rode the rest of the way in silence. As we passed the park near the Baltimore Zoo, I could see the tops of trees with their red and orange foliage. It was early fall; another season was passing.

We stopped at the entrance of the old hospital, and when the ambulance doors opened, a blast of cold fall air rushed over me. The paramedics quickly wheeled me inside, parking me near a radiator.

"The clinic is full right now," the red-haired paramedic explained, flipping the pages of my chart. "We're going to leave you here in the lobby until they can admit you." He wrote something on the chart, then placed the pen behind his ear.

"You okay?" he asked once more.

"Yeah."

"Well. They'll take good care of you from here." With that, he left.

I turned my face toward the radiator. I enjoyed the warmth and listened to people's muffled conversation resonating off the high ceiling and their footsteps crisscrossing the marble floor. *So this is the famous Johns Hopkins,* I marveled, scanning the high, dark-cherry paneling and heavy crown-molding that led to one stairwell after the next. I gazed upward and saw the stained glass of the dome above me. Then I turned my head to see what the middle of the lobby looked like, and—

"Oh, my," I gasped. My heart skipped a beat.

There it was, dead center in the lobby, rising over fifteen feet above me: a huge statue of Jesus Christ, carved from creamy-smooth marble and mounted on a mahogany pedestal. His head was bowed and his arms were outstretched in a gesture that urged, "Come."

This was the resurrected Christ, wearing a robe that half-covered his chest. I could see the scars in his side and the palms of his hands. Gazing at his arms spread so wide, I found myself in his orbit, feeling as though he was looking directly at me. "Oh, my ... oh my ...," I kept repeating.

I strained to read the words on the plaque at the base of the statue: "Come unto me ... and I will give you rest."

A million people could have passed me in that long, sustained moment—masses of disinterested souls distracted by appointments and commitments, others chattering and striding to the cafeteria, their shoes clicking on the black-and-white marble floor; all of them moving through a world so different from mine. I never would have noticed them. In the midst of it all, Jesus had eyes only for me.

I felt I was back in Judea two thousand years before, lying on a stretcher against a shady wall. The day wasn't cool and windy like this one—it was hot, dry, and dusty. For I was lying by the pool of Bethesda, and somehow, some way, a chunky, red-haired, freckle-faced man in the crowd had parked me at Jesus' feet.

"You didn't forget me after all," I whispered, staring at the Lord's hands. "You didn't pass me by."

The statue's face was frozen in stone, but I was sure I heard him say, "I love you. Don't worry. If I loved you enough to die for you, don't you think my love is great enough to see you through this?"

Something was happening, something for the first time since Jacque lay next to me in the night, singing "Man of Sorrows": I was caught up in God's thoughts about me, not my thoughts about him. I was lying in a stream of sunshine, consumed by his compassion for me, not by my anger and doubt about him. My thoughts didn't even matter now—only his did. Only his mind, his heart. And his mind and heart were communicating clearly, as clearly as all those visionary moments I rode the horse trail, brushing past tree limbs, as clearly as all those nights by the ocean, under the stars. And he was saying, "Come unto me. Let me give you rest."

Yes, yes, I whimpered in my thoughts, *I need rest, I just want rest. Rest and peace.*

God was oh-so clever. During all the chaos in my life, he remained silent for a long, long time. And then—*voilà!*—he broke through with a quick-witted surprise, a keen twist, an unexpected but brilliant turn of events—like this statue. I would bang-bang-bang on heaven's door, firing daggers and darts, trying to manipulate him. I would blacken a white page with ink. I'd wail and sulk and thrash my head on a pillow to break my neck higher for spite. And then, this. God would answer, quietly and dramatically.

Lying there, I didn't try to analyze it much more than that. I simply looked into Jesus' face and basked in his blessing. I hadn't expected anything like this when I was wheeled into Johns Hopkins. I was here to get my nails cut out. But now I was thinking about other nails, staring at the scars they'd left in the hands of God's Son. *His nails for mine.*

Here was a God who understood my suffering.

The clinic finally sent an orderly to retrieve me. As he wheeled me under the statue, I tried to hold Jesus in my gaze as long as possible, desperate to hold onto this holy moment as tightly as I could. The wheels of the stretcher glided across the marble floor, passing me under Jesus' hand, under his jaw, under his arm, and finally behind his back. When the door of the clinic shut behind me, and the curtains were drawn to prepare me for surgery, it was okay. It was okay when they began to smear iodine on my fingers. They could remove as many nails as they needed to. It was just *okay.*

The following week at Montebello, I wasn't allowed to do much. The nurses didn't want my bandages to be disturbed. I was still able to go to occupational therapy, though.

"So, Miss Picasso," Chris greeted me warily. "What will you be painting today?"

"Hmmmm," I said, pressing my lips. "Christmas is coming."

"Next month," she said, brightening a bit.

"I think I'd like to paint some gifts for my family," I announced. "Maybe a few of those plaster-of-paris plates over there?"

"Really?" she said, surprised. "Then let's get to it. We'll fire them, and they'll make great gifts."

Chris unscrewed the lids of several jars of brightly colored paints and placed several clean brushes in the holder next to my easel. "Can you reach these with your mouth?"

"Mm-hm," I answered, grasping one of the brushes between my teeth.

For the next hour, I splashed red and green paint on several candy dishes and plates, sweeping broad, smooth strokes, trying to cover as many items as I could before my OT time ended. Every once in a while, I leaned back to admire my work and dabbed my brush into different colors to give the plates a holiday twist. I swept and swirled, moving quickly, adding a bit of white here and gold there. I moved fast, working largely and energetically.

I was a child again, safe and secure, sitting on my father's knee. I was at his desk, painting for his pleasure and approval, striving to please him. I was thinking about composition, about the balanced arrangement of squares and circles that lay beneath everything, like the bones under my skin, like the foundation of a house, like the Lord in my heart.

I finished up therapy at Rancho Los Amigos Hospital in southern California. And in April 1969, I was released from rehabilitation. Jay was there to celebrate with me on that final day of rehab. She took me to get my hair cut and colored, have my nails done, and have my portrait photographed.

We wanted to round the day off with something big and fun, so we decided to go to Hollywood. We opted for a play that had just opened on Sunset Boulevard, the musical *Hair.* Neither of us was that keen on it, but this was California—wild and crazy California. So, with a "Why not?" shrug, we scarfed down dinner and rushed to make the show.

The play was three hours of chaos: smoke, screechy guitars, hot-red flashing lights, pop posters, and peace signs. Three hours of profanity against the pigs and the war, of LSD and LBJ, of making love and daisy chains. And then, out of the fog, the actors and actresses dropped their tie-dyed clothes and stepped forward, naked and shameless.

What happened next was no surprise: I smiled. The way one smiles out of pity, or maybe of sorrow. I was never so glad to be repulsed by a play.

I don't belong here, this isn't where I fit.

And I knew it with joyful certainty.

Chapter Sixteen

But for you who revere my name, the sun of righteousness will rise with healing in its wings.

Malachi 4:2

The flames warmed our faces and the Canadian night air chilled our backs. I breathed in the heat of the burning logs as I sat in awe of my father, standing in a swirl of smoke, his face underlit by flame. He was no longer the strong and commanding prophet by the campfire. In his seventies now, he was slightly bent from arthritis and had to lean on his arm-cuffed crutches for support. Yet he could still weave a good story, and on this wonderful late-summer night in Alberta, he spun images of my family and me packing up the mules and following him and Angus Budreau along the steep trails of Wind River Canyon in search of gold.

As I listened to him tell his story, I could tell how happy he was in these glacier-scarred peaks. He was in his element here, much more himself than during the days when I was in the hospital. Back then I heard him come click-clicking down the hallway on his crutches. He'd knock on my door, smile, and say, "Hi-eee, Joni," with the same lilt he'd had since I was a kid. He'd hobble close to my bed in his faded blue jeans, red suspenders, and plaid shirt, looking out of place next to all the chrome and the white sheets. His callused hands would grasp the guardrail, hands that had handled rocks and mortar all day long. And he'd search, even fight, for words. He didn't know how to lead his youngest daughter, his pal, down this frightening new trail.

But I had been out of the hospital now for almost two years. It was 1971, and this was my family's first cross-country trip since my accident. Daddy was thrilled. Here in Jasper Provincial Park in the northern Rockies, he felt at home.

I leaned back in my wheelchair, looking up to see if I could find any familiar constellations through the grove of Douglas fir surrounding us. I couldn't remember a night as clear as this one. I couldn't even make out Orion for all the stars spilling across the night sky, stars that looked like white spray-paint on black velvet. A full moon was on the rise. The fire popped, causing sparks to fly upward, and I inhaled the cool, crisp pine air.

Many things about me had changed. Quadriplegia was now a fact of life, although my family and I had barely scratched the surface of all that meant. I wasn't at Western Maryland College, where I'd planned to go after high school. Instead, I was earning a few credits at the University of Maryland and taking art lessons.

But other things hadn't changed. I still loved a roaring campfire and listening to Daddy's stories. I loved drinking spring water from a tin dipper, the echo of birds in the woods before dawn, and the sound of crunching pine needles under my—well, my wheels now. The twilight silhouette of a distant, brooding mountain could still break my heart. And it was good to feel my heart break for reasons other than a broken neck.

Our Winnebago, parked near the base of Whistler's Mountain, served as our rectangular little home, as well as our trail base. One morning I watched Kathy and Jay strap on their hiking boots for a walk as far up the mountain as they could go, while Mom and Dad went into the village for supplies.

"You going to be all right while we're gone?" Jay asked, parking my chair under a picnic table. She placed a book in front of me and carefully dog-eared its pages so I could turn them. My shoulder muscles weren't very strong, and I had no movement or feeling in my hands, but with a shrug and a bicep-swing I could nudge things, like pages, with my armsplint. "Sure," I said, buoyed by the beautiful surroundings, "I'll be okay."

I watched my sisters until they became specks on the dirt trail lining the ridge. The day was breezy and bright, and I settled in to read my book. But on the very first turn of the page I shrugged too hard. My book slid off the table and plopped on the ground.

For a moment I stared at it, sick that I had miscalculated my arm angle. I sighed and looked around. The other camper trailers were quiet. No one was around to help.

Darn it. I felt resentment begin to rise up. *Of all times for this to happen.*

My face began to flush, and I knew I was on the brink of another Feel-Sorry-For-Joni-Day. Yet I couldn't let a stupid book ambush me. I wouldn't allow self-pity to take me down the grim, anxious road to depression. I was more fearful of that than of my quadriplegia.

And I had good reason to be. In the twenty-four months since my discharge from rehab, I had experienced the true horrors of deep depression. There had been days, many of them, when I chose to stay in bed, asking my mother to turn off the lights and shut the door. Then in the dark, I let the steady hum of the air-conditioner transport me to previous times when I was on my feet. Times when I would stand straight and erect in choir, belting out my alto part with plenty of air to spare. Times when I felt my fingers peeling an orange or my leg muscles burning from practice laps. I traced back over every sensation: my toes squeezing mud, my thighs pressing against a saddle, my fingers plucking guitar strings or gliding over the cool ivory keys of my piano. I recalled every touch, every sensual pleasure: my hand holding my boyfriend's, my lips touching his, my fingers fumbling for buttons, my palms stroking his bare back.

Then suddenly, I would be jarred awake. And I'd realize I was sliding deeper into the same miry pit I'd thrown myself into time and again. I also knew that the bottom of this pit had no light nor air, and was the same evil place where all those demons lived, the ones I used to see in the intensive care unit. I would frantically claw up the sides of the pit, begging God to rescue me, to keep me from hitting rock bottom where I knew I would lose my sanity, lose my grip on reality altogether, and be swallowed by my demons.

Yet when my mother came back to turn off the air-conditioner and turn on the lights, the reality at the top of the pit was almost as frightening. There was the wheelchair. A life without use of my hands and legs, of not feeling anything below my shoulders, of having people blow my nose and wipe my backside. All that was horrible.

But not as horrible as the bottom of that claustrophobic pit. And so, on that breezy, sunny morning in Jasper Provincial Park, I deliberately chose to rein in the self-pity that beckoned me to the edge of the abyss.

"Please, dear God," I pleaded, "come rescue me by this picnic table." I squished the back of my limp hand against my eyes. "Please help me. I know you can."

A few leaves twirled in a gust of wind, and I listened to the trees rustle. It seemed to me heaven was trying to speak. So I prayed one more time.

"If I can't go hiking and get out into your wonderful creation ..." I paused, getting an idea, "—then would you bring your creation close to me? Bring a butterfly. A caterpillar. Anything. Just show me you are here."

I sniffed and waited for several minutes. Then I began looking around again. Nothing moved. Not even the pine branch over our campsite.

For half an hour or so, I waited and hoped, searching the skies for an eagle, searching the ground for a chipmunk, the picnic table for an ant. But nothing stirred. The afternoon was as still and quiet as a sultry day back on the farm.

It seemed forever before my sisters returned. They walked up, untying their bandannas and sloughing off their vests, then plopped down on the picnic bench and pulled off their boots to compare blisters.

"Wasn't that view from the ridge incredible?" they said, excitedly comparing notes, "Did you see that deer?" As Jay wiped her face and arms, she turned to me and asked, "How'd it go?"

I glanced at the book on the ground. Jay picked it up, brushed it off, and put it back in front of me. "You didn't get very far."

I dropped my head.

"I'm sorry, Jon," she said tenderly.

"I am too," I said. "When the book fell on the ground, I thought about you guys enjoying yourselves. So I prayed and asked God to bring his creation close to me. But nothing's happened. I haven't even seen a caterpillar."

Jay stood listening, picking the day's dirt from under her finger-nails. "Well, maybe he hasn't answered yet," she said.

"Yeah, maybe," I said, not too hopeful. I'd always been told that God answers prayer. Sometimes it's with a yes and at other times, no. Then again, God may wait awhile before he gets back with a reply. Or he may answer quickly but in a way that's different from what's expected. I was convinced God was listening today and ready with a reply for me. I was over that hump. *But it sure seems I'm getting a lot of "no" answers, lately,* I thought.

That evening, after hot dogs in the Winnebago with Daddy and Mother, Jay stayed inside to wash dishes while Kathy started a fire in the pit. Tonight we were going to roast marshmallows. As the flames crackled, Kathy positioned me on one side of the pit, away from the smoke, then sat on a log on the other side and whittled a stick to a sharp point. She ripped open the bag of marshmallows, speared a couple, and held them close to the glowing hot coals. In a minute, they were hot, burnt, and gooey, just the way I liked them.

The heat of the fire felt good, and I could hear crickets in the gully and Jay humming in the camper. Kathy and I joined in Jay's tune, and before long we were singing a hymn. The countless stars were shining again tonight, and the moon was full and large behind the trees. Then, as Kathy pierced another marshmallow, I thought I saw something move in the dark behind her. I squinted, focusing a few feet beyond her back. Yes, something large and black was swaying slowly—maybe a dog.

"Kathy—," I whispered. My sister didn't hear me—she'd just begun the second verse and kept holding her stick over the fire.

Before I could get any words out, the giant dog rose slowly to its back feet. *Dogs don't do that.* This was no dog. The giant *thing* paused right behind her and—

"Kathy, don't move!"

My sister gave me a queer look.

"There's a bear right behind you," I warned in a urgent whisper.

"Jo-o-oni," she groaned, "quit with your dumb jokes." She shook her head and muttered, "Beanhead."

The bear-shadow bobbed his head, sniffing for marshmallows. Suddenly, he rose higher.

"Kathy, listen to me! There's a bear—and he's right *there*." I was afraid to make any sudden movement, so I directed my gaze behind her. Kathy put down her stick, slowly stood up, turned, and came within inches of a shiny black nose.

"Oh no—," she stifled a scream. She sat back down, tightly grasping the log. "There's a bear right behind me," she whispered, without moving a muscle. Smoke blew into her face, but she could only squint her eyes and try not to budge.

"Don't move. Don't move!" I hissed.

The bear sniffed Kathy's back and grunted. He turned aside and focused his attention on the bag of marshmallows at her side. When he saw a few burnt ones in the dirt, he began licking them. Now he was in the firelight, and we both could see him: black coat, huge head, large, flat paws. As he chewed the marshmallows, we caught the gleam of shiny teeth.

Now he started my way. The bear lumbered around the fire pit and began snorting at the foot pedals of my wheelchair. I couldn't believe it—a bear was practically in my lap. I was frozen with excitement and fear. I tried very hard not to move my head or shoulders.

When he meandered closer to the picnic table, Jay must have heard our whispering. She threw open the door of the Winnebago and yelled, "Bear? Where?" At that, the animal whirled around, nearly knocking the picnic table over. Pots and pans went flying and clattered to the ground. Frightened now, the bear lunged past Kathy and disappeared into the night.

"There he goes. There he goes!" I cried, nodding toward the woods. Jay and Kathy scrambled for the Polaroid camera and rushed after him. A jumble of scurrying and shouting followed, with my parents warning my sisters to come back. A screen door from a nearby trailer slammed, and soon flashlight beams crisscrossed the woods. The whole camp had been stirred.

"What happened?" my mother asked excitedly.

"Joni and Kathy saw the whole thing," Jay said, huffing as she returned.

"You did?"

We all stayed up late, going over every detail of the bear's visit: how Kathy was doing this when I said that, how he stood up behind Kathy, how he came over and paused by me. "I knew he wouldn't hurt me," I assured my mother. "That's one good thing about this wheelchair—I sat really still."

My sister and I were instant celebrities. We squeezed out every ounce of excitement over our tale until the moon sank behind the mountains. It was very late when my sisters put me to bed. Only after the crickets stopped chirping outside my screen window and the night was deathly still, did it strike me: *Oh, my—Lord, you did it. You answered my prayer. And what a first-class answer! This was no butterfly or caterpillar. This wasn't a little answer. This was gigantic.*

"A bear," I whispered into the night. I couldn't wait for the morning to tell my family about the way God answered my prayer.

This wasn't just a favorite vacation memory for me, to be hashed and rehashed by countless flips for that special page in the photo album. It was an affirmation of God's faithfulness. He answered. The Lord of creation had answered. And it was such a "yes" answer—such a big yes—that it made me forget all the other times I'd prayed and God had said no. I realized this was peace—the kind, I'd read, "which transcends all understanding, [and] will guard your hearts and your minds in Christ Jesus."

He gave not only a bear. He gave peace.

Too many endorphins must have been coursing through my system, because I woke up the next morning before dawn, as happy as the night before. I lay still, welcoming the sounds of the morning outside my camper window. Birds began calling high in the trees, and the darkness inside my room began to lighten to gray. A breeze caressed the tops of the trees and made a soft, cheery sound.

The next day my family and I boarded a chairlift that cabled us to the top of a rugged mountain overlooking the wilderness reserve surrounding our campground. There our eyes met the spectacle of majestic, dark-green forests, blanketing ridge after distant ridge. The terrain was wild and craggy, dotted here and there by turquoise lakes that glimmered like jewels. Shivering under our down jackets, half from the icy cold and half from the awesome view, we yelled our delight to one another over the roaring of the violent wind. Far beyond our ledge, an eagle circled. Barely a speck, he swirled and dove, and I admired his grace and ease.

My family did what we always did at such moments: we sang, "Then sings my soul, my Savior God, to Thee: How great Thou art; how great Thou art!" It flowed from our hearts and lungs so naturally, the only thing to do in view of such majesty. The scene was just too beautiful to enjoy alone, and a shared hymn was the best way to share it together, the only way to reach out and somehow become a part of the moment, the experience.

When the hymn faded, I whispered a verse I'd learned in Young Life: ". . . Those who hope in the Lord will . . . soar on wings like eagles; they will run and not grow weary, they will walk and not be faint."

I wasn't able to walk, nor was I able to run. But I was soaring. I couldn't account for why. I'm sure being in the mountains under a clear blue sky had something to do with it; but the power that had ladled out those lakes, carved out that river, and puckered up that mountain range was more moving than the scenery. It was power so personal, it sang along with our hymn. So compassionate, it touched the heart of a girl sitting shivering in a wheelchair. So merciful, it reached down into the slime of my daydreams and readily plucked me out. I was soaring on the inside, not merely because of nature or the indomitable human spirit. I was simply opening my heart more to God.

So much so that when I returned home from Canada, I dove deeper into the Bible. Jay had invited me to stay with her on the farm—Daddy had sold off most of the Circle X Ranch, and Jay and her daughter, Kay, lived in the old stone farmhouse by the barn. Jay's husband had recently left, and everyone agreed my move to the farm from Poplar Drive would be a good arrangement.

The old house was a miniature replica of the home we'd grown up in: stone fireplaces, a vaulted ceiling, adobe walls, and wood floors. Daddy's Indian rug hung on one wall in the living room and a cowhide hung on the other. Besides that, living with my blond angel-sister was all that I hoped it would be. Jay did her best to help me adapt to life in a wheelchair, and her farmhouse became a sweet, restful haven.

After feeding me bacon, eggs, and coffee in the morning, my sister set me up for either drawing or reading. I was heavily into reading, especially the Bible. Jay would place a black music stand in front of me, set my Bible on it, and put a rubber-tipped dowel in my mouth so I could turn the pages. I spent my days flipping this way and that, devouring as much as I could. Every verse I read resonated with the same truth that first struck me in Young Life.

Something rose up in me when I came across verses that had to do with healing or God's promises. "If you remain in me and my words remain in you, ask whatever you wish, and it will be given you." "By his wounds we are healed." I didn't talk much about these truths, but they worked their way into my subconscious. Naturally, they showed up in my drawings. I sketched page after page of people's bodies: striking women with strong arms and legs, with beautifully shaped breasts and thighs, all of them stretching or running.

"Is that supposed to be you?" Jay asked.

"Do you think this is what I would look like," I asked in turn, "if I were on my feet?"

She whistled, "I wish *I* looked like that!"

Maybe I've learned the lessons God wanted to teach me, I started to assume. *I'm doing okay in this wheelchair. The suicidal thoughts are gone. Depression comes less frequently. My whole family is a lot closer to the Lord. I'm a bit more patient, and hey, I think I'm doing pretty well without use of my hands.*

I kept thinking about those verses: "Ask whatever you wish, and it will be given you."

But how should I ask for healing? It seemed so—incredible.

I thought of my horse when I was a young girl, of how I had to learn to catch her to put the halter on. No horse wants to be caught—if they see you coming, they gallop away. So when I got within a few yards, I turned and sat waiting with my back to her. Sure enough, within minutes I felt her muzzle on my back, sniffing and nudging. I slowly turned, stroked her forehead, and gently slipped the halter over her head.

Maybe God is that way—maybe he's waiting for me to turn my back on my wish for a healthy body. Or to turn my back on wanting to catch him. I began to wonder if I should just release my angst, just let it go. Maybe that way, he would come up behind me and give me my wish.

Jay and I heard that Kathryn Kuhlman, a famous faith healer, was coming to the Washington, D.C., Hilton ballroom. Stories had reached us about cancer-ridden people who'd been cured in Philadelphia at one of her crusades. I wondered if I should go to the healing service in Washington, D.C.

One morning, when Jay was putting my legs through my range-of-motion exercises, Ernest Angley came on television. He was an odd sort of man who wore a bad wig and ill-fitting suits, and Jay and I rather enjoyed his antics. My sister and I stopped the exercises and watched as people dropped their crutches or got up out of their wheelchairs, many raising their hands and declaring they were free from pain.

"Do you think God could heal you?" Jay asked, staring at the screen.

"Maybe it *is* time," I replied.

I decided for sure later when I read Psalm 37: "Delight yourself in the LORD and he will give you the desires of your heart."

I've been delighting myself in the Lord this year, I reasoned. *Learning lessons, praying more, reading more. Maybe now God will give me the desires of my heart—a body that works. A real miracle!*

Jay and I arrived at the Hilton early and waited in a long line at the elevator to go to the ballroom. When we got there, we were greeted by ushers who escorted us to the wheelchair section. The expansive ballroom was quickly filling with people, and even the wheelchair section was getting crowded. The buzz in the room got louder and louder until finally the lights dimmed and a piano began to play. The air became charged. Everyone was tense and expectant.

After the crowd was led in a few hymns, the music crescendoed, and Miss Kuhlman swept from behind the curtains and into the spotlight in a long, flowing white gown. My eyes got wide and my heart began to pound. Someone on the platform read some Scripture passages, and a few people offered testimonies. Then the spotlight turned on a person at the far end of the ballroom. The man seemed to be experiencing a healing. Suddenly, there was a small commotion in another section, and the light veered there. Then there was another, and another. Evidently, healings were taking place all around us.

My cohorts in the wheelchair section became restless. We all were thinking the same thing: *Hey, over here! Here, where the hardcore cases are. Where the cerebral palsy is, and the multiple sclerosis is. Isn't the Spirit going to come our way?*

It was just like the Pool of Bethesda: all the hope and anticipation, all the thoughts of "Please don't pass me by" and "Over here!" All the anxiety of "Won't someone push me over there, where he is?" Yet I didn't want to grab at my miracle or act presumptuously. I wanted to release the angst, let it go, and simply wait for God to maybe come up from behind and surprise me.

But after an hour, it was clear the miracles were winding down.

"Maybe it doesn't happen all at once," my sister whispered consolation to me.

Ushers came to escort us wheelchair-users out early, to escape the crush at the elevator. As I sat there, number fifteen in a line of thirty-five people using chairs, braces, and walkers, I looked up and down the line. *Something's wrong with this picture*, I thought.

Something *was* wrong. I knew my condition wasn't a matter of not having faith or not believing hard enough. People in the ballroom had prayed over me, "In the name of Jesus Christ, be healed," and I had strained to move my legs, had strained to believe. I also knew it wasn't a problem with God's power or ability to miraculously heal. No, it went much deeper than that.

I believed it was all a matter of God's will—his purpose, design, intent. Yes, I had delighted myself in the Lord, and he had definitely chosen not to give me the number-one desire of my heart—at least he hadn't in the last four years since my accident.

So what gives, God? What is your will?

"You know why she didn't get healed, don't you?" a distant cousin said after my trip to Washington. "It's because of Uncle John."

My dad?

"You know, the family doesn't talk about it much, but he *was* divorced."

I couldn't believe the stupidity of his comment. I knew the verse he was referring to in Deuteronomy 5:9, that God would punish later generations for the sins of the fathers. But he'd neglected the rest of that verse: "showing love to a thousand [generations] of those who love me and keep my commandments."

Whatever sins my father had committed, God had separated them from him as far as the east is from the west. And he had blotted out all my transgressions too.

No, you don't play tit-for-tat, I told God in my thoughts. *But if I'm not going to get healed, you'll have to clear this up for me about your will. What God of compassion wouldn't want to heal a young person in a wheelchair?*

I knew the answer would come in time. For now, God had me wedged into his will for me on the farm with Jay and little Kay. Every morning six-year-old Kay would sit on the edge of my bed and learn to count to my "stretching" exercises. And my sister and I swapped clothes, explored new recipes, baked cookies, and led Brownies. Jay was den-mother of Kay's troop, and we planned exotic adventures, cookouts, and sleepovers.

The afternoons were full of painting for me and gardening for Jay. She included me in her canning of pickles and planting tomatoes, talking with me through the window as she tended the tender young plants. I felt I was right there with her, knees down in the black garden soil. And in early spring, our home became a hothouse: hundreds of little, brown seed-pots lined the plank boards against the dining-room windows. When the first small shoots of green sprouted, it was cause for celebration. That summer, we gave friends *our* tomatoes. I'd discovered the meaning of "vicarious" from Jay, in all its joys and pleasures.

Our evenings were times of Bible study with friends or of warming tiny glasses of Amaretto by the hearth and singing along with John Denver. Sometimes when the moon was high, Jay wheeled me down River Road, past the barn and the honeysuckle bushes that smelled so sweet in the damp night air. And we sang in left-right, left-right rhythm to Jay's steps, "Heaven . . . is . . . a wonderful . . . place . . . filled . . . with . . . glory and . . . grace . . . I'm gonna . . . see my . . . Savior's . . . face . . . Heaven is a . . . wonderful . . . place!"

One winter evening, when the snow was falling outside, my sister saw me pining by the window. "I bet you'd like to be out there," she said, squeezing my shoulder. I nodded and marveled at the winter wonderland forming on the front lawn.

"I think we can do something about this," Jay said and disappeared. The next thing I knew, I was sitting outside on her patio, a couple of old blankets wrapped snugly around me, my feet covered, and a wool hat pulled down over my ears.

"Are you warm enough?" she asked, dusting off her hands. Again, I nodded, this time with a big smile. She patted my shoulder and went inside, leaving me alone to enjoy the heavy, winter quiet.

Daddy's old street lamp above made everything sparkle and swirl, and I nearly cried for the beauty of it all. I watched my breath become tiny crystals and listened to the whisper of snow falling. I leaned my head back and let the flakes stick to my lashes, and every once in a while I puffed away the snow from my blanket. After a while, Jay popped her head out the door: "Want to come in yet?"

I shook my head no. "Give me a little longer," I said.

That night, after she tucked me in bed and turned out the light, I stopped her. "Jay?"

She turned to me.

"Thank you. Thank you for everything."

"Goodnight, Grundy," she smiled and blew a kiss.

Jay helped my friends feel at home around my wheelchair by virtually making them family. Always generous and hospitable, she spread a large, red gingham cloth over our farmhouse table, lit the candles, and set out generous bowls of steaming corn and asparagus from her garden, with the best hot-baked potatoes this side of Idaho and hamburgers that made your mouth water. After dessert, we would pull our chairs around the fire and sing until midnight.

I owed my sister so much—more than I could ever hope to say. At my most fragile time, she was standing by me, cajoling and coaxing me out of discouragement with gingham, grace, and a friendship that only sisters share.

One summer evening in 1972—almost a year after our excursion to Washington, D.C.—Jay and I sat together on the back porch, enjoying the full moon. She pulled her rocker next to my wheelchair so she could help me with my cup of tea. We didn't talk much. We just watched the fireflies float over the creek and listened to the squeaking of her rocker.

"Remember last summer, when that silly bear came to camp?" she chuckled.

"I sure do. And you with your Polaroid."

"Remember, you said that bear was an answer to your prayer?"

"Yeah," I said, not sure where she was going with the memory.

"Well, I've been thinking. There was more to that whole thing than God sending you a bear instead of a butterfly."

"What do you mean?"

She kept rocking and creaking, her blonde hair swinging in rhythm. Finally, she said softly, "It seems to me that if God could answer a little prayer like 'Bring your creation close to me,' then he can answer the big prayers. The big things. Like prayers about the future."

I waited, wondering what she meant. Was she thinking about little Kay, without her father? Or about me—what I would do, where I would eventually live, and whether or not I would find a job?

"Like prayers for—" she searched for words, "—a *deeper* healing."

I wondered at my sister's country-wise way. All this time, I'd been experiencing peace and rest on the farm, I'd progressed with my drawing, I'd gotten good grades in my classes at the University of Maryland, where Diana took me. My life with Jay had become so normal that at times I was hardly even aware of my wheelchair. And now, for a little perspective, Jay was nudging me that maybe, just maybe, God was giving me the desires of my heart after all.

With crickets calling under the willow and the moonlight shining on Jay's golden hair, we lifted our voices to an old hymn:

> *There is a fountain filled with blood,*
> *Drawn from Emmanuel's veins;*
> *And sinners plunged beneath that flood,*
> *Lose all their guilty stains.*

We didn't need a dulcimer. We didn't need a fiddle. I slid my harmony underneath her melody, and our voices—soft as country down—blended into the night, making our praises to God as sweet as star jasmine. Once again, peace and safety flooded my heart. And it was enough. It was *okay*.

So many years have passed since those days on the farm. But still, when Jay and I get together, we almost always launch into that favorite hymn. And when we hit the high notes, I'm back in that soft summer night on the porch, watching my sister's blonde hair swinging in rhythm with the rocker. It was the night we sang with no sheet music, like angels with our feet firmly planted in the clouds.

It was the night God sneaked up from behind and surprised me. It was the night I realized I had been healed.

CHAPTER SEVENTEEN

I consider everything a loss compared to the surpassing greatness of know-
ing Christ Jesus my Lord, for whose sake I have lost all things. I consider
them rubbish, that I may gain Christ. . . . I want to know Christ and the
power of his resurrection and the fellowship of sharing in his sufferings,
becoming like him in his death.

Philippians 3:8–10

Wheeling slowly down the corridor of St. Agnes Hospital, I turned right toward the cancer ward. I hated being back in a hospital, but this time I was a visitor. I was here to see my old friend Mr. Cauthorne.

I bit my lip, wishing I had words for him, wanting so much to be strong for him. I wished he weren't here—I wished he were back on his estate, saddling up his big thoroughbred to go riding with me. I would swing up on Augie, and together we would ride, ride, ride with the wind, hot on the heels of the hounds. Or we'd kick up clods of mud on the path alongside the Patapsco, bounding up over the bank and onto the road by his big red barn and white-columned mansion. I would rein Augie toward the wooden gate in the Cauthornes' pasture, spur him to it, clasp his mane, and up and over we'd sail, clearing the fence with feet to spare. But that was then. Augie was gone. And soon, Alex Cauthorne—his body riddled with cancer—would be gone too.

I paused outside his room to gather my thoughts before I entered. When I went in, he lay in bed, thin and frail under a white sheet, his handsome face gaunt and ghostly pale. He looked so out of place here, in the gray, cheerless hospital room, more so because he wore a flowered hospital gown.

Ever the gracious gentleman-farmer, he stretched his thin, purple-veined hand toward me. It shook a little, and he smiled through the pain. Our eyes became damp. I knew as he looked at me that he wasn't seeing me in my wheelchair. In his mind, he was waving to me from his porch as I jogged up the road bordering his farm. And I wasn't seeing him on his deathbed—rather, we were on our thoroughbreds, cantering across the fields, our eyes damp because of the bracing November air.

"Do you remember that Thanksgiving Day, Mr. Cauthorne?"

"Yes," he said, smiling weakly. "You were quite something on that horse of yours. . . . He'd take those fences in stride . . . like he was jumping sticks."

His words summoned images that brought warmth and color to the gray room. And so, as horse people do, I recited for him how my big thoroughbred would enter a show ring and quietly dance and prance in one place, never pulling against the reins, ears flicking backward and forward awaiting my command, well aware that hundreds of eyes were on him. I described how I never had to tug on Augie's head—I just held his snaffle-bit firmly against his mouth, keeping the reins low and taut. Whenever I wanted him to move ahead, all it took was for me to tighten my knees, and—*flash!*—off he would go. To the first fence, the second, swing to the right, a triple-bar-spread, left to a water jump, back round the other way, leaping through a complex maze of fences. Almost never did he shy away.

The old man was quiet yet happy. He'd been transported for a moment beyond the four walls of his room. "I bet you miss that horse," he offered wistfully.

"I do, that."

He turned his head to follow the memory a little further. It was a bit odd—our shared experiences had always centered entirely on horses. We never had reason to discuss anything other than bowed tendons and cracked hooves, the most suitable kinds of bridles and bits, or how my riding had improved since I was a little girl. Now here we were, no longer characters in *National Velvet*. Rather, we were in a stale-smelling hospital room, I paralyzed and he staving off death—both a little awkward, a little nervous, not knowing what else to talk about. And the clock kept ticking.

Finally, I remembered my purpose in coming. "Here I brought you a gift." I motioned to the book wedged next to my knee. "It's a Bible."

"Oh-h-h." His eyebrows raised as he slowly reached for it.

"When I was in the hospital, I sometimes read the Twenty-Third Psalm," I told him.

He rested back as I recited from memory, "The Lord is my Shepherd, I shall not want. He makes me lie down in green pastures. He leads me beside still waters; he restores my soul. He leads me in the paths of righteousness for his namesake. Yea, though I walk through the valley of the shadow of—" I stumbled. "—the shadow of death," I repeated, quietly, unsure how to proceed—

"I will fear no evil," Mr. Cauthorne breathed.

I cocked my head. Then—

"For Thou art with me," we said in unison, "Thy rod and Thy staff, they comfort me ... surely goodness and mercy shall follow me all the days of my life and I shall dwell in the house of the Lord forever."

Mr. Cauthorne had made his peace with God. He seemed to understand that he had lived a rich life and that he'd used happily all the days allotted him. Now, just as you'd expect from a wise and gracious old man, he wasn't afraid. He had placed his faith in Christ, and he had accepted God's will in his life. No, not just accepted—he had embraced the will of God.

His eyes drooped, and I watched him doze off. They were right: he was not far from death's door. *You look so peaceful,* I told him in my thoughts, *and I wonder ...*

I wonder if accepting death is sometimes easier than having to accept life.

Alex Cauthorne died a few weeks later and, with him, the beauty and grandeur of his lovely old farm. The horses were sold and the place was leased. Soon a housing development began to encroach on the outer fields. Vines and ivy invaded the columns on the house and the porch, and weeds grew up around the barn. Finally, the place was sold to the state park.

They might as well have sold my childhood. Half my problem in accepting life was watching my past wither and die as time wedged itself between my memories and me. To me, Mr. Cauthorne was still the man in a red hunting jacket and leather boots. Pepper and Augie were still waiting for us to saddle them up. I could feel the reins and smell the leather, breathe in the aroma of freshly mown hay and sweet-feed in the trough. The really painful part was watching these memories fade like old home movies. The farther the present distanced me from the past, the more dim and fuzzy those images became. I knew that in time even the smiles on the faces would vanish.

I had no right to feel badly, though. There were others who had it worse—who hardly had time to tuck years, let alone childhood memories, under their belt. It was from such people I learned how to accept my life.

My six-year-old niece, Kelly, was Linda's youngest, and, as the typical tomboy on the family farm, she'd been given lots of responsibilities around the house and barn. Kelly had become a strong, resourceful, independent little girl.

One day Daddy noticed Kelly limping up the driveway of the farmhouse, dragging her foot slightly. Linda immediately took her to the hospital. We were shocked and stunned when her doctor discovered an enormous cancerous tumor in her brain. Surgery could only do so much, and within a month Kelly was partially paralyzed on one side of her little body. After a long hospital stay, her doctor suggested we take her home. Her care required more time than Linda was able to give, so Dad and Mom opened up their home in Woodlawn to help Kelly around the clock.

Now there were two wheelchairs around our dinner table: mine, adult-sized, and Kelly's miniature one. The entire family poured love and attention on Kelly, and as she grew weaker we did everything we could to make her as comfortable as possible. Daddy would sit for hours by her bedside and share his many renditions of *Goldilocks and the Three Bears*. It was amazing to see the change in Kelly, in her spirit and attitude. No longer was she the tightlipped, I-can-do-it-myself tomboy. She softened into a sweet and wise child, memorizing virtually all the dialogue in the *Goldilocks* story, endlessly playing tea with her cousin Kay, and most of all, letting her imagination run wild when it came to heaven. The notion of heaven utterly fascinated her, and she couldn't wait for weekends when she could go to Sunday school and learn more.

Kelly tired easily during those last few weeks, and she spent more and more time in Kathy's and my old bedroom, the one with the angels. Just as we did when we were kids, Kelly lay in bed looking up into the faces of the three smiling angels, who kept watch through the night. One evening, Jay and Kathy beckoned me to the bottom of the stairs. "Listen," they said softly as they leaned on the banister.

"Jesus loves me, this I know, for the Bible tells me so," Kelly was singing in a half whisper from her dark bedroom. Our eyes turned liquid. The lilting little song from the top of the stairs transported us to some other world, where six-year-olds lay down with lions and lambs and where little children really did lead the way.

Yet I was touched even more deeply by something else.

"I like your wheelchair, Aunt Joni," Kelly told me softly one evening. The two of us were sitting alone at the dinner table, waiting for the others to join us.

"You do?"

"Yeah," she said, giving me her endearing grin. "I want one like yours when I grow up."

She caught me up short. All I could do was smile and shake my head at those impish eyes and thick eyelashes, the mop of brown hair cropped from the surgery, the freckles that flattened over her nose and cheeks when she laughed. Kelly scrunched her shoulders and leaned forward in her wheelchair, repeating, "Can I have one like yours?"

I gulped hard. In her eyes, my wheelchair was more to be desired than a new collection of *My Little Pony* dolls or a spiffy new tea set for her and Kay. My chair was a joyride, a passport to adventure. Kelly assumed that my wheels had initiated me into a very special club, a club in which she wanted membership. Yet she didn't seem to have a clue about the price one actually pays to join such a club. She seemed to discount the pain and the paralysis, the disappointment and the broken dreams. She utterly disregarded the dark side—it wasn't even worth considering. All she longed for was a chance to be like me, to identify with me, to know Aunt Joni better.

But something else was going on too. Those wise eyes of hers gave it away. Kelly wanted *me* to desire my wheelchair as much as she did. My niece wasn't just admiring it—she wanted me to do the same. All along I had been trying to cheer her up, to tell her stories and play games with her, even be an example to her. But I had it all wrong. She was leading *me*. Out of the mouth of this babe, God was showing me how to embrace his will.

"Your wheelchair's neater than mine. I like *yours* best," she said again.

And you should too, she was saying. Kelly knew—at least, she sure seemed to know—that I was still bogged down by broken dreams. She sensed I still struggled with the dark side, that I didn't quite know how to accept where I sat. For her, though, it was a cinch. Life had been hard on the farm, her parents argued a lot, and up until the diagnosis of cancer, you couldn't get her near a tea set. But her suffering had pushed her into the arms of Jesus, and her gracious, openhearted way of accepting—no, embracing—his will had cracked open heaven's floodgates of blessing. All my niece wanted to do now was talk about Jesus and his heaven, where she would pet giraffes and eat all the ice cream she wanted. Where she would ride bigger ponies, douse ketchup on everything, converse with Papa and Mama Bear, play with Baby Bear, and become an instant grownup.

"I'm glad you like my wheelchair," I finally answered. "And I'm happy you want one like mine when you grow up."

"Good!" she nearly jumped.

"But Kelly, soon you won't need one like mine. You won't even need yours."

She nodded, understanding completely what I meant. So I asked in a low, serious tone, "Kelly, when you see Jesus, would you please tell him that I said 'Hi'? You won't forget?"

She smiled, hunched her shoulders again, and nodded.

Later that week, Kelly said to her mother, "Mommy, I want to go home."

"But, honey, don't you want to be at Grandmom's and Grand-dad's anymore?" Linda asked.

"No, I want to go home with Jesus," she whispered hoarsely. "Would you pack my suitcase?"

It was nearly 2:00 A.M. on a pitch-black night. I was in the room directly beneath hers, and I could hear footsteps above and muffled talking. As Kelly requested, the family was stuffing her favorite toy animals around her and packing a suitcase with her jeans and dresses. Everyone knew her passing into heaven would happen at any moment, but I was unable to get up the narrow steps to say good-bye with the others. I lay there wide awake, staring out the large bay window and straining to hear the hushed conversation going on above me.

Then, all of a sudden, I saw a brilliant, golden shape flash pass the window.

"Aauah!" I cried aloud.

It was a dazzling form, and it moved upward from the ground. My eyes quickly searched for a car that might be driving by, but nothing was out there.

A moment later, Jay called down the steps, "Kelly's gone!"

A few family members came downstairs. When I told them exactly what I'd seen, they sank into their chairs in amazement. As we worked out the timing, Jay breathed, "That happened just at the moment she was praying, 'If I should die before I wake, I pray the Lord my soul to take.'"

"It was real," I kept repeating. "It actually happened."

We knew I must have seen a large spiritual being—an angel?—sent to escort Kelly's soul home. "Yea, though I walk through the valley of the shadow of death," we whispered together, the familiar Twenty-Third Psalm, as though pronouncing a benediction, "I will fear no evil. For Thou art with me."

I couldn't shake the reality of Kelly's death. Or Mr. Cauthorne's. One moment, these lively, happy people were here, and then suddenly they weren't. One minute they were struggling, and the next minute they let go of life and embraced death. Or maybe it was the other way around: maybe they let go of their struggles to embrace life. A different kind of life, on the other side of a thin, transparent veil—life that was invisible, yet rock-solid real.

I also couldn't shake the reality—the crystal-clear actuality, the certainty—of that other world. I had actually seen its power and influence. Those suitcases and toy animals stuffed around Kelly weren't just wishful thinking. It wasn't a nostalgic longing or a vague hope for something on the other side. It was an actual passage from the land of the dying to the land of the living. And

I'd tasted that land's joys, through Kelly's changed life, and through the peaceful face of Mr. Cauthorne. I had read about it in 2 Corinthians 4:16–18:

> Therefore we do not lose heart. Though outwardly we are wasting away, yet inwardly we are being renewed day by day. For our light and momentary troubles are achieving for us an eternal glory that far outweighs them all. So we fix our eyes not on what is seen, but on what is unseen. For what is seen is temporary, but what is unseen is eternal.

I looked down at my paralyzed legs and repeated, "What is seen is temporary ..." Then I lifted my eyes. "... but what is unseen is eternal."

I had always acknowledged that heaven was part of what it meant to be a Christian. Yet it had always been buried in paragraph fourteen on page three of an eternal insurance policy. It had existed only as a part of the culture of my faith, more of a mental tip-of-the-hat than an actual realm that encroached on the present, infusing its power and hope into everything. That changed for me with Kelly's death—or, I should say, life. Everything changed with the sight of that glowing spiritual being and those verses from 2 Corinthians. I wanted to fix my eyes on things eternal. And I wanted greater faith to believe *more*—the kind of faith described in Hebrews: "Faith is being sure of what we hope for and certain of what we do not see."

I wanted to be sure, to be hopeful. To be certain of something I couldn't see. I knew I needed faith that large to accept life in a wheelchair.

Dear Lord, will this wheelchair ever be a joyride? A passport to adventure? Will I ever be able to disregard the dark side? Discount the pain and the paralysis as not worth considering?

I sensed, just as Kelly had, that I was in a very special club. A club that, up to now, I wanted little to do with. Like it or not, though, I was a member—enrolled in the fellowship of Christ's suffering.

"Joni, you're on the right track. You're heading in the right direction. This wheelchair is your chance to identify with Christ," Steve Estes told me.

Three years younger than I, Steve was virtually a Bible scholar. And he was just the person I was looking for. Diana had done her best to help me with my questions, but she knew I needed more help. So she introduced me to her church friend, Steve—a tall, somewhat gangly but incredibly winsome teenager. After Diana made the introductions, Steve promised to come to the house regularly to help me study the Bible. The only condition was that I keep him stocked in RC Colas and my mother's BLT sandwiches.

That summer, I plunged into the Bible with Steve alongside, coaching and guiding me with every flip of the page.

"This wheelchair is your passport to become like Christ, to know him better," he underscored, flipping the pages of his big black Bible back and forth, searching for a verse.

A small bit of fear reared up within me. "Listen, I once asked God to draw me closer to him," I pointed out, "and look what I got." I looked down at my chair. "If this is the way he answers—"

"Don't be afraid," Steve said softly. "He *is* answering." He placed his hand on the armrest of the wheelchair. "This *is* part of his will. Listen to this verse in Philippians."

He read—

> I consider everything a loss compared to the surpassing greatness of knowing Christ Jesus my Lord, for whose sake I have lost all things. I consider them rubbish, that I may gain Christ. . . . I want to know Christ and the power of his resurrection and the fellowship of sharing in his sufferings, becoming like him in his death.

I didn't get his point.

"Joni, don't regret that you prayed to get closer to God," Steve said. "It's worth anything to know him. Everything else is a loss in comparison—we both know that. And those who know God best are the ones who share in his sufferings."

"No wonder he has so few friends," I joked.

"Kelly was his friend," Steve countered.

My eyes dropped in embarrassment.

He continued, "Think of what your wheelchair is doing. It's like, well—a jackhammer, breaking apart all your rocks of resistance. It's sandblasting you to the core, obliterating all the pride and independence. It's like a sheepdog snapping at your heels and driving you to the cross. Joni . . ." He paused to look straight at me, ". . . this wheelchair is getting you ready for heaven. Like Kelly got ready. And considering this world can never keep its promises, considering that it will always disappoint us—your wheelchair is not a bad thing. It may even become a blessing."

This was going somewhere. It rang true somewhere in me. So often I had been the stoic, plowing and plodding two steps forward and three back with my head against the wind of God's will (and however it was connected with my wheelchair). My family recognized that in me whenever I stubbornly refused to feed myself or became sullen or moody after I passed a full-length mirror. Even Kelly had seen it in me. So often I had dared not believe my wheelchair could be a passport to joy. Instead, I'd reined in my hopes, bridled my heart, and buckled up my thoughts, put a martingale on my mind and a tie-down on my dreams. I would not let go—I would not be free. I wouldn't release myself to believe that the joy of the Lord was big enough to enrapture and enthrall me, despite a lifeless, limp body. Instead, I chose to resign myself to a situation, my condition—and my heart always seems to get a little harder. Or I'd whine and end up feeling defeated.

"You will never accept your wheelchair," Steve said while pouring more cola into his glass. He took a sip then added, "You'll never adjust or cope or even yield or submit to it."

A lump rose in my throat. He had stated what I hadn't wanted to admit. But—where was he going?

Steve took one more swallow, wiped his mouth, and said emphatically, "But you *can* embrace God."

I was beginning to understand—maybe.

"Think of a greater affliction—*his* affliction," he added. "As you do, you can't help but embrace him. And as you embrace *him*, you can't help but love his will."

That meant something. It was being sure of something I hoped for—being certain of something I couldn't see. It was, I realized, what having greater faith meant. Not faith in my ability to accept a wheelchair, but faith to embrace Christ, to trust him in spite of— no, because of—my problems.

Again, I recalled the first time I tasted the power of the gospel that night in the hills of Virginia. *How could I doubt the one who gave his life up for me?* I remembered my friend Jacque singing to me in the hospital, the statue at Johns Hopkins, my pleasant life with Jay on the farm, Kelly—and, as always, the stars above the campfires. They were all part of the path Jesus had led me on thus far. *How could I not believe him?*

Steve was leaning back, watching all this happen in my head. I grinned to him, *I got it.*

"May I have a sip?" I asked. As Steve tilted the glass to my mouth, I gave him a good-natured wink. I had not only connected with what he was saying—I had connected with the open book on the table. I knew it would be my passport to adventure. And I knew I was in for a joyride because my faith was in the right place—or rather, the right person.

"C'mon," Steve said, slapping the table. It was nearly midnight, and my folks were in the other room watching a late movie, but that didn't stop us. A full, pale moon beckoned us outside, and Steve opened the side door, tilted back my chair, and wheeled me full speed into the night: me on my two back wheels, and him huffing and pushing. The yellow orb cast long shadows through the trees; it was a night much like the ones when Daddy took us horseback riding. Steve bumpity-bumped my wheelchair over the front lawn, parking me in a large swatch of moonlight, the biggest and brightest spot on the lawn.

He stood back, flung his arms wide, and let loose a coyote yell, "Ow-ow-owwwwl!"

"You're crazy," I laughed, "you're insane!"

That just egged him on. With his face awash in moonlight, he threw back his head again, "Ow-ow-owwwwl!"

It was the most ridiculous thing I'd seen in years. But I hadn't had this kind of zany fun since high school hockey antics. So with the sheer abandonment of a kid, like cowboys-and-Indians, galloping bareback with my arms spread like wings—like days when I was on my feet—I leaned back as far as I could in my chair, threw my head up, and howled at the moon, "Ow-ow-owwwwl!"

We howled like a pack of happy coyotes. "Ow-ow-owwwwl!"

"Ow-ow-owwwwl!"

"Ow-ow-owwwwl!"

I was making memories—new ones, fresh and cheery memories. Everything about the night—the tall, dark trees casting jagged shadows, the stars like jewels, the tinkling of wind chimes, the moon continuing to climb—it was all ethereal and otherworldly, as if Steve and I had reached through a thin, invisible veil and touched the joy of heaven. Maybe our faith *had* parted the veil—and heaven had poured out its joy on us in a blessing.

I went to bed that night feeling safe and satisfied. "Goodnight," I heard Daddy whisper. Or was it God?

My thoughts in the half-awake world just before sleep transported me to other happy moments—places where distance and time hadn't tarnished the sights, sounds, and aromas. Once again I was sitting atop my big horse, about to enter the show ring. I could feel him beneath me, prancing and dancing in place, never pulling on the reins, ears flicking backward and forward, awaiting my command. I tightened my knees against him and—*flash!*—off he cantered toward the first fence, anxious to respond to me, his rider holding the reins. Over the first fence, the second, and third we flew, leaping through a complex maze of hurdles and hedges. Not once did he balk or shy away. It didn't matter whether he understood the course set before him; he showed no concern over how hard the stone walls appeared. He simply loved to jump. And because he trusted my judgment, he loved to do my will. His confidence in me was absolute and complete, and he was eager to obey in an instant. It was the joy of his great heart to please me.

Oh, how I wanted to please God with all my heart. Unsnap the bridle and buckles. Release the tie-down and uncinch the martingale. I would let go. I would be free to believe his joy and peace could outweigh the dark side of my suffering. I would believe he was leading me, reining me, into the adventure of knowing him, pleasing him. I would trust his judgment in the course set before me. My confidence in him would be absolute and complete, and he would be the joy of my heart.

It was still a dream. But I was sure of what I hoped for and certain of what I was barely able to see.

Chapter Eighteen

They did what God's power and will had decided beforehand should happen.

Acts 4:28

Alma Redemptoris Mater, quae pervia caeli
Porta manes, et stella maris, succurre cadenti,
Surgere qui curat, populo: tu quae genuisti,
Natura mirante, tuum sanctum Genitorem

I had no idea what the words meant, but Diana and I and a handful of other friends sang it just as we had in high school. We'd learned the ancient antiphon in choir, and now as we revisited the harmony and melody, we intertwined our voices as if braiding a rope, filling the entire hall with the wistful chant in minor key. The music was sublime and elegant, transporting us with breathless wonder as we sang with heads back and eyes closed. It was an antiphon fit for the grandest of cathedrals. I know, because our audience was just as enraptured. There they sat: a homeless guy and a couple of sailors.

It was Friday night, and we were in the huge waiting room of the old Pennsylvania Railway Station on Charles Street. The granite lobby was cavernous and virtually empty. If not for the occasional clickity-clack of trains passing beneath us, we might have been in a cathedral. It even had that musty, damp smell mingled with the scent of lemon oil from the wooden benches. Our little group had found a quiet corner under the marbled columns and magnificent domed skylight. We had come here to sing.

It was one of the things I could still do, and do well. I'd never let it go.

Once, my parents had begged a visiting consultant from California to come to the state institution to examine me. The expert stood by my bedside, poking me with a pin in my feet and ankles, trying to determine if I had much potential for improvement. He slowly worked his way up my body, asking, "Can you feel this?" and I would shake my head, no. "This?" and another no. He reached my waist, then my chest, and I still couldn't feel anything. But I wanted to assure him I could do a lot more than his pin indicated. So when I still couldn't feel the pin-prick near my collarbone, I blurted, "I can't feel that. But—but I can sing! Wanna hear me? Really, I can!"

I could always find a song. Hymns and Young Life songs, cowboy and sailor songs. Love songs gleaned from listening to Mother sing along with Arthur Godfrey on CBS Radio or any of the twenty-six moon songs she knew by heart. Songs from Kathy's old Broadway musical LPs. Every Beatle and Beach Boys tune that hit the top ten on WCAO. Even Latin chants from high school choir—especially the Latin chants. And particularly this one, "Alma Redemptoris Mater," composed in the eleventh century by Herman Contractus, better known as Herman the Cripple. I liked that.

It was not unusual for Diana and me to hunt up a few choir cronies on a weekend night just to sing. Sometimes it happened in my parents' living room, with its wood floor and high ceiling, other times at the glass vestibule at the entrance to a mall—anywhere that would echo. On this particular Friday evening someone suggested we try out the acoustics down at the old rail station because it would probably be deserted at that hour anyway.

We weren't disappointed. When our little choir parted with the last glorious note, we paused to listen to it reverberate off the domed ceiling. The homeless man took a swig from his paper bag, wiped his mouth, and smiled. The sailors grinned and applauded lightly. A janitor working nearby nodded as he rested on his broom. We were a hit.

Then a uniformed guard appeared. "Okay, okay, enough of this now," he said gruffly. "This isn't any church here. This is a place of business, and you young people need to clear out."

"Aw, do we have to?" Diana whined in jest.

The guard didn't think she was funny. "I said, enough. Gather your things and get going. And *you*—" he pointed at me menacingly in my wheelchair "—you put that back where you found it."

"You mean her wheelchair?" Diana asked.

"Yes, I mean the wheelchair," he said as though we were mocking him. "Get out of it, missy, right now!"

This was too funny to be true. "Sir, I wish I *could* get out of it, but I can't," I answered. "It's mine."

"Don't you sass me. It belongs here. Now, put it back!"

Of all the crazy things—I must have looked so "normal" that this guy thought I could get up and walk.

"Sir, my friend really is paralyzed," Diana said. She demonstrated by lifting my limp hand. "See?"

He still wasn't convinced. He thought we were just a bunch of unruly teenagers playing a trick.

"Honestly, I'm paralyzed," I said, trying to keep a straight face. "I really am!"

Suddenly, he turned red. "Okay, okay, just get out of here, all of you," he said, shooing us with his hands.

As Diana revved the engine, my friends tossed me in the front seat of the car, and we screeched out of the parking lot, hitting every green light on Charles Street. We rolled down the windows and, making a beeline for home, let the night breeze carry our laughter in our wake. I was sitting head-level with my friends, intoxicated by the night's music and fun, having played so hard and happily that no sad thought could possibly enter my head. And how I'd fooled the guard!

I wished my niece Kelly could have seen it. I was on a literal joyride, wheelchair and all, my passport to adventure.

"Ow-ow-owwwwl!" I howled, and the rest of our pack joined in.

I was making memories again.

I had always looked back on childhood days as the best of times, feel-good reminders of another time, another place. But now fresh, new moments were taking place, and they took on that same time-less feel. This night was brimming with joy—much more than an earthy joy. It carried a fragrance from another world, a world of eternity.

God knew I needed it. It was 1974, and I had put seven hard years between my diving accident and the life I lived now. I had rope-and-tackled my way up the walls of the miry pit, slipping and sliding, only to find footing for a short while, pause, grab a breath, wipe my brow, and scale higher. But now, this seventh year was my jubilee. I had reached a broad, spacious plain, and God must have known I needed rest and refreshment. Life was tough, yes, but God's grace was tougher. And in the brutal spaces came great moments of blessing—moments that were so *ordinary.*

One summer morning, Jay and I decided to have tea with an elderly friend, Grandma Clark, at her big house on the end of Main Street. We opened the kitchen screen door and were greeted by the aroma of hot cake from the oven. Grandma Clark had placed crisp, white linen on a table by an open window, and a breeze lifted the lace curtains, wafting in the scent of roses. As Jay and I sipped Earl Grey from porcelain cups, Grandma Clark leaned back, smoothed the tablecloth, and spoke of heaven. Her words were filled with pining, almost an ache.

A sudden gust snapped the curtains like flags, and she held up her hand against the wind, smiling and squinting. The air eddied around the table, and the dappled sunlight danced on the tablecloth, making our spirits dizzy and light. The moment was delightfully strange—and it vanished as quickly as it came, settling us back, and leaving in its trace the same fragrance of heaven.

Such moments were so filled with eternity, I forgot all about my wheelchair. Or, if I didn't, at least I laughed about it. One summer evening Diana and I, with some other friends, arrived at the beach in Ocean City just as the sun was setting, and the nighttime crowds began to emerge. We wheeled up to the corner of 18th Street and Boardwalk, on the edge of the Honky Tonk section down by the end of town. Even at that distance, we could hear the laughter of people on the Ferris wheel and the shrieks of others on the roller coaster, and we smelled the aroma of hot, salty french fries.

Diana set me up next to the pilings, and as she and the others settled on them, we enjoyed our favorite evening-on-the-boardwalk pastime: chewing cotton candy and watching the world go by. Bikers and roller skaters whizzed in and out of parents pushing strollers and elderly couples walking arm-in-arm. Teenage girls in jeans and skimpy tops strutted along, showing off their new tans, while their boyfriends prowled close behind. Dads carried toddlers on their shoulders, and mothers ambled along behind in twos, talking and relaxing. Most of the passersby looked our way, and occasionally, when their eyes met mine, I smiled.

Yet after a half hour or so, we all began to feel a bit unsettled. It was obvious I was being stared at. That's when Diana snapped her fingers and beamed, indicating, *I've got an idea!* She shot off the piling, rushed back to the hotel, and came back plopping down an armful of items. She pushed me into the middle of the boardwalk, among the stream of people.

"What are you doing?" I blurted.

Without answering, Diana threw a blanket over my legs, grabbed my hand, and entwined my limp fingers around the handle of a tin cup.

"If people are going to stare, we're going to make them pay," she declared. She promptly sat back down on the pilings, leaving me by myself in the boardwalk traffic.

I couldn't believe her. "Diana, will you quit—" I glared with irritation.

Clunk! In shock, I looked down and saw a quarter spinning in my cup. I glanced over my shoulder to my friends, bewildered, and—*clunk!*—someone dropped in another quarter. People thought I was begging!

I shrugged and threw myself into the act, pleading, "Alms for the poor." My girlfriends split their sides in laughter. "We're not rescuing you 'til you've made enough for pizza!" they taunted.

Their jeering drew shocked expressions from more passersby—which, in turn, resulted in more quarters.

Later, as we finished eating the last piece of pepperoni, we wondered aloud if people had given quarters to play along or if they really felt sorry for me.

"Who cares?" I said, gulping my last slice, then licking my friend's tomatoey fingers. "Begging pays!" We left the pizza parlor and joined the stream of people walking the boardwalk, our high spirits matching the neon lights and the circus sounds from the carousel calliope.

Once again, my wheelchair had been a passport to adventure. We had entered another ordinary, brown-paper-packaged moment and unwrapped it, discovering a hidden grace—grace that was able to suffice, atone, and make up for anything I might have lost. Whether howling like a coyote over some newfound truth in the Bible or blending my voice with others' in an ancient Latin antiphon, the moments kept whispering, "Hang on. One day you'll bathe in joy like this. Satisfaction will shower you, peace will encompass you—and it will last forever."

Such moments were happening more often. And one by one, they were creating a string of pearls, connecting one day to the next with joy and confidence, helping me see how life could be lived. I didn't know how to account for it all except that maybe this was my jubilee. It was God's doing; my pursuit of him was no longer something extraordinary—it was part of my everyday routine.

It was quite ordinary to find me parked in front of a Bible with a rubber-tipped dowel in my mouth, flipping from one end of the book to the other, searching and studying. I was following Steve Estes' lead, learning to embrace God rather than self-pity. My Friday night Bible studies with him spilled over into weeknights as I pelted him with more questions:

"Do things happen by chance?"

"Was my accident just that—an *accident?*"

I had long ago given up asking *Why?* with a clenched, angry fist. Now I asked the same question—"Why?"—with a sincere curiosity, a deep need to know. Empty bottles of RC Cola cluttered the table as we searched and studied late into the night, Steve always bending over his Bible with pencil in hand, marking this verse and that, me always leaning in, asking, "Let me see that . . ."

It didn't matter how late the midnight oil burned—I was always energized. One night, as the fire from the hearth cast a cozy warmth throughout the room, I was poring over the twelfth chapter of the book of Romans.

"Steve, look," I noted, "it says here that God's will is 'good and acceptable and perfect.' How can a good God allow so much suffering?"

Steve leaned forward on the table, a deep furrow in his brow. He stared past me, slowly drumming his fingers and softly repeating my question. Then he looked up—something had registered. "Joni, let's take a look at your question this way," he pondered. "Let me ask you—do you think it was God's will for Jesus to suffer?"

I gave him a puzzled look, wondering if it was a trick question.

Steve switched tacks. "Well, think about this. It was Satan who gave Judas the idea to betray Jesus. And it was Pilate who held that kangaroo court. Surely it was the devil who must have incited those drunken soldiers to beat Jesus. They pulled his beard out. They struck him with rods. Who knows what else they did to him in that back room. And what about the mob in the streets who screamed for his blood? How can *any* of those things be God's will?"

He had me there.

Steve held up his fingers and checked off a mental list.

"Treason. Injustice. Torture. Murder."

He paused, as if to let the shock sink in with me. "Joni, we say the cross was part of God's plan, but . . ." he paused again, perhaps this time for himself, ". . . but we forget it included evil things like these."

It was a sobering thought. I didn't see how God could allow torture—especially that kind of torture—in his will for anyone, let alone his Son. I could see the devil being involved—but God?

"Listen to what it says here," Steve said, his finger moving down the page in the book of Acts. "'They did'—that is, Judas and the rest—'they did what God's power and will had decided beforehand should happen.'"

He closed his Bible and looked straight at me. "Joni, God didn't take his hand off the wheel for a nanosecond. He permits things he hates—*really* hates—to accomplish something he loves. He allowed the devil to instigate the Crucifixion all because he had in mind our good. The world's worst murder became the world's only salvation."

I knew this was no ordinary lesson.

"So, what does this say to you?" Steve asked, leaning back and folding his hands behind his head.

I connected the dots. *God permitted something he hated*—my quadriplegia—*to accomplish something he loved*—my growing need of him. "You mean this paralysis wasn't an accident at all?" I asked.

Steve let a brief moment pass. "What do you think?" he responded. He began to gather the empty soda bottles and take them to the kitchen.

"I think—I believe that—I think God doesn't take his hands off the wheel for a nanosecond."

I let it sink in.

A quick yell came from the kitchen: "It's too late tonight to call out the pack of coyotes."

It was an extraordinary moment nonetheless. My diving injury . . . It wasn't some flip-of-the-coin in the cosmos, some turn in the universe's roulette wheel. It was part of God's plan—*for me.*

That fact alone was able to allay my fear about the future. God was in control—and he had brought me to a broad, spacious plain. In 1974, I had risen to a higher plateau. So that year, my jubilee of rest, I did something extraordinary: I embraced the will of God.

I showed Steve the verse I'd marked in my Bible long ago, about physical healing: "Delight thyself in the Lord and he will give you the desires of your heart."

"So," Steve asked, "has he done that?"

"Oh," I answered, "he's done that, and much more. Yes, he's given me the desire of my heart. He's given me . . . himself."

———

My jubilee year was extraordinary in another way. It started casually enough, with exhibitions of my artwork in a few local festivals. But then a Baltimore news channel did a story on me, and—*bang!*—I soon found myself on the set of *The Today Show* in New York, facing Barbara Walters. I gazed at the NBC set behind her while she pointed to my artwork, hanging on a wall behind me.

"Tell us where you get your inspiration," she asked. "Would you call yourself a religious person?"

I stumbled over my answers, marveling a bit at what was happening. The interview ended with me autographing a drawing with a pen in my mouth, and I exited the sound stage during a commercial break. On the ride home, I realized that I had no idea what I'd gotten myself into. All I knew was, when I got back home, I kept hearing the question, "How did you make *that* happen?"

Of course, the point was I *didn't* make it happen. It just *happened*, as if it were another in this growing series of ordinary things. I felt funny when friends made a big deal about the national morning show. And I felt the same way the following week, when a publisher called.

"I saw your interview with Barbara Walters," he told me. "I liked what you said."

My mind scrambled to remember. *What did I say?*

"Miss Eareckson," the publisher said, "you told the world that you weren't a religious person."

"That's right," I recalled.

"Well, would you mind explaining your comment?"

It felt like a test in Mrs. Krieble's class. I thought of all I'd learned from Steve Estes and finally concluded, "I don't think Christianity is about religion. It's about a relationship. A relationship with Jesus Christ."

"But, doesn't your quadriplegia affect that?"

I knew where he was heading. He assumed my disability should have driven me away from God and made me bitter, rather than toward him.

"Yes, it does affect my relationship with the Lord," I answered. "It makes me need him more."

There was a long silence at the other end.

"Well, Joni," he said, "—may I call you by your first name, Joni? We would like you to share that perspective with others."

The next week, a contract was in my mailbox. Jay opened the envelope and placed the legal document squarely in front of me on the dining room table. Now *this* was totally out of the ordinary— the idea of a book about my life sounded so preposterous. With my mouthstick, I flipped open the contract. Its language was about as indiscernible as what lay ahead for me if I signed the dotted line.

This called for a pow-wow with Steve, even though he was now away at college. "Do you think I should do this?" I asked.

There was a long pause on the other end of the phone. I couldn't tell if Steve was stumped or if this was something he thought I should decide for myself.

"Just make sure you keep pointing people to the Bible," he finally offered. "Your life story can't change anyone, but God's Word can."

Six months later, at the same dining-room table, I sat staring at a manuscript. It was odd to think my turbulent, noisy life— especially my last eight years in a wheelchair—was now condensed into a stack of paper eight inches wide by ten inches long and three inches high. I began reading, "The hot July sun was setting low in the west and gave the waters of the Chesapeake Bay a warm red glow. . . ."

My stomach fluttered. *Oh boy—I hope I'm doing the right thing.*

In the fall of 1976, a hardcover book called simply *Joni* appeared. I smelled the fresh ink on the crisp pages, and marveled at how it had all happened. That's all I could say about it—it had just . . . *happened.*

And this may be as close as I'll ever come to giving birth to something, I thought. I smiled, knowing others were now responsible for its upbringing. "Now," I told myself, "I can get back to my normal life on the farm."

Before that could happen, though, I received a phone call—from Billy Graham.

Jay nearly dropped the phone. "He wants you to share your story on one of his crusades," she croaked hoarsely. She covered the receiver and added in a whisper, "Can I go?"

It was a cool October night when Jay and Kathy wheeled me onto the field of the Pontiac Silverdome near Detroit, Michigan. Somewhat dazed by the glare of the stadium lights, we kept turning our heads to take in the overwhelming scene. The stadium was packed with thousands upon thousands of people.

"Over here, girls," Judy Butler pointed. She was a secretary to one of the Billy Graham Team members, and that authoritative fact, coupled with her proper British accent, prompted us to pick up our pace.

Judy directed us to our seats on the platform, and Billy Graham came over to greet me. I had never been so close to anyone that famous, except maybe Barbara Walters. Yet I had no cause to be nervous. Mr. Graham squeezed my shoulder, and put me at ease immediately with his warmth and sincerity.

That night, before Mr. Graham spoke, I had eight minutes to share my story before the huge crowd. I had worked hard the preceding weeks to condense it, and I closed with this short statement: "Even paralyzed people can walk with the Lord." I was taken aback by the ocean of applause.

After Mr. Graham finished his sermon, he followed his usual practice by encouraging people to turn from their sin and open their hearts to Christ. I watched, stunned, as hundreds began slowly streaming down the stadium aisles and onto the field. Yet I knew exactly what they were feeling and thinking. I vividly recalled that first night when, as a fourteen-year-old, I decided to quit going my own way and follow Jesus. As I looked out over the sea of people before me, I could hardly believe that was only a little over a decade ago.

Look at all that's happened in my life since then. And now, God, you've brought me here?

When it was over, Judy had a challenge on her hands herding us sisters back to the car. Jay, Kathy, and I were like kids in a candy store, alternately running back to the stadium, people-gazing, grabbing extra croissants from the green room, and peeking into the production trucks. When Judy finally rounded us up and jammed us in the car, she slumped into the backseat and pronounced to the driver, "Home, James, and don't spare the horses!"

At the hotel that night, I looked into the bathroom mirror and asked myself, "Why are *you* here, and not someone else?" I didn't know the answer, but I was beginning to realize I'd been given a special trust—something I knew I had to hold lightly, treat with respect, and give back to God when all the fanfare was over.

But it showed no signs of letting up. With a bing-bang-bong, the *Joni* book was soon published in French, German, and other languages, and I was being asked to travel to Europe to tell my story. I had never flown across the ocean, and as Jay and I packed, I kept thinking, *How will I empty my leg bag? Those little airplane trays are so tiny—will I be able to feed myself with my bent spork in my armsplint?*

It looked like my ordinary days of life on the farm might be over.

Later in the trip, Kathy would join us, but for now, Jay and I, along with my friend Betsy from Young Life, were off to Europe—lifting me out of my wheelchair, into my plane seat, and bunching pillows and blankets to prop me up. A happy bunch of girls in our twenties, we kept singing, "How 'ya gonna keep 'em down on the farm, after they've seen Par-ee!"

We arrived in Austria, hitting the ground with my wheels literally spinning. Our first stop was in the midst of a thunderstorm, for a stay-over at a cold, damp medieval castle.

"Why can't they put us up in a hotel?" I whispered to Jay and Betsy, as they lifted me out of the car in the pouring rain. "Good grief, the publishers flew us over here … they should be able to find us a place with an elevator."

The castle's emphasis was definitely on "medieval": high stone walls, turrets, and a heavy wood door straight out of *The Bride of Frankenstein.* We arrived late, due to the storm, and had to wait outside in the rain while the proprietor, whom we awakened, fingered slowly through his big ring of keys. Finally, the great door creaked open. There he was in his night shirt, mumbling something in German, indicating his irritation.

Our interpreter—a female Arnold Schwarzenegger—quickly manhandled our luggage to the second floor. When she reappeared, she directed us to our bedroom.

"Up doze stairs," she instructed.

Betsy wheeled me closer to the small, corkscrew staircase in the corner.

"You mean this—this firehouse thing? These twisty little steps? You want *us,*" she pressed her chest, "to carry Joni up *there?*"

As if on cue, lightning flashed, casting a pale aura over the circular stairwell. It looked like a turret leading to Dracula's lair.

"You Amerrikans are strong. You can do it," the interpreter said matter-of-factly. She turned on her heel and walked briskly to her own room to retire.

We had no alternative. So Jay clasped my upper body from behind, and Betsy grabbed my legs, the three of us squeezed into the entrance to the circular staircase. Jay and Betsy haltingly took the first step upward, barely able to see the way in the dim glow of the wall light. Every so often, lightning flashed again, illuminating the stairs. Each step creaked, and halfway up we started giggling, causing Betsy to lose her grip. She had to sit down.

"What are you doing?" Jay hissed.

"Stop, I can't breathe," I cried, "from *laughing.*"

"We can't stop, we'll get stuck!"

But Betsy was on her side now, laughing uncontrollably.

A bedroom door above us cracked open, sending out an accusing beam of light. Someone said something softly in German.

"No prrrob-lem, no prrrob-lem!" Jay muttered, faking a German accent.

The door closed, darkening the staircase again. From that point, I was dragged like a sack of potatoes by my cackling carriers, my backside bumping up each step.

As they hauled me into bed, rain beat down loudly on the roof, adding to the already spooky atmosphere. Jay and Betsy unpacked while I gazed around, exploring our bedroom by the glow of the table lamp. It had massive floor-to-ceiling windows, with ornate crown molding and casements and billowy sheer curtains. Whenever the lightning cracked, great gusts of wind filled the curtains, blowing them upward like giant ghosts.

"Woo-o-o-o," Jay menaced, crouching above me naked, having sneaked in from the bathroom. She whispered in her best vampirish tone, "I am cah-ming to get you!"

Just then, another flash struck, and the electricity went off. I let out a blood-curdling scream. A voice called out from down the hall, "Vat ist wrong? Vat ist it?"

We heard footsteps scurrying toward our room, then an urgent knock at the door. Jay panicked and grabbed a sheet to cover herself.

"Vat happened?" the man demanded when she answered. "Vhy did you screaming?" he asked, glowering at this gaggle of silly, noisy American girls who arrived way too late, with way too much luggage.

"Oh—," Jay stammered, clutching her sheet, "oh, it was just— it was Dracula."

The man looked skeptical. "Dra-cu-lah?"

"Yes, but—but it's okay now," she said. "It's over, he's gone." She waved at the rest of the room. "See? Gone. Really."

The man looked around carefully until he was satisfied. Then he glared at Jay, muttered a "Hmmph!" and shuffled back down the hall to bed.

My silly, naked sister jumped into bed next to me, while Betsy nestled into the bed by the open window.

"You know what we are?" I mused in the dark, under the sound of the falling rain. "We are crazy and silly. A bunch of crazy Americans."

"But we're having fun," came Betsy's reply.

"As long as Dracula doesn't get us," I said in a stage whisper.

That kicked off more giggling, which, in turn, gave way to a flood of shared childhood memories. Jay and I told Betsy about the werewolves that lived in Linda's closet and relived Daddy's stories about the Flying Dutchman. We reminisced about *The Creature from the Black Lagoon* and every other bogeyman that ever scared us, until finally we conked out. Despite the rain, the clunky furnishings, the gruff proprietor, and jokes about vampires, I felt utter joy with my sister and my good friend. The presence of God in it all was heavenly.

It was happening again. This brown-paper-bag moment—a girlish pajama party—had me living once more above my wheelchair.

When we got back home, however, something not so ordinary was waiting for me. *Joni* was going to be made into a full-length feature film.

"Wow, they want to do a *movie* about you?" Word spread quickly around Woodlawn and Sykesville, and people began to assume I now had it all together, that I never had bouts of depression or frustration anymore. After all, why else would the Billy Graham people want to do a movie about this girl in a wheelchair?

I couldn't blame anyone for thinking that way, but of course they were wrong. The truth was, I knew I would always struggle—I would always feel weak and needy of God. And that was okay. It was *supposed* to be that way. I was supposed to be dependent on him. I'd become convinced, thanks to Steve Estes, that only as I recognized my weakness and dependency on God would I gain his strength. And *that's* what they wanted to make a movie about.

What was *extra*-ordinary about it was they wanted *me* to play *Joni*.

The only thing I'd ever "starred" in was the Horse and Dog Club's production of *Oklahoma!* I'd been a witch in *Macbeth* in junior high, an Indian to Kathy's cowboy in the horse pageant, and an apple in my ballet recital. And many were the times I sold toothpaste to my bathroom mirror. And oh yes, I did pretend to be a beggar on the boardwalk. But that was it—who was I kidding? I didn't know anything about acting.

Yet if the real person plays the real part, I wondered, *might it have a real impact—for real people, with real problems? Lord, I don't know what to do.*

"I know if I say yes, it'll change my life. Forever," I soberly told Steve, and Jay, and Kathy, and my family and other friends. If I agreed, I was afraid it would mean the end of coyote moments under the moonlight or midnight moments in a railway station. It would mean the end of those ordinary, brown-paper-bag evenings sitting on the back porch and singing hymns with Jay. All the lazy, happy days on the farm would be gone. Moving to California for six months would mean a huge change. I thought about Daddy, as he now pushed seventy-eight years of age. I thought about my dear mother, whom I'd drawn so much closer to since my accident. *Do I really want my life to change? Would things ever be* ordinary *again?*

I was at a fork in the road. One path was well worn and predictable: I could stay on the farm, continue my classes at the University of Maryland, and maybe become a real artist in a few years. An ordinary path.

The other path was anything but ordinary. I wasn't even sure I could call it a path. I imagined it more as God standing on Pikes Peak, pointing to a faraway wilderness, and saying, "See that? Go blaze a trail." I had no idea what was out there. Where would it lead? After the movie *Joni*, would I be the same . . . Joni?

It was an extraordinary predicament. So I took it to the person I'd always shared my questions with.

Steve's response came in a letter postmarked "Columbia, South Carolina" where he was in Bible college.

"I've been able to lead you deeper into God's Word, Joni," he wrote. "But when it comes to the will of God with this one, I can't tell you what to do. . . .

"This one's up to you."

CHAPTER NINETEEN

This is what the Sovereign LORD, the Holy One of Israel, says: "In repentance and rest is your salvation, in quietness and trust is your strength."

Isaiah 30:15

Tanned hands grasp the edge of the raft, and in one graceful motion, the girl lifts her body out of the water. She reaches up and smoothes back her blond hair, wringing it in a tiny knot. She tugs at the elastic of her swimsuit and shakes the water from each leg. In another fluid movement, her knees bend, arms swing, and she pitches forward in a dive. Her body slices the surface of the water. She is under.

"Cut! That's a print!" the director yells from a rubber raft floating nearby.

His shout jars me back to reality. Or is reality the dive I just witnessed?

No, it wasn't real—because the girl who just dove is an actress, and I'm sitting on the shore, surrounded by cranes and crew members. I've signed on to the extraordinary and have come to California to play my part in the *Joni* movie.

Now it's my turn. I am to be placed in the water to pick up where the actress left off. Sitting on the beach, a breeze lifts the towel off my lap, exposing my leg bag and catheter. My corset is buckled around the outside of my suit, so I can breathe while I wait. The strap of my suit slips off my shoulder, but I can't pull it up.

"Okay, we're ready for Joni. Let's get her out here!"

The crew members position lights and reflectors, and the camera and sound equipment are floating by the raft. Paramedics lift and carry me out into the water, past the camera operators, sound men, and the director. Everyone looks a little nervous.

"Not to worry, you'll do fine," the property master calls from the shore.

"It'll be all over in a flash," the assistant cameraman waves from the crane above. The actress who just completed the dive wades closer and watches intently. The director tries to find a comfortable seat on the edge of the raft from where he can see everything.

The paramedics lay me on my back in the cool water. Shivering a bit, I float, lightly supported by their arms underneath. We're waiting for everyone else to get in position.

The camera starts rolling, and so does the sound deck. The director gives a nod, I take a giant breath, and the paramedics flip me over. I am face down, and in the underwater acoustics I can hear the director yell, "Action!"

I strain to hear the "Kathy" actress call my name. I hear her splashing, her muffled voice calling for me. But seconds tick by. The bay is cold and dark, and my lungs are hungry for air.

I'm scared. I almost start shaking my head—a prearranged signal to warn the paramedics that I need help. I try to hold on a little longer. *I can do this . . . no, I can't. I can't breathe. I need air!*

In the next second, "Kathy's" hands grab my shoulders and lift me from the water. I sputter and gasp for breath. I am genuinely struggling and frightened, but wait—oh yes, I'm supposed to act.

"Kathy . . . I can't move. I . . . I can't feel," I manage to gurgle my lines.

The actress says her lines, all the while trying to support my heavy body. She begins to carry me to shore. A camera crane follows. A sound man holding high a boom mike wades alongside us. People on shore take notes, and gaffers tilt reflectors.

"Cut! It's a print!"

The whole crew and cast heave a sigh of relief, me included. The paramedics lift me from the arms of "Kathy" and carry me back to my wheelchair, where Jay and Judy Butler—on loan from the Graham Association to help me—quickly pat me down with warm towels.

The scene has come and gone so fast. The reality we just filmed is now at a distance, recorded neatly on a strip of celluloid and encased in a can. The unit manager shouts, "Take ten," and the cooks from the catering truck set out snacks. Everyone gravitates toward doughnuts and coffee. I glance back at the now-lonely raft still anchored off shore, rocking slowly on gentle swells.

"Want a doughnut?" my mother asks, balancing her paper plate while giving me a hug. She and my father are here in southern

California, to watch me film the first couple of days of the *Joni* movie in the back bay behind Newport Beach. "Here," my mother urges one more time, "have a bite."

"Mom, I can't," I shake my head, "remember? They told me to lose weight."

The director is concerned I look too full-cheeked for the upcoming hospital scenes, and encouraged me to stay out of the sun and lay off doughnuts.

Over the next few days, I skip breakfast and only nibble lunch as we film the hospital scenes on the sound stage back in Burbank. After the wrap on Friday, Jay, Judy, and I start to make our way back to our little rented house seven or eight blocks away. But after a block or so, we realize we're coming up on a soup-and-salad restaurant.

"Let's do salads tonight," I pipe up.

Dinner that evening is lettuce and tomatoes with no salt or oil, half a baked potato with no butter, diet soda, and absolutely no dessert. From then on, we decide to crash-diet.

"Hey, I've got an idea," Jay says one Saturday, as we drive along Ventura Boulevard. "There's a T-shirt place. You know, where they print anything you want on the front?" She pulls to the curb to park, and she and Judy disappear into the shop.

I look in the front window at the shirt styles, colors, and slogans. In a short while, Jay comes out and announces, "Joni, you now have the perfect answer for those crew guys who want to stuff doughnuts into your mouth."

She holds up a T-shirt that reads DON'T FEED ME!

"But," she quickly adds, "you're not the only one who needs to lose weight here." She whips out another T-shirt from the bag. It reads OR ME.

Judy emerges from behind her, displaying a big grin and yet another shirt, this one reading NOR ME. And later, my friend Betsy, who's able to take Jay's place to help me for a while, gets a T-shirt too: I'LL TAKE THEIR SHARE.

The shirts do the trick. So does movie adrenaline. The pounds begin to melt off me, and I feel fit, lean, and energetic. Most of all, I feel focused.

I lie in bed one night, thinking about the extraordinary fork in the road I've taken. The windows in our little rented house are open, allowing the cool, wet scent of gardenia to float in from the yard. From my bed, I gaze at my empty wheelchair in the corner of the room. I ponder the times it has been my enemy, other times a prison, others a miry pit. Yet over the last couple of years, it has become a passport to adventure. And now, with my slacks draped over its back and my corset and armsplints resting on its seat cushion, it looks like an odd friend. It has been a stern schoolmaster from which I've learned so many lessons, tutoring me in patience and perseverance. Now God is about to use it to show others that they too can trust him in their weakness. Who knows how many thousands of people might see the movie and be uplifted. From my vantage point, the wheelchair appears to be a strange but beautiful—

"Gift," I say softly in the dark.

It has taught me many good things. So much so, I can't call my paralysis "suffering." *It's a gift*, I think—*isn't it, Lord? Like the Bible says, "For unto you it is given in the behalf of Christ, not only to believe on him, but also to suffer for his sake."* That wheelchair, parked there in the dark corner across the room, is a gift.

The next morning I pass up breakfast again and head to the studio early. We're filming more hospital scenes today.

"Hey, you're looking pretty good," the director smiles, admiring my thinning face and neck.

I'm pleased my diet is beginning to pay off. I calculate my calories for the day: a salad with no dressing, no cream in my coffee. No breakfast tomorrow, and no doughnuts at the studio. Maybe a light lunch and a small piece of grilled chicken for dinner tomorrow evening. *I'm not really hungry anyway*, I realize. I'm living on energy— so much nervous energy that I can hardly get to sleep that night.

The days blur quickly into weeks, and more weight drops off. "Hey, c'mon, you're making extra work for us," the wardrobe mistress kids. "We've got to take in all your shirts and jeans for these scenes." Secretly, I'm pleased.

I don't relax in the evening. Instead, I focus on learning the script for the next day. "Get a load of this!" Jay notes, reclining on the couch, crunching an apple while flipping through my script for the following week. "They've got a kissing scene in here, and guess whose name is on the call sheet." She rises to show me the page, wearing a Cheshire-cat grin.

The script describes the scene in less than half a page. I have a line or two. Cooper—the actor playing my boyfriend's part—has even less to say. The rest is action. Only a half page for all those memories when my boyfriend would come to Montebello State Hospital. There was no place for us to be alone—the solarium was filled with visitors, and the auditorium was off-limits. The only place we could escape from my six-bed ward was the elevator. We'd catch an empty one, press the third floor button, and flip the "stop" switch between floors. There we had plenty of privacy—until a nursing supervisor tracked us down.

"I'm glad they've included that in the script," I tell Jay. "It'll add a fun moment to all those other drab hospital scenes."

"Yeah, and you'll be having all the fun." My sister tousles my hair.

But will it really be fun? Doing a kissing scene in front of a movie crew, with an actor I hardly know? Cooper is nice, very nice, but I know nothing about him beyond his eight-by-ten-inch press photo tacked to my dressing room wall with those of the other cast members. I haven't kissed anyone in ages. That night, when I'm alone, I practice the best kisses I can remember—on my wrist.

In the following days, Cooper and I are thrown together frequently, acting our way through various scenes. Always, I wonder what he's thinking: *Has he read ahead in the script? Does he have the same silly thoughts I do about the elevator scene? Probably not. He's a Hollywood actor—he must kiss leading ladies all the time.*

The Day of the Kiss arrives, and we go on location at a local hospital. An elevator is rigged with stage lights, microphones, and electric cables. The large camera is anchored on a tripod in the corner. Cooper walks up behind me. "Think we'll fit in there?" He pops a breath mint into his mouth.

When all is ready, I'm pushed into a corner of the elevator. The director pulls Cooper next to me and briefs us on our few lines. "Remember now, you two are boyfriend and girlfriend. This is Montebello State Hospital, and it's 1968, okay? The rest will come naturally," he says, smiling.

Cooper carefully squeezes next to me, taking cues on how close he appears to be with me through the lens. The script lady grabs her clipboard and pulls up a stool to within a few feet of us. She is ready to record every word and movement for the editors, who will piece the film into one smooth scene.

"Action!"

The actor turns toward me, brushes my cheek with his hand, and tilts my chin. His lips touch mine and, out of nowhere, a jolt shoots through me. The foreignness of feeling lips on mine melts immediately, and I forget about the lights and the camera. The director calls for a cut, and Cooper breaks off his embrace, leaving me in mid-emotion. The script lady on the stool fans us with her script—it's getting warm under the lights.

"Boy, you kiss well," Cooper laughs, patting my hand.

"Okay, let's do another take," the director calls.

Once more, Cooper leans toward me, only this time I'm quicker to respond. I'm surprised at how easily I relax into his kiss. And we linger a bit longer past the "Cut!"

"We don't need another take, you two," the director breaks in, and everyone laughs. I glance at the cameraman and the script lady and nervously laugh along. Do they know? Do they realize that it wasn't all acting?

I purse my lips, and they feel hot. My insides surge with passion—another foreign feeling. In the next instant, guilt rises, and the rush vaporizes. I smile, still a little shaky—after all, God knows I haven't kissed anyone in a decade. The thought of never kissing anyone for another decade registers, and my smile quickly fades.

That night, in our little house, I yearn to toss and turn in bed, but I can't. I'm itchy and vexed and full of nervous energy. I keep rehearsing the kiss like a broken record, until a muscle in my neck begins twitching. I thrash my head on the pillow. All sorts of restless emotions bubble up: *When will I ever be kissed again? Will anyone ever love me? Really love me? Will I ever marry?*

My head feels like it's exploding. I begin to second-guess the idea that quadriplegia is a gift. Feelings of being trapped constrict my throat. I hate not being able to move, and the whirlwind of mixed emotions clash and keep me awake long past midnight. *Maybe it's the caffeine*, I wonder. *Or that I'm exhausted.* It's barely two months into the filming, and I'm dangerously thin and running on empty.

The director warned that once this movie began, we'd be on a greased slide—movie lingo for "fast, downhill, unstoppable action."

He was right. The first eight weeks have been a wild initiation, like living life in constant déjà vu.

The next day, I find a quiet moment in the studio courtyard to look at the script on my lap, opened to a new page of dialogue. I didn't write these lines, but they are mine, and somehow I'm acting—yet I'm not. The script is about my life ten years ago, but the scenes are much too close for comfort. In front of a camera, I seethe, "I can't stand not being able to use my hands!" Hours later in a restaurant, I'll find myself saying the same words when food falls off my bent spoon and onto the floor. Things like this, little slips of the mind and mouth, are beginning to happen too often. *I must remember why I'm here, why I'm doing this movie!*

Suddenly, the sun beating down on the courtyard begins to burn, and my skin prickles again with anxiety. The shade of a small potted tree nearby offers a little relief. I retrace my steps over the last year, thinking about Diana and Steve, the farm, Jay and Kathy and Linda, and I wonder, *Why do they feel so far away? Why am I filled with such anxiety?*

I have been praying, concentrating on the crew and actors and the people who'll be inspired by the film—but prayer for myself? Many Christians have warned me about the massive spiritual attack I would face by doing a movie in Hollywood, even a Christian one, but I haven't taken it very seriously. I haven't prayed for protection and covering as I might have. I realize I've assumed my past is so far behind me that it can't touch me. Now I'm not so sure. Am I to learn lessons about singleness and self-image all over again? I don't think I can—I'm so tired. And my Bible. For the past three weeks, I've barely opened it. Oh, I've rehearsed in my mind a few familiar verses on my way to the set each morning, verses memorized from long ago. But nothing new, nothing fresh. Lots of things are beginning to slip on the greased slide.

"Joni, got a minute?" Rob, the assistant director, jars me out of my thoughts. We're on the set, and I quickly erase the tiredness from my face and switch gears back to movie-making. Rob motions me into the screening room and spreads sheets of music on the carpeted floor. He sits at the piano and begins toying with a melody.

"What do you think of it for the close of the film?" he asks, and dives into a song:

> *Father, set my soul sailing like a cloud upon the wind,*
> *Free and strong to carry on until the journey's end.*
> *Each mile I put between the past and the future in your hand*
> *I learn more of your providence and find out who I am.*
> *I want to thank you for the gift of your Son,*
> *and for the mystery of prayer,*
> *and for the faith to doubt and yet believe that you're really there.*

Rob turns to me as he finishes the song. "The director wanted me to run it by you," he says. "Get your input."

"I like it," I mused, hesitating. "But, tell me more about that line— 'I want to thank you ... for the faith to doubt, and yet believe that you're really there.'"

Rob gathers the music sheets and taps them together on the piano. He smiles mysteriously and says, "Jon ...," then pauses as if deliberating whether to speak, "... you know, it *is* possible to doubt, and yet believe. Christians can doubt, you know. God is big enough to handle our questions."

I don't like his answer. It's a weakness to doubt. Doesn't the Bible say a man with doubts is like a wave of the sea, carried forward by the wind one minute and pushed back the next?

Yet as much as I hated to admit it, it described me perfectly. *That kissing scene with Cooper,* I brooded—I couldn't for the life of me shake the feeling of that kiss, even if it were fake. It felt like all those hot Friday nights with my high school boyfriend. And now I was rehearsing all those memories more than I wanted to admit. I was digging up every sensual pleasure I could and turning it over, time and again. So much so, I felt I was back in the dark bedroom with the drone of the air-conditioner, sinking further into the old pit.

I realize a distance is growing between the image I project and the turmoil I'm experiencing. I'm saying one thing and feeling another. I have it together in public, but alone I'm a basket case. It's like I'm *living* a movie, as if I'm made of celluloid, and about as shallow and fragile. Yet so many people have such big expectations, they have so much invested in this movie, I feel compelled to keep up a façade of peace and confidence in myself and in God. In reality, I'm shriveling on the inside, becoming disconnected from the outer Joni who's relating so well to everyone.

"Jay! Judy!" my voice is urgent. I've been awakened in the middle of the night by a pounding headache. I know something is desperately wrong with my body.

Jay stumbles into the room, "What is it?" She reads the panic in my eyes. "Oh, Joni, you're sweating buckets!"

"I think it's my catheter. It must be blocked or kinked or something." I breathe deeply, trying to control my heart rate. Jay shifts into high gear, throwing back my covers and turning me on my side. My bed is soaked. I'd drunk two quarts of water before bed, a necessary part of my nighttime routine. It's clear I haven't gotten rid of that fluid, and I'm in dysreflexia—a dangerous reaction in spinal-cord-injured people that can result in cerebral hemorrhage.

"I'm going to change it," Jay says, "we don't have time to fool around." She scrambles through the dresser for a new catheter, syringe, and scissors. My head is still hammering, and I know my blood pressure is shooting higher. I try not to think about things like a stroke.

Within minutes, Jay has the new catheter inscrted. "C'mon, c'mon. Drain bladder, drain," Jay urges nervously, scanning my clear urologic tubing for any flush of urine.

"What's happening? Why isn't it working?"

"I don't know, I don't know! I've checked everything. It must be a faulty catheter."

Now I read panic in Jay's face. She knows how dangerous this is. Doctors have warned us about it, and we've read about it in medical books. But this is the first time it has happened.

I feel like a tight band is squeezing my head. "Oh, God, forgive me, forgive me," I mumble, thinking I'm at death's door and need to make amends. "Please don't let this happen."

Jay fumbles for the phone and calls the movie's transportation captain. "Get the paramedics for Joni, quick!"

"Praise the Lord ... praise the Lord ...," I repeat, as much as my pain and labored breathing will allow. I wait—either for the paramedics to arrive or for the rising pressure to stop or for my brain to snap.

As I'm rushed to the hospital, some of the pressure across my skull subsides. My bladder must be draining. I know I'm soaking the sheets and the stretcher, but I don't care. I'm just happy not to have a stroke. In the emergency room, I'm fitted with a new catheter, and my blood pressure is monitored for an hour to make sure everything is stabilized.

By the time we're headed back to our own beds, it's 2:30 in the morning. I joke with Jay and Judy about looking bright-eyed in just a few hours, for the morning's shooting schedule.

"You can't be serious," Jay replies, stunned. "Don't you think you ought to take the day off? The production can wait. Nobody will mind, Joni."

I consider her concern, but I know I'll feel better if I don't lie around worrying about what could have happened. "Okay, let's compromise," I say. "We'll sleep in. We can ask the director if he'll let us start filming at noon."

Back in bed, I rush only a quick prayer of thanks to God. After all, I have got—I have *got*—to get to sleep for tomorrow's schedule. I fight off guilt and hope he'll understand.

Later that day, as we arrive on the set, the crew is unusually quiet. No "How ya doin' there, kid!" Obviously, they've heard about my middle-of-the-night emergency. I suppose I must look tired, so Judy floods my eyes with Visine to cover the redness. Because time is short, we move quickly to the first entry on the schedule: Scene 648, a scene near the end of the movie where I realize life would never be the same.

JONI: "I'm okay. I can still feel."

Cut to Jay.

JONI: *(continuing)* "And I guess I'm alive. I just wanna be alone for a while."

After the scene is shot, I curtly dismiss Judy's suggestion that I take a nap or an early break. She and Jay just don't understand. I've got a job to do—I can't let the cast and crew down. I can handle the pressure.

In fact, I appear to handle the pressure for the duration of the filming—more than six months. On the final day, the production company holds a big party to celebrate the final wrap. Trays of hors d'oeuvres are everywhere, along with bottles of sparkling apple cider and bowls of punch. Everyone is laughing and toasting the film's hoped-for impact on those who'll see it.

I heartily agree and take pains to thank each and every cast and crew member for their help. But inside, behind my smile, I'm utterly exhausted. I have expended every last ounce of energy, and I can't *wait* to go home. Not to the little rented house in Burbank, but to the farm in Maryland.

On the TWA flight back east, I lean against the headrest, thinking about what lies ahead. The movie is no longer a part of my life. Other people will take it from here: editors and color processors, musicians and technicians. Eventually, it will be handed to promoters and distributors. People will pray over its effect on viewers and that the movie's message, just as Billy Graham predicted, will change lives.

But for now, the veneer of that seventeen-year-old girl on the screen, and her long-ago experiences, must be pried off. Somehow, I have to pick up where I left off a year ago.

Hours later, the plane drops within sight of the snow-covered fields of western Maryland. Our farm will be a picture-postcard of white drifts shouldering up to the stone house, with its candlelit windows. Horses in their winter coats will be stamping their feet near the barn trough, and pine trees dressed in heavy white will frame the entire scene.

Jay drives us from the airport through the snow slush on the highway till we reach the country lane of the farm. Once inside the house, I glance around the corner into my study, where my art easel is still standing. My desk and books are just as I left them, along with a new stack of letters that need my attention. The mason jars holding my brushes and paints await my return. My sketch pad lies open on the easel. The page is blank.

It's the dead of winter, 1978, and oddly, I feel blank too.

The next day, I decide to reconnect myself with where I left off. Phone calls to friends don't produce anything—some are at work, others are still in school, some have holiday commitments. Steve Estes is still at college, and the weatherman predicts a cold rain for that evening.

I decide I need to get back to my art easel—it's been months since I've drawn anything. I'm rusty and out of practice, and as I begin sketching, everything looks wrong. Every time I try to press my pencil against the paper, my neck starts twitching violently. *Why can't I relax? What's wrong with me?*

A few days pass, and still I find it hard to draw. Can't seem to focus on reading either. One night in bed, I pass the time watching an old Burt Lancaster movie, *The Birdman of Alcatraz.* His story of life imprisonment strikes me, and a lump comes to my throat whenever one of his little birds flutters beyond the bars of the cell window. The camera focuses on the birdman's face as he watches his precious friends fly beyond the bars, then back in, then out again. His face is so easy to read: *Oh, how I wish I were free to fly away!*

Once again, a movie is hitting close to home—too close. Panic and claustrophobia grip my chest, and I have trouble breathing. The old horror of lying flat on my back and not being able to move seizes me.

"Jay, come quick!" I gasp.

Within seconds, Jay is there. "What is it?"

"Sit me up, sit me up!" Jay gets her arms around me and heaves me up to a sitting position.

"Press on my abdomen. Help me breathe!"

She does. A minute later, the flush and panic evaporate.

"What happened?" Jay asks, slowly laying me back down.

"I don't know," I breathe, "I just . . . feel like . . . I'm in . . . prison."

Jay stares at me for a while. She smooths back my hair from my forehead and says softly, "You're okay. Everything's going to be okay."

A few days later, I'm back at my easel again, but I'm having little if any success. I wonder if I've lost my talent or if I'm too worn out to ever be creative again. I mess up half a sketch pad, and my old nemesis, panic, begins to rise. I glare at my feeble, amateurish attempts, which mock me on the sketch pad. *I can't even draw a straight line!*

Suddenly, fear overwhelms me. "Jay—," I start to half-call my sister, but I can't get my breath. I spit the pencil from my mouth and stare wide-eyed at the shaky lines on the sketch pad. I feel I'm being pushed over a brink. The next thing I know, I'm lodging my shoulder against the easel and sweeping my arm across the desk.

Pad, pencils, books—everything goes flying, crashing against the wall and onto the floor. The noise alarms Jay, who is vacuuming in the next room.

"I can't draw! I can't do anything!" I scream hysterically. Jay stands dumbfounded, looking at the mess on the floor, her hands and eyes open in a question.

I shake my head, sobbing, "I don't know who I am ... I don't know who I am ... I don't know who I am...." My nose runs, and, helplessly, I look at my sister and repeat, "I don't know who I am...."

The summer of 1979 seemed to sweep in on the scent of apple blossoms. June isn't apple blossom time in Maryland, but it felt like it was. I was back to being the sapling, thin and green but growing a little stronger each day. Every once in awhile, when I gained a pound or two, I could feel the knife-point of the graft, cutting deeper into the damp wood of my soul.

Doing the movie hadn't been the smooth, easygoing process I had thought it would be. I would realize much later that I'd been seriously depressed during the final months of filming. But that was then. I was gaining back weight now and getting rest. Sometimes I found myself humming an old hymn, "Jesus, I am resting, resting in the joy of what Thou art.... I am finding out the greatness of Thy loving heart." Oh, how I needed rest. I came to know the words of Isaiah as my clearest need: "This is what the Sovereign LORD, the Holy One of Israel, says: 'In repentance and rest is your salvation, in quietness and trust is your strength.'"

With rest came repentance. A lot of sucker shoots had sprung up during the year the movie was made, and just as my Uncle Don would do in his orchard, I took inventory of what was worth keeping and what needed to be cut away. Things like neglect of God's Word ... trifling in prayer ... cherishing a puffed-up idea of my own importance ... most of all, feeling I could run my life on cruise control. I repented of it all and asked God to give me his strength.

The *Joni* movie went on to enjoy a life of its own. It would be translated into fifteen languages and viewed by millions around the world. As people witnessed the struggle of a young girl coming to terms with her hardships and gaining trust in God, hundreds of thousands would embrace Jesus Christ for the first time.

That news would humble me tremendously. I knew it was all God's doing, and certainly not mine; I was still learning the very lessons I wrestled with in the film. So, whenever I was asked about doing a follow-up to the movie, I replied, "No, there will be no _Joni II_, or _Revenge of Joni_, or _Son of Joni_, or _Beneath the Planet of Joni_." I was glad I did . . . one milestone I would never revisit.

There was, however, a new milestone I reached—one as significant as any other in my twenty-nine years. It was summed up in the line from Rob's song, the line I originally didn't like: "I want to thank you . . . for the faith to doubt, and yet believe." I may not have understood it at the time, but I did now. _Lord, thank you that you're big enough to handle not only my doubts, but my sin. Bless you for forgiving me._

Another line in Rob's song completed the new milestone. It said, "Each mile I put between the past and the future in your hand, I learn more of your providence _and I find out who I am_." I'd found out the answer to my sobbing plea.

Something in me had died during that movie-making process. It was the Joni I thought I was—having it all together spiritually, in control, able to handle pressure. Once I died to that Joni—once the sapling was cut back to the basic root—I discovered something else: the closer I got to Jesus, the more I found out who I am, good and bad. The more I found out who I'm supposed to be.

Lo and behold, it's the real Joni. Not a fake one, not a movie image, but a real person. In quietness and in rest, the "Joni" I was supposed to be slowly began to unfold. "Each mile I put between the past and the future in your hand, I learn more of your providence _and I find out who I am_."

I find out who God wants me to be. Who Daddy always hoped I'd be, as he spoke softly to me through mosquito netting . . . who my mother hoped I would be, as she tucked me in bed under the three angels. The answer to my cry "Who am I?" seemed to come on a scented breeze from a pine grove or in a whiff of apple blossoms in the spring, whispering this truth: _For you died, and your life is now hidden with Christ in God._

Who I am . . . is hidden in Christ.

The chair is a gift after all. It's still a passport to adventure. And the best is yet to be.

The
GOD
I LOVE

Part Four

CHAPTER TWENTY

If the Spirit of him that raised up Jesus from the dead dwells in you, he that raised up Christ from the dead shall also quicken your mortal bodies by his Spirit that dwelleth in you.

Romans 8:11 (KJV)

Didn't she know she would die on that ice floe?" I asked innocently. I couldn't shake the image of the old Eskimo woman, sitting in the midst of the swirling snowstorm.

Daddy had taken my sisters and me to see a movie called *The Savage Innocents*, but none of us knew it would contain such a troubling scene. An aging Eskimo grandmother was too feeble to migrate with her family across the snow-covered wilderness. She was left behind to die.

"She just knew it was her time, honey," my father tried to explain. I held tightly to Daddy's hand as we walked back to the car. I wondered how many years he would have before he'd be as old as that Eskimo.

We talked about it on the way home, and although I can't remember my father's words, I knew that if he had been that weathered old Indian, Daddy would have chosen the same path. We—his Eskimo children—would have begged and pleaded, but just like the woman in the movie, he would have folded his arms, grunted, and sat down on the ice floe. That was the way he was—never afraid of death, not even when he faced it on Pikes Peak.

I forgot about that Eskimo movie, until the spring of 1990. The image of the old woman had been our long-feared nightmare while growing up, and my sisters and I had always pushed it from our minds. Yet now our father, at the age of ninety, was dying. How could Daddy be this old? When did it happen? *1990*—where have the years flown to?

It was sunset and evening star. He was about to see his Pilot face-to-face; he was about to cross the bar.

It meant twilight and evening bell for a million memories, all of which Daddy was about to take with him...

Remember when I sat at your feet with my coloring book, and tried to copy the way you'd paint? How your hands lifted me on top of Thunder? The times at the beach when you'd snap me into my orange life vest, so I could ride the crests of the waves? The way you said "Laard" and harmonized on "Let the Lower Lights Be Burning"?

I remember the night I was awakened by a cacophony of buzz-buzzing coming from the trees beyond my bedroom window. Daddy and I leaned on the sill as he beamed his flashlight out into the dark. There, I witnessed the wondrous migration of the seven-year locusts, struggling up out of the deep earth and climbing the trees to look for a mate. "It only happens once every seven years," Daddy marveled.

Memories like these were already fading like photographs. Now I was afraid their images might all but disappear with him. *Oh, this can't be true. My daddy will soon be gone.*

Our beautiful, rustic house—the home of painted angels and a thousand echoes of little feet playing hide-and-seek—was put up for sale. The gift my father had built for the family, the great timber-and-brick home of massive fireplaces and vaulted ceilings, of bear rugs and backdoor dinner bells, the driveway on which we sketched hopscotch in chalk—all of it would be gone. It was simply too difficult for my mother to care for Daddy in that huge, rambling house.

Mother moved with Daddy to Florida, where he resided in a cheery little nursing home, and she stayed at Uncle Eddie's house a couple of blocks away. Mom walked from my uncle's house every morning to care for Daddy's needs and returned at night only after he was put to bed. My sisters and I often visited them, frequently stretching the visits to help out however we could.

My mother did exactly what she had done for her mother, for Aunt Lee when she had cancer, for Kelly, and for me during my months in the hospital. She bound herself to Daddy, and to the nursing home staff, through a thousand filaments of compassion and sympathy. If Bingo was on the afternoon rostrum, she made sure every resident was invited. When Sunday afternoon church service was on the slate, Mother managed to triple the attendance. No one was more deserving of the Volunteer of the Year plaque she received from the staff director.

But there was nothing my mother could do to stave off the encroaching specter of death. Daddy's withered, bony frame was but a shadow of his former strapping physique, and a constant series of small strokes continued to claim his bright countenance. Only once in a while did his undaunted spirit sparkle from his blue eyes.

As I sat by his bedside, looking at him over the guardrail, I was so grateful for all the times he cheered me on in the geriatric ward of the state institution, when I thought I was doomed. He would stand by my bed, white-knuckling the guardrail, and whisper to me with tears welling in his eyes, "Joni, every day you're getting better and better and better. . . ."

In my heart of hearts, I'd hoped he was right. I hoped the doctor had told him something I didn't know, that soon the paralysis would wear off and I really would get better. From a pragmatist's point of view, I never did. But that's not the way my daddy chose to look at it. In retrospect, he was right. Every day I did get better—maybe not on the outside, but on the inside.

"Oh, Johnny," I whispered to my father, "I wish you could get better."

I watched the sheet covering him rise and fall with his heavy breathing and thought of all the other times he cheered me on after my accident. He was so proud the night the *Joni* movie premiered at the Baltimore Civic Center in 1979, and he couldn't believe he got the chance to meet Billy Graham. He cheered me on as I gained my strength back and, with Judy's help, started a ministry to handle the deluge of letters, invitations, and inquiries from all over the world. We called the fledgling organization *Joni and Friends*.

He gave me the thumbs-up when I moved into a home in southern California and set up an office nearby. He was glad to see me taking art lessons from Jim Sewell, the art director on the *Joni* movie. He applauded me when I announced I was learning how to drive a van. And he hardly blinked an eye when I said, "And it doesn't have a steering wheel!" Most of all, I was grateful he had lived long enough to walk me down the aisle to give me away.

No one was more supportive than my father and mother when, in 1980, I introduced them to a young man named Ken Tada, whom I'd met at church. They liked him but couldn't help wondering what about this strong, handsome man drew him to their wheelchair-bound daughter.

In the summer of 1981, we decided to go camping together to get to know one another better. Dad and Mom watched this Japanese-American Ken-guy like a hawk as we packed up my van. With Ken at the wheel—or rather, the joystick—we climbed out of the San Fernando Valley, onto the plateau of the north desert, past the little town of Mojave, out of the hot plains, and into the back side of the cool High Sierras. When we arrived at Mammoth Mountain, we found our little campground nestled in its shadow. We would pitch our tents between two turquoise-blue lakes at the base of a grove of towering Ponderosa pines.

Daddy's arthritis kept him from driving the tent pegs, so he sat at a distance and watched Ken skillfully swing the flat head of his hatchet. Later, I wheeled beside my father as we traversed the campgrounds foraging for firewood and pine cones. My wheelchair made the perfect truck to haul small branches, and Daddy smiled when he noticed Ken had caught up with us to help.

"Would you like to go fishing on the lake tomorrow?" Ken asked. Daddy beamed. For all his outdoorsy adventures, my father had never really fished much.

The next morning, Ken rented two boats at the Lake George boathouse—one for my parents and Judy, and one for the two of us. It took only minutes for him to wedge an old beach chair into the bow, and my father's eyes widened as he watched Ken ably lift me from my chair at the water's edge and set me in the boat. We pushed off in our boats and motored slowly toward the shady edges at the far end of the lake, where we'd heard the fish were big and fat.

Once we picked a spot, Ken chained the bows of our boats together. Then he began to hook and bait two rods, using words like "casting" and "reeling." My parents looked at him as though he were speaking a foreign language. He readied a rod for me too and cast its line far out into a shady spot. "Here," he said, lodging it in my beach chair. "This is for your fish."

"But I didn't cast. You did."

"Yeah, and you won't reel in the fish either. But you're still holding and watching, and that'll make it yours."

Our two boats drifted together on the wind-rippled lake, as we chatted and drank sodas. Then, all of a sudden, Mother shattered the calm with a shriek. A fish was splashing and fighting on her line, and she turned away to hide her eyes. Ken grinned and gently explained how to reel it in. Mom obediently cranked in the line, still refusing to look. Ken netted the trout for her, and we tried to conceal our excitement so the distant fishermen who looked our way wouldn't think we were novices.

I was designated Keeper of the Fish. Ken strung the trout by their gills through a metal clothespin and snapped it to my arm-splint. I dangled my hand in the water, watching my captive fish swim alongside our drifting boat. I felt sorry for them and gave them each a name, hoping to persuade Ken to have steaks for dinner instead of fish fillets.

Nothing was more relaxing than hearing the water softly lap against the boat and feel its gentle rocking. Every once in a while, I found myself staring at Ken, who sat up front, focused on the water's surface where his line disappeared. His thick black hair framed dark-brown almond eyes. His smile was ready and his back strong. Judging from the way he'd handled this camping expedition thus far, he was patient too. His character seemed as clean clear through as this lake. *He knows the Lord. And he loves my family. Hmm.*

We had been dating a little over a year. This was the man who first caught sight of me when I spoke at a Young Life banquet near Los Angeles and asked me out to dinner. When I was confined to bed for a month because of another pressure sore, Ken set up my art easel over my bed so I could keep painting. And it was Ken who talked me into riding the Matterhorn at Disneyland—he set me in the bobsled, hopped in behind, grabbed me around the waist, and that's all I remember. My eyes remained shut, and I screamed the entire ride. Now he looked for me in the gallery of Racquetball World whenever he was in a tournament. We had forged a fast friendship, and lately, only lately, he had been dropping hints of marriage.

"Okay, everybody, I'm going for a second one!" Mother was beginning to get into this fishing adventure and cast her line for another trout. Meanwhile, Ken and I noticed that my father, with his back turned to us, seemed preoccupied. Occasionally, we heard him mumbling and looked up to see him shaking his head. Finally, Ken stepped into their boat to investigate and, in dismay, held up a tangle of knots looped around Daddy's reel. My left-handed father had reeled in his line backward, and Mother, Judy, and I burst into laughter that rang across the water. Ken shook a finger at Daddy and proceeded to untangle the mess as we broke for lunch, enjoying sun, scenery, and sandwiches.

An hour passed as Ken worked steadily and patiently, pulling a bit through here and looping a line there. Mother insisted that he stop and relax, but he was committed to his task. And the more I watched him at work, the more impressed I became.

After we caught a mess of fish, Ken reached over and unhooked the chain that linked the two boats. As our vessels drifted apart, my parents and Judy hardly noticed—they were still casting and reeling and recounting fish stories.

Ken took a seat near the stern, slid the paddles from their sleeves, and gently rowed until we were some distance away from the others. Then he laid the oar across his knees and let our boat drift. We turned slowly in the water until Ken's head eclipsed the late afternoon sun, making a golden glow around his face. I couldn't see his features, only his dark glasses and the white of his smile. He cut an appealing figure in his fishing vest, khaki shorts, and the red bandanna knotted around his neck.

"Want to hear something I've been writing in my head?" I ventured.

Ken nodded.

"It's a song. I'm not finished with it yet, but it goes—"

> *Oh the High Sierras, white-capped spires of age,*
> *Painted alpine meadows, paintbrush, pine all praise*
> *the God who made you, and your redwood trees.*
> *Speak your mystery to me, High Sierras, just for me.*

"That's beautiful," Ken whispered. Then, without missing a beat, he said, "I love you, Joni."

I smiled but didn't answer.

"Ever since I saw you over a year ago, that time you spoke at that banquet."

I raised my arm from the water, dragging the line of fish for him to see.

"Don't change the subject," he said.

I plopped my arm back into the water.

"Well, you know what?" I said. "I love you too."

Now it was his turn to smile and say nothing. We let the boat drift, enjoying the quiet and each other's company. After a few moments, Ken spoke up.

"It could work, you know."

I looked up questioningly.

"I've been watching Judy help you all these months. I know I can do the things she and others do for you."

"You're talking marriage?"

"Our life together—" he began.

The thought gave me goose bumps! I noticed it did for him too.

"—it could be a real ministry for the Lord." He leaned forward and squeezed the toes of my moccasins.

I shook my head cautiously.

"You just said you loved me."

"Yes, but . . . ," I nervously smiled, "well, marriage is a big step. I mean, I'm a quadriplegic. I can't use my hands or legs. There's the disability, and . . . and . . . and Joni and Friends, and . . ."

It was the sort of conversation you dream about having all your life, and suddenly, when it arrives, you stumble as if you've never given marriage a thought. Handling marriage would be one thing— handling it with quadriplegia would be another entirely. It meant not relief but being plunged deeper into the thick of things. Sacrificing over and over. Thinking of the other constantly, day in and day out. Having to find things we could truly *do* together.

I didn't want a "yes" to Ken to be dependent on finding out the answers to all these concerns. It wouldn't be a "yes" at all if it had strings attached.

Summer faded into fall, and one rainy afternoon that November of 1981, Ken walked into my art studio. He paused to admire the pot of red geraniums I was painting. Red was everywhere—tubes of red, stains on rags, tinted brushes, color tests tacked on the wall, the oil on the canvas. He put his hand on top of my easel, sighed, and turned to me.

"Joni, will you marry me?"

Suddenly, the room glowed with the aura of all the warm, red color. The phenomenon almost took my breath away before I could answer Ken, "Yes."

For the next eight months, until July 3, 1982, my every waking moment was spent preparing for marriage. Bridal showers were a part of it, and the first one began with me feeling awkward in my bulky wheelchair among so many delicately wrapped gifts and dainty decorations. Everything was piled high around my foot pedals, and two little daughters of friends had the honor of opening each present for me.

People had given pots and pans, a coffee grinder, casserole dishes, and an ironing board. As one of the little girls struggled to lift a new iron out of its carton, she used both hands to hold it high for everyone to see. Then she turned to me and asked sincerely, "How can you use this, Joni? Your hands don't work."

The room fell quiet.

"Well, I'll use that iron the same way I'll use those oven mitts over there."

"How's that?" she said, setting down the heavy iron.

"By borrowing someone's hands. Like I'm borrowing yours to open these gifts."

She thought for moment, until she seemed satisfied. As she turned to the next box wrapped in lacy paper, a universal sigh of relief went up. Soon the little girl held up an exquisite, long, black-satin negligee. Again, everyone became quiet.

I sensed their unease. "Don't worry, ladies," I quipped, "other hands will take care of this one." A roar of laughter filled the room.

I realized this was monumental. Somehow God had brought me not only to embrace him and his will but even other people's fears.

After the gifts were opened and punch and cookies were served, it was time for me to respond. I glanced at these wonderful women—new friends I'd met since moving to California after the movie—and I decided to make a confession.

"When I was first injured, back fifteen years ago, I dreaded the idea of marriage. I think one of my biggest fears back then—this is going to sound silly—was having a bridal shower. I was so afraid of sitting in front of a room full of ladies and not being able to open my own gifts. Not even being able to untie the ribbons."

At that point, punch glasses stopped being collected. Several girls wandered in from the kitchen. I stared at the carton of crumbled wrapping paper by my wheelchair.

"I was so scared that if I got an iron, everyone would know I couldn't use it. But as the Bible promises, 'Perfect love casts out fear.' And I can say I feel such love from you—from every one of you."

I looked around at Ken's mother and sister, at my new California friends, at my sisters, and a few high school pals from back east.

"*And,*" I added, glancing at the black negligee, "I can love what God is doing in my life, whether my hands hold an iron or not."

Ours was a wedding unlike any other, I'm sure. It started in the church bridal salon, with my girlfriends laying me down on a couch. They had to shift my paralyzed body this way and that in order to pull my voluminous gown over me. After I was corseted, buttoned, and lifted back into my wheelchair, my gown was gingerly draped over a thin wire mesh that covered my wheels, so the fabric wouldn't get caught in the spokes.

When the organ music began, I wheeled toward the door, stopping for a moment in front of a full-length mirror. I looked a little like a float in the Rose Parade.

The glass doors of the sanctuary opened, and I positioned myself at the top of the aisle, breathing deeply to steady my nerves. Daddy looked resplendent in his gray morning suit and a Windsor cravat. I'd never seen him so formally attired, nor he me. He smiled in a way that told me, *You're not my little pal anymore, not my cowgirl. And I'm glad!*

I leaned toward his ear, and above the organ music I explained in a loud whisper that I would wheel slowly so he could keep up with me. He handed Judy one of his crutches and held onto the armrest of my chair for support.

"You're marrying a good one, honey-girl," he told me.

From my vantage point, I could see John MacArthur, the pastor of our church, and Steve Estes standing up front. Steve had flown all the way out from Pennsylvania to help officiate, and I grinned as I recalled images of our fireside Bible studies, flipping and sipping and howling our delight for God. *That was ten years ago,* I realized, *and here he is, a pastor, married, his quiver full of kids. Now he's ready to pronounce Ken and me "husband and wife."* At any other event, I would have done the coyote yowl.

Just before the wedding march began, I looked down at my gown. *Aauugh!* I groaned—I had wheeled over the hem and left a huge, greasy tire mark. It didn't help that my dress hung clumped and uneven. And even though my chair was spiffed up, the wheels and gears were still visible through the wire mesh. My bouquet of daisies was off center on my lap, because my hands couldn't hold them. I was not a picture-perfect bride.

I hated greasy marks. Old battles started rushing back, as I was reminded of stains on my soul. I'd often wondered, even after the incredible events of the past few years: *does Christ see anything lovely in me?* I knew I had been cleansed from my sin, but I was still unclean. I was justified before God, but I had miles of sanctification to go before I slept. I was in his household but far from home. My eyes had been opened, but like everyone else, I saw only through a glass darkly. I felt so—*unworthy*. And I felt that especially now, as I sat at the top of the aisle.

As my last bridesmaid finished her walk, the organ pipes crescendoed, and I inched my chair closer to the last pew, wanting to catch a glimpse of Ken. Suddenly, I spotted him down front, standing at attention and looking tall and elegant in his tuxedo. I looked down, my face hot and my heart pounding. It was a flush of nerves I'd never felt before. When I looked up again, I saw him craning to look up the aisle, to find me. Our eyes met, and—it was amazing—from that point, everything changed.

How I looked no longer mattered. I forgot all about my wheelchair. Grease stains? Flowers? No longer did I feel ugly or unworthy. The love in Ken's eyes washed it all away. I was the pure and perfect bride—*his* bride. That's what he saw, and that's what changed me.

On the way to the airport, I asked my husband if he'd seen the grease marks on my gown. I wondered if he felt funny that his bride had been far from Emily Post picture-perfect. "Did you notice my daisies had slipped off my lap? And the tire track on my hem?"

He shook his head. "No, I just thought you were gorgeous. Really."

He didn't know it, but Ken had just raised me to a higher plain. That day, the day of our wedding, he helped me get a little closer to heaven.

And so had my wheelchair. Once again, my chair was turning out to be a strange but beautiful gift, my passport to adventure. It taught me it's not half-bad to feel unworthy, even on your wedding day. And one day—on that bright, eternal morning—all the stains of earthly life will be purified away, just by one look from God's eyes. We'll be transformed forever by his gaze upon us. And my face will flush, my heart will pound, and it will be more than I ever dreamed of, more than I ever longed for.

"Oh, Daddy, do you remember my wedding day years ago?" I said softly, trying not to wake him. Nurses walked quietly down the hallway, and occasionally someone made an announcement over the intercom.

"You handed me over to Ken. You gave your princess to another king. All the dreams and hopes you had for me—they're coming true."

I sat there for a long time, telling him about Ken and all that was going on at Joni and Friends, the people I was meeting, the places I was traveling to. "We have an actual staff now, Daddy," I whispered, "and in a few months we're holding the first International Congress on the Church and Disability."

Daddy didn't respond.

"And next month, I'm going to the White House. Can you believe it?"

I realized my father, even if he were awake, probably couldn't connect with any of my adventures.

"Thank you for helping me find the center. For showing me how to be a lower light. I'm letting the light shine, Daddy. I'm showing the way to safety."

I gently began the old hymn that Anna Verona had taught her boys—the one Daddy, in turn, had taught his girls around the campfire. And while I sang, Cap'n John softly snored.

In a span of less than two weeks, his health had failed dramatically. My mother and sisters had camped on couch pillows by his bedside, trying to keep him comfortable. Then, on May 17, 1990, I received a phone call from Kathy: our father had finally crossed the bar.

Her voice was filled with sorrow yet laced with joy. "You won't believe what happened, Joni. For the first time in days, Daddy turned to Mom and opened his eyes really wide. They've been rolled back in his head for so long, but now they looked so blue. I mean, a blue I've never seen. And his cheeks were no longer sunken. Suddenly, his ashen skin became rosy and his face full.

"And then he smiled—oh, my goodness—the sweetest smile I've ever seen. He kept looking past us, as if he were seeing something beyond where we were standing. He gave a big, full smile again, and then he languished for a moment in this—this incredible *glow*. It must have been the glow of God's presence because then, he was gone. I tell you, Joni, it was a miracle."

Afterward, my mother, sisters, and a recreational therapist-friend held hands around his bed and sang the Doxology. Then my sisters canvassed the hallways, telling people, "Daddy just went to heaven to be with the Lord. Daddy has gone to heaven!"

Weeks later, after Daddy's funeral, Kathy, Mother, and Ken and I took a trip to Colorado Springs. As our van crested the hill above town, we caught our first sight of that massive, imperious mountain range with peaks resting like silent giants. We found the turn-off to the old dirt road that leads to the top of Pikes Peak. At the crest, Ken helped me out of the van and into my wheelchair.

The day was bright and blue, and we could see the tops of clouds below us. The view hadn't changed since we were children—the Sawtooth Range was still to the south and Denver to the north. And there, near the little trading post, rested the mound of stones that Johnny Eareckson had missed by just a few feet in that blizzard of 1933.

The four of us found a private place near the edge of a cliff. Thousands of feet beneath us spread green-and-golden valleys, patchworked by sun and cloud-shadows. The icy wind whipped our hair, and Kathy and Mother held onto their wool hats. An eagle hangglided nearby as Ken opened the Book of Common Prayer and read:

> Forasmuch as it hath pleased Almighty God, in his wise providence, to take out of this world the soul of our beloved father, John Eareckson, we therefore commit his body to the

ground; earth to earth, ashes to ashes, dust to dust; awaiting the Resurrection at the appearing of our Lord Jesus Christ; at whose second coming . . . the earth and the sea shall give up their dead; and the corruptible bodies of those who sleep in him shall be changed, and made like unto his own glorious body. . . .

Ken turned to a verse from Romans and read us this assurance: "If the Spirit of him that raised up Jesus from the dead dwells in you, he that raised up Christ from the dead shall also quicken your mortal bodies by his Spirit that dwelleth in you."

He closed the book. "Okay, Mom," he said, "it's your turn."

With that, my mother stepped closer to the edge. The wind whipped strands of her gray hair, and she faltered a little. Yet the cold did not diminish her smile—nor her tears. Ken produced a small vial, opened it, and tapped some of my father's ashes into my mother's open palm.

She turned toward the cliff, paused, and threw the ashes to the wind. I watched with teary eyes as a gust carried my father's ashes up and beyond the clouds. Ashes to ashes, and dust to dust.

"That's the last hike I take with you, Cap'n John," Mother said in a confident voice. Never one to fear the future, she shielded her eyes and waved good-bye.

CHAPTER TWENTY-ONE

Now the Lord is the Spirit, and where the Spirit of the Lord is, there is freedom.

2 Corinthians 3:17

A re you going to use these little packets of butter?"

It was an odd question for Jan, our Dutch contact, to ask. We had nearly finished breakfast, and Ken and I, along with Jay and Judy, were hurrying to leave our Amsterdam hotel. We were bound for the airport and a journey that would take us across several borders into Romania. There we expected to meet government officials on behalf of Joni and Friends, but the true focus of our visit was the Christian church and people with disabilities.

Our trip had all the makings of a hazardous plan, for this was 1982 and the Communist dictator Nicolae Ceausescu still held a vicious grip on the country.

"How about these little jars of jelly?" Jan asked, pulling a few from the basket on our table.

"What's with the butter and jelly?" Ken said, wiping his mouth.

Our Dutch friend paused for a long moment, then smiled. "You'll see," he answered. "Just be sure to stuff a few in your pockets before we leave the restaurant."

I was more worried about passports than packets of butter, but Ken grabbed the little packets and jars and jammed them deep into my handbag. Before we left, we managed to scrounge a few hotel soaps, and once at the airport we bought a small can of Dutch coffee.

As we boarded the old Aeroflot plane, we were transported back into an old James Bond movie. The flight attendants' uniforms were straight out of the sixties, and instead of hearing the usual Muzak on the intercom, we located our seats to the tune of Elvis Presley's "Heartbreak Hotel." Safety procedures were nil, and we noticed a stewardess stuffing cartons of Kent cigarettes into one of the overhead bins.

"What do you bet that's for the black market," Ken whispered.

As we flew over Germany and Austria, we marveled at the glorious, green landscape dotted with tidy villages and neat hedgerows. Halfway through our flight, however, the world below changed to rusty brown. Even from an altitude of 15,000 feet, we could tell the towns were poor and unkempt, the roads mere dirt and badly rutted.

"We just crossed the Iron Curtain," I realized.

A flight attendant glared at us.

"Shhh," Judy cautioned, "we're not supposed to say that."

As the sun set on the West, we landed in Bucharest. Gazing out the window, Ken could hardly contain himself as he spotted armored vehicles and soldiers carrying guns on the tarmac.

"Sir, you must put away your camera," the stewardess said gruffly. "No photos are allowed."

Our plane taxied up to the terminal—an old, gray, rundown building. I had to be carried down flights of steps, after which we had to haggle with immigration officials, whom we later learned were looking for a bribe. We found our luggage on a rusty old rack, and once outside the airport, we gazed out on a different world.

Our recent time in Holland seemed like a planet away—America, another galaxy. We were in Romania, a ravaged and denuded land, where the grand old boulevard leading to Bucharest was potholed and populated not so much with cars but horse-and-carts, their drivers slump-shouldered and sad. Old-fashioned streetlights lined the boulevard, but not one was lit. The only lights in the city, it seemed, were the stoplights at intersections, but not all of them worked. The few people we saw appeared like ghostly shadows in gray garb. So did the buildings.

As we drove down the boulevard, I imagined the city in the 1800s, when it was the glorious toast of central Europe. A melody began to play in my head, sounding a bit like a Strauss waltz, and I pictured viscounts and countesses passing by in sleek black carriages pulled by high-stepping horses. I saw ladies wearing bustled dresses, strolling down the sidewalk with parasols. The small parks behind ornate iron fences were filled with picnicking patrons and children at play, students reading books together, and lovers sitting under the trees. I imagined yellow and red flowers and lavender carts on street corners and men toasting each other in outdoor cafes.

Yet now, street after street revealed these same parks and grand old baroque buildings to be crumbling and crusted with dirt. Trash and stray dogs were everywhere. A literal cloud, thick and dismal, hung over the once-magnificent capital, heavy with the smell of leaded fuel and coal dust.

We were on our way to the Intercontinental Hotel, where we'd been ordered to stay. We assumed it would be a nice, well-lit place that might live up to its name. But it too was another drab, dirty building, built only in the fifties. We were given a room on the second floor near the end of the hallway, and it was nice enough. But we had been warned ahead of time by Jan to be careful before talking in the room. We first had to turn on both water faucets in the bathroom, so the noise of the filling tub would prevent bugging devices from picking up our voices. Even in our own room, we couldn't let slip a name of any of our Christian contacts.

As Judy started to remove my coat, Ken whispered, low and urgent, "Look!" We watched as he tried to move the mirror on the wall above the dresser. It didn't budge. He tried to peek behind it with no success. He stepped aside, out of its view, and mouthed to us silently, "It's a part of the wall."

We looked at each other, stunned. Then we remembered the strange door to the room next to ours: it didn't have a regular room number. We realized we were, indeed, in another world—a world full of unseen eyes and ears.

The next day we were up early to meet with staff from the American embassy, as well as leaders from the Romanian departments of health and education. "We want to take you to a school for rehabilitation of children," the Romanians said officiously. During the drive we peppered them with questions but couldn't seem to break through their cloak of suspicion and secrecy.

When we arrived, we were escorted into a roomful of teenagers dressed in blue uniforms, sitting erect and in silence. One showed me his leg brace, and another his amputated arm. Judy, Jay, Ken, and I glanced at each other, mystified. These were the disabled?

"And now we shall go to another rehabilitation center."

When we pulled up to this one, I noticed high curbs and steps to the front entrance. "How can this be a place for disabled people?" I whispered.

A large, brawny man was waiting for us—he had been assigned to carry me up the steps. Inside, the dingy hallways were lit by only a few dangling light bulbs. We were taken to one of the many white-tiled side rooms and shown a few old-fashioned prosthetic legs and braces. In another, a forties vintage film about war-wounded soldiers projected onto a sheet nailed to the wall. I kept straining to look down the long hallways, thinking, *Where are the people in wheelchairs?*

Toward the end of our visit, a few disabled people, one in a chair and the others on crutches, were ushered into the hallway to meet us. Try as I could to strike up a cheerful conversation, they were timid and fearful. It was obvious everyone couldn't wait for us to get out of there.

We drove away in silence. I leaned on my elbow and gazed out the window again, thinking back to the lessons I'd learned about Communism so many years before in Modern and Contemporary History. I remembered how afraid I was of the people behind the Iron Curtain, as if they were of a different race, all stalwart and strong, like those imposing Leninist sculptures of farmers holding sickles and workers wielding hammers. I was sure they were ready to stream across the border to suppress the West, if given the chance.

That evening, we climbed into the little red car of our host contact, Pastor Sarac. He had invited us to dinner at his home, and I was to speak at his church afterward. We took a circuitous route, until we finally drove through two large wooden gates and into a small courtyard. His home was on the left, his Baptist church next door.

I was still amazed by the day's events. I asked Pastor Sarac, "There were so few disabled there. There have to be more than that. If they aren't in those rehab places, then where are they?"

"I wish I could say," he said sadly. He seemed to know more than he was letting on but was clearly reluctant to say more. After he turned off the ignition, he simply sat in the car. I wondered why we weren't getting out. Finally, he turned to warn us: "Please—do not ask these questions in my house. It is okay here in the car. We know that in here," his eyes scanned the interior, "it is safe. No one is listening. But in my home, it is not so safe. A few weeks ago, workers came. We don't know what they left behind."

We nodded obediently, each drew in a breath, and followed him inside.

We took our seats on one side of the dinner table as our hosts sat facing us. Everyone smiled awkwardly across the table, until Ken quietly slipped a jar of jelly from his pocket and onto the linen tablecloth. Pastor Sarac glanced quickly at his wife. Jay and Judy followed Ken's lead, emptying their handbags of our little jars of jellies, butter packets, and a few small bars of hotel soap. Ken arranged the items in a tidy line, and behind them another row of jellies, a couple of candy bars, and the small can of coffee. Pastor Sarac's wife's eyes were wide and bright.

"Oh, this is so kind of you," our pastor-friend said tenderly. He silently divvied up the goods for the families represented at the table. "We must share," he said with a soft smile.

After a blessing, platters of garlic chicken, steaming sausage, and onions were served by two elderly women dressed in long skirts and wearing babushkas. We later learned these women and several others from the church had taken turns standing in long food lines to make sure they got two chickens and some onions.

Rain began to fall outside. "We must hurry to get into the church," the pastor said, wiping his hands on his napkin.

"But the service doesn't begin until nine o'clock," I reminded him. "It's early yet."

"Oh, I do not think so, dear sister," he grinned.

Once we stepped outside, we were speechless at the sight before us. Rain was pelting down on a sea of people. Clogging the path to the church entrance were elderly men huddled beside their wives, young mothers holding babies, fathers clasping the hands of their children—all of them smiling and staring wide-eyed at me, oblivious to the pouring rain.

"Hello, hello," I said cheerily, as Ken and I slowly pushed our way through the crowd. "Please, you do not have to welcome me out here in this weather." Jay and Judy shook hands vigorously with everyone and kept insisting, "Thank you, yes, please, let's go inside the church!" Except to make way for my wheelchair, no one budged.

Once inside the church, we found out why. The place was jam-packed. Elderly people crowded each pew, while younger ones stood in the aisles, shoulder-to-shoulder, three abreast, in row after row up the middle aisle. On the stairs to the balcony, children were packed like sardines, and the upper section appeared to sag from the weight of many more. The air was hot and steamy, and when I glanced to see if the windows were open, I was greeted by smiling young children and teenagers sitting on each sill. Behind them, even more people stood outside in the rain, jostling to get a view.

Pastor Sarac said a few words in Romanian and led everyone in hymn singing. I'd never heard such sweet, robust worship, and as the harmony crescendoed, tears filled my eyes.

This was the persecuted church.

After the introductions, Ken wheeled my chair to the front, and I turned to face the crowd for the first time. As if on cue, women and children began bringing forward flowers, placing them on my lap and around my wheelchair. My soul was stirred to a depth I'd never known—yet not just because of the gesture. On my left and right, lying on thin mattresses and mats, and sitting in homemade wheelchairs made from bicycle parts, were men and women with twisted legs and spines. Maybe they had polio, maybe spina bifida. I recognized cerebral palsy in one or two. My eyes lingered on a short young woman leaning on a cane. All of them strained to see their American counterpart.

I had planned to speak about trusting and obeying God, hoping to use the story of my old thoroughbred, Augie, as an illustration. I'd intended to describe how, in the show ring, my horse always trusted me with the reins, that his obedience was absolute and complete despite the confusing maze of hurdles set before him. But I realized these people had a different use for horses.

"As I was coming into your city," I began, "I noticed the many horses plodding and pulling their carts with heavy loads. I love horses, and I've been around them all my life." The people seemed happy to know that I too had an old horse and tire-wheeled wagon back in America. "These horses of yours are obedient, staying on the straight and narrow road as they labor. They respond to their driver, stopping and turning whenever he tells them to. A horse yields to the one who holds the reins in his life. It's called trusting and obeying."

After an hour of speaking, I summed it up with this verse: "'So then, those of you who suffer according to the will of God, commit yourself to your faithful Creator and continue to do good.' Committing yourself to God is trusting him. Continuing to do good is obeying him."

As I spoke, I tried to make eye contact with as many people as possible. Yet my gaze kept returning to the short young woman leaning on her cane near the window. Her liquid black eyes sparkled with intelligence, and she seemed to hang on every word. After the meeting, I stayed to greet many people, glancing up every now and then to see the young woman with the cane waiting patiently at the end of the line.

Finally she hobbled up. "Oh, Joni," Maria said in English, "I always knew, I always felt that we were very much alike, very much one in the Spirit of Christ."

I clumsily lifted my arm in a gesture that said, "Let's hug," and she propped her cane against my chair to embrace me. As I buried my face in Maria's shoulder, I cried to think that I had more in common with this girl from Romania than I did with my neighbors on my block in California.

Maria stepped back in respect when Pastor Sarac came up. "This is a very special friend," he told me, placing his hand on Maria's shoulder. "She has translated your and Steve Estes' book *A Step Further*"—my face lit up—"and she did it all on her typewriter at home."

Maria blushed a little. She rode with us back to the hotel and explained to us how the Romanian edition of *Joni* had touched her. Someone then had given her an English copy of *A Step Further*, the book in which Steve and I detailed the lessons I'd learned from our Bible studies years ago. "I just had to translate it into our language," Maria said, "because so many people here need to know that God is in control. This fact has changed my life. I have learned afresh that my limp and shortness are nothing to be ashamed of."

I was exhausted by the time we arrived at the hotel but wanted to hear more. "Come inside and have coffee with us," I said to Maria and Pastor Sarac, a light drizzle still falling. Happily, Maria limped up to the front door of the Intercontinental Hotel but paused when she saw the doorman.

"Maria?" I asked.

Her eyes became serious and a little fearful. They darted to the doorman and back to me.

"Is something wrong?"

Pastor Sarac, still holding an armful of flowers, leaned down to my ear. "They will not allow her in here, Joni. She is a cripple."

My jaw dropped.

"They don't permit people like her to be seen in a place like this."

I felt shock—then indignation. "What about me? I'm like her," I said, loud enough for the hotel clerk to hear me.

"Please," our pastor friend cautioned me, "remember what I said in the car. It's different here."

I wheeled back into the misting rain to give Maria one more hug and say good-bye. "They may think you're not worthy, but God thinks otherwise," I said in a choking voice. "Like you said—he's in control. He permits what he hates so that his power can show up in people like you and me. Do you hear?"

I wanted so badly to run over the toes of the doorman, but I knew that would only cause trouble for Maria and her church. I watched her disappear into the night, and then I sat listening to the dripping rain. My eyes scanned the boulevard, taking in the eerily dark, quiet buildings, and I inhaled the stench of wet coal dust and fumes from leaded gas. The misty mountains of Transylvania lay just beyond the city and now a half-joking comment from Jay earlier in the trip came back to me with haunting irony: this was the land of Dracula—a prince of darkness.

Back in our room, my sister smoothed her wet hair behind her ears. "I nearly got trampled leaving the church," she said, breathing a sigh. "People were desperate to reach you, Joni, and they kept shoving these little notes at me. Look at all this," she exclaimed, unloading handfuls of tightly folded pieces of paper from her pockets. She spread the notes onto the bed.

Judy and Ken had been given notes too, and together they formed a massive pile on the bed. We sat down and started to read through the scores of brief, edited stories of these people in halting English—all pleading for hope or help, some wanting us to mail letters, others to send back news. A few asked for knowledge of a medical cure for mental retardation or spinal cord injury or stroke or brain injury: "Can you help my son who has spastic palsy?" "My daughter needs a wheelchair, please."

After a while, we looked at each other knowingly. We knew we'd seen something few Westerners were aware of. And we all felt the same thing: it was as if someone had laid a mantle on our shoulders, a burden of responsibility.

With no running tap water to drown out our words, the four of us gathered in front of the mirror and prayed. "Lord, the disabled people we met this evening don't begin to scratch the surface of so many more thousands we know must be out there. Please, somehow, use us to reach them with your love."

Back home with our team at Joni and Friends we realized we had much to learn—especially when I was told authorities had interrogated Maria and confiscated her typewriter after I'd written to thank her for translating *A Step Further*. Our trip ended up being the first of several behind the Iron Curtain. And on each return trip, we became a little more savvy, gathering more information and bringing more help. On one occasion, that help came in the form of arm-splints for a teenage quadriplegic in Poland. Another time, it was a seat cushion for someone in Czechoslovakia. With every visit, we were sowing seeds of hope and shining the light of encouragement.

Some places, however, were almost impervious to hope.

On one trip, we decided to visit Auschwitz, the Nazi death camp in Poland. Hope seemed very distant as Ken wheeled me under the heavy iron gate, into the grounds of bare bricks and barbed wire, gallows and guard towers, and crumbling remains of gas chambers, ovens, and chimneys. We toured a small museum near the entrance, and I sat for a long time in front of a glass-enclosed display containing huge mounds of eyeglasses, canes, crutches, prosthetic shoes, braces, hearing aids. Beside the mounds were stacks of yellow, dusty record-books that neatly recorded the names of thousands of people—people with disabilities—from whom these life aids had been taken.

I read a placard telling how, in the early years of the Holocaust, Hitler's medical teams quietly searched through institutions for the mentally handicapped. They specifically noted people who had no family or received no visitors. These unfortunate ones were hustled from their beds at night, loaded onto cattle cars, and sent east to the gas chambers. Yes, the first victims of the Holocaust were people with mental or physical disabilities. People like Maria and me.

After our experience at Auschwitz, we journeyed the short distance to Birkenau. Here, trainloads of Jews and dissidents were emptied into the freezing night. Children were herded one way, their mothers gun-butted the other. Men were separated into groups of the old and young. Virtually all of them, millions, ended up in one place: the incinerator, now crumbled and overgrown at the end of the camp.

I thought of Arvin Solomon and Alan Silverstein back at Wood-lawn Elementary—Arvin and Alan who used to come to class on Jewish holy days wearing their yarmulkes. I tried to imagine kids like them—kids who played ball, entered spelling bees, licked ice cream, and played with friends like me—being stripped and led to their deaths here. And I recalled the time our sixth-grade class cheered when we heard the news of Adolf Eichmann's capture. We had no idea, absolutely no idea.

We paused at the huge new memorial that had recently been erected alongside the ruins of the brick incinerator. In the middle of it, carved in stone, was a single word: *Remember.*

For a long while, I sat there trying to remember, working hard to recall the anguish I'd felt in my own suffering. How it felt to question God, to call him into court, to demand that he give an account for all the unfairness, all the disappointment. I tried to taste again the bitterness when, so many years ago, I couldn't believe that God could still be good and yet allow something so awful as paralysis to happen. *Others who visit this place must feel the same way*, I thought.

Yet I realized, too, that many people—people just like me—get it backward. We rant and rave against God for the evil we have to endure but hardly blink at the evil in our own hearts. As I glanced over my shoulder at the brick incinerators, I remembered that God, in allowing all this, had merely permitted men to pursue their own wickedness.

How awful the enemy of men's souls is, I half-prayed, *how dark our own hearts are. And how desperately we need to be rescued. Sin is a monster that constantly shadows us, intermingling with our every thought. Were it not for your hand of grace and mercy, O Lord, holding back the flood of evil, we would live in a constant Holocaust. How this world needs your help, your hope, God. We are lost, we are depraved, without you.*

I scanned the vast compound once more. Nothing had been left standing. The train tracks and railroad ties were rotted and uprooted, and what little barbed wire remained was rusted. But one thing struck me: the light, airy daisies carpeting the rolling acres where the death-chambers and barracks once reigned. These smallest of daisies were swaying and dancing in the gentle summer wind, bobbing as far as the eye could see. And their out-of-place presence here touched me as nothing else did. They were waving like a million happy little flags, staking claim on this territory for its rightful Ruler.

Years later, we would see a shocking television report on ABC's *20/20* that revealed just where all those disabled Romanian people had been during our first visit to Romania. The sunken faces of naked children—some deaf, others blind or mentally disabled—stared at the camera from filthy cribs and cold cages. Obviously, the evil that had been unleashed in Auschwitz and Birkenau had not diminished. It was still fermenting in these orphanages, and who knows how many other institutions.

The images so stunned us that Joni and Friends launched an effort called Wheels for the World. It would return us to Romania with wheelchairs, physical therapists, and even more open eyes, ears, minds, and hearts. It would be the first tangible answer to the prayer that Ken, Judy, Jay, and I offered in front of that hotel "mirror." And it would not be the last.

With Wheels for the World giving wheelchairs and Bibles, and a strong desire to shine light into the darkness, I felt Joni and Friends was beginning to wave thousands of happy little flags, reclaiming the territory of disability and disappointment for the kingdom of God.

Our van was stuck in the middle of a long caravan of vehicles, inching slowly toward the border back into Austria from Romania. A sense of foreboding filled the van as each yard brought us closer to the ominous lookout towers and massive concrete walls separating us from the West. The guards ahead, brandishing machine guns, swaggered slowly up and down the lanes of traffic, while others stood by, holding leashes on big German shepherds.

"Look," Ken nodded, his eyes pointing us to a smooth stretch of sand along the towering walls and chain-link fences. "There are no footprints in that sand. They keep it clean, so if anyone gets close to the fence, they'll spot their tracks."

"Shhh," our guide warned us. "Keep your voices down. We are getting nearer to the crossing, so you must not say anything about the security. Don't look out the window, and don't look up at the guard towers. Just talk amongst yourselves, and try not to draw any attention."

"Why be quiet now?" I asked in a loud whisper. "We're at least fifty yards away from the checkpoint."

The guide answered very softly: "Do you see that blackened glass in the towers? They point highly sensitive microphones at the cars to listen in. Be quiet now," he said, closing the conversation. He kept both hands on the wheel and looked straight ahead, as we all held our breath.

An hour later, we turned off the motor at the checkpoint. Guards took our passports, looked underneath our van with mirrors, questioned us, made us open our trunk, and rummaged carefully through our bags. I wondered if they would say anything about the Czechoslovakian crystal vase I'd bought for $12, or the few Bibles we still had. Finally, after a half hour, they gruffly waved us on.

As the spy towers faded behind us, and another visit to Romania became history, I mused on what happens to a culture when God is exorcised from it. We had witnessed the dark, broken soul of a country where the weak are forgotten, the lame are cast aside, the elderly and poor are abused, and corruption riddles every stratum of society. Evil goes unchecked, with everyone suspicious of his neighbor, unraveling every thread of decency.

Yet we also saw the opposite. We witnessed the preserving power of the gospel when it is shaken out like salt, preserving and sustaining what little life is left. It had awakened a taste for the goodness of God here, and we marveled at how the life of Christ brought light to sullen eyes, hope to faint hearts, and peace to troubled souls. We saw what happens when eternal truth breaks the power of the prince of darkness.

Now the Iron Curtain was beginning to fray in places, and God's hope, light, and peace were starting to awaken hearts under dictators even as ruthless as Romania's Nicolae Ceausescu. "Demagogs always end up in the backwaters of history," I remembered Mrs. Krieble saying.

The barbed wire of oppression was safely a mile or so behind us now. And soon, as we crested a small ridge, opening before us lay a scene of beautiful Austrian fields, filled with ripe, golden grain, rippling as far as the eye could see. Without a word, we all rolled down our windows, let the wind whip through our hair, and burst into the best freedom song we knew:

> *Oh beautiful for spacious skies,*
> *For amber waves of grain,*
> *For purple mountain majesties,*
> *Above the fruited plain!*
> *America! America!*
> *God shed His grace on thee,*
> *And crown thy good with brotherhood,*
> *From sea to shining sea!*

CHAPTER TWENTY-TWO

*O righteous God, who searches minds and hearts, bring to an end the
violence of the wicked and make the righteous secure.*

Psalm 7:9

Today on December 8, 1987, a historic breakthrough
occurred," the anchor announced. "Mikhail Gorbachev
and President Reagan signed the INF Treaty, eliminating two classes of weapons systems in Europe, and allowing each
nation to make on-site inspections of the other's military installations. The world is becoming a safer place."

In the Soviet Union, Gorbachev was advocating *glasnost* and
perestroika, restoring private ownership of land, decreasing censorship, and instituting free elections. History was on a fast track, a
greased slide leading toward sweeping changes, not only in the
Soviet Union but in eastern Europe, as Soviet troops slowly withdrew from Poland and Romania. Whenever I saw news reports of
Solidarity leaders in Poland or citizens in Romania waving flags, I
thought of Maria and the other lame and blind people who came to
Pastor Sarac's church that night. I prayed that soon, very soon, the
winds of freedom would bring change for them.

That change swept in like a gale in 1989. Even in forbidding
China, university students held marches that quickly grew into large
demonstrations in Beijing's Tiananmen Square.

When I traveled to Manila to serve in the Lausanne Congress on
World Evangelization, I was amazed to meet pastors from the
People's Republic of China as well as the Soviet Union. "It took three
days for us to get here," one Russian pastor said excitedly, grasping
my hands. "*Three days!* But we made it, praise God. We made it!"

What was God doing?

I spoke at the Billy Graham Association's historic crusade in
Hungary. The July air was humid as I wheeled into the immense
soccer stadium in Budapest, and at four o'clock in the afternoon

thousands of people were already pouring into the stadium. Word had spread like wildfire that many of those flooding into the stands were refugees from Romania and East Germany who had slipped across the border. Biding their time while hoping to find passage into Austria, they had come to hear the great evangelist.

The wind churned the huge cumulus clouds that floated above the stadium, and with every rumble of thunder in the distance, everyone could feel the barometric pressure rising. We could also sense another pressure building up: everyone's expectations were at a fever pitch. The feeling was almost tangible: *Something's about to break open. Something's about to give way here.*

Scanning the stadium, hearing the laughter and applause and spontaneous singing, I could feel . . . *freedom.* I saw the euphoria on every face, in every song, and in the dazzling rays of sun that, like in a painting, burst through the clouds to stream heavenly blessings on the gathering. I shook my head in wonder.

As the stadium continued to fill, I did a sound check, rehearsing a Christian song I'd learned in Hungarian. As Judy wheeled me off the platform, she asked, "Shall we head back into the green room, inside the stadium?"

I looked out onto the crowds, and I saw something that stopped us in our tracks. "I can't, Judy," I said. "Look. Look around the track."

Gathering on the stadium floor were blind people, lame people, men and women on crutches and in wheelchairs, and parents holding their disabled children. Hundreds, maybe thousands, of disabled people were hobbling into the giant stadium through every entrance. Some took seats in the stands, but most were unable to climb the steps, so they remained on the track. Many were being carried by family or friends, some were dragged in on straw mats, and some families lugged in mattresses, on which they tenderly laid their child or elderly parent. Soon these people were lining the entire perimeter of the stadium.

"How did they all get here?" I asked an organizer.

"The Billy Graham Association provided them free passage on all the trains and buses," he explained. "They knew these people wouldn't be able to get here any other way."

Judy and I stayed on the stadium grounds, gazing upon these people whom I'd been investing my life in at Joni and Friends. I had traveled to nearly twenty-five countries at that point, taking hundreds of wheelchairs to the Philippines and ministering in Czechoslovakia, East Germany, Poland, Romania, and other countries where I knew that people like me were often on the lowest rung of the social ladder. I had to be with them now.

I wheeled slowly around the track to welcome these friends, to learn their names and where they came from, and to identify with their plight. They told me, "Oh, we read your book in Bulgarian," or, "Your story is in Russian" ... "German" ... "Polish" ... "Lithuanian." I answered many, "Listen closely to Mr. Graham tonight. His message is all about freedom—the freedom you can find beyond a wheelchair."

A few hours later, the stadium was overflowing with more than 110,000 people—the largest public evangelistic service ever held anywhere in Communist-governed eastern Europe. As we filed onto the platform, lightning flashed in the distance, clouds loomed, and the wind blustered. A choir began the service, and as soon as they finished, a conductor rose and tapped his baton. The Hungarian orchestra came to attention—each bow, trumpet, flute, and clarinet raised and ready—and the conductor gave the downbeat.

The music swelled slowly, and at first I didn't recognize the piece. It was clear, though, this wasn't just any performance. I saw a tear trickle down the face of a violinist, and the same happened with a cellist. The musicians were playing with an unusual passion, and as I strained to listen, something powerful and familiar struck me. They were playing the sweet, heartbreaking strains of Bach's "Now Let All the Heavens Adore Thee."

As flags snapped overhead, I began to sing along with the orchestra. I knew every phrase by heart. And as I added harmony to the violins' melody, I was transported back to the wood-paneled choir room in Woodlawn High. Mr. Blackwell had always emphasized the classics, and he made sure we all learned this chorale. Its beauty had made me cry then, and it made me cry now.

Now let all the heavens adore Thee,
Let men and angels sing before Thee,

With harp and cymbal's clearest tone;
Heaven's gates with pearls are glorious,
We there shall join the choir victorious
Of angels circling round Thy throne.

It felt so right, so free to sing. And the freedom I sensed in the air matched the wide-open space in my heart. *How is it that you brought me here, God?* I pondered as my eyes swept the awe-inspiring sight of tens of thousands of people. *Who am I, to be here at such a point in history? Who am I to be a steward of this gift?*

I couldn't account for it. All I could do was continue to share what I knew: the liberating truth that freedom comes with a painful price. I had seen it that night in Romania, in front of the Intercontinental Hotel, when Maria's tears mingled with the rain. And I'd seen it for myself the first time I gazed at the cross and began to barely grasp the enormous price Jesus paid for my freedom. I'd learned that you can't wear a crown unless you bear a cross—that if our Savior had learned obedience through suffering, we should expect the same.

Something did break open that night, something did give way. More than 35,000 people ran—not walked, but ran—forward to embrace Christ for the first time. They believed, when Billy Graham read from the Bible, "Where the Spirit of the Lord is, there is freedom."

Not everyone reveled in the changes, however. In the fall I received an award in Washington, D.C., from the National Institute of Rehabilitation, and each award winner got to choose a foreign embassy that would honor him or her with a special dinner.

"So," Ken asked, "which embassy would you like to go to?"

I had just witnessed television scenes of Berliners gathering in large groups outside the Brandenburg Gate. I was moved by the images of young Germans holding candlelight vigils in front of the Berlin Wall, protesting the twenty-eight years their city had been separated.

The decision seemed made for me already. I told Ken, "Let's go to the embassy of East Germany."

We arrived early at the ambassador's home, the tall, impressive columns of the old Georgian mansion giving every appearance of political importance. As soon as we entered, we were whisked into the study and invited to watch television until the ambassador returned. Every channel we flipped to showed crowds of people, young and old, flowing toward the Brandenburg Gate, waving flags and cheering.

After a short while, the ambassador arrived and walked briskly into the study where we were seated. He offered a brief greeting, then explained that he had just returned from taping *The MacNeil-Lehrer Report* on public television. "We must change the channel," he said and proceeded to turn to the PBS station.

Ken and I sat with the ambassador, watching him being interviewed by Robert MacNeil. The journalist asked, "And what is your response to the great numbers of protesters we are seeing in your country?"

The ambassador, standing beside us, looked closely at his response on the screen.

"It is a passing fad," he said, squirming slightly under the hot studio lights. "This will die down. This will go away. You will see."

My eyes darted between the television and the ambassador. I was watching an old guard from an old era, stuffy and pompous, trying desperately to hold on to a shattering empire by his fingers and toes. The ambassador, and other Communist leaders like him, couldn't believe, couldn't *conceive* that their regimes were crumbling. I saw the fear etched on his face—he had to know his days were numbered.

And they were. Three days later, on November 9, 1989, East Germany opened the Berlin Wall and allowed free passage between the two parts of the city. Berliners climbed atop the wall with bottles of champagne, dancing and waving flags long into the night. Families rushed through what once had been heavily guarded checkpoints, reuniting for the first time in decades. Border guards stood and watched as Berliners pounded away at the despised wall with sledge hammers. A short time later, Ken and I would find ourselves at the foot of that same wall, a hammer in my husband's hand.

In December the Romanian regime would also collapse. When I heard the news, I remembered the hungry, anxious faces I saw that hot, rainy night in Bucharest. And my thoughts turned to Maria. I smiled at the thought of her perhaps marching, her head held high, into the Intercontinental Hotel.

It was 1991 by the time we made it to Moscow. Our trip came via another invitation from Mr. Graham, asking me to speak at the citywide outreach. Gorbachev was long gone now, and the former Soviet republics were, for the most part, very open. Our Joni and Friends team ministered in hospitals and orphanages and among disability groups. Some of these groups had been organized by mothers of disabled children, including one located in an art center, housed in an old brick building down an alleyway. The mothers invited us to sit around the edges of the small room, as their children enjoyed a performance by a Russian dance troupe.

The show began with the troupe taking center stage—tall, strong-looking men and women dressed in brightly-colored peasant costumes and black boots. As the music started, the troupe slowly started circling, clapping, dancing, and singing. Their pace quick-ened as the mandolins played faster, louder, faster, louder, the dancers circling until they were a whirlwind of color and sound.

This was more than a dance—it was an earthquake of boots stomping, a tornado of colors flashing, a symphony of singing and cheering, pinning us against the wall by its jet-blast of joyful sound. I realized it was the first time I'd experienced the beauty of real dance—the performers giving it their all, heart and sweat and soul, creating something transcendent, something never to be repeated. And it left us panting as breathlessly as they. We were witnessing passion and poetry, the shear pathos of the Slavic heart, wrenching itself inside out, all for the sake of the dance.

The day before the Billy Graham Mission, we took wheelchairs to Hospital 19, a famous Russian institution I'd heard about back when I was first injured. The hospital was rumored to be on the cutting edge of researching cures for spinal cord injury. And now, some twenty-four years later, I couldn't wait to get inside to see it all for myself.

But that was then—1991 was a different story. When we looked down the drab hallways, and were shown medical displays long out of date, the renowned hospital's reputation quickly sank.

"You say you are a quadriplegic?" one therapist asked me, as we moved down the hallway.

"Yes, my hands and legs. I've been injured over twenty years."

"May I see your hands?" she asked. She held them tenderly in hers, rubbing and massaging. It was a nice gesture, although I couldn't feel anything. After stroking my palm for a moment, she said, "I want you to try to move this finger when I gently pull it."

"Pardon me?" I asked in disbelief.

"Just try to focus on moving this finger," she said again.

I tried to explain that my spinal cord had been severed, but she shook her head no. "Look at these people," she said, pointing to some paraplegics pushing themselves in wheelchairs. "If they can do it, so can you."

I was shocked, but a light began to dawn. Obviously, the therapists in Hospital 19 rarely saw a quadriplegic—people like me just didn't survive. These therapists had only worked with paraplegics, and their idea of rehabilitation was to teach a patient how to "think" his fingers into moving. It was such a naïve technique.

When the night of the Billy Graham Mission arrived, the scene at the stadium was a virtual replay of Budapest a few years earlier. Hordes of people streamed inside in numbers so vast that the organizers were forced to close the gates. Great crowds continued to press in from the outside, until finally a shout went up—a great cheer we heard from inside the stadium—because giant television screens were switched on at the entrances, so those who didn't make it inside could listen and watch.

My interpreter was a Bible student named Oleg Shevkun, a young man with an extraordinary grasp of English. He was also extraordinary in another way: Oleg was blind. Together, we sat on the platform with Billy Graham as the choir of the Russian National Army—the infamous Red Army—stood tall and erect in their brown uniforms, singing "The Battle Hymn of the Republic." Their rousing and robust chorus brought tears to Oleg's blind eyes as they belted out, "Glory, glory, hallelujah!"

The moment was not lost on Ken. He whispered to me, "This week marks the thirtieth anniversary of the Cuban missile crisis."

I gasped. Listening to the booming chorus of these Russian soldiers, I realized we were watching, feeling, experiencing a moment that rose above the historic, that transcended everything we'd known about our world to that point. I was seeing a pinnacle in time that was perfect yet completely impossible, something that couldn't simply be assigned.

Afterward, Mr. Graham stood and shakily made his way to the pulpit—Parkinson's disease was already encroaching. At that point, Oleg leaned over and said, "Joni, just think—tonight God is using a blind boy and a paralyzed girl to reach my nation of eleven time zones."

I glanced at Mr. Graham. "Oleg," I added, "tonight God is using a blind boy, a paralyzed girl, *and* an elderly man with Parkinson's to reach your nation."

After Mr. Graham had preached and given an invitation, tens of thousands opened up their hearts to freedom in Christ. I mused over the same thoughts I had in Budapest: *Lord, this is too momentous. I'm not able to handle the stewardship you've given me, the responsibility of what I'm seeing. Why is it me who's sitting here next to Oleg, behind Billy Graham, and not someone else?*

The same feeling came upon me when I attended the premiere of the *Joni* movie in a civic arts theater inside the Kremlin. *This is the Kremlin,* I kept thinking, *where Khrushchev presided. All those times we did duck-and-cover under our desks in elementary school—and now they're showing a Christian movie in the Kremlin.*

The lights dimmed, the crowd quieted, and once again I watched the tanned actress swing her arms and take a dive. I saw me floating face-down, saw the Kathy-actress grab my chest and heave me up out of the water, sputtering and gasping. However, this time it was in Russian. The film had been dubbed, and I was "speaking" in a foreign language.

As I glanced over the balcony rail at the packed house and saw the crowd gazing at the giant screen, I couldn't bear it any longer. If my hands had worked, I would have covered my face. *This is too much! Oh God, you say that "To whom much is given, much shall be required." I can't bear this kind of responsibility.*

I knew that truly responsible stewardship over this kind of powerful event required an utterly sanctified life. And that just wasn't *me*. Sometimes I wished God would give me less freedom. Sometimes I hoped he would force me to do the right thing, that he would *make* me holy. It would be much easier that way.

I knew God was requiring me to make choices. He was revealing walls in my life he wanted to tear down—not Berlin-sized walls, such as confinement to a wheelchair, but small ones: pride that raised its ugly head, the temptation to rehearse successes, my still-fierce competitive spirit, the constant itch to have things my way. Now Jesus was taking a sledgehammer to my despised walls, reminding me that his freedom doesn't mean merely, "Obey my rules," but, "Obey *me*." The old guard was crumbling, and God himself was breaking the grip of iron-rule-keeping. This was the God I was beginning to fall in love with—the one whose commandments were not burdensome, the one who was changing my heart.

In the summer of 1990, I was on the front lawn of the White House as a member of the National Council on Disability. We were there for President George Bush to sign the landmark Americans with Disabilities Act (ADA), which our committee had drafted.

Later at the hotel, at a small reception, our little crowd urged the executive director to make a speech.

"This is a great era of rights and privileges that we live in, a great time to be alive, to be free. But let's remember . . ."

He paused and cleared his throat, as if he might choke on his next thought.

". . . this new law may increase job opportunities, but it's not going to change the employer's heart. It'll provide for new mechanical lifts on buses, but it won't change the bus driver's heart. It'll assure that ramps will give us access to restaurants and theaters, but it won't change the waiters' hearts."

He stopped and looked around the room, making eye contact with us all.

"Here's to changed hearts," he said, silently lifting his glass.

To changed hearts.

His words were all the reminder I needed: *The gospel is all about changing hearts.*

When the winds of change at the turn of the decade finally died down, many eastern European people were left feeling frustrated. Some grated under the demands of democracy. They had assumed that freedom guaranteed unlimited rights. Now they were learning that you can't dress up your own willful determinations as "rights" in an attempt to pass them off as dignity.

True change happens only in the heart. And that change comes by the Spirit of God. I thought of the apostle Paul's words again: "Wherever the Spirit of the Lord is"—whether in my heart, or around the world—"there is *freedom*."

CHAPTER TWENTY-THREE

Brothers, I do not consider myself yet to have taken hold of it. But one thing I do: Forgetting what is behind and straining toward what is ahead.

Philippians 3:13

The test came back, Joni," the specialist said over the phone.

I gulped, waiting for the news.

"It's—it's negative," he sighed.

My heart sank.

"Listen," he said, "it has nothing to do with your spinal-cord injury. You're just one of those type-A women who can't conceive."

The words hit me like shrapnel.

Ever since Ken and I married seven years earlier, we had been trying to start a family. Now, on the verge of my fortieth birthday, in October 1989, we'd gotten the final news.

I called Ken on his lunch break at school. "I'm not pregnant," I said numbly.

I'd always heard about the sorrow of women who were barren. Now the heartache of it hit home. I pictured the stuffed animals, the children's books, and the games I had tucked away on the top shelves of our bedroom closet. I thought of the sketch I'd drawn for turning my art studio into a little nursery, of how we would bolt a baby's car seat to a lap-board on my wheelchair. I thought of the girlfriends I had lined up to help out. And the little pair of faded-blue overalls folded in the bottom of my dresser.

People get married in order to have a family. How will Ken and I handle this?

I let large, silent tears roll down.

Sorrow hung heavy that night like a humid mist, as Ken and I lay in bed. We small-talked, but mostly, we let the silence do the speaking. Although I couldn't feel it, I knew he was holding my hand, and I was comforted by the steady rhythm of his breathing.

"So," my husband asked softly, "where do we go from here?"

For several years, I had sensed this moment creeping up. Up to now, the road had been predictable: Joni gets married, Joni has a baby—my spinal-cord injury, merely a medical bump in the road. Now it was forking off into one of those interstate highway overpasses that end in midair, waiting for somebody to come and lay the next mile.

Where would it lead?

Or maybe it wasn't a fork in the road at all. Perhaps it was a clover-leaf, curving me back around onto an interstate highway with a hundred different off-ramps that lead all over the world, each mile billboarded with the faces of thousands of people I'd met over the years.

Many of those faces were children's. I pictured the Filipino girl dragging her legs behind her as she walked on her hands. The blind child in Poland who clutched a tattered copy of *A Step Further* to her chest, gushing, "This changed my life!"

Then there was the little tow-headed pixie I met in Hungary, on our journey through that country, East Germany, and Czechoslovakia. We went from Wittenberg, where I spoke in Martin Luther's church, to Liepzig, where I talked in Bach's church. We presented the gospel in one church after the next, never for less than two hours at a time. So when we arrived at our last stop, a large church on a hill overlooking Budapest, Hungary, I was running on empty. I arrived at the church early, but people were already there, packing the pews. It took me forever just to reach the front of the church, and I prayed in exhaustion, *Lord Jesus, give me fresh words to say here.*

God answered. The event ended up being a wonderful outreach, and afterward, as I slowly made my way back down the crowded aisle, I paused to greet people with the little bit of Hungarian I knew.

Suddenly, a blonde-haired child elbowed her way forward, jabbering excitedly in Hungarian and tripping over the adults around her. Men and women stepped aside, amused by this child-on-a-mission.

"I can't understand you," I pleaded with a smile. It didn't matter. She threw her arms around me, burst into tears, and kept muttering to me.

"What did she say?" I begged everyone. "What's her name?"

No one responded to my English. Finally, the fair-haired child pulled herself away, shoved something in my lap, and, wiping her eyes, stepped back into the crowd.

"Stop," I said, "what is your name?" I scanned the crowd for my interpreter, but by the time I looked up again, the girl had disappeared. I gazed down at the gift in my lap. It was a little, faded-green terry cloth rabbit, with a slightly worn ribbon around its neck. I could tell it was hand-sewn. From the looks of it, I figured it had been this child's playmate for a long time.

I kept the terry cloth rabbit on my lap, christening him Rabbie, all the way back to the hotel. As we bounced along the rutted roads, I gazed at his threadbare body and wondered whose hands had stitched him, what sort of secrets the little girl whispered in his ear, if she took him on trips and showed him new sights, and whether she had an older sister who teased her about her rabbit-friend. I wondered what the child's room looked like. Did her daddy read her fairy tales from a big red book? Did she share a bed with a sister? Did she snuggle with this terry cloth friend under her blanket?

Maybe I was exhausted. Or maybe I had regrets about being too driven, too much the type-A personality to conceive. Or maybe it was guilt, knowing that my rigorous travels had probably hindered my ability to have a baby with Ken. Whatever the reason, something about the rabbit and its child awakened in me a deep longing.

Suddenly, I just wanted to bring into the world a little girl. A child like my fair-haired Hungarian friend, who would learn to trust, wonder, and appreciate God's gifts. A girl who would enjoy beach camping and horseback riding and playing cowboys-and-Indians. Who would sit with me under the stars and learn the constellations, and who would sit next to me as I painted and ask, "What's a composition?" A child to whom I could point out the different trees and birds and read *Black Beauty*. A little girl who wouldn't mind dressing in a frilly frock for a piano recital, and who would be pleased to have me sit and listen to her practice "Tarantella." We could harmonize on songs and hymns, and sit on a balcony and listen to the crickets at night.

"That's all I want," I half-whispered to Ken. He turned in bed to face me. "But it's not going to happen."

"What's not going to happen?"

"A family," I said longingly. "My hopes and dreams for a family. I've got to let it go."

Ken brushed my hair with his hand.

"We've got to look at the future," I sighed.

Now the interstate highway took me down another off-ramp. This one carried me back to times with other children. I thought of Nicole in her pink, junior-sized wheelchair, with bicycle streamers on the handles. I met her at one of the Family Retreats that Joni and Friends had been holding for families affected by disability—five days of wheelchair hikes, swimming, arts and crafts, Bible study, and prayer times. During an ice cream social one evening, I powered my wheelchair over to visit little red-haired Nicole in her chair, Tiffany, her friend, and Rachel, standing next to her in leg braces. Soon we were playing a game of tag—wheelchair tag. Before long, a boy in a walker joined us with his sister, then a child with Down syndrome and her brother. We laughed as we weaved in and out around the legs of the adults, we laughed as our foot pedals clunked together, bumping and bouncing like dodge'm cars.

After the ice cream began to melt, our retreat director looked at his watch and tried to herd the families back to their cabins. But the children and I kept playing. We were so caught up in the game that I lost all track of time.

When we finally said goodnight, Nicole reached up to give me a hug. We pressed our warm cheeks together, and I rocked and hummed in her embrace. Halfway through our hug, I realized she had pulled me over too far. I had lost my balance and was resting against her shoulder.

A full minute went by. "Have we finished hugging?" I asked.

"Why?" she said, her voice muffled by my sweater.

"Because when we're done, you're going to have to push me back up in my chair."

Nicole squirmed out from under our hug and began giggling. With her child's strength, she tried to push me back up in my chair. "You can't make yourself sit up?" she asked.

"Nope," I answered, trying to raise my head off her shoulder, "and that's why I need your help."

"Hey," she brightened, "I can do something for a grownup!"

Only after we waved goodnight to each other did I realize that this night was like heaven. It was another joy-filled moment in a brown paper bag, whispering, "Hang on. One day you will bathe in joy like this. And it will last forever."

Before I entered my cabin that night, I looked up at the stars and thanked God for filling the void not only with himself but with *children*. I was connecting with boys and girls who had spina bifida, cerebral palsy, autism, spinal-cord injury, Down syndrome, and osteogenesis imperfecta. I cheered them on the sidelines as they entered heartily into every game, every dive into the pool, every chance to sit on a horse. And my heart warmed when they'd lift their eyes and clamor "Watch me!" and "No, watch *me!*" as though I were a mommy.

The sweet memory of Nicole and her hug began to dissipate the sorrow still hanging over our bed, as Ken and I lay awake in the darkness. And a sunny thought began to dawn: even though we couldn't conceive our own baby, we were enjoying the children of others.

"Are you still holding my hand?" I asked.

Ken raised it so I could see.

I inhaled deeply. "If we're not going to have a family of our own," I proposed, "then why not expand our idea of 'family'?"

He turned his head on the pillow. "What are you talking about?"

"Well, couldn't it mean .... your students? Caring about them. Having them up here for barbecues. Following them up as they go to college."

He thought for a moment. "Mm-hm."

"And look at all the countries we've visited," I continued. "The symposiums in Europe we've led. The wheelchairs given. And the orphanages for disabled boys and girls. We may not be able to have our own children—"

"But we have the children around the world," he finished the thought.

"Yes, disabled children."

Ken looked up at the ceiling, thinking further.

"So," I whispered in the dark, "so why not invest our time, invest ourselves, in *them?* Oh Ken," I said as he moved closer to me, "let's invest ourselves in the children. May we please—can we not love the children of the world?"

Suddenly, the fork in the road didn't seem intimidating. That night, Ken and I decided to not live one life, but a thousand lives, offering ourselves for service in kingdom work, no matter where God sent us. The following week, I gave away most of the stuffed animals and toys in my closet, and I trashed the little sketch of my art studio-turned-nursery. We gave away the little pair of blue overalls. We decided to focus our energies on Joni and Friends and the connection we could have with even more boys and girls.

As we did, God filled my heart with more children.

I met little Hannah Slaight and Joey, her brother, at our Joni and Friends Family Retreat near Chicago. The moon was high, the night was balmy and breezy, and I had just wheeled outside after our opening-night celebration. I spotted Hannah and Joey in their zippy little wheelchairs and—eyeing the long, gentle slope back to our rooms—I challenged them to a race.

"A race?" Hannah asked.

"Yeah," I said with a competitive edge. In the moonlight, I could see the question on their faces. "Haven't you ever raced anyone in your chairs?" They shook their heads with a little embarrassment.

They must be newer to their chairs than I thought. Before I could say, "Ready, set, go," they zoomed ahead, laughing and glancing back over their shoulders. I had to jam my chair on "high gear" to catch up. All the way down the hill we sped, nearly crashing into each other at the bottom. We were three happy-spirited campers, cavorting and cutting up under the moonlight.

Little did I realize just how new to their wheelchairs these two were. A year earlier, Hannah and Joey were running up and down the stairs, preparing for their first day of church camp, along with their younger sisters, Hope and Haley. The four children were singing a camp song as their parents, Jim and Janet, drove the van down the street. Only a mile and a half from home, a drunk driver crashed head-on into their vehicle at 92 m.p.h. The youngest, Hope, died at the scene. Haley suffered terrible injuries to her face, and required a bone fusion for her broken back. Jim and Janet incurred multiple broken bones and internal injuries. Hannah's and Joey's spines were crushed in the collision—they would never walk again.

When someone sent me a newspaper article about the Slaight family, I responded with a letter, gently suggesting they join me and the Joni and Friends team at our upcoming Family Retreat. Never could I have dreamed how this retreat would be an answer to the Slaights' prayers. Timid, tenderhearted, and still shaky, nine-year-old Hannah had been praying she would find a girlfriend with a spinal cord injury—someone who would understand what it was like to lose the ability to walk at such a young age. On the first day of the retreat, Hannah got her answer. She met eleven-year-old Abby in her junior wheelchair.

The "mother" in me watched with tender eyes as Hannah and Abby parked themselves by the lake. It looked like they were making daisy chains. A breeze tousled Hannah's hair; she looked so contented. The girls giggled and showed each other their progress. I wondered if Hannah resented the fact that she would never toe-dance or play dodge ball like the other kids at recess. Did the weight of the accident burden her? It didn't seem so as the girls tossed daisies into the lake. *So where is your anger, Hannah? Where is the spitfire and spiting God?*

I swallowed hard. Watching two little girls disregard the dark side and enjoy the blessing of contentment over the smallest of pleasures—counting he-loves-me, he-loves-me-not by a lake—made me so proud of them. So proud of God. He was bending over backward to alleviate her pain, straining to dry the tear, lighten the load, heal the heartache, and show the path to peace, joy, and contentment. God was doing everything from his side.

And I saw something in Hannah that I was missing when I was first injured: she was doing everything from *her* side. The next day, she announced to her mother, "They asked me what I was thankful for, and I said I was thankful for my disability. I *really* mean it this time. I've met so many new friends who have it worse than me and they're so happy! If they can be thankful and happy, how can I complain? I have my arms, I can feed myself. For the first time, I'm thankful for what my disability is."

Little Hannah, in her sweet, wise way, was teaching me something about true wisdom. It's found not in being able to figure out why God allows tragedies to happen. True wisdom is found in trusting God when you can't figure things out. I never did that when I first landed in a wheelchair. Less than a year into *my* paralysis, I was driving my wheelchair into a wall, slamming it in reverse and forward, again and again, until the plaster began to crumble, all to spite the Lord. But that's not what Hannah and Nicole were doing. These were kids who skipped the spite-the-Lord stage. These were the children who would blossom into young women who could step out in faith and embrace God through willful thanks.

God, you are amazing, I smiled to myself, as I watched Hannah and Abby abandon their play to wheel to the gazebo. *Your grace and your power to sustain these children humbles me.*

It happened again during a trip I had to take back east for a medical appointment. Judy and another friend, Francie, took me to downtown Baltimore for a urologic checkup at the University of Maryland Hospital. After the appointment, I wheeled down a few familiar hallways. The walls echoed with the same sounds—the padding of nurses' shoes, voices on the intercom, the creaking of juice carts rolling. I was hoping to visit my old room, but reconstruction and new coats of paint had changed everything. More than thirty years had passed, and the ICU where I'd spent so many weeks was long gone.

"I know a place that I bet still looks the same," I piped up.

We loaded into the van, drove a mile to the other side of downtown, and parked in front of Johns Hopkins Hospital. "Follow me," I told my friends, as we headed down the labyrinth of hallways toward the oldest part of the hospital, its center.

"Where's the old lobby?" I asked a security guard.

With Francie and Judy behind me, I wheeled ahead, anxious to see if the lobby had changed. I rounded the back of a stairwell lined with mahogany paneling and rolled onto the smooth marble floor. It opened up into the large old lobby I remembered, the one with the tall domed ceiling. There in the middle stood the marble statue of Christ. On the left was the same paneled wall where the red-haired paramedic parked me on my stretcher, so many years ago.

"They brought me here to pull out my fingernails," I told my friends. "I was so depressed, feeling so lost back then...." I explained how I used to imagine myself sitting at the Pool of Bethesda, waiting to get healed, waiting for Jesus to show up. "I didn't see any improvement, and I would beg the Lord to come and help me. To show himself in a real way. But Jesus seemed to be passing me by. That is, until they brought me here," I said quietly, gazing at the huge statue. "They placed me right here, at his feet."

I wheeled over to the base of the statue and read the familiar words: "Come unto me ... and I will give you rest." The arms of Christ were still outstretched, still beckoning and welcoming. And for a while, as nurses and visitors brushed past me, I lost myself in the memory of what it was like to be a teenager, so young and frightened. What it was like to be fighting off bitterness, thinking God had forgotten me, that surely my plight was more tragic than anyone else's. To be looking for a friend my age with whom I could identify, someone who would understand what it was like to lose the ability to walk at such an early age.

In the corner of the lobby was a wooden stand with a large, leather-bound guest book. I wheeled over to it and saw that visitors had written down their impressions after seeing the statue. As I glanced over the names, I noticed they were from all over the world. A few people wrote prayers. One or two said thank you. I asked Francie to pick up the pen and write the following for me:

"More than thirty years ago a frightened seventeen-year-old girl was paralyzed in a diving accident. During her rehab, she was brought to this hospital for minor surgery, her stretcher placed at the base of this statue. It was an answer to prayer. A prayer that God would show me that he hadn't forgotten. That he still cared. I'm happy to say, years later ... he still does."

An hour later, as we sat in the hospital cafeteria, a woman approached me and asked, "Are you ... *Joni?*"

I nodded.

"My name is Glenna," she introduced herself. "What are you doing here?"

"We were at another hospital earlier today, but I wanted to show my friends the statue of Christ. Have you seen it?"

"Oh, I can't believe it's you," she enthused, wringing her hands. "Your books have helped me so much. I'm here all the way from Ohio, with my daughter, Angela. She has spina bifida. We're waiting for her to go through another operation. She's been here many times for surgery."

In a flash, for just a brief second, I saw my own mother in this woman. I thought of Mom trekking daily to the hospital to see me. And I saw the same desperation, the same holding onto hope like the thin string of a kite.

"Would you have time—do you think you could please come up to the children's surgical unit and see my daughter?"

I didn't blink an eye. As soon as we finished lunch, we took the elevator to the fourth floor to see Angela. I wheeled down a colorful hallway and made a right-hand turn into her room. She had soft brown hair and a tender smile, and she looked groggy with tubes running in and out of her body. When I said, "Hi, my name is Joni," her eyes brightened.

"I know who you are," she said, her voice weak but happy. "I listen to you on the radio all the time."

I spotted a junior-sized wheelchair in the corner. It was black and pink and resembled a small racing chair with a low-slung back. I remarked on how snazzy it looked. "Yeah," she agreed, "and I gave my last wheelchair to *Wheels for the World.* I wanted some other kid to have it, some kid in Africa or somewhere."

There you go again, Lord—blessing me with the courage of a child!

God was using Angela—just as he did Nicole and Rachel, Hannah and Joey, and that little blonde Hungarian girl—to fill my barrenness. Now, I realized, there was hardly an emptiness to speak of. I was as proud of Angela as a mother would be—a spiritual mother. It was all I could do not to burst for joy over this resolve of a girl with spina bifida, holding onto grace, hanging onto hope in Christ, all the while thinking of how she might help some other child.

Before we left Johns Hopkins, I couldn't resist one last visit to the statue. As I sat in the corner, watching the people hurry by, I shook my head, wondering where the years had flown to. Rarely had I thought, truly thought, about those difficult days when my mother and I struggled with surgeries and catheters, blood tests and pressure sores. I looked down at my fingernails now, small and pale blue from years of uselessness. *Lord, help me remember that pain,* I half-whispered.

As the statue of Christ loomed above me, unchanging in its peaceful grandeur, I bore down hard to revive old images ... memories of when I was first paralyzed like Nicole or Hannah, when I had to face yet another surgery like Angela. I recalled the face of the red-haired paramedic and the bloody bandages on my fingernails that day—but I could not revive the real horror. As I sat now at the feet of Jesus, the mental movies I tried to play were full of blips and blank spaces—nowhere near the painful drama of three decades ago.

Time is slippery stuff. The past always looks different than it did "back when." It chooses only a few highlights of lasting importance of all that happens. In 1968, when I lay on that stretcher, gazing up at the marble statue, I simply didn't have the perspective I had now. All I had then was a mustard-seed-sized bit of hope, a thin, tattered kite string. There was no way I could understand how it would all turn out. Back then, I was looking for a road that would lead me out of the pain—and I wasn't finding it. But on this day, the day I met Angela, so many years later, I could see the whole interstate highway system, with all its exits and on-ramps. And I could see the billboards lining the highway, scores of them ... all filled with the faces of children.

I'm glad I can't remember the pain, I thought as we drove out of Baltimore. All that remained were the results, the things of lasting importance—things like the empathy I felt for Angela. It's the empathy and courage, I realized, the encouragement and the heavenly perspective, that rise and remain like stepping stones above raging waters. These are the things that carry me to the other side of suffering, to the present, to the place where I have a sense of arrival, where I'm more *me* than I was when I cried, "I don't know who I am!"

The God I love is continually trying to show me life this way. He's steadfastly implanting the perspective of the future into my present, like a voice counseling me, "This is the way it's all going to turn out. This is how it will all seem when it's over—a better way. I promise." It's a view that keeps separating what will last from what must fall by the wayside. "Blessed is the man you discipline, O Lord," the Bible says. And blessed is the child whom God disciplines—even if it's a bruising of a blessing.

I don't remember who ended up getting the little pair of blue overalls. I can't recall the name of the infertility specialist who worked with Ken and me. So many friends my age have children who are working on their second master's degree or who are having children of their own. I do not miss being a grandmother, or a mother. Those dreams, too, have fallen by the wayside. I can hardly visualize the sketch I made of my art studio-turned-nursery; it seems like a faded photograph in my memory. That's because Angela, Hannah, and the rest of the children in their wheelchairs keep filling my heart. They keep me focused on what's important: the peace and contentment, courage and commitment. They show me, in case I ever have a doubt, that God is awesome to inspire loyalty in the midst of so much loss. And because these children help me so, I treasure them, pray for them, and embrace them just as if they were my own.

Proof is propped against the lamp next to my bed. There snuggles a small, faded-green terry cloth rabbit with a worn ribbon around his neck. The threadbare rabbit keeps his vigil on my bedside table, reminding me to remember the children. Never forget the children. God has given me so many children.

For of such is the kingdom of heaven.

"You should have seen Dad today," Ken said, throwing his duffel off his shoulder and onto the kitchen table. "I got him to eat a whole bowl of sushi rice and to drink half a glass of green tea!"

It was late on Sunday night, and Ken had returned home from helping his mom take care of his ailing father in Burbank. Dad Tada's triple bypass surgery, followed by several small strokes, had left him completely dependent.

"It feels so strange," Ken said, "I'm doing the sorts of things for my dad that he used to do for me."

Ken's father had always been a strong, tall, no-nonsense Japanese businessman in the import-export industry. He had been a tough disciplinarian with Buddhist convictions, and my clearest memories of him always had him dressed impeccably in a double-breasted suit with a large black pearl tie tack. Dad Tada had not taken kindly at first to his son dating a girl with quadriplegia, but over time many things had changed. His love for me had grown, but his health had gotten weaker. Now, years later, he had traded in his suit for pajamas, his fancy car for a wheelchair.

He traded in something else too.

"I read the whole Sermon on the Mount to him today," Ken said, smiling. Dad Tada's tough religious exterior had begun to crack under the pressure of his many ailments. Mostly, it cracked under the pressure of his son's love. Weekend after weekend, for nearly four years, Ken gave up fishing for the pleasure of feeding and helping his dad. No longer could his father ignore such extraordinary care and compassion. And now, if Ken happened to forget a Bible reading, his dad would nudge him.

One day, after Ken had finished wiping his father's mouth from lunch, he looked deeply into his eyes. "I love you, Dad," he said, his face flushing red.

His father mouthed back, "I love you too."

The father had become the child . . . the child, the father. And in this strange role-reversal, this odd parent-son switch, a void was filled in Ken's heart too. He finally received so much of what he missed as a little boy growing up—a daddy's tender touch and words of love. Dad received something, as well—he opened his heart to Christ before he died.

The God Ken and I were growing to love more and more was a paradox. He kept closing doors so we would find the open window. And always, the window had a much, much better view.

CHAPTER TWENTY-FOUR

*His mercy extends to those who fear him, from generation to generation.
He has performed mighty deeds with his arm; he has scattered those who
are proud in their inmost thoughts. He has brought down rulers from
their thrones but has lifted up the humble. He has filled the hungry with
good things but has sent the rich away empty.*

Luke 1:50–53

I was sequestered away behind a closed door, glued to my computer, when Judy burst into my office waving a *USA Today*. "Look at what I just read while at lunch," she said. "We can win this. I know we can!"

"Win what?" I asked, without looking up.

"It's a contest—the 'Bridge the World' contest sponsored by KLM Airlines," she said. "They're celebrating their seventy-fifth anniversary, and they're sponsoring an essay contest. The prize is twenty-five free airline tickets, and all the cargo space we need, to fly to anywhere we want to 'bridge the world' of differences between people. All we have to do is write a 750-word essay, telling how we would use the tickets and the trip to 'bridge the world'!"

Judy was out of breath as she held out the newspaper for me to read. I peered over the rim of my glasses to examine the full-page ad about the contest, taking in all the details and deadlines. When I finished, I looked up at Judy, and we grinned simultaneously. I agreed heartily: "We can win this!"

We sped into the hall, where we nabbed John Wern, director of Wheels for the World, to show him the ad. By this time, Wheels for the World had developed into an international ministry program. Through it we collected used wheelchairs, had them restored in prisons, and recruited Christian physical therapists to travel with our teams overseas, where we fit the wheelchairs to needy disabled children and adults, and also gave Bibles and offered training for disability ministry in local churches.

"John, look at this," I said, jabbing the newspaper with my hand.

"I could easily write about how our ministry bridges the world of disability-differences between handicapped people around the world."

As he read through the ad, the same sly grin spread across his face.

"Come on, John," I said, "surely you can use those twenty-five free tickets. You can go anywhere in the world with wheelchairs and Bibles. So, tell us, what country should I write about?"

He rubbed his chin and said, "I know just the place."

Earlier in the year, John had led a Wheels for the World team on a trip to Ghana, West Africa. The team had traveled north of the capital of Accra to reach the town of Kumasi, and the journey hadn't been easy. The weather was hot, damp, and oppressive, and the dirt roads were badly rutted. To make matters worse, a civil war was raging just north of the town, and that had made the journey not just wearying but dangerous. Yet our African sponsors had told us the needs among the poverty-stricken people in that region were desperate.

"We found a large concrete pavilion with a tin roof, so we unfolded the wheelchairs there," John told us. "No sooner did we get things set up than a line of people started streaming in. We knew right away that more people were showing up than we had wheelchairs for. Mothers had walked miles, carrying their disabled children in slings on their backs. They came hoping and expecting. Joni, it broke my heart to tell them we didn't have any more chairs left."

John then described a certain African woman who had carried her twelve-year-old disabled boy on her back. She was black and beautiful, he said, but years of heavy labor had etched deep wrinkles in her young face, and her back was swayed from the weight of her child. When John told her that the chairs had run out, she smiled, undaunted. "That is no matter," she said with an air of assurance. "You will return. You will bring us more chairs."

John was taken aback by the confidence with which she spoke. He looked at her doubtfully.

But the woman merely nodded at him, her smile growing bigger. "We know you will come back," she said.

"In the face of all that disappointment," John told us, shaking his head, "those African women were so hopeful. They'd trudged all those miles, only to find they'd come in vain. Yet they weren't angry. They just had this air of assurance, saying, 'We will pray that you will return to us. God will send you back to us with more wheelchairs.'"

"So," I said, "what did you tell them?"

"I promised them we'd come back."

"Why did you say _that?_" I gasped. "Ghana's not on the schedule. Another trip to Africa isn't in your budget. All of those families will be disappointed, and—"

I stopped. The three of us looked at one another knowingly. Then, with hardly a word, I wheeled straight to my office, parked at the computer, and began writing.

The words flowed effortlessly. I made my case to the KLM contest committee, asking them to award the tickets and cargo space to Wheels for the World, so we could return to Kumasi:

> Dear Friends at KLM ... People with disabilities here in the U.S. have so much; some of us, even two wheelchairs. Yet there are needy individuals living in Africa who survive on the street and crawl in the dirt for lack of a wheelchair. Would you please help us bridge the gaping chasm between people like me, here, and friends over there? A gift of twenty-five tickets and cargo space will enable us to make a huge difference in their lives!

A couple of hours later, the essay was complete, and we mailed it off to the KLM headquarters in Amsterdam, Netherlands.

Two days after that, Ken, Judy, and I boarded a KLM 747 for Budapest, where Joni and Friends was holding a conference for disability leaders in eastern Europe. We had to make a transfer through Schipol Airport in Amsterdam, and as we wheeled through the terminal, we saw "Bridge the World" contest posters everywhere. There was one posted on each gate, along with balloons and streamers. With each gate we passed, my confidence grew, and I looked up at Ken and said, "See that? We're going to win that."

"Yeah, sure," he waved me off, "and I'm Ed McMahon from Publisher's Clearing House Sweepstakes."

But Judy and I remained undaunted. So did John Wern. We tried to convince our coworkers that we were in the running to win, but it wasn't easy. Some scoffed and insisted the odds were against us. But our hopes surged when we received a form letter from the contest office in Amsterdam. It announced, "You have been picked as a finalist."

I wheeled through the office, telling everybody, "We're a finalist! We made it to the last round." A few heads popped up over the office dividers, and one or two people came over to examine the form letter—one even swiping the letter's signature with a wet finger to see if it was real. But mostly, people shrugged their shoulders and went back to their computers. "We'll believe it when we see it," was the prevailing response.

They didn't have long to wait. A phone call followed a few days later with the news: my essay had won.

I almost jumped out of my wheelchair. Out of 15,000 entries from around the world, my appeal for transporting our wheelchairs to Kumasi had been chosen as one of the grand prize-winners. We were now free to start sketching plans to return to Africa.

In June of 1995, our team of twenty-five arrived in Amsterdam, where we were greeted and congratulated by KLM executives bearing gifts, T-shirts, and free cameras for our trip. Then, within a couple of hours, we were off to Africa, in a KLM jet loaded with wheelchairs for disabled children, as well as other equipment for blind and mentally handicapped people.

As we flew south over the Sahara Desert, I gazed over the endless expanse of pink sand. Exotic and beautiful, it stretched as far as the eye could see, underlighting the clouds in a soft, rosy glow. I leaned against the window and wondered about the people I would meet on this off-ramp of the interstate highway God had us on. I kept thinking about the families in that little town of Kumasi. I thought about the photos I'd seen of the huts with banana-leafed roofs, and the small houses made of rusty tin. Of boys and girls with cerebral palsy, who had lain for years on straw mats in dark corners. Of the rumors and taboos attached to these children by witch doctors, who insisted their ailment was a curse from the animist spirits. *So much darkness and heart-wrenching poverty,* I brooded.

When our KLM jet landed at the Accra airport, and our plane taxied in, I took in the surrounding area. The edges of the runway were old and crumbling, with weeds growing between the cracks, and the small terminal looked run-down. When we parked on the tarmac, I realized there weren't any jetways. Instead, a couple of African men in street clothes rolled portable stairs to the jet door.

When we exited, I sucked in a deep breath of hot, wet air. I could smell the ocean only a few miles away, as well as the scent of damp earth. Meanwhile, jungle trees and vines were encroaching against the chain-link fence surrounding the airport. Then suddenly, our team heard clapping, laughter, and music coming from the other side of the terminal. I turned with a puzzled look to one of the stairway ramp workers in street clothes. He smiled and happily informed me, "It is a welcome party for you."

By the time we left the terminal, the equatorial sun had set behind the jungle, tinting the clouds above in broad stripes of orange and red. The colors didn't last long; because we were on the equator, nighttime came fast, leaving us in a sultry, hissing darkness that made the drums sound exotic and mysterious. We stepped from the terminal's crumbling sidewalk into a large circle of happy Africans, finding ourselves in the middle of a worship service. Several cars angled in, their headlights providing enough light to see, and in the glare I made out flashes of brilliant color, beads, and swirling skirts. Some of the dancers were visible in the headlights, while others were silhouetted in black. It was a jumble of darkness and light, color and shadow, droning harmony and staccato of syncopated hand-claps, and soon I was surrounded by tall, hand-some women, swaying, swinging, and clapping in tribal rhythm, while a larger circle of drummers and men danced around them. It was a wild and captivating celebration, and I did not dare move. My breath quickened and my heart raced, but I gave myself over to the moment and shed my Western inhibitions, bobbing my head, smil-ing, and swinging my arms in rhythm to the dance.

"Welcome to Africa, where our God is bigger!" a pastor said with arms spread wide.

The party lasted nearly thirty minutes. Afterward, while the wheel-chairs and supplies were being unloaded from the plane, we settled into a hotel near the airport. I could hardly sleep that night. *We're in Africa*, I whispered into my pillow. Sounds of frogs, crickets, and shrieking animal calls filled the night outside my window, and I wished that Daddy were here. *He would love this,* I kept thinking.

I also thought about the amazing circumstances that had brought us here. *Lord, thank you for honoring the hopes of those women in Kumasi who got John to promise he'd return.* That was two years ago. So much time had passed. *Just a few months ago, it seemed an impossibility. But here we are! And it's all because of you, Lord Jesus, and an incredible contest. Who would have believed it?*

We separated into groups and fanned out into different villages along the coast. I was part of a team that took several wheelchairs and medical equipment to a small AIDS clinic on the outskirts of Accra. We were met by a British doctor and several African interns and nurses, who led us into a plain, low-slung, cinder-block building. The sun at high noon was oppressive, but once inside, the bare concrete hallways were cool and damp. "There is one woman I wish you to see," the doctor said, directing me to a room at the end of the hall. "Her name is Vida. She is a prostitute, and she's dying of AIDS."

I wheeled into the small room. It was like all the other rooms in the clinic: bare cinder block—clean, but bare. Vida, bone-thin and gaunt, was stretched uncomfortably under a thin sheet. With her hand resting on her forehead, I could see she was in pain.

"Vida, we have come to give you some things," I said softly as I wheeled closer. A friend deposited some perfume, toothpaste, a bar of soap, and some other items on her bedside table.

She mustered a smile and extended a hand to me. I was unable to grasp it, so I leaned forward and simply rested my hand against hers. Her eyes remained fixed on my face as I started to sing an African chorus I had learned the first night we arrived.

> *Cast your burdens upon Jesus, 'cause he cares for you.*
> *Cast your burdens upon Jesus, 'cause he cares for you.*
> *Higher, higher, higher, higher, higher, higher . . .*
> *Higher, higher, lift up Jesus higher.*

I remained by her bedside for a long time, allowing her eyes to drink in this strange, white visitor in a wheelchair. I tried to imagine the circumstances that landed her here. Just that day, I had read of a row of thatch-covered stalls behind a market, where prostitutes sold themselves for fifty cents a man.

I bit my lip as I studied Vida's face. She wasn't an attractive woman, perhaps in her early thirties; the side of her face showed tribal scars, and her eyes looked tired and swollen. I wondered how many years she had been selling herself. When I told her my story of how I broke my neck, she winced in pity. *Isn't this something, Lord. This woman is dying, and yet her heart is going out to me.*

"Do you know Jesus?" I asked, pointing to my heart. "Vida, do you know him, *here?*"

She nodded. The doctor later told us that Vida's family had disowned her, and she had no visitors or friends. "Your visit today meant the world to her," he said. "And don't worry for Vida. God will take care of her."

Oppressive heat, AIDS running rampant, I thought as we drove away. *Polio survivors dragging themselves along the sidewalks. Children abandoned because of their cerebral palsy. Endless poverty.*

Yet the Africans who embraced Christ—many of them like Vida, others with disabilities—were full of joy. The doctor's words kept ringing in my ears: "God will take care of her."

Here in the sub-Sahara, it seemed that the weaker people were, the harder they had to lean on God—and the harder they leaned on him, the greater their joy. It was so different in America, I thought. In the West, we think God exists to make our lives happy, more meaningful and trouble-free. Suffering is a hateful word, and we do anything to eradicate it, medicate it, circumvent it, or divorce it, building hospitals and institutions to alleviate suffering. But in Ghana, people seemed more ready to come to God in empty-handed spiritual poverty, taking from his hand whatever he might offer.

"The faith of Christians here is so big," I said to Ken over the phone that night. "Yet they have so little."

I found my own faith growing in Africa, not just from others' experiences, but firsthand. One afternoon, the KLM executives arranged for me to meet the president of Ghana. After a press conference, we sat with President Rawlings in his tropical garden under a sprawling, moss-laden tree. Macaws and parrots echoed in the thick jungle growth beyond the gate, and philodendron the size of elephant ears hung from branches above. Every once in a while, a breeze from the ocean nearby stirred the heavy, warm air, wafting in the scent of fruit and flowers.

"This castle here," President Rawlings said, pointing to the white, sun-drenched walls behind him, "was built by the British in the seventeenth century. It was here that our people were held in chains, awaiting the slave ships." There was no hint of bitterness in his voice; he understood that we all held slavery to be wrong. He was simply giving us the history of his land. "And your Mr. Lincoln was quite a president," he said, spreading his arms wide.

After refreshments, President Rawlings asked if he could do anything to help us on our mission in Ghana.

"As a matter of fact, there is," I replied, a little surprised at his offer. "The idea for this whole trip began with a promise made to a woman in Kumasi."

"Kumasi? We have been fighting rebels in the region north of there."

"Well, we would like to go there very much—I would, especially," I said. "But they tell me the road is rutted deeply and washed out in places, and the drive would be too hard for me."

Without hesitating, the president turned to his aide and spoke in his native tongue. After they deliberated for a few moments, President Rawlings turned to us and announced, "Tomorrow you will have the Air Force at your disposal."

It was becoming hard for my faith *not* to grow in Ghana.

Yet there was one more person, at least, whose faith was far greater.

The next day, as I waited to board the plane for Kumasi, John Wern was already well on his way north, taking the long, bumpy drive. The plan was for him to arrive ahead of me and set up the wheelchairs for distribution. Once he arrived and began the process of unloading them, a woman in beautifully colored tribal dress approached him. She was carrying a disabled son in her strong arms.

"Do you remember me?" she asked John, flashing a wide smile.

John looked up from his clipboard as the sway-backed woman hiked her son on her hip. "You have something for me," she said with a confident smile, "I know you do."

John's eyes widened in recognition. "Yes, I know who you are," he said, smiling. "You insisted we would come back." He set down his clipboard in amazement. "And here we are. Isn't it incredible?"

"Incredible?" she answered in the now-familiar African-British accent. "Why is that so? I knew you would return. We prayed that you would."

Her tone was so matter-of-fact, it caught John off guard. She had no inkling of all the levers and pulleys God used to get us back to her country. She knew nothing about the contest—yet even if she did, I know it wouldn't have surprised her to learn that we won.

"God always answers our prayers," she continued. "We knew he would bring you back."

We were in Africa, where people are convinced of a big God. Then again, he always seems bigger to those who need him most.

Africa showed me that God is attracted to the weak, he is drawn to the needy, and he is near to those who acknowledge their spiritual poverty, like the woman who walked two miles to Kumasi with her son on her back. Africa underscored to me that God always lavishes his grace on those who consider themselves undeserving— such as Vida and others I met in the AIDS clinic. And Africa illumined the words of Jesus to me with a new depth: "Blessed are the poor in spirit, for theirs is the kingdom of heaven," and "Listen, my dear brothers: Has not God chosen those who are poor in the eyes of the world to be rich in faith and to inherit the kingdom he promised those who love him?"

The images of those joyful Christians I met in Africa have retained their clarity for me over the years, much more than most. The edges haven't gotten fuzzy with nostalgia—they've remained sharp and definitive. Life in Africa is raw and bruising in its poverty, and there's nothing sentimental about an AIDS clinic there. It's hard to see anything romantic about a woman's long journey on foot with a heavy child on her back. In Africa, people require God earnestly, because they know they need him drastically.

Several months after the KLM trip, after I was back home in America and settled in, I was still speaking about Ghana wherever and whenever I got the chance. From one conference to the next, I told the stories of the people I met—the African boy who dragged himself on his hands for three miles to come to our wheelchair distribution, the bright and full smiles of worshippers, the singing and the drums, the clapping, swaying, and dancing of tribal people celebrating God. And wherever I spoke, I remembered Vida.

During a break at one such conference, I darted to the restroom. As I waited in line, my eyes wandered over the cool, Italian marble counters and the bronze faucets, the nicely folded towels and the little soaps in shell dishes. One well-dressed woman, putting on lipstick, caught me in the mirror and remarked, "Oh, Joni, you always look so together, so happy in your wheelchair. I wish I had your joy!" Several women around her nodded. "How *do* you do it?" she said as she capped her lipstick.

I glanced around at the women, all sharply dressed and studded with jewelry, and took note of their *Jones of New York* outfits and red-manicured nails. This conference was drawing from the wealthier surrounding suburbs. Then an image of Vida and her leathery, dark skin stretching over thin bones flashed through my mind.

"You want to know how I do it? The truth is, I *don't* do it."

A few eyebrows raised.

"In fact, may I tell you honestly how I woke up this morning?"

At that, several women leaned against the counter to listen.

"Here is an average day for me," I breathed deeply. "After Ken leaves for work at 6:00 A.M., I'm alone until I hear the front door open at 7:30 A.M. It's a friend coming to get me up. While I hear her make coffee, I usually pray, 'Oh Lord, my friend is about to give me a bath, get me dressed, sit me up in my chair, brush my hair and teeth, and send me out the door. But, Jesus, I don't have strength to face this routine one more time. I have no resources. I don't have a smile to take into the day. But you do. May I borrow yours? I urgently need you, Lord. I require you desperately.'"

Suddenly, the women before me relaxed. From their expressions, I could tell that underneath the makeup and jewelry, they were carrying burdens too. They were weary, some of their hearts bruised and numb. And they were curious to know more: "So, what happens when your friend comes through the bedroom door?"

"I turn my head on the pillow," I sighed, "and I give her a smile sent straight from heaven. It's not mine—it's God's. Whatever joy you see today—," I said, gesturing to my paralyzed legs, "—was hard won this morning."

The restroom was silent.

"Ladies, it's the only way to live. It's the *Christian* way to live. And maybe the truly handicapped people are the ones who don't need God as much."

I knew that most of those women would go home that evening to broken garbage disposals, indifferent husbands, swollen ankles, and sore feet. God willing, they would remember to go desperately and urgently to the Lord for grace. The lesson that the women in Kumasi taught me has come back to me many times since: the weaker we are, the harder we must lean on God—and the harder we lean on him, the stronger we discover him to be.

Chapter Twenty-Five

He was despised and rejected by men, a man of sorrows, and familiar with suffering. Like one from whom men hide their faces he was despised, and we esteemed him not.

Isaiah 53:3

July 30, 1997, arrived not with an anniversary cake but a cupcake with a candle on top.

"Make a wish," Ken said, half-joking. He'd wanted to mark the thirtieth anniversary of my diving accident with a bit of humor. After all, there aren't many people who would celebrate breaking their neck.

Yet we both knew I was still learning from my wheelchair. And it had kept me leaning hard on God. "Hurry up, the wax is getting on the icing," Ken urged, licking his fingers.

I didn't know what to wish. *Wow, three decades since I broke my neck . . . since I graduated from high school. . . .*

"I've got it!" I announced, as Ken pushed the cupcake nearly into my face. "I wish you'd go with me to my thirtieth high school reunion."

"Awww," he groaned. "Do you *really* like going to those things?"

"Yes," I declared, "and I want you there with me, so my friends can finally meet you."

He gave me a smirk as I blew out the candle.

It had been years since I had touched base with my peers from choir, clubs, Young Life, hockey, and lacrosse. And I looked forward to seeing the girls who'd stuck closest to me after my accident, mainly Jacque and Diana. I had to chuckle as I thought of the time they tossed me into the front seat of Jacque's Camaro like a sack of potatoes. We didn't even know enough to wear seat belts, and when we braked for a stoplight, I virtually slid on the floor.

That reminded me of the time Diana sat with me in a boat on Disneyland's *Pirates of the Caribbean* ride. We were floating along just fine until we heard a waterfall ahead, and looked up to see the boat in front of us diving straight down. Diana quickly leaped on top of me, pinning her body against mine, and together we screamed all the way down, plunging to the bottom of the waterfall. I never went on the ride again.

Those had been carefree days—and, of course, the days before that weren't so happy. I remembered the long-ago night when, as a frightened seventeen-year-old, I lay face-up in a shadowy hospital room wondering if God had abandoned me. The hallways were dark and visiting hours over. And then Jacque—my friend, my sharer of milkshakes, hockey sticks, and boyfriends—climbed into bed next to me. She'd instinctively known the only thing that would bring comfort, and in the midst of that dark night, she sang:

> *"Man of Sorrows!" What a name!*
> *For the Son of God who came*
> *Ruined sinners to reclaim!*
> *Hallelujah, what a Savior!*

Over the past three decades, whenever anyone asked me, "When was the turning point?" I described that moment. It was the best thing anyone could have done for a paralyzed girl. Lying for long hours in bed, I had recited verses about God's purposes in suffering, but their truths never reached the core of my anguish. Answers and reasons, good though they are, weren't reaching the problem where it hurt—in my gut and heart.

I was asking God "Why?" like a child looking up into the face of her daddy. I wasn't looking for answers so much then as I was looking for Daddy. An Almighty image of my own father, who would pick me up, pat-pat me on the back, and tell me everything would be okay. My unspoken plea was for assurance—Fatherly assurance—that my world wasn't all nightmarish chaos. I was in need of a Daddy bigger than my own father, to cover me and give me himself.

I didn't realize it then, but my heavenly Father was doing just that. He was being my Rock and Deliverer, whenever Diana read to me from Psalm 18. He was being my Wonderful Counselor, when she read from Isaiah 9. I didn't grasp it at first, but if God is truly the one at the center of the universe, holding it together so it doesn't split apart at the seams—if everything moves, breathes, and has its being in *him,* as it says of God in Acts 17:28—he can give us no greater answer or reason or gift than himself.

That's what Jacque helped me to grasp that night. God didn't give words, he gave the Word—Jesus, the bruised and bloody Man of Sorrows.

I telephoned the chairman of the high school reunion committee to make reservations and ask who else was coming. When I asked about my hockey friends, there was a long pause at the other end.

"Joni, I'm sure you didn't hear—"

"Hear what?"

"The news that's going around. Jacque's teenage boy, Josh, had really been struggling. He—Joni, he took his life."

I was breathless with shock.

After I hung up, a flood of memories washed over me. How, on the bus home from a hockey game, Jacque and I sang until our throats were hoarse. How as seniors, we cut class to drive to Washington, D.C., to buy a beer. How she, Diana, and others had stayed close by me, learning my bed and bath routines and leg exercises. And how happy Jacque was on the day of her wedding.

I felt large tears beginning to stream as I thought of all the innocence, all the simple-hearted unguardedness that marked our high school days. Never could we have anticipated, as we strolled to the showers after hockey practice, that our lives would be broadsided by death and disability.

I tried to call her but couldn't get through. I had to do something. I wanted so much to climb into her heartache as she had mine. So I wrote a letter:

Dear Jacque ... Ken and I are planning to be home for the reunion, and I'm hoping we can see each other. If so, I would want to hold your hand, as you once held mine in the hospital, and I would softly sing to you, as you once sang to me, "Man of Sorrows, what a name ..." I don't know what else to say. May the Man of Sorrows be your comfort. And, as in the hospital, I would hope you would sense what I felt and what I still remember to this day. Peace. Not answers, but peace. Do you remember that night more than thirty years ago? I have never forgotten it.

Weeks later, Ken and I were back in Baltimore, sitting across from Jacque at a private dinner table. She didn't feel she could face all the questions from old classmates, so she'd dropped by early to see us before we went to the party. Although her eyes were sad, the thirty intervening years, a divorce, and the death of her son still hadn't diminished the winsome, youthful optimism in her smile.

When I asked how she was doing, my old friend grew serious. She pressed her fingers to a cross that hung from her neck. It was of brushed gold with beveled edges and was threaded on a fine, delicate chain. Jacque gripped it as she quietly said, "I hate what has happened. I can't talk to God. I can't pray. I'm angry. But I still need my connection to him."

The reunion was somewhat subdued that night. It was still good to see everyone, though, even Benjamin Wallace, who used to pretend he was a race car zooming down the hallway. As I looked around, I saw that red hair had turned to gray, and blonde hair showed dark roots. Crewcuts and thin ties were no more, and most of the fellows were paunchy and a little bald. Now and again, the subject of Jacque's son came up.

But whenever the DJ played an oldie-but-goodie by the Supremes—favorites that Jacque and I used to dance to—I recalled her face from earlier in the evening. And I replayed the way she held the cross around her neck—not just an object of beauty or a nice piece of jewelry but something that in reality was all about dried blood, gore, buzzing flies, and spiked hatred. The cross that Jacque holds is no longer some cleaned-up jeweler's version, not an answer, not a reason—but the place where God gave *himself*.

Jacque is discovering all that that means. Just like her paralyzed friend.

CHAPTER TWENTY-SIX

A man may be chastened on a bed of pain with constant distress in his bones.

Job 33:19

The sun was low, casting a soft pink haze over the Dutch countryside. The outline of windmills and willows and cows grazing in the distance gave the impression we were part of a painting, a picture-perfect setting in which all was well in 1997. Swans glided along the canal, and white herons picked their way through the pastures. We were at the country home of Jan, our good friend, and as we relaxed around his dinner table graced with candles, china, and tulips, and as guests on either side talked and dined, I knew I couldn't stay in the picture any longer. I suddenly announced, "I'm sorry, but I have to leave the table. I must lie down."

The table became quiet.

Please, I whispered anxiously to Ken and Judy, *I have to lie down.*

A painful throb between my shoulder blades was beginning to stab like a knife. I'd held it at bay most of the evening, but sometime between dinner and dessert, it had become unbearable.

They found a couch in a side room, laid me down, unbuckled my corset, and propped pillows under my back. I took in deep breaths and tried to release what I felt was an ice pick buried deep between my shoulders. Judy tried to make me as comfortable as possible. As we waited and listened to the soft conversation in the next room, I chewed my lip nervously. This was the first time the pain had succeeded in ambushing me. It had tried before, but I'd been able to grin and bear it, push through and plod ahead. Not anymore. It was now unmanageable. As I heard laughter from the next room, I was afraid that life, as I had come to enjoy it, was slipping away.

I had always lived with general discomfort, like a constant, low-grade fever. In the last six months, however, I was twitching and squirming more often in my chair, excusing myself early from long meetings, and going to bed at eight o'clock rather than nine. I was also getting Ken up in the middle of the night more often to turn me.

"Suffering is like a sheepdog that snaps at your heels and keeps driving you toward the Shepherd," I would say confidently from the platform to a large audience. "Let it drive you into the arms of the Savior." And I meant it. But when I would go back to the hotel room and look into the mirror, I saw the eyes of a worried woman. *Will I be able to sleep tonight? Will the pain be this bad tomorrow?*

"Let's make a doctor's appointment as soon as we get home," Ken said.

"I've already been to the doctor," I said, demoralized.

"Well, we'll go again."

When we got back to the States, I lined up a series of tests. There were urology exams and a CAT scan, blood samples and X-rays. We thought we had it narrowed down to gallstones, but on the evening of the sonogram, the technician whispered helpfully, "Hey, good news. Everything looks fine."

"Oh, no," my spirits sank.

"You're not happy?" she said, her eyebrows raised above her glasses.

"I was so hoping we would pinpoint the source of the pain," I sighed. "Now we have to keep looking."

More tests ensued. A fractured bone somewhere? No. Cancer? No again. Aspirin and Advil gave no relief. Not even Vioxx helped. As months wore on, my hopes began to falter. *What if they can't find the problem?*

My doctor scratched his head. He was stumped but not daunted. "I want you to see a physiatrist," he said as he jotted a prescription. "Dr. Hedge, over at the Spinal Cord Injury clinic at Northridge Hospital."

I made an appointment but wasn't enthusiastic. I had seen lots of doctors.

The pain was now razor-edged and ruling my days, deciding what I did and where I went. I couldn't paint. Couldn't look down to read. Driving was out. Writing projects were postponed. The agony became all-consuming. "Joni? *Joni?*" a coworker would say, leaning over my shoulder. "Did you hear what I said?"

"Yes . . . er, no." Truth was, I couldn't focus. *Oh Lord, please help me get through this*, I prayed, but the plea wasn't heartfelt. It was a statement of exasperation, not a request.

Like a low groaning and creaking in the bowels of a ship, the core of my confidence in Christ was being rattled. The sovereignty of God that had always illuminated my life—"*I want you all to know my accident was no accident at all*"—was turning dark and foreboding. And scary.

Sunday mornings I would sit in church, wanting very much to listen intently to the sermon or to sing wholeheartedly with the congregation. But halfway through the service, I was swallowing hard, squirming left and right, hoping I could simply make it to the benediction. It seemed unfair. I, if anyone, needed the benefit of hearing the Word, but unlike the rest—including Ken who sat comfortably, attentive and relaxed—I couldn't hear the message for the pain.

One night, my fear was overwhelming to the point of suffocation. Ken had turned me on my side and situated my pillows before climbing into bed. His alarm was set for 5:30 A.M. I fell in and out of sleep until 2:00, when I was awakened by the same searing pain in my neck. By now, it was affecting my shoulder, the shoulder I was lying on. I twisted my head back for relief. I was only able to move a little, but I could at least squeeze an inch or two to the side, in order to drop my shoulder more. It didn't help.

I didn't want to wake up Ken—he had already turned me once. I tweaked my neck further back, deciding to remain positioned at that awkward angle, although it offered minimal relief. *Here I am, a quadriplegic lying in a contorted, stiff position, and the only part of me that can feel hurts like crazy.* I wanted to pray but could only repeat the name of Jesus.

"Jesus, Jesus, Jesus," I moaned softly. "I want to trust the Father with this, but he's so . . . so sovereign. And that's scary. I'm afraid to trust him. I can't, I can't," my thoughts trailed.

Sleeplessness kept my mind buzzing. *God, you're the one who's allowing this. You screened it and decided it could touch me, hurt me,* I groaned inwardly. *How can you permit this terrible pain in addition to quadriplegia!*

I thought back to more carefree days, before my accident, when the sovereignty of God seemed harmless and helpful. When I was in high school, it was a Band-Aid to be applied to a disappointing Friday night without a date or a blow-up with a sister over a borrowed blouse. It was useful. That's the way I treated scores of Christian doctrines back then. I'd flip through the Bible to find something that buzzed, resonated, or spoke to my latest experience. I'd dip into a chapter, read a few verses, pick out the data that benefited me, and close it up. I would grab Romans 8:28 and pour it like alcohol on a wound, grimacing but knowing "that in all things God works for the good of those who love him, who have been called according to his purpose."

I wasn't desperate for God back then. I was desperate for answers, for something that would fix my problems.

Then I broke my neck. I found myself on the high wire of a permanent handicap, a tightrope-walker gingerly stepping out over a deep chasm, holding onto the balancing pole of Romans 8:28 for all I was worth—still believing that all things, even paralysis, could fit together into a pattern for good. I believed God was at the other end of that high wire, with arms outstretched, saying, "You can do it—come on, you can make it." And miracle of miracles, I *was* making it. Years were passing, and I was maintaining my balance, cultivating patience and endurance, and watching things fit together for good.

No longer. Mind-bending pain had begun to jiggle the wire, and I'd lost sight of God at the far end. *Or maybe he's disappeared. Maybe he's gone.* Worse yet, maybe *he* was the one shaking the wire. *Maybe he's about to cut it,* I worried. I looked below me and saw no safety net, no everlasting arms ready to catch me.

Suddenly, in the dark, around 2:30 or so, I heard a soft, small voice in my heart. It said, *You can trust me. Trust me. I am the Man of Sorrows, acquainted with grief. I am the Friend of sinners and the Lifter-up of heads. I know pain. I know it well. Turn your eyes off your pain, and turn them on me. Place your confidence in me.*

I gritted my teeth, straining to listen in the dark. The thought—the inaudible voice, whatever it was—was fleeting, and I wanted to hear more. But there was nothing. Just high-pitched whining in my ears.

My spirits brightened a bit when I finally got in to see Dr. Hedge. I identified with him—he was another quad. He would understand. After reviewing my X-rays and charts, he wheeled back in and examined my sitting position.

"I can't find anything medically wrong, Joni," he said, "but we're going to try one more thing. I recommend that you see my associate, Paulette, a physical therapist. She's had a lot of success with patients in pain. She specializes in something called myo-fascia release."

Three days later, I was lying face down on my bed with Paulette standing over me, exploring my vertebrae and shoulder blades with her thumbs. She pushed and kneaded my muscles, thinking out loud, "Hum-um," and then, again, "Hum-um." After fifteen or twenty minutes of probing, she announced, "I think I can have you all better in five sessions."

"You can *what?*" my voice muffled against the mattress.

"Your problem is a mechanical one. You've been sitting wrong. Painting at funny angles. Throwing your shoulder back to drive. A little scoliosis. The muscles you have left are knotted very badly. But it's not hopeless."

At that word—*hopeless*—my face flushed, and I began to sob softly. "Oh, I do hope you're right," I sniffed, wetting the sheets, "I hope you're right."

I hadn't felt the freshness of hope in a long time. And I didn't exactly feel it then. But here was someone using that word—the H-word—holding it out to me with the faraway notion that things would get better.

With my face still pressed into the bed, I slowly recited a verse I had memorized long ago: "And we rejoice in the hope of the glory of God. Not only so, but we also rejoice in our sufferings, because we know that suffering produces perseverance; perseverance, character; and character, hope. And hope does not disappoint us. . . ."

"My, that's beautiful," Paulette said. "Is that from the Bible?"

"Yes. The book of Romans."

"And what does it mean?" she asked, continuing to knead my shoulders.

I realized this was one of those times I could either respond with something I'd learned by rote or make it personal. I chose the latter. "Remember the movie *Shawshank Redemption?*"

"Mm-hm."

It was a heart-wrenching story revealing in brazen detail the evils behind prison walls. The main character, Andy—an innocent man framed for a murder he didn't commit—escapes after decades of planning how he might not only thwart but also expose the evil warden. Andy flees across the Mexican border, makes his home in a village on the edge of the Pacific, and prepares for the time when his old friend from prison, an elderly black man named Red, will be paroled.

In the final scene, Red is at last released and discovers a letter Andy has left for him. In it, Andy urges Red to follow a secret route to the little Mexican village where he'll be waiting for him. Red hesitates but then reads the words: "Hope is a good thing—maybe the best of things. And no good thing ever dies."

The old man puts down the letter, smiles, and heads for the bus station. As he leans out the window of the bus, Red knows that crossing the Mexican border will either return him to prison for breaking parole or free him for the rest of his life. He's scared, but he dares to hope, thinking, *I feel the excitement that only a free man can feel—a free man at the start of a long journey whose conclusion is uncertain. I hope to see my friend and shake his hand. I hope the Pacific is as blue as it has been in my dreams. I hope. I hope.*

The first time I saw the movie, I too kept hoping: *Red has to make it across the border, he has to find his friend. Then his troubles will be over. You can do it, Red, you can make it!*

The last scene was worth the previous two hours and thirty minutes of prison horrors. I felt tears flow as I watched Red sling his coat over his shoulder and stride across the wide, white Mexican beach. Andy looks up from sanding the hull of a boat, spies his friend in the distance, and waves, rejoicing that Red decided to follow the trail of Hansel-and-Gretel hope he'd left for him. As the closing shot panned up and out until the turquoise blue of the Pacific Ocean filled the entire screen, I felt I was looking at heaven.

"It was a story of hope and redemption," I murmured. Then I repeated the line I'd memorized, "'Hope is a good thing—maybe the best of things. And no good thing ever dies.'"

"It *is* the best of things," Paulette underscored, as she continued to work on my back.

"I want so badly to have hope like that," I said softly. "The Bible says we can know for sure that God will help us glorify him, no matter how wretched the pain."

"Including this pain in your neck?"

I hesitated before offering a weak yes. As Paulette packed up after our session, she patted my shoulder, saying, "You'll be fine. You'll see." I felt as if she were Andy and I were Red, hoping against hope that she really knew the way of escape from all this horror.

For the next several weeks, in between sessions with Paulette, my emotions seesawed about God and his sovereignty. I wanted so much to be able to relax in his control of things, but every time I tried, fear seized me. My pain had warped my perception of the God who promised me in his Word, "'For I know the plans I have for you . . . plans to prosper you and not to harm you, plans to give you hope and a future.'"

I wondered about that promise now.

I wondered if other believers—especially those in places like war-ravaged Bosnia—were struggling with feelings of fear about God. The Balkan nightmare had left 300,000 people dead. And it wasn't over. Instead, the war had simply moved south to Kosovo. *Lord, I know—I truly believe—you hate the evil that's happening there and that if you weren't in control, it would be so much worse. But still, old women are starving in caves, and young girls are held down in barns to be raped. You're asking them to bear the unbearable.* Then, the inevitable question: *How can you expect them to trust you?*

The more I thought about it, the more I wondered for myself: *Who's to say you wouldn't ask me to bear the unbearable?*

I wished God were like he used to be. A few notches lower. I wanted him to be lofty enough to help me but not so uncontrollable. I longed for his warm presence, as in the times when Steve Estes read the Bible to me by the hearth. When Jay and I sang our hymns under the moonlight on the back porch. Times when he seemed more . . . safe.

Where's the safety now? God—who are you?

In my fog, I recalled someone else asking those same questions. It dawned on me it was the character Lucy in C. S. Lewis's fantasy, *The Lion, the Witch, and the Wardrobe*. The book tells the story of two children searching for their brother, who's under the spell of a wicked white witch. As Lucy and her sister Susan hide in the home of Mr. and Mrs. Beaver, the Beavers speak in hushed tones of a rumor: Aslan, the long-gone Lion King of Narnia, has been spotted and is on the move again. The Lion is symbolic of Christ, the God-man.

"Is—he a man?" asked Lucy.

"Aslan a man!" said Mr. Beaver sternly. "Certainly not. I tell you he is the King of the wood and the son of the great emperor beyond the sea. Don't you know who is the King of beasts? Aslan is a lion—_the_ Lion, the great Lion."

"Ooh!" said Susan, "I'd thought he was a man. Is he—quite safe? I shall feel rather nervous about meeting a lion."

"That you will, dearie, and no mistake," said Mrs. Beaver, "if there's anyone who can appear before Aslan without their knees knocking, they're either braver than most, or else just silly."

"Then he isn't safe?" said Lucy.

"Safe?" said Mr. Beaver. "Don't you hear what Mrs. Beaver tells you? Who said anything about safe? 'Course he isn't safe. But he's good. He's the King, I tell you."

God is not safe. I let the thought sink in. And as I did, I felt the high wire give way beneath me. Falling, falling . . . down and down, into a dark chasm, down back into the old miry pit. I kept repeating, _But he is the King, and he is good._

"Oh God, you _are_ good, you _must_ be good. Who have I to turn to, but you? You are the only one who has the words of life," I prayed. Just then, as if caught by invisible arms, an old, familiar assurance buoyed me up as it had so often in the past: _Joni, if I loved you enough to die for you, then I can see you—I can sustain you—even through this. You're safe. You're safe._

"Then, Lord," I answered, "please keep your everlasting arms underneath me. Please give me strength to hope—not that I'll get better but that you are enough. I need hope that you are enough."

The darkness didn't instantly become light, and I was not transported to picture-perfect tranquillity—but that was okay. It was _okay._ God had descended into my hell and rescued me. I felt his arms, and that was enough.

Five sessions later with Paulette, a dramatic change occurred: I noticed a drop in the level of my pain. I had to change my sitting position, drink more water, wear my corset looser, and stretch more often, but Paulette was right—I wasn't a hopeless case. Never would I have believed it, but I was better. Much better. I would wheel outside and be grateful for the sunrise. I would sleep straight through the night and wake up amazed. I'd pick up a paintbrush with my teeth and thank God I could still work at my easel. And I'd feel a lump in my throat whenever I looked at the little gold cross hanging on a necklace by my bathroom mirror. Suffering had, once again, revealed the stuff of which I was made—and once again it was not pretty. I fell apart when it pushed me past my limits. I panicked when it gave me more than I could bear. But I knew it was all so that I would lean on him, and him alone. It was all that I might be convinced he *is* enough—and that I might not be afraid.

Lord, one thing is for certain: I can no longer be confident of my love for you—but I am confident in your love for me. Still, I wondered what I would do if the pain came back. *I'll cross that bridge when I come to it. All I can say is, I've learned to cling to you today, God. Desperately!*

"I can't allow myself to slip back into life as it was," I told Steve Estes on the phone. "That whole pain experience was a crisis of faith."

"Remember that lesson we did years ago?" Steve reminded me. "The one on Philippians 3?"

"Yeah," I sighed, grinning as I thought of those years spent by the fireplace in my parents' home. "It was about wanting to know Christ and the power of his resurrection."

"And the fellowship of sharing in his sufferings. Well, there's more to that verse, Joni. It ends up saying, 'I want to know him ... and become like him in his death,'" Steve noted. "When you were describing your pain like being on a high wire and looking down at that chasm, you got a taste of what it means to become like Christ in his death."

I leaned against the receiver and closed my eyes. Jesus died on the cross for my sins—that, I knew. Now I must take up *my* cross and die to sin. Die to any hollow, casual trust in God. Die to faithlessness, to every doubt and fear, to all anxiety and worry. To having control and assuming that my trials should neatly fit into my Day-Timer, that God should space them out in moderate doses. Die to pride and self-sufficiency, to self-resourcefulness and self-reliance. Die to self, self, self, me, me, me.

As months wore on, I kept in touch with Paulette, making appointments for her to work on my neck and shoulders to keep the pain at bay. One day after a session, she reached into her duffel bag and pulled out a gift-wrapped package. "This is for you," she smiled and began to untie the ribbon for me. "You've shown me something about hope, too, and I wanted to return the favor. So my husband and I asked a friend to write this out for you. She had to rent the movie and rewind it a few times, but it's all there."

Paulette held up a hand-calligraphied plaque in a wooden frame. I read the message aloud:

> *The old man unfolds the letter and reads: ". . . Remember Red, Hope is a good thing. Maybe the best of things. And no good thing ever dies."*
> *Red reflects upon the letter and tells himself,*
> *"Get busy living or get busy dying."*

I got busy living again.

The next several years were the busiest ever, and by the time 1999 arrived, I was sitting in the wings of a theater stage, behind the heavy, velvet curtains of the Thousand Oaks Civic Arts Plaza, just up the freeway from the office of Joni and Friends. I was waiting for my cue while listening to little Kara in her wheelchair finish her speech in the stage spotlight. This child with the small voice was explaining to the crowd that she wanted to give her old wheelchair to Wheels for the World.

"I want some little girl in Africa or Asia to have the chance to know Jesus, and to use a wheelchair!" she exclaimed. Then Kara's mother pushed her old chair out from the shadows, so everyone could see the beautiful, big, gold ribbon her daughter had tied around it. The audience of over a thousand burst into applause.

There was a lot to applaud about. The gala event at the Civic Arts Plaza was a celebration of the twentieth anniversary of Joni and Friends. As I watched Kara take a bow in her chair, I kept thinking of the thousands like her who were getting help through Family Retreats and Wheels for the World. The ministry was growing fast, with area offices springing up all around the country, and international disability organizations signing up as Joni and Friends charters or affiliates. At that point, we had distributed over seven thousand wheelchairs and as many Bibles, trained countless Christians in churches around the world, and were adding more Family Retreats every year. I couldn't believe what God had started—and what he was continuing to do—through that diving accident so long ago.

And the best, and busiest, times were yet to come.

Thankfully, I was able to keep my pain at bay, as Francie, Judy, and I boarded a jet for the interminably long flight to China, with side visits to Japan and Australia. We and the Wheels team were taking three hundred wheelchairs to three cities in that sprawling nation of more than one billion people. The gift of those chairs to the disabled people of China didn't amount to a drop in the bucket, we knew, but we looked at this visit as a "starfish" trip. As the story goes, an old man and a boy were walking along a beach cluttered with stranded starfish after a storm. The boy picked up a starfish from the sand and threw it back in the ocean, then another, and another. The old man chided him, "What difference can you make? There are thousands of these stranded up and down this beach!" The child picked up another starfish, tossed it in the ocean, and replied, "I made a difference to that one."

That's how we viewed China: we would make a difference in one life at a time. A life like Dr. Zhang Xu's, a man who lived far beyond the mountains north of Beijing, where the arctic air can sweep down across the Mongolian plain and freeze his hometown of Anshan in an icy grip. Inside the town's hospital, on the third floor, Zhang Xu sits by a window. He's one of the few spinal-cord-injured quadriplegics who has survived in this difficult environment.

I couldn't wait to meet this wonderful starfish.

Zhang Xu had been an orthopedic surgeon who had worked for the Chinese government in the Middle Eastern country of Yemen. On a weekend break from his hospital routines, he went to a lake with friends and took a fateful dive like mine. His coworkers scrambled to keep him alive, but infection quickly set in on top of the quadriplegia, and Zhang Xu's parents were told their son wouldn't survive. They begged that he might die in their beloved China rather than in some desert outpost. So when he was sent home on a stretcher, his friends at the China Rehabilitation Research Center in Beijing worked fast and furiously to save him. Slowly, with the help of his family, he gained strength.

During that time, a Japanese therapist—a Christian—gave Zhang Xu a tattered, old copy of the *Joni* book in English. At night, while cold winds rattled the hospital windows, his mother held the book for him by the soft light of a bedside lamp, and he began reading. Here was a story he could identify with. Here was someone like him asking the same questions. And here were answers. The Answer.

Dr. Zhang's heart was strangely warmed. Immediately, he decided to begin translating the story into simplified Chinese text. He dictated while his mother, a journalist, painstakingly penciled down every word. Soon they had a thick, heavy handwritten manuscript to show for their efforts.

After many months of countless emails, faxes, personal connections, and conversations—with a physician at the Beijing American Embassy, with a ministry partner in Bangkok, with the foreign-rights staff at Zondervan, and our team at Joni and Friends—the book rolled off the press of a Chinese publishing house, with the story and Scriptures intact. It was, in fact, the first Christian book ever published by a government-run publishing company in China. And that meant a wider distribution in secular book shops there.

We arrived in Beijing energized by the many new sights and sounds and a people whose language and culture were so different from ours. I was relieved Ken was able to join us in time for our trip to the Great Wall. He and two men hauled me in my wheelchair up the many steps to reach the top. It reminded me of the way Ken had lifted my wheelchair up to the Parthenon years ago in Athens for the Greek premiere of the *Joni* movie. Then, as now, I sang a hymn for the occasion: "Love Lifted Me."

When the day came for Zhang Xu's and my book to be officially introduced at a press conference at the Rehabilitation Center, media executives and officials from the government and the University of Peking had gathered to give speeches, reviews, and congratulations. The large room was completely clogged with lights, microphones, cameras, and dignitaries, and the air was hot and stuffy. Far in the back, disabled people sat quietly in wheelchairs next to supportive family members and did their best to stay out of the way. No one paid much attention to them, but each had been given a Chinese *Joni* book, and a few silently leafed through it. Every so often, they looked up and flashed a smile our way.

All was dignified, all was official as the press conference began, and one speech followed another. But the hour dragged on, and the air became hotter and stuffier. Finally, it was time for Zhang Xu to give his speech. As I leaned toward my interpreter, I heard him describe the details of a long journey of pain and disappointment. As he spoke, I noticed that the back row of people in wheelchairs were growing more and more restless. Finally, when Zhang Xu told how the *Joni* book helped him, I started to hear sniffles. I peered around the lights and cameras and saw most of the people in the back crying.

"I thought I was alone," Zhang Xu continued in Chinese, "but I learned through this woman's story that there is a God who cares." As I gazed around the room, I saw that others who had been touched by deep suffering were weeping too. A little boy with cerebral palsy and his parents. A mother and father of a brain-injured child in the third row. An old man who had survived a stroke. Dr. Zhang was touching many chords. Or, rather, the Lord was.

I'm always astounded at how far we are able to go on a little bit of hope. And at how most people are either busy dying . . . or busy living. Perhaps when that press conference started, most people were busy dying. But by the time Zhang Xu finished, the hot, stuffy air had lifted. I think—I'm *sure*—it was because of hope. God had used the broken body and tender voice of this Chinese "hero"— not the words of an American in a fancy power wheelchair—to sweep away discouragement and blow across everyone the fresh air of hope. I could see it in the eyes of the little boy with cerebral palsy, in those of the parents of the brain-injured child, and many more.

Suddenly I felt a tissue on my cheek. Dr. Zhang's mother was bending down to wipe my eyes, which by then were spilling over with salty tears. Her gentle touch made the tears flow even more fully.

I see the God of all comfort keep raising up people like Zhang Xu on every continent, in every land—willing witnesses to how his power shows up in weak, needy people. The Father of compassion picks up starfish one at a time and casts them into his ocean of love.

CHAPTER TWENTY-SEVEN

Again he said, "What shall we say the kingdom of God is like, or what parable shall we use to describe it? It is like a mustard seed, which is the smallest seed you plant in the ground. Yet when planted, it grows and becomes the largest of all garden plants, with such big branches that the birds of the air can perch in its shade."

Mark 4:30–32

And what are these?" a girlfriend asked one morning, as she helped me get ready for the day. We were in my bathroom, and she'd lifted the lid on a small porcelain pillbox on the vanity. Inside were a few dry, crusted seed pods.

"Ah, those are mustard seeds." I had almost forgotten about them, it had been so long.

"But they look too big," she frowned, poking through them. "I thought the mustard seed was the smallest of all seeds."

"I once said the same thing," I said, smiling at the memory. I explained to her how the pods were merely casings for the mustard seeds. But now, after sitting on my bathroom counter for ages, the pods had shriveled into dry shells. There was nothing inside them.

"Do you want to keep them? Or shall I throw them away?" she asked, holding the pillbox over the wastebasket.

I shook my head. "I'll keep them," I said. Even though the mustard seeds had disappeared, the faith they had stirred hadn't.

It was the fall of 1998, and Ken and I, along with Judy and another friend, Bunny, were visiting Israel. We were driving along the narrow, winding road behind the Mount of Olives when Jan, our Dutch host calmly warned us: "We are moving out of Israeli controlled territory now. Things will look a little different."

He was right. We saw fewer tanks and soldiers and a lot more donkeys and Arab goatherders. The road twisted and turned for several miles before it dipped into Bethany, a small, white-washed village a few miles east of Jerusalem. As the others found out while exploring the town, Bethany hadn't changed since the days of Lazarus, Mary, and Martha. Meanwhile, as Bunny and I waited in the van, she spied an old, bearded Arab down the street sitting at a small table.

"I'm going to go see what he's selling," she said, hopping out.

Moments later she returned, her face aglow. "Would you look at these," she said, holding out dried, brown pea-sized seeds. "They're mustard seeds. If we have faith the size of one of these, " she said, picking one up, "we can move mountains."

"But they look kind of big," I said. "I thought the mustard seed was the smallest of all seeds."

"I said the same thing to that old Arab," Bunny said. "Let me show you what he did." She cracked open one of the pods and gently spread its contents across her palm. "Look at them," she said, cupping her hands slightly so the breeze wouldn't disturb them.

I had to lean forward and focus to see them, but there they were: infinitesimally tiny black specks—mustard seeds. A single pod contained thousands of them.

Bunny dusted off her hand and sealed the package of pods. "We're going to scatter these wherever we pray on this trip!"

We pulled out of Bethany, wound our way down into the Jordan River valley, and entered the Palestinian town of Jericho. Arab children, dirty and poorly clad, clamored around us, offering beaded necklaces for sale. We purchased a couple, said a prayer for the village, and continued our drive north. Bunny blew a handful of mustard seed-dust out the window.

Soon we entered back into Israeli territory. We cringed as we passed more soldiers and tanks. Bunny rolled down the window and scattered a few more seeds. With each dusting of seeds, our resolve—our faith—seemed to grow. This was a land that needed prayer. And a people who needed peace.

Within an hour, we reached the Sea of Galilee. We parked our van in a spot overlooking the wide, blue body of water, and wandered through a field toward a natural amphitheater tucked on the side of the hill. It was late in the day, and the tour buses had all departed. Summertime crickets hissed in the tall grass, and a breeze rustled nearby trees. We found ourselves on the slope above the ruins of Capernaum, very near the site where Jesus preached the Sermon on the Mount.

A dry wind tossed Ken's hair as he clasped his hands behind his back, faced the setting sun, and began to recite: "Now when he saw the crowds, he went up on a mountainside and sat down. His disciples came to him, and he began to teach them, saying: 'Blessed are the poor in spirit, for theirs is the kingdom of heaven—'" The wind carried his words, caressing the land with the same blessings Christ once pronounced, "'—Blessed are the peacemakers, for they will be called sons of God.'"

Ken had been memorizing these three chapters from the Gospel of Matthew for some time. But neither of us had anticipated that we would actually see, let alone stand, where Jesus uttered those words. As Ken continued reciting, I was amazed not only to be where Jesus was at one time, but also to be where he was at that moment—shining through my husband's eyes, resonating with every fiber of his being, filling his voice with virtue and courage, making him stronger and more handsome to me than ever.

"Blessed are the peacemakers!" I shouted to Ken.

"Blessed are the peacemakers," Bunny echoed from where she stood on the hill. She blew on her open palm, scattering more mustard seeds.

Ken turned and took in the scene before us. All was quiet and, on the surface, peaceful, but underneath we could sense a restlessness, an uneasiness. We heard it in the sighing of the wind through the trees. We felt it in the heavy silence of the ground beneath our feet. We sensed the longing in the agitated whitecaps on the Sea of Galilee. We even saw it in the graffiti on the trash container near the parking lot. And we couldn't ignore it in the tense faces of the young soldiers we'd seen everywhere that day. The planet was far from peaceful. It was waiting for God's feet to again touch the earth to bring peace forever. As we left the hills above Capernaum, twilight washed the landscape in a moody, dusty rose.

We planned to spend the next day in the Old City of Jerusalem with our guide, Fanny, a street-savvy, seventy-three-year-old Dutch Jew and Holocaust survivor. She told us we'd do well to begin at high noon when most visitors would be gone.

"This will be a day you will not forget," Fanny announced as we stood outside the Jaffa Gate. The aroma of baked almond bread and hot sausage welcomed us, as did the sounds of Arabic music.

"Come," our guide beckoned us down the narrow streets.

I passed by one kiosk after the next, sniffing baskets of dates, figs, grapes, and olives. There were colorful beads, Persian rugs, and wood-carvers displaying their creations. Bearded vendors weighed sacks of cumin and henna on their scales, bartering with groups of women. Legs of lamb hung from hooks, and a baby goat bleated from its tether. Several cats watched from perches while fishmongers filleted the morning's catch. A man knelt by a small round oven, spreading meat on a flat pita. He then cracked an egg in the middle and slid the pita into the oven. For all the dirt and smoke, the finished delicacy smelled savory and spicy. This was Jerusalem just as I'd hoped it would be.

Only one thing looked out of place: the constant presence of soldiers carrying large sub-machine guns. They were young and handsome, and many were women. They looked serious and alert, scanning faces in the crowd for the slightest hint of trouble.

Fanny waved us into a small gift shop. "This store is run by Palestinians," she said, "and this is my old and good friend." She grinned with pride as she embraced an elderly woman about the same age as she. The two could have been sisters, exuding the same tanned, weathered good looks, broad smiles, and gray hair. Their hands were strong and veined, their eyes wise and kind. They turned to each other and spoke in a little Arabic and Hebrew. And I thought again of Jesus' words, "Blessed are the peacemakers."

As we left the shop, Fanny told us, "There is one more place you must visit."

We drove around the walls of the Old City, passing more soldiers, and arrived at a checkpoint. Around us were heavy concrete roadblocks, traffic police, and military personnel checking IDs. Every soldier carried a machine gun. Every man and woman wore a somber expression and had searching eyes. Bags and purses were checked as the people ahead of us funneled through the guard gate. I wondered where Fanny was leading us.

When we left the checkpoint behind, the street opened out into a spacious plaza. It was bordered at the far end by a huge, ancient wall made of massive stone blocks.

"This is a sacred place for us Jews," Fanny said reverently. "This is the Western Wall—or, as some call it, the Wailing Wall. It's the last structure still standing, the retaining wall, from the ancient Temple. The Arabs may have control of what's on top," she said, pointing to the Mosque of Omar resting on the Temple Mount, "but this is the place of all our hopes and dreams."

Huddles of Jewish worshipers, many wearing black hats with prayer shawls, were scattered across the plaza in front of the wall. For years this area was controlled by Arabs, and during those decades Jews were not permitted to worship here. All that changed after the war in 1967, when Israel gained control of East Jerusalem. Now Israelis flooded to the wall, pressed their hands and faces against its cool stones, kissed it, and let their tears fall upon it.

Fanny crossed her arms and gazed wistfully at the structure, as if she were the one who had rescued it for her people. "Would you like to pray at the wall?" she asked me. "You can go to its base, there on the right side. That's where women are allowed to pray."

I wheeled into the wall's shadow, followed by Judy and Bunny. Immediately, I felt the unmistakable weight of Jewish history. Of Macabbean Wars, of the Diaspora, the Babylonian captivity, the annihilation of the Warsaw Ghetto, the wars of King David, and especially Auschwitz and Birkenau. When I reached the base, I rested my head against the cool stone. On the left, beyond a separating chain, young men were bowing and rocking, reciting Scriptures they cupped in their hands. All around me, women wept, leaning their arms against the stones. The air was filled with the droning of prayers and psalms.

Looking up, I spotted several soldiers near the top of the wall. I thought of the neighborhoods just beyond this wall, where rage simmered. I thought of the timeless struggle between the Allah of Ishmael's line and the Jehovah God of Isaac's.

Suddenly, I was startled by flittering sounds and a rustling of branches above my head. I looked up and saw a large bush growing out of a crack between the stones. I strained to see what was making it move.

"Look, girls," I said to Bunny and Judy. "It's a little sparrow."

We stood quietly, watching the bird busy herself, darting in and out of the branches. Bunny opened her Bible to Psalm 84 and read: "How lovely is your dwelling place, O LORD Almighty! My soul yearns, even faints, for the courts of the LORD; my heart and my flesh cry out for the living God. Even the sparrow has found a home, and the swallow a nest for herself, where she may have her young—a place near your altar, O LORD Almighty, my King and my God. Blessed are those who dwell in your house; they are ever praising you. . . . For the LORD is a sun and shield; the LORD bestows favor and honor; no good thing does he withhold from those whose walk is blameless."

Here we were in the courts of the Lord, looking at a sparrow who made her home in what was once the dwelling place of God. Bunny closed her Bible. For a long while, we watched the little bird. Then we turned our attention to the people who were folding written prayers and wedging them into cracks in the wall. This was a place where people brought their dreams, their hopes.

That's it, I thought. "Judy, do you have a piece of paper?"

As Judy held pen and paper, poised to write, I dictated our mission statement at Joni and Friends: "To communicate the gospel and to equip Christ-honoring churches worldwide to evangelize and disciple people affected by disability."

When Judy finished writing, she folded the slip of paper, and I quietly led us in prayer: "Lord Jesus, you are the Prince of Peace. You bring healing where there's sorrow. Break down the dividing walls of hostility. Remove the barriers. And use us, Lord, to reach those who are hurting the most—people who are bewildered and confused by physical and mental disabilities. Amen."

Bunny turned to the wall and located a spot just underneath where the sparrow was still rustling the branches. She found a small crack and pushed the folded paper in as far as it would go. As we left the wall, our hearts were set afire by a fresh spark. We had a mission to accomplish—a mission to tear down walls and bring peace to the paralyzed, people paralyzed by handicap or by hate.

That evening before bed, Bunny scattered another handful of tiny mustard seeds into the night.

Three days later, we arrived in Bosnia. A damp, smoky haze blanketed Sarajevo as we passed one bombed-out building after the next. We had come to this splintered society with towns separated by barbed wire, concrete emplacements, and fields of land mines. We had come to offer hope and help to those disabled from the war.

We were awakened the next day by a muezzin's call to prayer over a loudspeaker from the mosque down the street.

"I think we have an answer for that," said Bunny. She scurried to the window in her robe, carrying her bag of mustard-seed pods. "This is the day the Lord has made," she said insistently, as she threw open the curtain sash, leaned out the window as far as she could, and scattered the tiny seeds to the breeze. She looked up and down the empty street and began singing like a muezzin in a minaret, "Our Father . . . who art in heaven . . . hallowed be thy name!"

Our real mission began the next day. As we drove to Tuzla, the road wound through deep mountain passes and green cow pastures. All along the country road, we spotted small farms and cottages. We passed one or two, brightly painted and with flowers all around; then, only fifty yards up the road, we drove by a blackened shell of a structure, with a half-burned roof and walls pock-marked from gunfire; then another house or two, spared; then a couple more, bombed out.

"Ethnic cleansing," our sponsor remarked. "They were very selective."

Ethnic cleansing. The phrase made my skin crawl. It was a cold, feeble attempt to sanitize a distasteful reality. *A little like calling paralysis a "mobility impairment,"* I thought, shaking my head.

One thing I couldn't shake was the selectivity of the targets. Two farms burned and ravaged; then three untouched, with white fences and flowers; another farm destroyed; the next, skipped over. *These people used to be friendly neighbors,* I thought as we flew past more cottages. *They swapped stories and shared milk and cheese. Their animals grazed on each other's fields. Then one day, hell breaks loose, and they become bitter enemies.*

When we arrived at the hospital in Tuzla, the doctors and nurses—most of them Muslim—were skeptical of us at first. But as we sipped strong Turkish coffee together, discussing rehabilitation philosophy, laughing over the tactics of politicians, talking of common problems, they quickly warmed to us. Eventually, they allowed us to visit with the disabled men and women in the hospital. We saw near-naked men lying on old mattresses on floors. Later, as we were departing, the doctors asked if we could return with wheelchairs. They smiled warmly. We were ministering, after all. Walls of hostility were beginning to come down.

I had no idea, however, that on this trip God wanted to swing the wrecking ball at walls in my own heart.

It started with Dario, the young Bosnian-Croat soldier who was assigned as our driver. As we drove through the pillaged countryside, past more charred and crumbling villages, I gently probed him with questions.

I learned that Dario had served as a commander of a small unit during the war. For three years, his was a world of killing and carnage. As I put together his story with the news reports I'd seen back home, I wondered about the raping and murdering. I felt revulsion. I couldn't look at him. As my imagination put pictures to his words, I wondered: *How could this man have done those unspeakable things?*

Riding in the car next to him, I sensed an invisible wall beginning to rise between us. I couldn't help feeling I was a better person than he. I reasoned that my sin was minor compared to his. Yet as soon as that thought flashed, I was convicted by it. No, I hadn't killed anyone, but I had "killed" people in my heart.

I listened to Dario's slow and halting speech, the horrors of the war having blocked his ability to speak clearly. His stuttering qualified him as one of those "disabled from the war." Softly, Dario described the land mines exploding around him by day and in his head by night. At one point, his voice drifted off, as though he had no strength to call up more morbid memories.

As we traveled to more meetings and receptions, Dario continued to share bits and pieces of his story. The more he unfolded his heart, the more mine broke for him. And the more I felt our common bond: we were both sinners, broken people, and we knew it. The wall between us was crumbling.

On the last day, as we drove to the airport in Sarajevo, Dario mustered strength to bring resolution to his tortured story. After we unloaded baggage and hugged good-bye, he wedged a letter in the side of my wheelchair.

"Read this later, if you like," he said with a slight smile.

On the plane, miles above and beyond the hills of Bosnia, I unfolded his note:

> *I asked a German missionary who visited me and my mother if is it possible that God can forgive even so big sins like mine. He answered to me that Jesus pays some 2,000 years ago ALL the sins from this world. Later that night I fall upon my knees and started to pray, crying and begging from God to forgive me and change my life. During that night I had hard nightmares. When I wake up next morning, I felt some very strange deep peace and joy inside me. It was nice sunny morning. I could hear birds singing. I wanted to pray more and to share that joy with Jesus with others.*

I leaned my head against the window of the plane. Dario's story symbolized the only solution for rich and poor, able-bodied and disabled, brown-skinned and white, Muslim, Croat, and Serb. It's the solution for the haves and have-nots, for the Jew and Gentile, for the urban and suburban, for the soldier and civilian. It's Ephesians 2:14–16:

> For [Christ] himself is our peace ... and has destroyed the barrier, the dividing wall of hostility, by abolishing in his flesh the law with its commandments and regulations. His purpose was to create in himself one new man out of the two, thus making peace, and to reconcile both of them to God through the cross, by which he put to death their hostility.

"Blessed are the peacemakers ... for Christ himself is our peace," I said to my girlfriend at my bathroom vanity, who was still holding the small, porcelain pillbox. "And before we boarded that plane, my friend Bunny—"

"—scattered more mustard seeds," she finished for me.

I smiled. She did too.

Before we exited the bathroom, we did what we always did—we prayed.

On that morning, we prayed for the people in Bosnia and Israel. We prayed for peace and for the seeds to take root and grow— mustard seeds, which would become the largest of all plants, with branches so big that no wall could stand against them.

How little we know just how much we need his peace, I mused.

I soon would find out for myself.

CHAPTER TWENTY-EIGHT

A good name is better than fine perfume, and the day of death better than the day of birth. It is better to go to a house of mourning than to go to a house of feasting, for death is the destiny of every man; the living should take this to heart. Sorrow is better than laughter, because a sad face is good for the heart.

Ecclesiastes 7:1–3

M is for the many things she gave me. . . . O is that she's only growing old. . . ."

I sang softly, hoping my mother was listening. It was a song she used to sing to Grandmom, and now, it was my turn to sing it to her.

" . . . T is for the tears she shed to save me. . . . H is for her heart as pure as gold. . . . E is for her eyes, they shine like diamonds. . . . R is that she's *r-r-right*, and right she'll be . . . put them all together, they spell 'MO-O-OTHER,'" I sang like Al Jolson, my arms spread wide as best I could, "the word that means the world to me."

Mother didn't budge. She sat stiff and cross-armed on the couch, giving no indication she heard me. She just kept staring vacantly through the rain as it spat against the sliding-glass door of her Ocean City condo.

Bunny, Judy, and I had come east to give my sisters a break from caring for my eighty-seven-year-old mother. It was Easter week of 2001, and we were tucked cozily away in Mom's end-apartment of the top floor of Harbour Island. The little vacation community was situated on a small barrier island facing west over the Sinepuxent Bay, with the Atlantic Ocean behind it. To step out onto Mother's balcony was to be on the bow of a ship heading northwest—you could shield your eyes and scan an uncluttered horizon from north to south.

I wheeled to the sliding-glass door to check if the clouds might soon part—no, rain was now pattering the balcony patio; bad weather was here to stay. Still, there was something quiet and beautiful about this bracing spring day by the ocean. I looked across the water—the sky and bay were the same moody gray-blue, separated only by the horizon, a thin purple strip of Maryland's eastern shore.

Mom began to softly snore, her head slowly drooping to her chest. I sighed with relief. Sleep was her one respite from constant pain and confusion. Yet sleep was also the escape that was drawing her further and further from me.

Our pace was slow. We'd get up in the morning, eat, exercise, do a bit of reading, drive to the boardwalk to watch the surf one day, relax in rocking chairs at Phillip's Hotel the next. Always after dinner it would be a game of Scrabble, but it was no longer the fun it used to be. Mother, once the word-game queen, now struggled to decipher the board. A series of strokes and heart problems had slowly eroded her bright and buoyant spirit.

It started back in 1998, when shortly after heart surgery she fell on the tennis court, breaking her shoulder while going for a backhand shot. She was never able to play again. I'm not sure which demoralized her more—the pain and stiffness that followed or not being able to play. It grieved her to grow old. "I'm just sorry I'm not going to be around to say, 'I told you so' when you get to be my age," was her standard joke. "Getting old ain't for sissies."

While Judy caught up on emails, Bunny read and Mother slept, I parked myself at the dining table to leaf through a tattered family album. There was my mother, Lindy Landwehr, the top medalist in a swim meet on one page; on another, first place in a tennis tournament. On every page were scotch-taped newspaper clippings of Lindy winning badminton and lacrosse honors. And if not her, then her sisters, holding onto the pool edge and mugging for the camera.

I studied a yellowed photo of Lindy on the tennis court. I grinned, remembering how I could always tell where Mom had played on any given afternoon by the color of her tennis shoes left at the back door. Orange dust meant the clay courts over at Leakin Park. Grass stains, the Mount Washington Club. Black tar, Woodlawn Senior High.

Another photo showed Mom and her sisters in short skirts, pearls, and straw hats, dancing to a big band. "You guys have got to see this," I whispered to Judy and Bunny, trying not to disturb Mother.

"Mrs. E. was a flapper?" Bunny's eyes widened.

"You should have seen her at the Dunes Hotel that Fourth of July," Judy said, rolling her eyes.

"Yeah," I added, "the piano in the tearoom started playing 'It's a Grand Old Flag,' and the next thing we knew, Mom had grabbed the Stars and Stripes from the lobby and started marching around the room, waving it and insisting others join her parade."

Bunny stifled a laugh, "You're kidding."

"Nope," I confirmed. "She got a good long line of people snaking behind her, and they all loved it. Ken and my niece didn't, though. They skedaddled before Mother could rope them in, too."

I paused, smiling and thinking of how Ken now looked back on that July Fourth and bragged of Mom's patriotism. "One lady leaned over to me, not knowing I was the daughter," I whispered, "and she asked me in all seriousness, 'Is she a retired showgirl?'"

"I bet they thought she was Carol Channing!"

"That was her, exactly."

"Joni," Judy corrected, "not even Carol Channing could match your mother."

"Yeah. There's no one like Mom," I mused. They turned a few more pages with me before going back to their email and book.

When we were little, it was true that my father was the sun around which we all orbited. I'd always felt closer to Daddy—he didn't discipline us as hard as Mom did. At the time, I never questioned his rationale when he came upstairs to spank us; I only put a pillow over my hiney hoping to soften the blow. Mother's discipline, however, was straight to the point. There was the time I said "damn" at the supper table—I can't recall why I did such a thing—and Mother was quick to jump for the riding crop as I dove under the table, crawled my way through, and raced to my room. She gained on me going up the stairs, though, and snatched my ankle just before I disappeared underneath my bed. "No, Mommy, no," I pleaded as I dug my nails into the wood floor. It was too late. Later, as I rubbed the welts on my legs, I decided no four-letter word was worth the pain.

Mother was tough, yet I never once doubted her tenderness. I remembered when a Canadian TV interviewer spotted her in the audience and asked her to join me in front of the camera. "Mrs. Eareckson, I know this brings up difficult and painful memories—," his voice dripped with sympathy—"but as Joni's mother, can you . . .

would you ..."—his eyes were pleading and teary, "... please tell us how you *felt* when you learned the news of Joni's terrible accident?"

I held my breath. Mother replied, "My first thought?"

The interview nodded with doleful eyes.

"My first thought," she declared, true to form, "was, 'How could she do such a stupid thing like dive in shallow water!' She'd just earned her life-saving certificate the week before. I couldn't believe it." She sat back, satisfied, chipper, and bright-eyed.

I couldn't believe it, either. Neither could the interviewer. But that was Lindy.

For Mom, expressions of tenderness were less huggy-kissy and more practical. Yet if ever I doubted my mother's affection before my accident, not once did I question it afterward. No other mother at Montebello State Hospital made the long drive north on Loch Raven Boulevard to see her daughter every day. No other visitor was at the front door of the hospital every morning, waiting for visiting hours to start, and hers was the last car in the parking lot at night. She smuggled in homemade crab cakes and kept me in fresh flowers. After she made sure everyone in our six-bed ward had clean sheets and hair washed once a week, my roommates donned her official Room Mother.

I looked up from the album to bring into focus another image. I saw my mother standing at my hospital bedside, holding a book open so I could read. Now, in my memory, I saw things I'd never noticed before. How she had to lean against the guardrail and keep switching hands to give her arms a break. Or how she apologized for the time she occasionally took to rub her lower back. These things didn't register with me back then. I was a teenager, and mothers always did that stuff. Or did they?

The afternoon light was beginning to wane, making it harder for me to read the faded clippings. I pushed the album aside—the photos were twisting my heart too much, anyway. My mother's smile in them, so youthful and dewy fresh, revealed a gallant young girl, undaunted and ready to swim, run, back-flip, and dance into the future. Now the future was here.

"Mrs. E? Are you warm enough?" Judy asked Mom, who continued sitting stiff and straight on the couch. "Shall we light a fire?" My mother didn't move.

A blast of cold wind flattened the rain against the windows, and we decided to light one anyway. The crackling tinder cast a cheery, dancing light over the room. Evening was upon us, and the gray monotone outside was quickly disappearing into dark. Bunny draped an afghan over Mom's legs.

"Mom E., we're going to have crab cakes tonight," Judy offered, leaning over and placing her hand on Mother's shoulder. "Would you like that?"

We held our breath to see if her favorite subject—cooking Maryland crab cakes—would register. All she did was move her empty gaze from the balcony to Judy's arm, as if to say, who are you?

"Mom," I suggested, "wanna help Judy cut up the celery and onion?" We were anxious to get her off the couch and focused on something other than the darkness beyond the sliding-glass door.

"You don't need my help."

We all were taken aback. These were her first words all day. And she uttered them so plainly, so cognitively.

I begged, "Mommy, we do need your help. Nobody makes crab cakes like you. Judy's from England, and Bunny's from Texas. You're the only one here from Maryland."

She turned and gave me an icy scowl. I drew back. I had seen her look the same way at my sisters. It was an eerie, alien glare, as if someone else were looking through her eyes. "Who are you?" she said flatly.

"I'm Joni, your youngest," I answered softly.

"No you're not," she muttered defiantly and turned her gaze back toward the rain.

My heart split open. *She really doesn't recognize me. How could she not know me?* I was grieved that my mother couldn't recognize her family—that she was lost, thinking her daughters had abandoned her to strangers.

Just as I started to choke up, childhood memories came rushing to the rescue, buoying me with nostalgia. Memories of Mother waxing our hardwood floors on all fours. Of me standing with her in the backyard to watch the sun go down. Hearing her cheery "Kitchen's closed!" every night after the dishes were done. Memories of her standing in the yard watering her beloved azaleas each summer night. Of playing hopscotch with me and harmonizing on "I'll Be Loving You, Always." Of her making BLTs until midnight for Steve Estes and my friends.

Memories of me asking Kathy to hold my hand in bed because I was afraid I'd wake up and my parents wouldn't be there, that Daddy would die in the night. Times when I felt so lost, so little, thinking, *Daddy, please find me. I'm here, please find me!* Now Daddy was gone. And soon—too soon—Mother would be, also. *Oh, Mommy, here I am—I'm Joni. Please know me.*

The rain began to pound the condo roof, sheeting the windows and blurring the distant lights, casting upon everything a nauseous surrealism. Our crab dinner was a success in that Mom sat at the table and actually ate something—the crab. But before we could stop her, she headed back to the couch.

And there she stayed.

By ten o'clock, we had tried repeatedly to get her to go to bed, but she refused. She assumed the same rigid position, her arms folded. "Please, it's time to go to bed," I asked her gently.

"Suit yourselves."

I decided to play her game. "Lindy!" I said sharply, "you must get up now. We all need to go to bed!"

She glowered and shook her head.

Judy looked at her watch. It was going on eleven o'clock, and Mother was still fully dressed. We were out of ideas and didn't know what to do next. Finally, I suggested, "Let's call Kathy." Mother had lived with Kathy for the past ten years. My sister surely had experienced this sort of thing. She'd know what to do. We used the phone in the other room.

After I described to Kathy our fitful day and exasperating evening, she asked, "Where is Mom now?"

"She's still dressed, sitting on the couch, and won't get up," I said in a low voice.

I heard a knowing sigh on the other end. "Well, feel free to leave her there. Just give her a pillow and swing her legs up, if she'll let you."

I couldn't believe my ears. "She still has her shoes and socks on. You let Mom sleep all night in her *clothes?*"

"Only if it's the last resort."

A strange relief washed over me.

"Joni," Kathy said, "Mom won't be with us forever, and we can't fight her on every point. If she wants to sleep on the couch with her shoes on, then let her. If she only wants ice cream for dinner, so be it. It's not worth the angst—for her or for you. Jay will tell you the same thing."

"Okay. We'll leave her on the couch."

Kathy added a qualifier: "But make sure she takes her medicine. That battle you need to win."

I hated the idea of winning any kind of battle. Just two years earlier, when Mother wasn't so debilitated, she had flown out to California and spent over three months with Ken and me. Tending to her needs back in 1999 didn't include any battles. She was happy to be with her daughter and son-in-law. She was tickled to be at the twentieth anniversary celebration of Joni and Friends, and to take part in my fiftieth birthday party. Most of all, she loved driving to work with me each day and being my helper.

"Pilot to copilot," I would say at a stop sign, "anyone coming up on the right?"

"All clear, roger," Mom would say.

"Taking off."

"Big rig coming up on your left," she'd warn.

"Roger," I'd respond. We were playing one of Daddy's games, but somehow it was now reality.

Once she heard a staff report at our office on our new partnership with Maersk-SeaLand, to ship our wheelchairs to seaports. The next day Mom gasped when a lumbering eighteen-wheeler passed us on the freeway with the name *MAERSK* on its side. "Joni, look!" she squealed, "There go our wheelchairs! Maybe to Africa, or maybe Peru!"

My eyes filled—we were a team, friends, little girls on an adventure. I didn't want to spoil her delight by telling her the truck was probably full of washing machines going to San Francisco. *Then again*, I thought as I watched the truck disappear down the 101, *it very well could be hauling our wheelchairs to China.*

In California, Mother and I were inseparable. The day she was to return to Maryland, we stood together in the kitchen with Jay, who had flown out to escort her back. Jay was as thrilled as I was that our mother had obviously enjoyed her visit. "Mom, you know, you really don't have to go back yet," I said, cutting a glance at Jay. My sister smiled and nodded. "You can stay here if you want," Jay said.

Mom looked at one daughter, then the other. Three months had been a long time to be away. Finally, she looked at me and said with a little jump, "I'll stay with you!"

I could hardly believe it. My mother favored me over Baltimore, the farm, and all her grandchildren and great-grandchildren. Not since my hospital days had we spent so much time together. No, not since I was a child—day in and day out, for over three months. I would have thought I'd be tired of her visit, that I would secretly resent her choice to stay. But I wasn't. I discovered I needed her still. Or, maybe, she needed me.

Her visit stretched for another two weeks. The morning before she was to finally leave, we stopped by the drugstore for some items, but when we returned to the van with our packages, I hit the toggle switch to open the van door, and the chain broke. We were stuck— me in a wheelchair and my elderly mother, in front of a broken vehicle.

"Mother, there's only one thing we can do," I said, "and that's pray." We must have looked like a helpless pair, holding hands and praying in the parking lot. But no sooner did I finish than a pleasant young man approached, sensing something was wrong. In less than five minutes, he had our van door fixed. He happened to be a professional cyclist and knew all about broken chains.

"May God take care of you after I'm gone, honey," my mother said as we pulled away.

"And may God take care of you, Mommy," I said softly, as Judy and Bunny turned out the lights. That night, the rain continued to fall as my mother snored away the hours on the couch. She had won that battle, but as I lay awake, I hoped she'd be brighter in the morning. I knew I'd have to win the battle of the medicine.

It felt odd to be worrying about her that way. But I was discovering something sweet about this role reversal—especially for me, a quadriplegic. For so many years people had helped—I mean, physically helped—me with bathing and dressing, brushing hair and teeth, hygiene and all the rest. My husband, sisters, friends, people at work—each one had bent over backward to make up for my lack of hands and feet. And now, for the first time in my life, I was responsible for another person's care. I would have to say, "Mom, have you taken your medicine?" and "Mom, would you like to do your exercises now?" I prayed there would be no battles in the morning.

It was hard to sleep. Every time the wind rattled the balcony door in the living room, I wondered if it was Mother trying to open it. I imagined her outside, standing in the night rain, clutching her sweater, bewildered and wet, and wondering where she was, all the while edging closer to the balcony rail. *Mom?* I yelled in my thoughts. *Mom, are you okay?* I hated that her dementia was so dangerous. She had lost so much in the last couple of months. The glass door rattled again as the wind howled. It sounded cold and lonely, like a death rattle, like the coming of the grim reaper.

Strange how we expect the parade of life to go on forever. And when it finally runs out of steam, we feel cheated, as if someone should have told us it was this short, this hard, this final. I didn't know what to make of my mother's plight. So I asked a pastor friend about it, a man who had lost his elderly mother.

"I've thought a lot about the horrible pain my mother suffered," he replied, rubbing his chin thoughtfully. "Maybe death is supposed to be hard. Maybe it's supposed to be a taste of hell."

His words made me reel.

"If 'the wages of sin is death,'" he continued, "I wonder if God has in mind for us to feel—really *feel*—a little of what the Savior bore. Or perhaps God wants to remind us of what sin would have earned us, had it not been for Christ."

We both sat quietly with that thought. Finally, he said, "Maybe the throes of death are our birth pangs before we enter bliss."

It was a sobering notion. Sometimes the facts of death seemed as harsh as the facts of life. I recalled the time I spoke to a small group of pastors and their wives in Germany. It was their chance to ask me, this woman who wrote on suffering, about why a good God would allow so much horrible suffering in the world. "That terrible flood that took place two weeks ago in Mexico," one woman mentioned, "and all those people perished, many of them children. What about them? Why did they have to die?"

I wondered about the premise behind her question. It assumed that those Mexicans were good, honest villagers who deserved better. But what did they deserve? What did the German woman, what did I, what did *any* of us deserve? Do we see the seriousness of our self-righteousness? *Dear lady*, I thought before I answered, *God is holy beyond your wildest dreams. And you—as well as those people in Mexico—have offended him beyond your ability to imagine. For each of us, the wages of our sins is death.*

I drew in a deep breath and answered, "When anyone dies, it should be like a wake-up call—an alarm clock, a red flag waving, warning us, 'Wake up! Examine yourself! Have you made peace with God?' And when a whole village of people perish, that alarm should sound louder. I can't say what God had in mind with that flood, or any other disaster. But I *can* say that we're all heading for the grave, some of us sooner than others. And that should make us sit up and take notice: what have we done with Jesus?"

My mind replayed that scene late into the night, until finally the wind quieted down. My mother's mental anguish and physical pain were not out of the ordinary. They were a preview of the hell she had escaped. *Thank God you're safe in Christ, Mother,* I thought. I also thought of several family friends, particularly one who had died recently, an agnostic. This man had suffered in his last days as much as my mother. *Were his sufferings a spoonful of hell come early?* That friend had always been proud of his fine, upstanding life and good deeds. But the Scriptures lay bare the truth about humanity all too clearly: "There is no one righteous, not even one; there is no one who understands, no one who seeks God. All have turned away, they have together become worthless; there is no one who does good, not even one." *Not even my mother's good, kind, charitable friend.*

Oh, thank you, thank you for this wheelchair! I prayed. *By tasting hell in this life, I've been driven to think seriously about what faces me in the next. This paralysis is my greatest mercy.*

My mind drifted back to wild junior high school parties, to loud music and soft couches in dimly lit basements. It drifted forward to high school graduation, to pride and independence, to rebellion and angry outbursts. To plans on how to "protect myself" with my boyfriend when I got to college. And then . . . my accident.

It was your roadblock, God, to keep me from totally messing up my life. Thank you, bless you. My sin would have only gotten worse in college. And I know, I truly know, I would have been lost to you forever.

It was odd how my mother's failing health was forcing me to ponder such heavy thoughts. Then again, it seemed natural and appropriate. Just as any parent would do to the dying end, Mother was making me *think*—making me consider, ponder, and weigh the consequences for my own good. On the other hand, it was odd: Mom had always despised getting old, the same way she never quite accepted my wheelchair. Watching me struggle as a quadriplegic, she grieved for herself and she grieved for me. *But, Mom, our suffering has taught us something, taught you something: our afflictions have shown us something cosmic is at stake. And just five minutes of heaven, I promise you, will make up for everything. It will atone for it all.*

The next morning, I was awakened by the aroma of bacon sizzling and coffee brewing. The sun poured into my bedroom, and I heard the soft conversation of my friends in the kitchen. I also heard Mother snoring on the couch. I wondered what kind of day was in store for us.

Mother was still sleeping after my two-hour getting-up routine. Once up, I wheeled over to take a look at her. She had stretched herself out, and during the night someone had placed a pillow under her head. She looked comfortable, even if she was still in yesterday's clothes.

"Mom?"

She squinted, letting me know she'd probably been awake for a while.

"How about some breakfast?" Judy asked.

It was the same as the day before. After much coaxing, she sat up and only nibbled at scrambled eggs and bacon. We turned on some morning music, spoke in happy, positive voices about the seagulls, and marveled together at how quickly the incoming tide was covering the sand bar in the bay.

"Those people clamming out there are going to get soaked, " Bunny exclaimed, "and they have a dog too. Mrs. E., come and look!"

We waited, hoping she would rise to her feet and join us by the window. She didn't.

The morning slipped into a slower, more quiet pace. Judy set up her computer, and we decided to work on my manuscript for this book. As she placed the first few chapters in front of me to reread, I looked back at Mom over my shoulder. I felt so sad that nothing seemed to be able to pull her back to reality. Nothing we'd done could lift the pall of darkness over her mind. I sighed and started to read chapter one:

> I dug my toes into the sand of the Delaware beach, hugged my knees, and drew as close to the campfire as I could. The flames warmed our faces while behind us the night air chilled our backs. Huddled with my sisters and cousin, I smelled the burning logs and breathed in the fire's heat. We all sat in awe of my father. He stood across the campfire from us, a figure a-swirl in rising heat and smoke, his face underlit by flame as if he were a prophet on Mount Sinai. We clutched each other as he weaved his story. And we didn't dare look over our shoulders toward the ocean, lest we catch sight of—
>
> "The Flying Dutchman!"

Suddenly, I had a thought. I asked Judy to place the chapter on my lap, and I wheeled over beside my mother. "Mom? Listen to this. Just listen . . ."

I began to read about the Sargasso Sea, and Daddy's little sailor jig, and my sisters and me singing, "Let the Lower Lights Be Burning." Every paragraph or so, I paused and asked, "Remember this?"

She nodded.

"Did I get that right?"

She muttered, "Mm-hm."

Judy and Bunny watched from the kitchen, holding their breath.

When I came to the passage about trekking back over the dunes to our tent, Mother shook her head and said softly, "This is great."

I gulped hard. I turned to my friends—they saw my relief.

I paused to flip to the next page. I was so pleased she'd been listening, I hadn't noticed that the glaze in her eyes had all but disappeared. I'd been concentrating so hard on reading well and with expression, I failed to see the faint smile on her lips. Suddenly, I felt her eyes on me.

"Mom?" I asked, encouraging, "is this the way it was? You and Daddy and us kids?"

"You are the real Joni," she said with wonder. It was as if someone had lifted a veil.

I was almost afraid to respond. I feared my voice would send her in retreat, pushing her back into that horrible darkness. Finally, I managed through tears, "Yes, Mommy, I'm the real Joni. It's *me*, the real Joni. I'm here," I urged reassuringly, "I'm here, it's me. Everything's okay."

There would be other such breathtaking moments of recognition and reality for my family until late August 2001, when my mother slipped away. But none were so riveting, so comforting and encouraging for me, as that bracing spring morning at Harbour Island, when Mommy found me among the sand dunes and tents, giggling and playing with Kathy, Jay, and Linda, looking for sand crabs and playing catch with the waves.

On September 1, 2001, Lindy was laid to rest next to her dearest and best. As we sat under the awning covering the grave and sang old hymns, I read the gravestone. *Cap'n John* was on the left side, *Lindy* to the right. In between was nestled *Kelly*. I looked at Linda— I could tell she was thinking of her little girl who, had she survived cancer, would now be in her late thirties. I looked too at Kathy— she and Jay, as well as Jay's daughter, had cared for Mom so faithfully during her last years. Now my eyes turned to Jay. She smiled back at me, and began singing, "Let the Lower Lights Be Burning."

After the graveside service was over, I wanted to show the old Eareckson homestead to a few California friends who had made the trip east. Ken drove us the mile or so through Woodlawn, to 2321 Poplar Drive and the house that Daddy built. I didn't know who lived there now, but it appeared no one was home. We got out and slowly ambled up the sidewalk.

"There's my old bedroom," I said, pointing to the little side-dormer window. "And that's the balcony where I used to play my guitar at night." We went a little further around, and I pointed, "See the living room windows? I used to open them on summer nights and let the breeze carry my piano music down the street."

I leaned back, looking up at the old oak trees that seemed as tall now as they did when I was little. "Listen!" I shushed my friends, as the wind made the leaves above us roar. I could have sworn I heard chimes.

I sat in my wheelchair by the driveway where Mom and I played hopscotch. Letting my eyes trace every nook and cranny of our beautiful, log-and-cedar-shingled house, and the massive stone fireplaces, I wondered how anyone could face the past without some sure hope of the future. How they could look so many sweet memories in the eye and not cave in?

Before we left, I trespassed as far as I dared, to see whether the old dinner bell was still by the side dutch-door—the door that led to the dining room where Steve Estes studied the Bible with me. It wasn't there. Then I remembered Jay had thoughtfully removed it before the house was sold. The empty brick wall where it once hung looked so bare, so different. Everything was different. Life, for me, was no longer here—it was in California. Or, more accurately, around the world. Or, better yet, beyond this world.

But wherever I would travel, wherever I would go, my roots would always be here. Always in the house with the room with painted angels. Angels that would always look out for us girls. *Oh Daddy, dear Mother . . . thank you for the life you gave us. Not just life and breath, but an Eareckson life. So very different. And just a little odd.*

During our flight back to California after Mother's memorial service, I literally felt the distance increase between me and my Eareckson roots back east. With both parents gone, I sensed I had moved up a rung on a ladder reaching up into the stratosphere. Lindy and Cap'n John had abandoned the top rung, just as their parents had before them. There were no more Earecksons—at least in my parents' line. And now, holding onto the family ladder as best I could, I was alone. True, my role as a wife to Ken was the vital thing now, but with Daddy and Mom no longer a phone call away, with their images only preserved in old photographs, and with my sisters having their own lives and families, I felt . . . alone.

By the time we arrived at our house, the hour was late, and Ken and I were exhausted. We dropped our suitcases and took a moment to thumb through mail, noticing what were probably a few sympathy cards. I opened the first one, addressed from Maryland. Something dropped out of the envelope. When I took a closer look, my chest tightened. It was an obituary from *The Baltimore Sun*. There, in print, I read: "Margaret J. Eareckson died August 21, 2001."

Hot tears filled my eyes. For the first time, I fell apart.

The word "homegoing," much like "passing away" or "going to be with Jesus," sounded easier. Easier to swallow than "death" or "died." But the bare facts in the obituary were as cold and hard as ice.

I shoved the clipping aside and opened another envelope. It was a sympathy card from a friend in Texas. At least, I thought it was a sympathy card. This one looked different. On the front were lilies, and on the inside were the words of the hymn, "Christ the Lord Is Risen Today."

It was an Easter card. And in it was written, "Joni, somehow this Easter card expresses more what I want to say. Your lively, happy mother is free from pain, and isn't it good to know that we will all be reunited at the resurrection. I'm so glad He rose."

> *Soar we now where Christ has led, Alleluia!*
> *Following our exalted Head, Alleluia!*
> *Made like Him, like Him we rise, Alleluia!*
> *Ours the cross, the grave, the skies, Alleluia!*

The warmth and joy of the resurrection melted the cold-as-ice fact of my mother's death. Never were there better words of sympathy than this reminder from my friend of the resurrection of Christ. *I'm not alone*, I reminded myself. *Yes, I'm an Eareckson and, yes, a Tada. But more than this, I'm a citizen of heaven. I'm heading home.*

"Mom and Dad, I'm hot on your heels," I said aloud to no one in particular. "One day down—one day closer to heaven."

CHAPTER TWENTY-NINE

I have told you these things, so that in me you may have peace. In this world you will have trouble. But take heart! I have overcome the world.

John 16:33

Ten days later, all hell broke loose.

"Joni, wake up!" Judy shook my shoulder hard at seven in the morning.

"Wh-what?" Through my grogginess, I immediately knew something awful had happened.

Judy clicked on the television and sat on the edge of my bed, huffing. I squinted, recognizing the World Trade Towers through huge columns of billowing smoke.

"Two planes flew into the buildings," she said tensely.

The words sounded like a nightmare.

"Was it an accident?"

Judy's look told me it wasn't. "They said on the radio it's hijackings. Another plane has slammed into the Pentagon. More could still be out there."

The TV reporters huddled against buildings, nervously fumbling for words, their microphones shaking, their stories staccatoed with terrifying facts: "The upper stories are an inferno. . . ." "Flames are belching from office windows. . . ."

None of their words seemed real. The live images were just as unreal: office workers huddling on ledges, camera angles confirming reports of people falling from windows, thousands fleeing down the streets, and—*oh, no, no*—the colossal towers rumbling, roaring, and now collapsing in a tsunami of smoke, like dying giants, falling and dragging hundreds, maybe thousands down with them.

My mind couldn't take in what my eyes were seeing.

I got up as quickly as I could and called my sisters back in Baltimore. I knew they were far from Washington, D.C., and the Pentagon, but the terror of what was happening made me, made us all, feel suddenly fragile and insecure and desperate for the sound of family voices. We consoled each other on the phone—"Are you okay?" and "Yes, yes, I'm okay. Are you?"—and I felt we were back in the basement of our old house on Poplar Drive, huddling with each other while the distant, eerie sound of the siren from the Woodlawn Fire Department warned us to take cover because the Russians were about to drop the bomb at any minute. We'd held our breath, waiting for the God-awful siren to stop, worried that if we whispered too loud, the enemy would hear us and burst through the back door.

That same fragility and fear gripped me now. But this was no civil-defense drill from the fifties. This was a new era, a millennium, with new enemies to fear. And although the devastating scenes on television bore a surreal resemblance to a *Die Hard* film, I had to keep reminding myself, *This isn't a movie.*

I didn't stop to think that millions like me were feeling, thinking, and doing the same things: telephoning family members, standing by television sets weeping and praying, waiting hour after hour, transfixed by the heart-twisting images, hoping against hope that those hundreds of firemen and policemen didn't really go into those buildings, that all those stock traders and brokers, cleaners and janitors surely made it out okay, that certainly those planes were empty.

There was a knock on the door, and I jumped. Then I remembered my appointment with our contractor to go over paint samples—we were putting an addition on our house. It all seemed so trivial, so I begged off. He seemed relieved too.

Yet I couldn't just sit at home in front of the TV all day. Ken was at school, teaching, and I wanted to be at Joni and Friends with my friends and coworkers. Besides, emails were already flooding into the office from around the world, expressing shock along with concern, as if the civilized world feared the United States was about to be blown away. Every message included the assurance, "We are praying for America and her people."

It was hard to concentrate on everyday work. Doing anything other than talking about the terrorists' attacks—it was being reported as terrorism—seemed innocuous. And so, as news flashes came in, we listed things to pray about on the whiteboard in the boardroom: survivors ... families ... firemen and emergency workers ... and the hundreds who obviously would be victims of burns and injuries. By four o'clock, we were numb and spent. We closed the office early.

Judy drove me home—I was too shaken to drive myself—and as we sped down the freeway, we listened to the radio. The whole nation was asking, *Who were these awful men who turned planes into missiles, killing thousands? Who was this enemy? Why were we the focus of so much hatred? Which other major cities would be next? Los Angeles?* A dark, ominous wave began forming on the horizon of my mind. I had never experienced such thoughts before. Thoughts of war. A war that wasn't being waged in the Persian Gulf or Vietnam, but one that had come home.

It felt strange to stop at the supermarket for something as ordinary as dinner, but as we pulled into the parking space, my attention was averted by a small group of six or seven spike-haired teenagers on skateboards, whooping and hollering and hopping the speed bump in front of the supermarket, all the while snubbing the sign posted directly above them: No Skateboarding Allowed.

"Look at those kids," I gasped to Judy, "I can't believe what they're doing on a day like this. Someone should stop them."

A pregnant pause passed. "Why don't you?" Judy asked.

Why not? I thought. I wheeled over to the group and mustered up a firm tone of voice. "Young men, may I talk with you a moment?"

The clatter of skateboards ceased. My sudden appearance—perhaps my wheelchair—stunned them into silence. I could tell they didn't know whether to run or start badmouthing me. So I ventured further, "Please let me have a few words with you."

"I'm afraid of you, lady," yelled one kid as he hopped on his board and began circling at a safe distance.

"Afraid of two older women, one in a wheelchair?" Judy called out, joining me.

His friends snickered. That was good—for a moment, I had their attention.

"Young men," I said again, hoping they would rise to this level, "this morning thousands lost their lives because awful people broke laws and had contempt for authority." At that point, my face became red and my eyes moist. "Seeing that so many died because of this, how can you with a clear conscience so flagrantly break this law?" I gestured to the sign with my eyes.

The boys were listening—some of them looking intently at me, almost relieved, while others stared at the ground. "Your behavior dishonors the people who died and those that tried to rescue them."

A lull settled over us. "Here, gather around me," I continued, "let's pray for the families. Come close now. Just bow your heads with me."

Each one shuffled forward. In the next moments, these spike-haired kids with tattoos and earrings held their skateboards and listened— or prayed, perhaps—as I asked God to comfort the families, and to be with the rescuers and all those who had been injured. I concluded by asking him to be large in the hearts of these young men, and to help them be good citizens, good role models to their friends.

"Amen," I said. I thanked them as they nodded then and wandered off in different directions, their common bond broken for the moment.

When Judy and I finished shopping and exited the market, we half-anticipated to hear the sound of skateboards. But as we reached the parking lot, there was no one in sight. Judy started the van, and I wondered aloud, "What'll we do if they come back?"

"You'll talk to them again," she said, smiling at me in the rearview mirror.

That strange encounter underscored that life on September 11 changed—instantly and dramatically. On one hand, I was invigorated, curious to test this peculiar boldness welling up within me, and wanting to encourage others to seek God in these never-before-experienced times.

On the other hand, the ominous wave was looming darker, churning with a terrible sense of doom. Privately, I worried about this new, sinister enemy. So much so, I found it impossible to sleep that night. A battle between courage and cowardice raged as I brooded, *If they attack Los Angeles, will our neighborhood be affected?* From there, I wondered about a rush on the food markets and water supplies, and the price of gas—the same kinds of things that kept me awake after the 1994 Northridge earthquake that shook our house like a toy. But that was a natural disaster, a one-time moment. This was so different, so evil, so unnatural. *Will life ever be the same?* I wondered, and from there thought, *What if the economy collapses? What if we have to close up the ministry office?*

The next morning, I wheeled into the garage to get into my van and drive myself to work. I took one look at the three-quarter-ton Ford Econoline van and froze. It sat there, monstrous and mechanical, looking like a weapon of mass destruction waiting to be detonated. I felt so fragile next to it that my breath suddenly got short. All I could picture was me driving down the freeway and slamming into the side of a skyscraper. I shivered, turned around, and called the office to ask for a ride.

As more reports surfaced of terrorist cells hell-bent on being willing to die to obliterate the Great Satan—the U.S.—the building wave of doom in my mind drew closer, darker, and higher. This was no ordinary enemy. It was an enemy without a face, without a name, and utterly devoid of any moral consciousness.

I found it hard to pray alone that night and the next. It was different when I prayed with others at the office, and I was okay while praying with friends around the television. But at night, when I was in bed and facing God by myself, in the dark and quiet, I choked. Once again, my confidence in God and his sovereignty was being confronted. It unnerved me that he could have prevented September 11 . . . and didn't.

President Bush asked all churches to open their doors for a nationwide prayer service that Thursday, the fourteenth, at noon. When I arrived at our church—a small, unassuming, prefab building with folding chairs—only a handful of people were there, most of them regulars. But soon the place was packed with teachers from the school down the street and employees from the water-and-power company across the road. Truck drivers and contractors walked in, taking off their leather gloves and hard hats, and found seats next to secretaries and waitresses.

Our pastor opened the service with a short greeting, a prayer, and then turned over the time to me. As soon as I began singing "God Bless America," everyone spontaneously joined in. After that, I asked several people to come forward and offer prayers on behalf of the families and the rescue workers affected by the attacks. We sang "America the Beautiful" and "Amazing Grace," and followed those with more prayers.

The next morning, I peeked into the garage. The yellow weapon of mass destruction was still placidly parked, waiting for me to drive it away. I shut the door and turned back to the phone to call for another ride. The talons of fear weren't about to release my heart overnight. All the way to work, I kept repeating, reinforcing, *God is sovereign, God is good. God is sovereign, God is good.* Yet all the while, I stared at all the cars speeding by—every one a missile, every truck a torpedo.

I knew enough about fear to know that I dared not run from it, suppress it, or ignore it. Daddy had taught me that, in the waves at Bethany Beach. "See that big one coming, Joni?" he said. "Swim toward it, not away from it. Get to it before it breaks, and dive under it!"

We'd start free-styling toward the huge swell on the horizon, as if our lives depended on it. I pushed aside my fears with every stroke of my arms, straining every muscle to reach the wave before it crashed. And always—I don't recall ever missing—we dove into the curl just as white foam appeared on its crest.

And so it was, I had to reach this wave.

We called our Joni and Friends team in eastern Pennsylvania and began putting our heads together about how we might help survivors who would be disabled. Although reports were sketchy, we knew hundreds of people would be maimed or injured by the rubble and flames at the Pentagon and the World Trade Center. Within days, we amassed hundreds of Bibles, as well as my books on heaven and suffering, and responded to requests from churches in New York and Washington, D.C. I would also travel east to speak to friends and family members of the fallen and accompany our teams to give the Bibles and books to volunteers, show them how to encourage people from God's Word, and visit hospitals and rehab centers.

As soon as the airlines were cleared to fly again, I boarded a United flight to New York—but it felt eerie being on a nearly empty plane. "I'm sorry about the loss of your coworkers," I said to one red-eyed flight attendant. No one talked or read magazines during the announcing of safety procedures, and I found my eyes flitting to several dark-skinned passengers. Everyone on the flight seemed to hold their breath until we landed on the east coast.

The city of New York was edgy and anxious. Our meeting at one midtown Manhattan church began with news of a bomb scare nearby, but even that didn't keep hundreds of people from coming, people with a lot of questions. "You're in a wheelchair, you've been dealt a blow with your quadriplegia," said one New Yorker. "Tell me, how can you say God is good? If he's good, why didn't he prevent *that?*" he asked, gesturing in the direction of Ground Zero.

It was a question everyone asked, from radio interviewers to the students at the Lower Manhattan campus of Nyack College. Even Larry King was asking the nation, "Where is God?"

At that meeting and in the rest, in New York and D.C., I realized it was familiar territory. I simply spoke of what I had learned from the Bible over so many years—that God doesn't say, "Into each life a little rain must fall," and then turn a fire hose on the earth to see who gets the wettest. On the contrary, he screens the trials that come at us. He's the stowaway on Satan's bus, always erecting invisible fences around the enemy's fury and bringing ultimate good out of wickedness.

"How does he pull it off?" I asked rhetorically at one packed church meeting across the river from Ground Zero. "Welcome to the world of finite humans trying to comprehend an infinite God. What *is* clear is that God permits lots of things he doesn't approve of. That fact doesn't sit well with us, but think of the alternative. Imagine a God who insisted on a hands-off policy toward the evil barreling our way. The world would be much, much worse than it is. Evil would be uncontrolled. But thank God he curbs it."

Everywhere we went—with every opportunity to speak, to share God's Word, to witness of the peace of Christ—we sensed courage rising. And fear was dissipating. By God's grace, we were diving under the wave.

"Please know, I'm no expert," I always confessed. "There are days I wake up and think, *I can't do this. I have no resources for this. I can't face another day dealing with total paralysis.* But that's when I plead, 'Lord, *you* have the resources I lack. I can't do this, but you can.' And he does. The truly handicapped among us are those who start their mornings on automatic cruise control, without needing God. But he gives strength to all who cry to him for help. So, who are the weak and needy? Who are those who need his help?" A brief pause in the dark shadow of recent events always allowed the point to come home. "It's you. It's me."

Bittersweet were the private times we had with people who'd lost friends, colleagues, and loved ones: the brother of a fireman. The wife of a stockbroker. A jogger who'd left her purse and briefcase on her desk on an upper floor, and begun taking her morning run when the plane hit. A little boy whose uncle perished. A woman whose husband was still missing and whose sorrowful tears betrayed a gratitude to God for being encouraged to face another day.

After the service at a crowded church in Queens, I spied a little Hispanic girl who seemed much too young to be in line. As she approached us and was given a Bible, I leaned down and asked, "Is someone missing in your family?"

For a moment, she froze. "This Bible is for my daddy."

"Oh really?" I asked gently.

"Yes, he has AIDS."

I looked into her dark, doleful eyes and saw the fear. Everyone has a story filled with private terror. Always, there is an enemy lurking—whether for Maria in impoverished Romania or Dario in war-ravaged Bosnia or disabled Albanians lying in bed for years in tiny concrete houses in remote villages. Or Liu Qiaoling in China, a little girl with spina bifida who, until we gave her a wheelchair, spent her days and nights on a slab of Masonite board by a window. These all lived with uncertainty, even with terror, every day. And so did this Hispanic child from Queens, New York.

"Don't be afraid, little one," I smiled at the child, pulling her to me. "Let me write something for your daddy in that Bible." She watched with wide-eyed fascination as a colleague put my pen in my mouth and I wrote down a verse. I can't remember exactly what I penned, but it should have been Ephesians 6:16: "Above all, take the shield of faith so you'll be able to quench all the fiery darts of the wicked."

Only one thing can ever—will ever—conquer fear: faith in God.

The war has not let up.

If anything, it's more terrifying than ever. There were anthrax deaths. Then a shoe bomber on an airplane. Then a plot to detonate a dirty bomb. There have been low alerts and high alerts, involving tanker trucks and shipping ports, cyber-terrorism and nuclear power plants. And I will not be surprised if something happens to dwarf even the collapse of the World Trade Center towers.

It feels apocalyptic. And, in truth, it is.

As I write this, last night there was another suicide bombing in Jerusalem. I'm not sure how many there have been now or how many casualties have been suffered in Israel and the Gaza strip and the West Bank. All I know is, Jan, our Dutch friend, called this morning to tell me that the young woman who met us coming off the plane in Israel was killed on that bus, with eighteen others. "Everyone is traumatized," he said. "Everyone feels so hopeless and helpless."

I wonder how Fanny, our elderly Jewish tour guide, is faring through it all. And I wonder about her friendship with the Arab woman in the little gift shop. When they embraced that day, their obvious affection for each other challenged all the entrenched hatred between their peoples, their love seeming to override history and provide hope for the future. *Has one of them lost a son? A nephew or a brother?* I brooded. *What of their love and friendship now?*

Never have the lines between the forces of darkness and light, of good and evil, seemed so clear. Never has the world, battered and bruised as it is, seemed so vulnerable, so fragile. So unsafe.

Over time—ever so slowly—in the months that followed September 11, 2001, something began to become clear to me. It was something I sensed just ahead, something that began to appear on the horizon and that grew with each day, with each speaking engagement, with each tear wiped away when a wheelchair was presented, a Bible given, a hug shared.

I'd been given eyes to see . . . an adventure.

In the long shadow cast by my wheelchair—the thirty-six years of my paralysis—I'd now been granted the *privilege* of living at such a time. No greater shadow had ever been cast in the earth's history, it seemed. Today, post-September 11, was an on-ramp to an ever-broadening highway. An opportunity to showcase God's grace, his gospel, in the midst of so many now-visible weaknesses and limitations throughout the world. It was a chance, a mandate, to remember the world's most vulnerable—the disabled—while power brokers shift the planet's levers and gears. It was an opportunity—

indeed, a gift—to witness the unfolding plan of a gracious God who draws near to the weak, stays close to the afflicted, and always seems bigger to those who need him most. It was an even larger, greater on-ramp to adventure.

And my wheelchair was taking me there.

It was broadening more than ever the adventure he'd already given me: to love my husband, Ken, and my friends, my family, my neighbors, my coworkers at Joni and Friends. To paint and write, sing and speak, as he gives strength—all on the road he laid out before me so many years ago.

Today, as I watch events play out in the Middle East, my thoughts turn to Israel, that dusty little country that's the focus of peace for the world. And I recall the special and personal peace I found there for myself. It was during that dry, warm, and windy day we visited Old Jerusalem with Fanny.

After meeting Fanny's Arab friend, we passed through the bazaar and found ourselves in a quieter, less congested part of the city. There, we slowly meandered down the cobblestone path toward the Sheep Gate. To our right, we saw the tops of the cedar trees bending in the breeze above the Temple Mount. As we turned left, we followed a stone path bordering a church built by Crusaders and leading through a small grove of olive trees. A warm wind rustled the branches, and flowers along the path bobbed. No one was around but us, and all was oddly quiet.

Suddenly, the path opened out into an acre or two of white stone ruins. A plaque on the guard rail read: "Now there is in Jerusalem near the Sheep Gate, a pool which in Aramaic is called Bethesda. . . . Here a great number of disabled people used to lie—the blind, the lame, the paralyzed. . . ."

I stared at the verse for a long time before lifting my eyes to explore the crumbled colonnades. The place was deserted. Ken decided to amble down to see if he could find any water left in the cistern below. Meanwhile, Fanny, Bunny, and Judy found a rock at a distance and sat down to rest. I stayed by the plaque on the railing.

A flurry of dust swirled at my feet as a warm, dry breeze rose and tossed my hair. I was speechless here. Large tears welled in my eyes, and I sniffed hard, as I imagined blind people clustered against the wall, and the lame leaning against the pillars. I could see paralyzed people lying on stretchers and mats, their eyes searching and their hands pleading. And I saw myself among them—just as I had pictured so many years ago—dressed in a burlap cloak, lying on a mat, squeezed somewhere between a shady, cool wall and the paralyzed man who had been there for thirty-eight years.

Another dry breeze touched my wet face. *Oh Lord, you waited more than thirty years—almost as many years as the paralyzed man you healed that day—to bring me to this place.*

I gulped hard, remembering the times I'd lain numb and depressed in my hospital bed, hoping and praying that Jesus would heal me, that he would come to my bedside as he did with the man on the straw mat, that he would see me and not pass me by. I remembered the times Diana would read to me about this place. I thought of the marble statue at Johns Hopkins. And Jacque lying next to me in the dark, singing "Man of Sorrows."

Ken waved at me from way down in the ruins.

"You won't believe how many times I used to picture myself here," I called, my voice echoing across the crumpled stones and columns. Ken nodded. He continued to explore below, and I leaned on my arm against the guardrail. I whispered, "And now . . . after thirty years . . . I'm *here* . . . I made it. Jesus *didn't* pass me by. He didn't overlook me. He came my way and answered my prayer— he said no."

I turned my thoughts, my words, heavenward.

"Lord, your no answer to physical healing meant yes to a deeper healing—a better one. Your answer has bound me to other believers and taught me so much about myself. It's purged sin from my life, it's strengthened my commitment to you, forced me to depend on your grace. Your wiser, deeper answer has stretched my hope, refined my faith, and helped me to know *you* better. And you are good. You are so good."

I let the tears fall.

"I know I wouldn't know you . . . I wouldn't love and trust you . . . were it not for—"

I looked down at my paralyzed legs.

"—for this wheelchair."

Ken returned to my side, his chest heaving and his hands cupped. "Look, I have something for you," he said excitedly, extending his hands. "Water from the Pool of Bethesda. I found it way down at the bottom of some steps. It was pitch black—and scary. But I got some for you."

A brisk wind rumpled our shirts as Ken placed his wet hands on my forehead. "Lord, I thank you for my wife."

I cried and laughed at the same time. Ken's prayer was like a capstone, a seal on a most remarkable day. We said good-bye to the Pool of Bethesda, and as we walked back up the path toward the Lion's Gate, I glanced back and shook my head in amazement.

It wasn't often I could presuppose God's motives, but I could with this one. He had brought me to the Pool of Bethesda that I might make an altar of remembrance out of the ruins. That I might see—and thank him for—for the wiser choice, the better answer, the harder yet richer path.

Ah, this is the God I love. The Center, the Peacemaker, the Passport to adventure, the Joyride, and the Answer to all our deepest longings. The answer to all our fears, Man of Sorrows and Lord of Joy, always permitting what he hates, to accomplish something he loves. And he had brought me here, all the way from home—halfway around the earth—so I could declare to anyone within earshot of the whole universe, to anyone who might care, that yes—

There are more important things in life than walking.

Answering The Call

*J*oni's memoir, *The God I Love,* has poignantly captured the way God has worked in her life to touch millions around the world. But the story is far from over. Through Joni and Friends, a Christian organization accelerating Christ's love in the disability community, Joni and her husband Ken work tirelessly to share hope and help among thousands of disabled people and their families. The heart of Joni and Friends lies in a worldwide team of committed staff and passionate volunteers who invest their labors in JAF's *Family Retreats, Special Delivery,* and *Wheels for the World* outreach programs.

Join the team!

If you would like to help Joni and her team spread Christian encouragement to thousands more disabled people and their families, contact Joni and Friends to learn how you can be involved.

Visit our web site or write us today:

Joni and Friends

P.O. Box 3333 • Agoura Hills, CA 91376
(818) 707-5664

www.joniandfriends.org

The award-winning story of a young woman who triumphed over devastating odds to touch countless lives with the healing message of Christ

JONI
An Unforgettable Story
Joni Eareckson Tada

In a split second on a hot July afternoon, a diving accident transformed the life of Joni Eareckson Tada forever. She went from being an active young woman to facing every day in a wheelchair. In this unforgettable autobiography, Joni reveals each step of her struggle to accept her disability and discover the meaning of her life. The hard-earned truths she discovers and the special ways God reveals his love are testimonies to faith's triumph over hardship and suffering.

This 25th Anniversary edition of this award-winning story—which has more than 3,000,000 copies in print in over 40 languages—introduces a new generation of readers to the incredible greatness of God's power and mercy at work in those who fully give their hearts and lives to him.

In a new afterword, Joni describes the events that occurred in her life since the book's initial publication in 1976, including her marriage to Ken Tada and the expansion of her worldwide ministry to families affected by disability.

Softcover: 0-310-24001-8
Unabridged Audio Pages® Cassette: 0-310-24040-9

ZONDERVAN™

GRAND RAPIDS, MICHIGAN 49530 USA

WWW.ZONDERVAN.COM

If God Is Loving, Why Is There Suffering?

WHEN GOD WEEPS
Why Our Sufferings Matter to the Almighty
Joni Eareckson Tada and Steven Estes

When suffering touches our lives, questions like this suddenly demand an answer. From our perspective, suffering doesn't make sense, especially when we believe in a loving and just God.

After more than thirty years in a wheelchair, Joni Eareckson Tada's intimate experience with suffering gives her a special understanding of God's intentions for us in our pain. In *When God Weeps*, she and lifelong friend Steven Estes probe beyond glib answers that fail us in our time of deepest need. Instead, with firmness and compassion, they reveal a God big enough to understand our suffering, wise enough to allow it, and powerful enough to use it for a greater good than we can ever imagine.

Hardcover: 0-310-21186-7 Softcover: 0-310-23835-8 Curriculum Kit: 0-310-24191-X

Are You Ready to Discover New Joy?

BARRIER-FREE FRIENDSHIPS
Bridging the Distance Between You and Friends with Disabilities
Joni Eareckson Tada and Steve Jensen

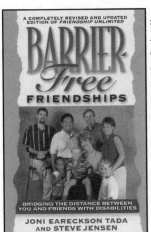

Each of us knows someone who is hearing, visually, or mentally impaired, or physically disabled. Millions more suffer from invisible disabilities that can be just as devastating. Writing from her own experience as a person with a disability Joni Eareckson Tada joins with her fellow disability advocate, Steve Jensen, to share how you can overcome obstacles that have kept you from becoming friends with those who may be limited by their bodies or their circumstances.

Joni shows you how to build mutually fulfilling relationships based on insights into how Jesus related to individuals with disabilities. She also offers story after story of the hope and joy of those who've crossed the barriers, from either direction, and found a lifetime of friends.

Softcover: 0-310-21007-0

Beautifully Presented Devotionals That Include Photos and Illustrations by Joni

MORE PRECIOUS THAN SILVER
366 Daily Devotional Readings

Joni Eareckson Tada

Has your heart been touched by silver? Joni Eareckson Tada peers into the treasury of Scripture — pure as refined silver, cleansing what it touches. *More Precious Than Silver* reveals surpassing wealth in the subtle things we overlook as we chase life's golden glitter. This year's worth of wise, insightful devotions will show you why nothing can compare to the riches of a heart that's known the silver touch of God's Word.

Hardcover: 0-310-21627-3

DIAMONDS IN THE DUST
366 Sparkling Devotions

Joni Eareckson Tada

This is a sparkling new collection of daily devotional writings from one of the most significant and popular Christian writers of our day. *Diamonds in the Dust* captures Joni Eareckson Tada's rare talent for taking the ordinary things of life as her subject matter and suffusing them with the love and grace of God. Day by day this truly inspirational writer provides a meditation on a selected Bible verse, a short prayer, and a "thought for the day," gently helping readers to look at their world in a totally new way.

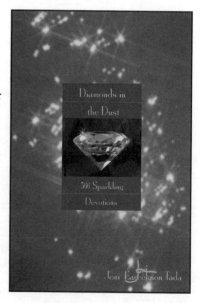

Hardcover: 0-310-37950-4

HEAVEN
Your Real Home
Joni Eareckson Tada

We all think about heaven—or at least we wonder what will happen to us after we die. For the Christian, these should be comforting, exciting thoughts. In this beautiful devotional gift book, Joni has chosen short excerpts from her book *Heaven* and arranged them around common topics, such as *Where is heaven and what is it like? What will we do in heaven?* Each inspiring and faith-filled meditation is paired with a verse of Scripture and a heart-felt prayer.

Hardcover: 0-310-24165-0
Softcover: 0-310-21919-1

A STEP FURTHER
Growing Closer to God through Hurt and Hardship
Joni Eareckson Tada and Steve Estes

Originally published in 1978, *A Step Further* is Joni's response to thousands of letters she received from people puzzled about the "whys" of suffering. Joni answers these questions by taking a personal look at how God has used circumstances, people, and events in her own life and the lives of others. *A Step Further* has been used by individuals, in hospitals and rehab centers, and in scores of countries overseas to bring comfort and peace to those who are suffering. It is available in over thirty different languages.

Softcover: 0-310-23971-0

THE LIFE AND DEATH DILEMMA
Families Facing Health Care Choices

Joni Eareckson Tada

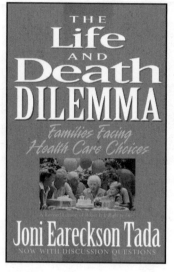

You might be standing by the bedside of an ill or dying family member, facing agonizing moral and medical choices. Or you may be struggling with a disability, asking questions that seem to have no answers. Where can you find practical encouragement and realistic perspective to help you make the best decisions?

Joni Eareckson Tada, herself a quadriplegic, helps you and your family tackle the hard questions about death, illness, and suffering, such as:

- Is it ever right to choose death, either for yourself or a suffering loved one?
- How can I make the best decisions in a medical crisis?
- Where is God in the unanswerable questions?
- Are our rights being protected?

Stories of real people who have faced life-and-death decisions, practical suggestions for coping in crisis, and scriptural insight on the meaning of life help you find hope and answers in difficult situations. From the legal facts to the human factor, Joni brings a unique perspective to what makes life worth living and how to make health care choices with dignity, wisdom, and compassion.

Softcover: 0-310-58571-6

ZONDERVAN™

GRAND RAPIDS, MICHIGAN 49530 USA

WWW.ZONDERVAN.COM

**A Moving Reminder of God's Gracious and
Unconditional Love and Care for His Children**

GOD'S PRECIOUS LOVE

Joni Eareckson Tada

Padded Hardcover: 0-310-98907-8

God's love is more precious, more amazing than we can imagine. Joni Eareckson Tada explores the depths of God's love for us in these beautiful, inspirational gift books. Each encouraging and uplifting quote is surrounded by the beauty of Joni's own unique artwork.

GOD'S TENDER CARE

Joni Eareckson Tada

Padded Hardcover: 0-310-98420-3

We want to hear from you. Please send your comments about this book to us in care of zreview@zondervan.com. Thank you.

GRAND RAPIDS, MICHIGAN 49530 USA

WWW.ZONDERVAN.COM